IP Telephony

IP Telephony

Packet-based multimedia communications systems

OLIVIER HERSENT

DAVID GURLE &

JEAN-PIERRE PETIT

Addison-Wesley

An imprint of **PEARSON EDUCATION**

Harlow, England · London · Reading, Massachusetts · Menlo Park, California · New York · Don Mills, Ontario ·
Amsterdam · Bonn · Sydney · Singapore · Tokyo · Madrid · San Juan · Milan · Mexico City · Seoul · Taipei

PEARSON EDUCATION LIMITED

Head Office:
Edinburgh Gate
Harlow CM20 2JE
Tel: +44 (0)1279 623623
Fax: +44 (0)1279 431059

London Office:
128 Long Acre
London WC2E 9AN
Tel: +44 (0)20 7447 2000
Fax: +44 (0)20 7240 5771

Website: www.awl.com/cseng/

First published in Great Britain 2000

The rights of Olivier Hersent, David Gurle and Jean Pierre Petit to be identified as authors of this work have been asserted by them in accordance with the Copyright, Designs and Patents Act 1988.

ISBN 0-201-61910-5

British Library Cataloguing in Publication Data
A catalogue record for this book is available from the British Library.

Library of Congress Cataloging in Publication Data
Applied for.

The programs in this book have been included for their instructional value. The publisher does not offer any warranties or representations in respect of their fitness for a particular purpose, nor does the publisher accept any liability for any loss or damage arising from their use.

Many of the designations used by manufacturers and sellers to distinguish their products are claimed as trademarks. Pearson Education Limited has made every attempt to supply trademark information about manufacturers and their products mentioned in this book.

10 9 8 7 6 5 4 3 2

Typeset by Pantek Arts, Maidstone, Kent.
Printed and bound in the United States of America.

The publishers' policy is to use paper manufactured from sustainable forests.

Contents

Foreword

VoIP is the fastest growing emerging telecom sector, even faster than mobile telephony was a few years ago. Manufacturers, carriers and IT managers need to adapt quicker than ever, but the learning curve is very steep and really requires an eduction strategy.

VON professional conferences provide an up-to-date view of the market and industry trends, but there is still a need for educational and reference material: the hype is very strong, and only a thorough understanding of the technology allows for sorting out hard facts from vaporware.

Gathering in a single book all of the background needed to get a complete picture of the VoIP technology is a challenge, as you need to explain state-of-the-art techniques in many different areas: speech coding, quality of service on IP, multicast ...

Olivier, David and Jean-Pierre have decided to face that challenge, with success.

The book embraces all of the fields that the VoIP professional needs to be aware of in a clear and organized way. The protocols section describes in details all of today's VoIP standards, with a protocol agnostic state-of-mind that is a great help in understanding the pros and cons of competing standards. The speech section will give you a detailed overview of both voice compression techniques and speech quality assessment. The IP networking section will help all IT managers cross the finish line, providing all the tools and information needed to actually deploy a carrier grade multimedia network.

This is in no way an easy read, but hey this is high tech after all! What is nice is that the authors have all actively participated in the development of these standards, and they really go to great lengths to always start from the basics – you'll even find a tutorial on cryptography in order to really understand VoIP security.

The only areas that the book doesn't cover are product reviews and the regulatory environment. But this is where the VON conferences & workshops will fill in the gaps!

I recommend this book to all VoIP engineers, analysts, and IT managers who really want to know what they are talking about on the net, enjoy!

Jeff

Jeff Pulver is the founder of the VON (Voice On the Net) coalition, and the founder and president of pulver.com

Preface

This book is about the newest service to arrive on the Internet: interactive voice and video. Since its first appearance to the market in 1995, it is amazing to note how fast the IP telephony technology has evolved. But this evolution alone wouldn't account for VoIP's growing success if there weren't a general recognition of the importance of the Internet in our day-to-day activities.

Flashback

In 1991, the Internet was still a maze without a map where only addicts really felt at home. As students we used to print and exchange our bookmarks – as soon as someone had found a really good ftp site with anonymous access, he would copy and distribute the listing. Any good book on the Internet inevitably ended with hundreds of pages of such bookmarks. The Internet was a nice tool, especially email and chat, but really you had to enjoy being stuck in front of your black and white computer screen for hours.

Then, in 1993, with the World Wide Web, came the first revolution. The Internet became colorful and our piles of paper bookmarks were instantly obsolete, replaced by links on web pages. Soon there were too many links for one person to keep track of. So two US students came up with the idea of keeping bookmarks up to date for other people and created Yahoo!. It was a good thing indeed. Thus, with all the bookmark sites and search engines, the Internet became less intimidating for non-UNIX gurus. It became feasible for a literature student to get an Internet account.

By 1996 every student had an email address and most of them actually used it. But for most people, the Internet was still a toy. It was too complex to reach the mass market, and would never really count outside universities and research labs. In one sentence: 'the Internet will really count when your grandmother can use it.'

It was around that time that we saw the first attempts to build an Internet telephony gateway. The first prototype was a strange hybrid. The telephone interface was a modem with speakerphone capabilities. The problem with this speakerphone modem was that there was no way to simultaneously play a sound and record from a PC. Actually you could use the modem only to dial the destination number. Some sound boards had a driver that made it possible to simultaneously play and record ('full-duplex'), but no telephone interface, so you had to wire the sound-board line-in jack to the modem microphone, and the modem speaker to the sound-board line-out jack. Of course, some software was needed to turn this into an Internet telephony gateway, but in 1996 there was already good Internet telephony freeware available, such as VAT, and adding some code to interface with the modem wasn't too difficult: when an incoming call arrives, pick up the line, play a welcome prompt, get the destination number with DTMF touchtones (the modem had that capability), relay the information to the destination gateway that would use the modem to dial the right number, and spawn the Internet telephony software.

This was only a very crude, one-line gateway, but its potential was immense. The telephone network is *the* example of a technology that really counts. There are over 800 million telephone lines in the world, and a five-year-old can use a telephone. Obviously, being able to carry even a small fraction of all telephone conversations over the Internet would have been a major achievement. Many research labs suddenly realized that it could be a second Internet revolution and tried to evaluate if it was possible to build a more sophisticated gateway.

This was only three years ago, but already today, there are more and more companies running their operations without the use of a single 'blackphone' of a PBX. And tomorrow, our grandmother may still use a regular analogue telephone, but the likelihood of this phone being connected to a Softswitch (IP Central Office) will be very high. By this time, there is no doubt that the full potential of Internet will eventually be reached. With its first www revolution, the Internet got a face, with the IP telephony revolution, the Internet has got a voice!

The technology

AT a first glance the technology behind the IP telephony may seem almost trivial. It isn't. In particular it is *much* more complex than one-way media streaming (used by TV or radio broadcasting on the net) because the latency between the talker and the listener must remain very low, while streaming applications can use very large buffers.

Here is a short list of some topics one needs to explore before understanding the subtleties of IP telephony:

- the characteristics of the human ear, especially its perception of echo and delay;
- the voice compression and packetization technologies;

- silence suppression and comfort noise generation;
- echo cancellation technologies;
- the shortcomings of the Internet protocol regarding real-time applications: delay, jitter, packet loss;
- the strategies to overcome these limitations: buffering, redundancy, time-stamps, differentiated services;
- the characteristics of packetized voice traffic, and how it cohabits with non real-time data flows;
- in band data transmission in the telephone network (DTMF, fax, modem);
- telephone signaling protocols (ISDN Q.931, SS7 ISUP, etc.), and all connection sequences (regular calls, calls to intelligent services, calls while the network is overloaded);
- IP telephony protocols (ITU H.323 and associated protocols, MGCP, IETF, MEGACO and SIP);
- politics, to better sort out technology-driven controversies and business-driven controversies.

Very soon in our exploration of VoIP, it appeared that it was really an area that brought together many different types of expertise in the networking, speech and telephony area. In order to build a good VoIP team, it would be necessary for each expert to update the others on the most essential aspects of his domain that are relevant for VoIP.

Audience

You will find this book useful if you face issues such as:

- which gateway should I choose for my corporate converged network? What standard?
- can I replace my backbone trunks with VoIP links transparently?
- can I get rid of all the telephone wiring?
- can I prevent VoIP from overloading my network? How does it get through firewalls?
- will my 2 Mbit/s IP access be sufficient for my brand new 100-operator VoIP call center?
- can I use VoIP on a network with dynamic DHCP addressing?
- How do I fax through the net?
- will I be able to use VoIP for multipoint conferences or broadcasting?

On the other hand, you will be disappointed if you look for a list of vendors and a discussion of each product, or simply a quick overview of the technology.

This book assumes a working knowledge of IP and ISDN networking. This doesn't mean that our reader should be familiar with all socket options or BGP4 routing, but we do not explain the basics of IP routing such as the significance of an IP address or TCP port. If you feel you need some clarification on the Internet protocol, we would recommend the books written by Christian Huitema. Similarly we assume the reader knows what Setup, Alerting or Connect ISDN messages mean, although we explain their role in the context of H.323.

Other than that, we have tried to avoid an excessive use of pointers to external documentation in the text itself. We know it can be extremely time consuming to download and read a full RFCs or ITU recommendations when you need to check only a detail, and therefore we have inserted small digests wherever they are useful. For instance, you will find descriptions of popular voice and video coders in the H.323 section. We have also provided a large list of definitions for the acronyms used in the book, as it seems that each new telecom application has to create its own vocabulary. Of course, the relevant pointers are gathered in the reference sections.

Relation to standards

In just three years IP telephony has evolved from one-port, do-it-yourself gateways to backbone hardware supporting 120 ports per PCI slot. And this is just the small part of the iceberg – standards are evolving twice as fast. It was even harder for us because we decided not to choose between the emerging standards and to describe H.323, SIP and MGCP. People are often confused and ask us: Who will be the winner? But in fact only H.323 and SIP can be seen as direct competitors: both aim at being implemented by 'intelligent' multimedia endpoints, and the common opinion that H.323 is 'much more complex' than SIP relates mainly to the fact that H.323 uses a binary ASN.1 encoding, which is not a serious obstacle for any programmer. MGCP is more an effort to create a light stimulus-based protocol for gateways and appliances and can be used in conjunction with both H.323 and SIP. The SIGTRAN group efforts are not described here, as they aim at transporting transparently SS7 signaling across an IP network, which means the Internet is used as a simple trunk. To us it seemed SIGTRAN would rather belong to a book on PSTN technology.

We have tried to keep the manuscript current, but there are unavoidable delays in the publication process, and by the time you read these lines we know that some standards will have evolved. In particular we have based some of the chapters on material gathered from IETF Internet drafts, which is explicitly discouraged by IETF because these documents are not stable. In practice though, people rarely rewrite drafts entirely, and we hope that the background material gathered in the book will be sufficient to allow you to catch the train and join the community of engineers who improve VoIP technology day after day.

We have provided pointers to most of the relevant standards, drafts, mailing lists and web sites. Nothing can really replace daily participation in the standardization process: for each line written in a standard document, there are perhaps 100 lines worth of emails, discussions and drafts that really put this single line into perspective. Sometimes a controversy arises and gives birth to one of those 'everybody's right' sentences (such as the paragraph regarding G.723.1 and G.729 in H.323) that nobody can understand without remembering the previous discussions. We have tried to take this 'behind the scenes' data into account in this book, but we encourage you to make your own opinion using the mailing lists.

The future of multimedia over IP

The speed at which IP telephony has become an industry is truly amazing, but we are far from having reached maturity.

There are still a lot of technical shortcomings in today's products. In general, products are about two years behind the standards. For instance, at the time of book there was just one gateway and one IP phone software that supported mid-call call redirection, although it was already defined in H.323v1. This is one of the most basic and most widely used services in today's PSTN. Everybody boasts 'added value services' and still, amazingly, nobody really has the basics right yet.

Another striking example is the lack of a standardized URL format to trigger an H.323 IP phone call. The very big software manufacturers have resisted any attempt to do so. Because of this you have to put a different button for each flavor of H.323 phone out there.

There are also some economic issues to resolve. Historically, almost all Internet sites were in the US. Consequently the ISPs in the rest of the world had to pay 100 per cent of the data leased lines to the US. The situation in the phone network is different: each carrier pays 50 per cent of the leased line. This situation is unfair and cannot last much longer: the web traffic imbalance is more in the 30/70 range, and of course interactive voice and video is symmetrical. Interestingly, voice over IP seems to develop equally fast in the US, Europe and Asia, which should help in the promotion of a truly international Internet.

Despite these minor issues that will quickly be resolved, the future of IP telephony and video seems bright. Soon the SDH and SONET transport networks will carry more data than voice (this is already the case on the BT network), and at this point using packetized voice is an obvious choice. Some will still argue that packetized voice doesn't mean IP. Why wouldn't we use frame relay or ATM? There are two simple reasons for this: soon 99.9 per cent of the data generated by individuals and corporations will be IP. Introducing an ATM or Frame Relay Layer to the end customer just for voice makes no sense. In addition, ATM and Frame Relay don't scale in terms of connectivity. Switched Virtual Circuits are too slow for today's sporadic data exchanges, where everybody pings everybody, and Permanent Virtual Circuits, although fine for backbones or intranets when there are only a few dozen nodes to connect, make no sense on an open network.

It is true that IP has a latency problem on low-speed links, but in tomorrow's networks with xDSL connections this issue will be resolved, and at this stage we will probably realize that large packets use bandwidth much more efficiently for video. If we project ourselves a few years forward, with these xDSL lines connected to multi-gigabit backbones, hardware IP phones with state-of-the-art echo cancellers, and a new wideband coder standardized by ITU, we will have a better sound quality than today's ISDN network, and of course video. This is not so far away. Already in Canada some fortunate people have 2 Mbps lines in their homes for less than $100 per month.

And we may have even greater surprises. Tomorrow's mobile telephony networks, such as UMTS, will basically be wireless data transmission units able to send and receive megabytes per second. Why invent protocols for the multimedia applications running on those phones when it is already obvious that they will have to talk IP? Maybe our next mobile phone will be an IP phone.

Acknowledgements

We need to thank many people for their contributions, support and help without which this book would not have reached its goals. Especially those who regularly attend, IETF, ETSI TIPHON and ITU SG 16 meetings and contribute to numerous IP telephony related mailing lists.

We are particularly indebted to those like Scott Petrack, Christian Huitema, Dave Oran, Louise Spergel, Dale Skran, Gur Kimchi, Jonathan Rosenberg, Henning Schulzrine, Jim Toga, Max Morris, Mike Buckley and Jeff Pulver who through their valuable contributions participated in setting up the Internet Telephony revolution.

In CNET, our thanks go to Michel Dudet, Gerard, Sylvie, Catherine, Marcel, Michel, Bernard, Bertrand, Cyril, Pierrick, Jean Jacques, Soleiman, Christope, Sebastien and Frank.

We would also like to thank folks in VocalTec, Elad Sion, Eran Barak, Lior Moscovici, Alon Cohen, Doron Zinger and Bayard Gardineer for their support and comments.

The Authors

THE APPLICATION LAYER
IP TELEPHONY
PROTOCOLS

H.323 and a general background on IP telephony

A little history

H.323v1 had little ambition. Noting the growing success of IP, IPX and Apple Talk-based local area networks in all kinds of companies, Study Group 16 of ITU-T decided to create H.323, 'Visual telephone systems and equipment for local area networks which provide a non-guaranteed quality of service', a LAN-only standard for audiovisual conferences. Originally the responsibility for multimedia communications was allocated to Study Group 15. The study group had already acquired a lot of experience during the development of H.320, 'Multimedia conferencing for ISDN-based networks'. This background had some good consequences for H.323, such as good interworking with H.320, and some bad consequences such as unnecessary heaviness.

H.323 didn't attract major interest from the market until VocalTec and Cisco founded the Voice over IP forum (VoIP) to set the standards for VoIP products. At that time the focus in the VoIP forum was given to the specification of endpoints using UDP-based signaling protocols. When major software and hardware firms realized the potential of Internet telephony they pushed the VoIP forum to become part of IMTC (International Multimedia Teleconferencing Consortium) and thanks to their market share and strength changed the focus of the VoIP activity group to tune H.323 to the specificities of Internet telephony. With a few minor changes, H.323 appeared to be quite suited for the most popular WAN environment of all: the Internet.

Soon the ITU SG 16 acknowledged that the success of H.323v1 called for a much broader scope, and the title of H.323v2 was changed to 'Packet-based multimedia communications systems'.

Work on H.323v1 began in May 1995, and this version was approved in June 1996. Version 2 was approved in February 1998 with three annexes: H.245 messages used by H.323 endpoints; procedures for layered video codecs; H.323 on ATM. Work on H.323v3 is ongoing and approval is planned for February 2000.

Where to find documentation

All ITU documents can be purchased on the ITU web site (www.itu.int). However, H.323 is still in a state of flux and the latest versions become available only some time after they have been approved. For those needing detailed and up-to-date technical information, the best option is to read the working documents of SG16, which are available on the following ftp site: *http://standard. pictel.com/webftp.htm*. However, you should be aware that all the documents found there can be copyrighted, and should not be copied without authorization. It is also interesting to monitor the discussions of the TIPHON (Telephony and Internet Protocols Harmonization Over Networks) project of the European

Telecom Standards Institute (ETSI). Originally ETSI was a members-only, Europe-centric organization, but TIPHON triggered a revolution. The focus of TIPHON is truly international, and its working documents and specifications are available on the web (*http://etsi.org/tiphon*).

H.323 is a complex standard, and still needs a lot of interpretation. The live discussions held at SG16 and TIPHON are invaluable for the expert who is trying to keep track of the updates. Much of the material presented in this chapter was gathered from those discussions and reflects the state of the art at the time of publication, but those readers who want a more detailed picture should refer directly to the ITU recommendations, the TIPHON specifications and the various working documents available on the web.

From RTP to H.323: a quick tour

RTP/RTCP (Real-Time Transport Protocol, Real-Time Control Protocol), described in RFC 1889, is the protocol suite that was used in the first conferencing tools available on the Internet: VAT – Visual Audio Tool – used RTP version 0. Since then, RTP has evolved into version 2. RFC 1889 describes a general framework of a protocol enabling the transport of real-time (or, more precisely, isochronous) data over IP (Internet Protocol). This protocol allows a level of tolerance for packet jitter and loss. Some profiling work is needed on top of RFC 1889 in order to build a specific application.

ITU-T H.225.0 does this profiling work (in fact, the entire specification of RTP/RTCP is annexed to it) for H.323 video-conferencing applications. In particular H.225.0 defines which identifiers are to be used for each type of codec recognized by the ITU (International Telecom Union), and discusses some conflicts and redundancies between RTCP and H.245. H.225.0 also describes the RAS (registration admission status) protocol which is used between a terminal and a gatekeeper, and the call signaling channel protocol.

H.323 is an umbrella specification describing the complete architecture and operation of a video-conferencing system over a packet network. H.323 is not specific to IP: there are sections on the use of H.323 over IPX/SPX or ATM (Asynchronous Transfer Mode). The framework of H.323 is complete, and includes the specification of:

- video-conferencing terminals
- gateways between an H.323 network and other voice and video networks (H.320, POTS, etc.);
- gatekeepers, which are the intelligent part of the H.323 network, performing registration of terminals, call admission and much more;
- MCU (Multipoint Control Unit), MC (Multipoint Controller) and MP (Multipoint Processor) functional blocks which are used for multiparty conferencing.

H.323 also describes how various communication protocols are used between those units:

- the 'Call Signaling Channel' which is used during the establishment and tear-off phases of the call will look familiar for anyone having studied ISDN networks; in fact, it uses the message format of Q.931 and extends it using the user to user information element. This call signaling channel is described in detail in H.225.0;

- the RAS channel, introduced above;

- the H.245 control channel which is opened at the beginning of the call to negotiate a common set of codecs, and remains in use throughout the call to carry some control messages.

H.245 is mainly a library of ASN-1 messages and protocol state-machines which are used in H.323. H.246 describes in more detail the operation of H.323 gateways. H.332 (loosely coupled conferencing) profiles H.323 and extends it for use in the context of a large conference with only a few speakers and a large audience. H.235 specifies a secure mode of operation for H.323 terminals, and refers to the SSL (Secure Sockets Layer) specification.

Because all messages are described using ASN-1 syntax, one must read X.691 (ASN-1 encoding rules, specifications of packet encoding rules) and X.680 (Abstract syntax notation-1) to actually code the H.323 PDUs (protocol data units). A small summary can be found at the end of H.245.

Normally H.323v2 systems have to use H.225 version 2 and H.245 version 3 or later. The protocol version is indicated in the protocol identifier information element of the messages (e.g. {itu-t (0) recommendation (0) h (8) 2250 version (0) 2}). The H.245 version can change dynamically during a call if third party rerouting is used.

Transporting voice over a packet network

A Darwinian view of voice transport

The switched circuit network

The most common telephone system today is still analogue. Analogue telephony uses the modulation of electric signals along a wire to transport voice (*see* Fig. 1.1).

Although it is a very old technology, analogue transmission has many advantages: it is simple and keeps the end-to-end delay of voice transmission very low because the signal propagates along the wire almost at the speed of light. It is also inexpensive when there are relatively few users talking at the same time,

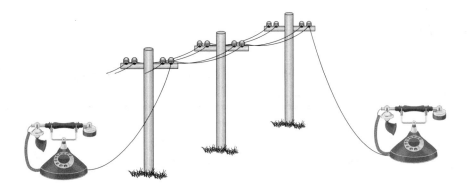

Fig. 1.1 : Analogue telephony

and when they are not too far apart. But the most basic analogue technology requires one pair of wires per active conversation, which becomes rapidly unpractical, and expensive. A first improvement of the basic 'baseband' analogue technology was to multiplex several conversations on the same wire, using a separate transport frequency for each signal. But even with this hack analogue telephony has many drawbacks:

- unless you use manual switchboards, the analogue switches require a lot of electromechanical gear which is expensive to buy and maintain;
- parasitic noise adds up at all stages of the transmission because there is no way to say what is the signal and what is noise and the signal cannot be cleaned.

For all these reasons, many countries today use a digital telephone network. In most cases the subscriber line remains analogue, but the analogue signal is converted to a digital data stream in the first local exchange. Usually, this signal has a bit rate of 64 kbit/s (one 8-bit sample every 125 µs).

Now many voice channels can be multiplexed along the same transmission line using a technology called time-division multiplexing (TDM). In this technology, the digital data stream which represents a single conversation is divided into blocks (usually an octet, also called a sample), and blocks from several conversations are interleaved in a round-robin fashion in the time slots of the transmission line, as shown in Fig. 1.2.

With this digital technology, the noise that is added in the backbone does not influence the quality of the communication because digital signals can be restored. Moreover, digital time-division multiplexing makes digital switching possible. The switch just needs to copy the contents of one time slot of the incoming transmission line into another time slot in the outgoing transmission line. Therefore this switching function can be performed by computers. However, a small delay is introduced by each switch because for each conversation a time slot is available only each T microseconds, and in some cases it may be necessary

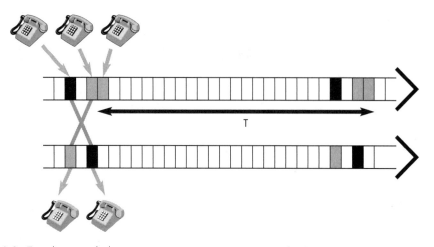

Fig. 1.2 : Time-division multiplexing

to wait up to T microseconds to copy the contents of one time slot into another. Since T equals 125 microseconds in most digital networks, this is usually negligible and the main delay factor is simply the propagation time.

Asynchronous transmission and statistical multiplexing

Unless you really have a point to make, or you are a politician, you will usually speak less than half of the time during a conversation. Since we all need to think a little before we reply, each party usually talks only 35 per cent of the time during an average conversation. If you could press a button each time you talk, you would send data over the phone line only when you actually say something, not when you are silent. As we will see later, most of the techniques used to transform your voice into data (known as codecs) now have the ability to detect silences. With this technique, known as voice activity detection, instead of transmitting a chunk of data, voice or silence every 125 microseconds, as is done today, you transmit data only when you need to, asynchronously (see Fig. 1.3).

When it comes to multiplexing several conversations on a single transmission line, instead of occupying bandwidth all the time, 'your' bandwidth can be used by someone else while you are silent. This is known as statistical multiplexing (see Fig. 1.4).

The main advantage of statistical multiplexing is that it allows the bandwidth to be used more efficiently, especially when there are many conversations multiplexed on the same line (see Chapter seven). But statistical multiplexing, as the name suggests, introduces uncertainty in the network. We just said that in the case of TDM, a delay of up to T could be introduced at each switch; this delay is constant throughout the conversation. The situation is totally different with sta-

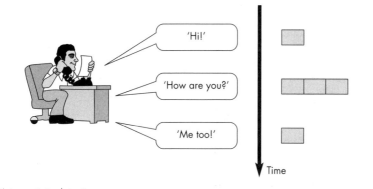

Fig. 1.3 : Voice activity detection

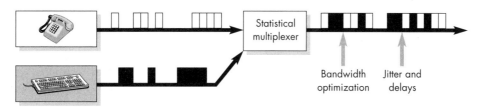

Fig. 1.4 : Statistical multiplexing

tistical multiplexing: if the transmission line is empty when you need to send a chunk of data, it will go through immediately. If, on the other hand, the line is full, you have to wait until there is some spare capacity for you.

This varying delay is caller jitter (*see* Fig. 1.5) and needs to be corrected by the receiving side. Otherwise, if the data chunks are played as soon as they are received, the original speech can become unintelligible.

The next generation telephone network will probably use statistical multi-plexing, and mix voice and data along the same transmission lines. Several technologies are good candidates, for instance, voice over frame relay, voice over ATM, and, of course, voice over IP. We believe voice over IP is the most flexible solution because it does not require virtual channels to be set up between the sites that will communicate. It scales much better than ATM or frame relay networks in terms of connectivity.

Voice and video over IP with RTP and RTCP

The reference for this chapter is RFC 1889 which can be found at *www.internic.net/rfc/rfc1889.txt.*

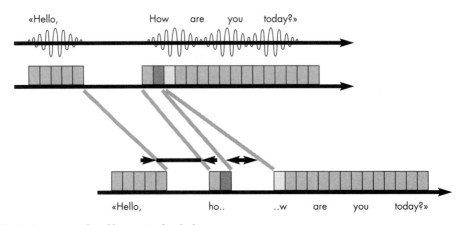

Fig. 1.5 : Jitter introduced by statistical multiplexing

Why RTP/RTCP?

We have seen that when a network using statistical multiplexing is used to transmit real-time data such as voice, jitter has to be taken into account by the receiver. Routers are good examples of such statistical multiplexing devices, and therefore voice and video over IP will face the issue of jitter.

The Real-Time Transport Protocol was designed to allow receivers to compensate for the jitter and desequencing introduced by IP networks. RTP can be used for any real-time stream of data, for instance voice and video. RTP defines a way to format IP packets carrying isochronous data and includes:

- information on the type of data transported
- timestamps
- sequence numbers.

Another protocol, RTCP, is often used with RTP, which allows the conveyance of some feedback on the quality of the transmission (the amount of jitter, the average packet loss, etc.) and can also carry some information on the identity of the participants.

RTP and RTCP do not have any influence on the behavior of the IP network; they do not control quality of service in any way. The network can drop, delay or desequence an RTP packet like any other IP packet. RTP must not be mixed up with protocols like RSVP (Resource reSerVation Protocol). RTP and RTCP simply allow receivers to recover from network jitter by appropriate buffering and sequencing, and to have more information on the network so that appropriate corrective measures can be adopted (redundancy, lower rate codecs, etc.).

RTP/RTCP's design allows these protocols to be used on top of any network layer. However, RTP and RTCP are mostly used on top of UDP because the TCP retransmission scheme is not adapted for data that needs to be carried with a very low latency, such as interactive communications. In this case RTP is traditionally assigned an even UDP (User Datagram Protocol) port and RTCP the next odd UDP port.

RTP

RTP allows the transport of isochronous data across a packet network which introduces jitter and may desequence the packets. It is typically used on top of UDP which provides the notion of port and a checksum. When it uses UDP, it can be carried by multicast IP packets, i.e. packets with a multicast destination address (e.g. 224.34.54.23): therefore an RTP stream generated by a single source can reach several destinations (see Chapter eight).

Some uses of RTP

Sequence number and timestamp. Each RTP packet carries a sequence number and a timestamp. Depending on the application, they can be used in a number of ways. A video application, for instance, can immediately deduce from the time-stamp which part of the screen is described by the IP packet. Even if it has not yet received packets before it, due to desequencing problems or loss, it may still use the packet to construct the part of the image that it describes.

An audio application cannot use it this way (because we would not understand garbled speech) and will use the sequence number and timestamp to manage a reception buffer. For instance, an application may decide that it is going to buffer 100 milliseconds of speech before beginning the playback. Each time a new RTP packet arrives, it is placed in the buffer in the appropriate position depending on its sequence number. If a packet doesn't arrive on time and is still missing at play-back time, the application may decide to copy the last frame of the packet that has just been played and repeat it long enough to catch up with the timestamp of the next received packet, or use some interpolation scheme as defined by the par-ticular audio codec in use.

Payload type (PT). The payload of each RTP packet is the real-time information contained in the packet. Its format is completely free and must be defined by the application or the profile of RTP in use. In order to distinguish one particular format from another without having to analyze the content of the payload, the header of each RTP packet contains a payload type identifier. For example, Table 1.1 illustrates the identifiers in use in H.225 for some standard codecs. Those are called static payload types, assigned by the Internet Assigned Numbers Authority (IANA). PTs 96 to 127 are reserved for dynamic PTs, i.e. the codec used with those PTs is negotiated by a conference control protocol dynamically.

Since RTP itself doesn't define the format of the payload section, each applica-tion must define, or refer to, a profile. In the case of H.323, this work is done in annex B of H.225.

Table 1.1 : Static payload identifiers

Payload Type	Codec	
0	PCM, μ Law	AUDIO
8	PCM, A Law	
9	G.722	
4	G.723	
15	G.728	
18	G.729	
34	H.263	VIDEO
31	H.261	

A few definitions

- **RTP session**. An RTP session is an association of participants which communicate over RTP. Each participant uses two transport addresses (in the case of IP, for instance, two UDP ports on the local machine) for each session: one for the RTP stream, one for the RTCP reports. When a multicast transmission is used, all the participants use the same pair of multicast transport addresses. Media streams in the same session should share a common RTCP channel.

- **Synchronization source SSRC**. Source of an RTP stream, identified by 32 bits in the RTP header. All the RTP packets with a common SSRC have a common time and sequencing reference.

- **Contributing source CSRC**. When an RTP stream is the result of a combination by an RTP mixer of several contributing streams, the list of the SSRCs of each contributing stream is added in the RTP header of the resulting stream as CSRCs. The resulting stream has its own SSRC. This feature is not used in H.323.

- **NTP format**. A standard way to format a timestamp, by writing the number of seconds since 1/1/1900 at 0h with 32 bits for the integer part and 32 bits for the decimal part (expressed as number of $1/2^{32}$ seconds, e.g. 0x80000000 is 0.5 seconds). A compact format also exists with only 16 bits for the integer part and 16 bits for the decimal part. The first 16 digits of the integer part can usually be derived from the current day, the fractional part is simply truncated to the most significant 16 digits.

The RTP packet

All fields up to the CSRC list are always present in an RTP packet (*see* Table 1.2). The CSRC list is present only behind a mixer and therefore will not be present in the content of H.323:

- 2 bits are reserved for the RTP version. It is now version 2 (10). Version 0 was used by VAT and version 1 was an earlier Internet Engineering Task Force (IETF) draft.

Table 1.2 : An RTP packet

V = 2	P	X	CC	M	Payload type	Sequence number
Timestamp						
Synchronization Source Identifier (SSRC)						
Contributing Source Identifier (CSRC) *not used in H.323*						
Profile dependent					Size	
Data						

0	2	4	6	8	10	12	14	16	18	20	22	24	26	28	30

- A padding bit P indicates whether the payload has been padded for alignment purposes. If it has been padded (P=1), then the last octet of the payload field indicates more precisely how many padding octets have been appended to the original payload.

- An extension bit X indicates the presence of extensions after the eventual CSRCs of the fixed header. Extensions use the following format:

```
 0 1 2 3 4 5 6 7 8 9 0 1 2 3 4 5 6 7 8 9 0 1 2 3 4 5 6 7 8 9 0 1
┌───────────────────────────────┬───────────────────────────────┐
│        defined by profile      │            length             │
├───────────────────────────────┴───────────────────────────────┤
│                        header extension                         │
│                             . . . .                             │
```

- The 4-bit CSRC count (CC) tells how many CSRC identifiers follow the fixed header. There is usually none.

- Marker (M): 1 bit. Its use is defined by the RTP profile. H.225.0 says that for audio codings that support silence suppression, it must be set to 1 in the first packet of each talkspurt after a silence period.

- Payload type (PT): 7 bits. Some static payload types are defined in RFC 1889 and in the 'assigned numbers' RFC. For H.323 the reference is H.225.

- Sequence number: 16 bits. Starts on a random value and is incremented at each RTP packet.

- Timestamp: 32 bits. The clock frequency is defined for each payload type, e.g. H.261 Payload uses a 90 kHz clock for the RTP timestamp. For most audio codecs (G.711, G.723.1, G.729, etc.) the RTP clock frequency is set to 8000 Hz. For video, the RTP timestamp is the tick count of the display time of the first frame encoded in the packet payload. For audio, the RTP timestamp is the tick count when the first audio sample contained in the payload was sampled. The clock is initialized with a random value.

RTCP

RTCP is used to transmit control packets to participants from time to time regarding a particular RTP session. Those control packets can include information about the participants (their names, email addresses, etc.) and information on the mapping of participants to individual stream sources. The most useful information found in RTCP packets in the context of H.323 is about the quality of transmission in the network. All participants in the sessions send RTCP packets; senders send 'sender reports' and receivers send 'receiver reports'.

Bandwidth limitation
All participants must send RTCP packets, which causes a potential dimensioning problem for large multicast conferences: RTCP traffic should grow linearly with the number of participants. This problem does not exist with RTP streams in audio-only conferences using silence suppression, for instance, since people generally do not speak at the same time (*see* Fig. 1.6).

Since the number of participants is known to all participants who listen to RTCP reports, each of them can control the rate at which he sends RTCP reports. This is used to limit the bandwidth used by RTCP to a reasonable amount, usually not more than 5 per cent of the session bandwidth. This budget has to be shared by all participants. RTP stipulates that active senders get one quarter of it because some of the information they send (for instance CNAME information used for synchronization) is very important to all receivers and RTCP sender reports need to be very responsive. The remaining part is split between the receivers.

Even for small sessions, the fastest rate at which a participant can send RTCP reports is one every five seconds. The sending rate is randomized by a factor 0.5 to 1.5 to avoid unwanted synchronization between reports. The average value is derived by the participant from the size of the RTCP packets he wants to send, and from the number of senders and receivers that appear in the RTCP packets he receives.

These guidelines are from the RFC (Request For Comment), but very few H.323 implementations actually care about such guidelines because there is no scaling issue if multicast is not used. It will be more important for H.332 systems, however.

RTCP packet types
There are various types of RTCP packets for each type of information:

- SR: Sender reports (*see* Table 1.3) contain transmission and reception information for active senders;
- RR: Receiver reports contain reception information for listeners who are not also active senders;

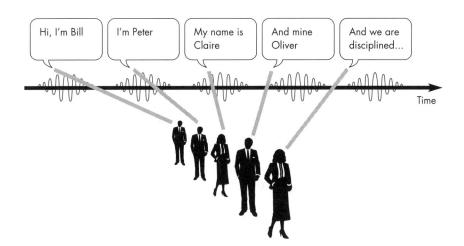

Fig. 1.6 : RTP traffic does not grow with the number of participants

Table 1.3 : A sender report

V = 2	P	RC	PT=SR=200	length
Sender				
NTP Timestamp (most significant word)				
NTP Timestamp (least significant word)				
RTP Timestamp				
Sender's packet count				
Sender's octet count				
SSRC 1 (SSRC of first source)				
Additional RR data				
SSRC n				
Additional RR data				

- SDES: Source descriptions describe various parameters about the source, including the CNAME;

- BYE: Sent by a participant when he leaves the conference;

- APP: Functions specific to an application.

Several RTCP packets can be packed in a single transport protocol packet. Each RTCP 'message' contains enough information to be properly decoded if several of those RTCP messages are packed in a single UDP packet. This packing can be useful to save overhead bandwidth used by the transport protocol header.

Sender and receiver reports
Each SR contains 3 mandatory sections. The first section contains:

- the 5-bit reception reports count (RC), which is the number of report blocks included in this SR;

- the packet type (PT) is 200 for an SR. In order to avoid mixing a regular RTP packet with an SR, RTP packets should avoid payload types 72 and 73 which can be mixed up with SRs and RRs when the marker bit is set (but normally a UDP port is dedicated to RTCP to eliminate that potential confusion);

- The 16-bit length of this SR including header and padding (the number of 32-bit words minus 1);

- The SSRC of the originator of this SR. This SSRC will also be in the RTP packets originated from this host.

The second section contains information on the RTP stream sent by this sender:

- the NTP timestamp of the sending time of this report. A sender can set the high order bit to 0 if it can't track the absolute NTP time and this is only an NTP measurement relative to the beginning of this session (which is assumed to last less than 68 years!). If a sender can't track elapsed time, it may set the timestamp to 0;

- the RTP timestamp, which represents the same time as above, but with the same units and random offset as in the timestamps of RTP packets;

- sender's packet count (32 bits) from the beginning of this session up to this SR. It is reset if the SSRC has to change (this may happen in an H.323 multi-party conference when the active MC assigns terminal numbers);

- sender's payload octet count (32 bits) since the beginning of this session. This is also reset if the SSRC changes.

The third section contains a set of reception report blocks, one for each source that this sender has heard of since the last RR or SR. Each of them has the same format, shown in Table 1.4.

Table 1.4 : Typical reception report blocks

SSRC of the source	
Lost fraction	Cumulated number of lost packets
Highest received sequence number	
Interarrival jitter	
Last SR (LSR)	
Delay since last SR	

- SSRC_n (source identifier): 32 bits – the SSRC of the source about which we are reporting;

- fraction lost: 8 bits – equal to floor (received packets/expected packets*256);

- cumulative number of packets lost (24 bits) since the beginning of reception. Late packets are not counted as lost and duplicate packets count as received packets;

- extended highest sequence number received: (32 bits). The most significant 16 bits contain the number of sequence number cycles, and the last 16 bits contain the highest sequence number received in an RTP data packet from this source (same SSRC);

- interarrival jitter: 32 bits. An estimation of the variance of the interarrival time between RTP packets, measured in the same units as the RTP timestamp. The calculation is made by comparing the RTP timestamp of arriving packets with the local clock, and averaging the results, as shown in Fig. 1.7.

- the last SR timestamp (LSR): 32 bits. The middle 32 bits of the NTP timestamp of the last SR received (this is the compact NTP form);

- the delay since the last SR arrived (DLSR): 32 bits. Expressed in compact NTP form (or, put more simply, in multiples of 1/65536s). Together with the last SR timestamp, the sender of this last SR can use it to compute the round trip time.

A receiver report looks like an SR, except that the PT field is now 201, and the second section (concerning the sender) is absent. It can be used by passive receivers which do not generate RTP flows.

SDES: source description RTCP packet

An SDES packet (Fig. 1.8) has a PT of 202 and contains SC (source count) chunks. Each chunk contains an SSRC or a CSRC and a list of information. Each element of this list is coded using TLV (type, length, value) format.

The following types exist but only CNAME has to be present:

- CNAME=1 (unique among all participants of the session) is of the form user@host, or the IP address or domain name of the host

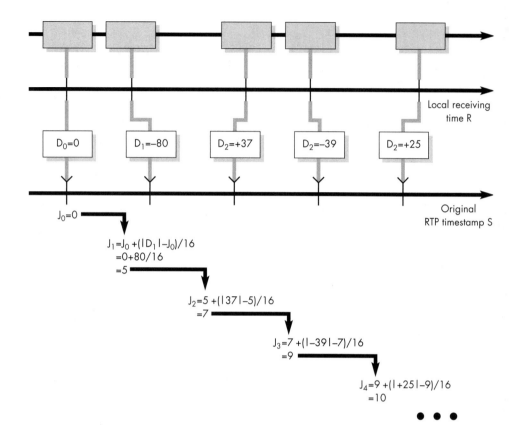

Fig. 1.7 : Calculating interarrival jitter

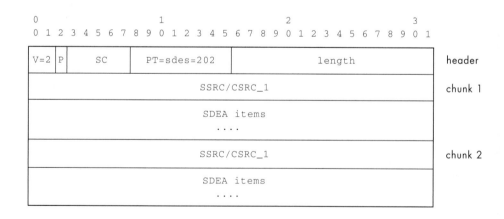

Fig. 1.8 : A source description RTCP packet

- NAME=2 common name of the source
- EMAIL=3
- PHONE=4
- LOC=5, location
  This packet is not used in H.323.

BYE RTCP packet

The BYE RTCP packet (Fig. 1.9) indicates that one or more sources (as indicated by source count SC) are no longer active.
  This packet is not used in H.323.

APP: application-defined RTCP packet

The application-defined packet (Fig. 1.10) can be used to convey additional proprietary information. The PT field is set to 204.
  This packet is not used in H.323.

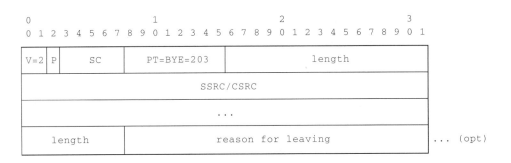

Fig. 1.9 : A BYE RTCP packet

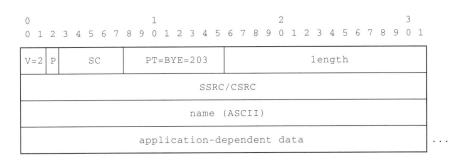

Fig. 1.10 : An application-defined packet

Security

Security can be achieved at the transport level or at the RTP level. At the transport level there are still no widely used standards for UDP, so most of the time encryption is performed at the RTP level. The RTP RFC presents a way to do it using Data Encryption Standard/Cipher Block Chaining (DES/CBC) encryption. Since DES, like many other encryption algorithms, is a block algorithm (see a more detailed description in the section on H.235), there needs to be some adaptation when the unencrypted payload is not a multiple of 64 octets.

The most straightforward method, padding (*see* Fig. 1.11), is described in RTP (RFC 1889 section 5.1). When this method is used, the padding bit of the RTP header is set. Other methods that do not require padding, called ciphertext stealing, can also be used and are also described in the H.235 section further on.

Authentication is not within the scope of RTP. It can be performed out of band using a Diffie-Helmann scheme (*see* p. 68) to negotiate a common secret, then using that secret for RTP encryption, as in H.235.

H.323 step by step

H.323 did not invent video conferencing over IP. Researchers and students have done it for years on the Mbone using RTP/RTCP. However, RTP/RTCP has only very basic signaling capabilities, as we have seen.

H.323 mainly defines the signaling needed to set up calls and conferences, choose common codecs, etc. The core of RTP/RTCP is still used to transport isochronous streams and get feedback on the quality of the network, but fancy RTCP features such as email alias distribution are not normally used by H.323.

H.323 tackles a complex problem, and consequently is quite complex itself. The set of documents that an H.323 engineer needs as a reference (Q.931, H.323, H.225, H.245, H.235, H.332, IMTC and ETSI TIPHON profiles, etc.) takes a while to read. Therefore we have chosen here not to paraphrase H.323 but to illustrate

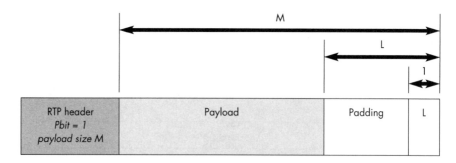

Fig. 1.11 : Padding

the behavior of H.323 entities in various configurations. We hope this will be a useful introduction. The examples are believed to be exact at the time of writing, but there are still ambiguities in the evolving H.323 specifications, so the reader should look at the latest H.323 specifications when in doubt.

I did my best to track inaccuracies, and various engineers have checked these lines. Still, all errors are mine, and there will be errors because the standard is new and I have only a couple of years' experience working with it. I thank in advance any reader who reports such errors (mail to: *book@netcentrex.net*) and helps to improve future editions.

The 'hello world' case: simple voice call from terminal A to terminal B

For this first easy example we assume that two users attached to two distinct IP terminals would like to establish a voice call. From a circuit switched network point of view, the users would have the same experience as if they were using two analogue terminals attached to their respective switches and willing to have a conversation. Other call-related aspects such as security, billing and management are not considered here.

Establishing a point-to-point H.323 call requires two Transmission Control Protocol (TCP) connections between the two IP terminals, one for call setup and the other for call control and capability exchange. The initial TCP connection is made from the caller to a well-known port on the callee and connection carries the call setup messages defined in H.225.0. It is commonly called the Q.931 channel or call signaling channel. Call control messages use a second TCP connection. Upon receipt of the incoming call, the callee listens for a TCP connection on a dynamic port; the callee communicates this port in the call acceptance message. The caller then establishes the second TCP connection to that port. The second connection carries the call control messages defined in H.245. Once the H.245 channel is established, the first connection is no longer necessary (in this simple call example) and may be closed by either endpoint.

The H.245 channel is used by the terminals to exchange audio and video capabilities and to perform master/slave determination. It is then used to signal opening the logical channels for audio and video, which causes RTP sessions to be created for the media streams. The H.245 channel remains open for the duration of the conference. It is also used to signal the end of the conference.

First phase: initializing the call

H.323 uses a subset of the Integrated Services Digital Network (ISDN) Q.931's user to network interface signaling messages for call control. The following messages belong to the core H.323 and must be supported by all terminals:

- Setup
- Alerting
- Connect
- Release Complete
- Status Facility.

Other messages, such as Call Proceeding, Status, Status Enquiry, are optional. Regarding supplementary services, only the Facility message is supported; all others, such as Hold, Retrieve, Suspend, etc. are forbidden. (The same functionality is provided by H.450)

In Fig. 1.12, John, logged on terminal A, wants to make a call to Mark, knowing Mark's IP address (10.2.3.4). Terminal A sends to Terminal B a Setup message on the well-known call signaling channel port (port 1720 as defined by H.225.0 appendix D) using a TCP connection. This message is defined in H.225.0 and contains the following information elements, which have been borrowed from Q.931:

- a protocol discriminator field set to 08H (Q.931 defines this as a user-network call control message);
- a 2-octet locally unique call reference value (CRV) chosen by the originating side which will be copied in each further message concerning this call. Here John's terminal has picked CRV=10;
- a message type (05h for Setup as specified in Q.931 table 4.2);
- a bearer capability, a complex field that can indicate, among other things, whether the call is going to be audio only or audio and video. ISDN gateways can place in this field some elements copied from the ISDN Setup message;
- a called party number and suborders, which must be used when the address is an E.164 number. This field contains a numbering plan identification. When it is set to 1001 (private numbering plan) it means the called address will be found in the user to user information element of the Setup message. If John knows Mark by his transport address (10.2.3.4:1720), the numbering plan will be set to 1001;
- a calling party number and subaddress, which can be present if the caller has an E.164 number;
- a user to user H.323 protocol data unit (PDU) which encapsulates most of the extended information needed by H.323. In this case it is a Setup information element which contains:
  - a protocol identifier (which indicates the version of H.225 in use);
  - an optional H.245 address if the sender aggrees to receive H.245 messages before connect;
  - a source address field listing the sender's aliases, for instance *John@myhouse.uk* (in case the sender has only an E.164 number it is the Q.931 calling party field);

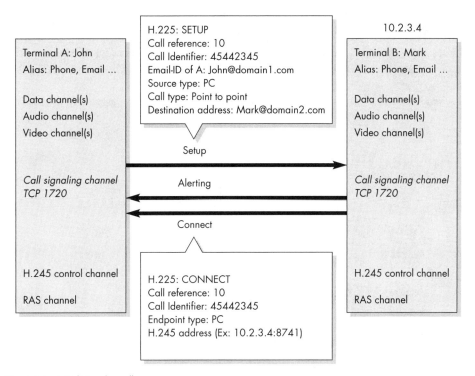

Fig. 1.12 : Initializing the call

– a source information field can be used by the callee to determine the nature of the calling equipment (MCU, gateway, etc.);

– a set of destination alias addresses. Several types are defined in H.323v2: E.164 which is a regular phone number using only characters in the set «01234567893#*,", H323-ID which is a unicode string, url-ID, transport-ID (ex 10.2.3.4:1720), and email-ID (ex: Mark@domain.org);

– a unique conference identifier (CID). This is not the same as the Q.931 CRV described above or the caller identifier (CallID) described below. The CID refers to a conference which is the actual communication existing between the participants. In the case of a multiparty conference, all participants use the same CID, and if a participant joins the conference, leaves and enters again, the CRV and CallID will change, while the CID will remain the same;

– a conference goal which indicates whether the purpose of this Setup message is to create a conference, invite someone into an existing conference, or join an existing conference. In this simple scenario, we simply want to create a conference;

– a call identifier (CallID) which is set by A, and should be globally unique, not only locally unique like the Q.931 CRV.

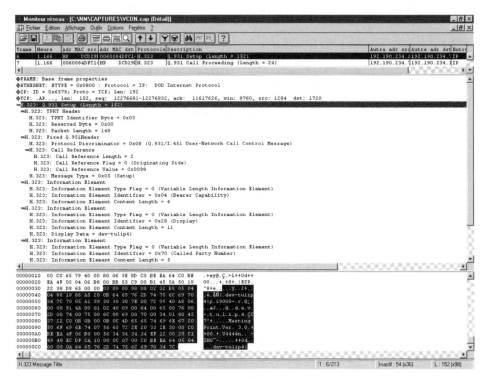

Fig. 1.13 : Capture of a Setup message (using Microsoft Network Monitor – French version)

Either Release Complete, Alerting, Connect or Call Proceeding must be sent by Mark's terminal immediately upon receipt of a Setup message. One of these must be received by John's terminal before its setup timer expires (in general after four seconds). Once Alerting is sent, the user has up to three minutes to accept or refuse the call. Capture of a Setup message is illustrated in Fig. 1.13.

As Mark picks up the call, his terminal sends a Connect message with:

■ the Q.931 protocol discriminator, the same call reference (10), and message type 07h;

■ in the H.323-PDU there is now a Connect user to user information element with:

　　– the protocol identifier

　　– the IP address that B wishes A to use to open the H.245 TCP connection

　　– destination information, which allows A to know if it is connected to a gateway or not

　　– a conference ID copied from the Setup message

　　– the call identifier copied from the Setup message.

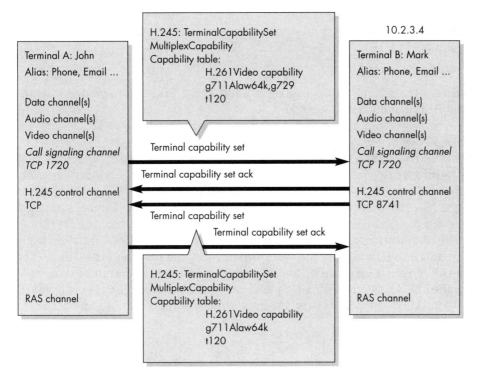

Fig. 1.14 : Establishing the control channel

Second phase: establishing the control channel

Capabilities negotiation

Call control and capability exchange messages are sent on the second TCP connection, which the caller establishes to a dynamic port on the callee's terminal (*see* Fig. 1.14). The messages are defined in H.245. The caller opens this H.245 control channel immediately after receiving the Alerting, Call Proceeding or Connect message, whichever specifies the H.245 transport address to use first. It uses a TCP connection which must be maintained throughout the call. Alternatively, the callee could have set up this channel if the caller had indicated an H.245 transport address in the Setup message. The H.245 control channel is unique for each call between two terminals, even if several media streams are involved for audio, video or data. This channel is also known as logical channel 0.

The first message sent over the control channel is the TerminalCapabilitySet, which carries the following information elements:

■ a sequence number;

■ a capability table which is an ordered list of codec configurations the terminal can support. Each codec configuration is a structure in which the terminal can express the codecs that can be used simultaneously and alternatively. For instance, a terminal could say: I can use (t120 and g729) or (t120 and H.261 and G.711Alaw);

■ capability descriptors.

The terminals send this message to each other and acknowledge it with a TerminalCapabilitySetAck message.

Master/slave determination

The notion of master and slave is useful when the same function or action can be performed by two terminals during a conversation and it is necessary to choose only one (e.g. choose the active MC, opening of bi-directional channels). In H.235, the master is responsible for distributing the encryption keys for media channels to other terminals.

The determination of who will be the master is done by exchanging masterSlaveDetermination messages which contain a terminalType value reflecting the terminal capabilities and a random number. The terminal type values specified in H.323 prioritize MCUs over gatekeepers over gateways over terminals, and MC+MP capable units over MC-only units over units with no MC or MP.

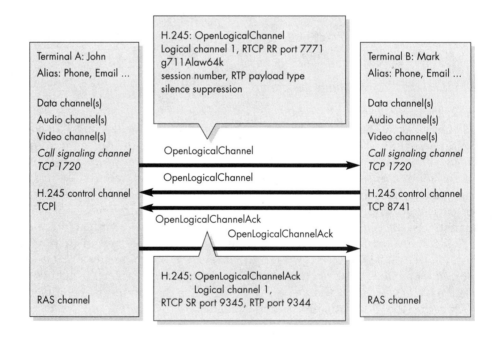

Fig. 1.15 : Beginning of the call

Third phase: beginning of the call

Now terminal A and terminal B need to open media channels for voice, and possibly video and data (Fig. 1.15). The data for these media channels will be carried in several logical channels, which are unidirectional except in the case of T.120 data channels. In order to open a voice channel to B, A sends an H.245 OpenLogicalChannel message which contains the number that will be given to the logical channel, and other parameters such as the type of data that will be carried (Audio G.711 in our example). In the case of sound or video (which will be carried over RTP), the OpenLogicalChannel message also mentions the UDP address and port where B should send RTCP receiver reports, the type of RTP payload, and the capacity to stop sending data during silences. This is also where the sender specifies how many codec frames are put in each RTP packet.

B sends an OpenLogicalChannelAck for this logical channel as soon as it is ready to receive data from A. This message contains the UDP port number to which A should send the RTP data, and the UDP port to which A should send RTCP data. Meanwhile, B may also have opened a logical channel to A following the same procedure.

Fourth phase: dialogue

Now John and Mark can talk, and see each other if they have also opened video logical channels (Fig. 1.16). The media data is sent in RTP packets. RTCP SR pack-

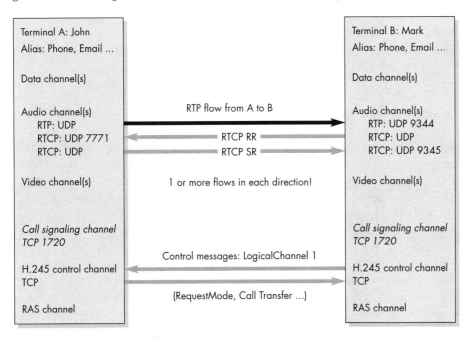

Fig. 1.16 : Dialogue during the call

ets sent by A are used to allow B to synchronize multiple RTP streams, and can also be used by B to evaluate the expected rate of RTP data and to measure the distance to the sender. RTCP receiver reports sent by B allow A to measure the quality of service of the network between A and B: RTCP messages contain the fraction of packets that have been lost since the last RR, the cumulative packet loss, the inter-arrival jitter and the highest sequence number received. H.323 terminals should respond to increasing packet loss by reducing the sending rate.

Note that H.323 mandates to use only one RTP/RTCP port pair for each session. There can be three main sessions between H.323 terminals: the audio session (session id 1), the video session (session id 2) and the data session (session id 3), but nothing in the standard prevents a terminal from opening more sessions. For each session there should be only one RTCP port used, i.e. if there is simultaneously an RTP flow from A to B and from B to A, the RTCP sender and receiver reports for both flows will use the same UDP port.

The end

How to hang up an H.323 call? Well, it is not that simple. If John hangs up, terminal A must send an H.245 CloseLogicalChannel message for each logical channel that A opened. B acknowledges those messages with a CloseLogicalChannelAck. After all logical channels have been closed, A sends an H.245 endSessionCommand, waits until it has received the same message from B and closes the H.245 control channel. Finally, A and B must send an H.225 ReleaseComplete message over the call signaling channel if it is still open, and this channel is closed and the call is closed.

Needless to say, many terminals are not so polite, and terminate rather than close calls.

A more complex case: calling a public phone from the Internet

In the simple case described above, Mark called John directly on his current IP address 10.2.3.4. This situation is convenient for showing the basics of H.323, but unlikely to happen in reality. If nothing else, a plain IP address is difficult to remember. In many cases it will even change – most Internet service providers (ISPs) allocate a dynamic IP address to their subscribers.

The next example is more complicated. Mark wants to call his grandmother, who has a regular phone and does not have the slightest idea of what an IP address is. This example will show the need for a new H.323 entity, called the gatekeeper.

The gatekeeper is the most complex component of the H.323 framework. It was introduced in H.323v1, but at that stage most people did not really understand how useful it would be. At best, the gatekeeper was considered to be a sort of directory mapping friendly names to IP addresses, and some companies had 'better ideas' on how to do it. Even today some 'H.323 compliant' software and hardware do not use the gatekeeper but use proprietary mechanisms ranging from IRC (Internet relay chat) servers to LDAP (lightweight directory access protocol) servers to find the transport address of another IP phone.

H.323v2 has clarified the role of the gatekeeper, and now it is widely acknowledged that the gatekeeper is *the* right place for all network-based services; i.e. those which need to be performed independently of the terminal or when the terminal is turned off. Those services include registration (the ability to know that someone has logged on and can be reached at a particular terminal), admission (checking the right to access to resources), and status (monitoring the availability of telephone-related network resources such as gateways and terminals). Finding the transport address to use to reach a particular alias is naturally also part of the gatekeeper's role, since this transport address might depend on the status of the called party (for instance, if the person is not logged on, the call should be redirected to an answering machine or a regular phone through a gateway), the identity of the caller (not everybody might be allowed to call Mark), or the status of a particular resource (if all ports on a gateway are busy, it might be necessary to instruct the caller's terminal to use another gateway).

Therefore in this section we consider that the caller has access to a gatekeeper, and show some of its features in action. The terminal and the gatekeeper use a specific protocol for registration, admission and status purposes, which has logically been named RAS.

First phase: where is the gatekeeper?

In simple configurations, the gatekeeper's IP address might be configured manually in the IP terminal. However, H.323 has developed a mechanism to dynamically find a gatekeeper (GK) on the network. This has a number of advantages, such as when someone has got a laptop and roams between several office locations. It also provides a way to introduce redundancy and load balancing in the network.

In order to find a gatekeeper, an H.323 terminal should send a multicast 'gatekeeper request' (GRQ) to the group address 224.0.1.41 on port 1718 (for more information on multicast, refer to Chapter 8). Within the GRQ message, it can specify whether it is willing to contact a particular gatekeeper. The terminal also mentions its aliases, allowing a gatekeeper to reply only to specific groups of terminals. Eventually a GRQ can be sent in unicast to port 1718, or preferably 1719, the default for unicast RAS messages.

This message should be sent with a very low TTL (time to live) initially in order to reach first the gatekeepers on the local network, and then use expanding ring search. This GRQ message tells the GK on what address and port the terminal expects to receive the answer, which type of terminal it is, and what the terminal alias(es) is (are).

Each gatekeeper should be a member of group 224.0.1.41 and listen on port 1718. Therefore one or more of those gatekeepers will reply on the address specified by the terminal with a 'gatekeeper confirm' (GCF) message which indicates the name of the gatekeeper, and the unicast address and port that this gatekeeper uses for RAS messages. It can also include the names and transport information of other backup gatekeepers.

The use of multicast for gatekeeper detection has caused much controversy. In fact, not many IP networks support multicast today. Multicast routing is not activated by default on routers, and many network administrators feel comfortable with static routes and are not really willing to experiment with a dynamic multicast routing protocol such as DVMRP or PIM. Moreover, most of the Ethernet hubs and switches installed today do not support multicast – at best some of those devices turn multicast into broadcast traffic. However, if you are still using an Ethernet coax network, multicast will work on your LAN segment and you do not have to do anything. In addition, the most recent switches support multicast (see Chapter eight of this book to see what it means exactly), so if you upgraded your network from shared 10 Mbps to switched 100 Mbps recently it is likely that multicast works on your LAN too.

In the near future, all switches will support multicast, and if you plan to support video conferencing and video broadcasting efficiently across your network, you will have to turn on some multicast protocol in your routers.

Because of the problem with multicast, most implementations are expected to use broadcast or static configuration instead. However, broadcast traffic will never be propagated on the public Internet, and in the near future you may want to outsource your gatekeeper to an external service provider (which may own gateways or provide additional services), so you should take care to choose software that can be configured to support multicast (see Fig. 1.17). The latest interop tests seem to show that gatekeeper discovery is being supported by more and more implementations – causing storms of GK responses in the labs!

If the terminal has received more than one answer, it chooses one and registers to the corresponding gatekeeper by sending a 'registration request' (RRQ) message (usually on UDP port 1719). This message carries one important piece of additional information compared to GRQ: the transport address which is to be used for call signaling. The registration request can be a 'soft state' if the terminal desires, in which case it also specifies a 'time to live' for the registration and will refresh its registration periodically by sending more RRQs.

The gatekeeper replies with a 'registration confirm' (RCF) message in which the gatekeeper assigns a unique identifier to this terminal which must be copied in all subsequent RAS messages. The GK can also assign an alias to the requesting endpoint in this RCF.

The set of all H.323 endpoints, MC, MCUs and gateways managed by a single gatekeeper is called a 'zone'. In our example, John's terminal and the gateway belong to the same zone.

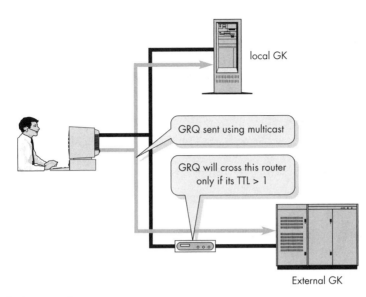

local GK

GRQ sent using multicast

GRQ will cross this router
only if its TTL > 1

External GK

Fig. 1.17 : Finding a gatekeeper

Second phase: requesting permission to make a new call

Now that John's terminal has found a gatekeeper and is registered, John still needs to request permission from the gatekeeper for each call he wants to make. In this case he wants to reach his grandmother at +33 123456789. His terminal will first send an 'admission request' message (ARQ) to its gatekeeper. This RAS message includes:

■ a sequential number

■ the GK assigned terminal identifier

■ the type of call (point to point)

■ the call model that the terminal is willing to use (direct or gatekeeper routed)

■ the destination information (in this case the E.164 address +33 123456789 of Grandma, but it could also have been Mark's email alias)

■ a globally unique CallID

■ an estimation of the bi-directional bandwidth that will be used for this call for audio and video. This includes audio and video that will be sent from the called party and is measured excluding network overhead. This is a *very* rough estimation because the codecs will be negotiated later. For instance, an audio-only terminal might indicate 128 kbit/s as a worst case if the two terminals negotiate a G.711 codec (64 kbit/s) for the incoming and outgoing audio logical channels. The endpoint may use 'bandwidth request' (BRQ) messages later to ask for additional bandwidth (e.g. if it needs to open video channels).

The two possible call models refer to the way the call signaling channel (carrying Q.931 messages) and the H.245 channel are set up between the endpoints. The calling endpoint can establish those channels directly with the called endpoint (the direct model), or it can establish those channels with the gatekeeper which will relay the call signaling and call control information to the called endpoint (there might be several gatekeepers routing the Q.931 and H.245 channels between the two endpoints). The latter is the gatekeeper routed mode.

In this simple example we will use the direct model, and will discuss the GK routed model later.

If it decides to accept the call, the gatekeeper replies with an 'admission confirm' (ACF) message which specifies:

- the call model in use;
- the transport address and port to use for Q.931 call signaling. This address can be the IP address of the called terminal directly (or the IP address of a gateway when calling a regular phone number) in the direct model, or it might be the gatekeeper itself if it decides to route the call. In our example the gatekeeper replies with the IP address of a gateway;
- the allowed bandwidth for the call;
- the GK can also request the terminal to send 'information request' (IRR) messages from time to time to check whether the endpoint is still alive.

Third phase: call signaling

The admission confirm message has provided John's terminal with the information it needed to complete the call (Fig. 1.18). Now the terminal can send a Setup message to the call signaling address and port specified by the gatekeeper – in our case a gateway to the phone network.

Before proceeding, the gateway may itself ask the gatekeeper if it is authorized to place the call using an ARQ/ACF sequence. The ARQ will mention both the calling endpoint alias/call signaling address and the called endpoint alias/call signaling address.

The gateway knows from the called party number information element of the Setup message which phone number it must call. If it is connected to an ISDN phone line, it will simply send an ISDN Q.931 Setup message on the D channel to initiate the connection on the ISDN. If it is connected to an analogue line, it will go off-hook, and dial the number using DTMF (digital tone multi frequency). Note that the format of the phone number may need to be changed, e.g. the country code may need to be removed depending on where the gateway is installed.

The gateway will send an H.225 Alerting message to the caller as soon as it has received an indication from the phone network that Grandma's phone is ringing, and will send the Connect message as soon as she has picked up the handset. If the gateway was connected through an ISDN line, those events will

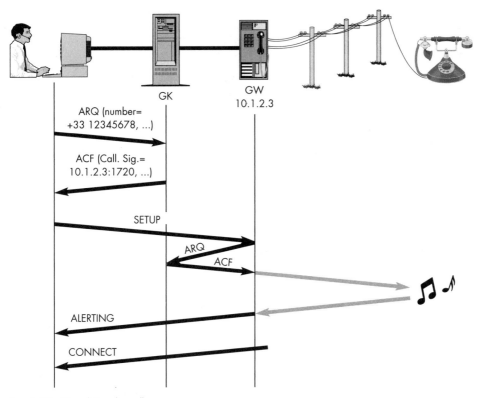

ARQ (number=
+33 12345678, ...)

ACF (Call. Sig.=
10.1.2.3:1720, ...)

SETUP

ARQ

ACF

ALERTING

CONNECT

GK

GW
10.1.2.3

Fig. 1.18 : Completing the call

be signaled by the phone network using similar Q.931 Alerting and Connect messages. If it is an analogue line, the gateway needs to detect the appropriate ring/busy/connect conditions.

The Alerting or Connect message contains a transport address to allow John's terminal to establish an H.245 control channel on which it can negotiate codecs and open media channels. This procedure is identical to the procedure used when John was calling Mark. Now the media channels are opened between the gateway and John's terminal. Note that the gateway also requests permission to secure and forward the call using another admission request message (ARQ).

Termination phase

■ whoever hangs up (e.g. the gateway) first needs to close its logical channels using the H.245 CloseLogicalChannel message (Fig. 1.19);

■ the gateway then sends an H.245 EndSessionCommand message to John's terminal, and waits to receive the same message from John's terminal. The gateway then closes the H.245 channel;

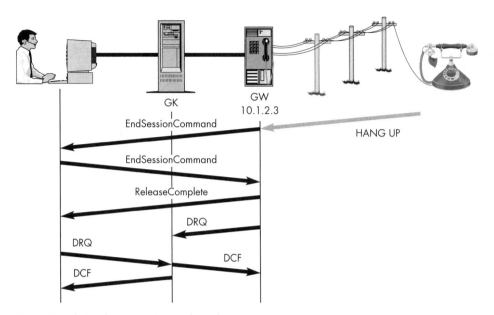

Fig. 1.19 : Closing the communication channels

- if the Q.931 channel is still open, each terminal must send a Q.931 ReleaseComplete message before closing it;

- then the terminal and the gateway must send a 'disengage request' (DRQ) message to the gatekeeper (this way the gatekeeper knows that bandwidth has been released). The gatekeeper replies to each with a 'disengage confirm' (DCF). If there is more than one gatekeeper and the gateway and the terminal are registered to different gatekeepers, each one sends a DRQ to its own gatekeeper;

- the terminal or the gateway might want to unregister (sending an 'unregistration request' (URQ) to the gatekeeper), but there is no reason to do so unless, for instance, John decides to close his IP telephony software.

If during the communication the gatekeeper wants to clear the call it can also send a DRQ to one of the endpoints. At this point the endpoint must send an H.245 EndSessionCommand to the other endpoint, wait to receive an EndSession Command, close the Q.931 channel with a ReleaseComplete, and send a DCF to the gatekeeper.

In order to prevent a terminal from pretending it is closing a connection with a gateway without sending an EndSessionCommand/ReleaseComplete to the gateway, when a gatekeeper receives a DRQ from the terminal first it will wait until it has received a DRQ from the gateway before replying with a DCF. If the gatekeeper receives a DRQ from the gateway (as in our example), it will wait until it has received a DRQ from the terminal before sending a DCF to the gateway. If the gatekeeper does not receive a DRQ from the terminal within a few seconds, it will ask the terminal to disconnect by sending a DRQ. The terminal is supposed to disconnect and send back a DCF, but if it does not do so within a few seconds (the PC might have crashed), the gatekeeper will send a DCF to the gateway anyhow. This procedure prevents fraud and unwanted operations due to unstable or non-conformant terminals.

H.323 across multiple domains

As the initial title of H.323 implied, the first version of H.323 did not consider issues that would occur in a wide area environment. It was assumed that all gate-keepers would get a complete view of the network and so would be able to respond to 'location requests' (LRQs) and admission requests. In this context it did not seem necessary to have an inter-gatekeeper protocol.

Now that H.323 is considered for all kinds of calls, it is obvious that there will need to be a gatekeeper-to-gatekeeper protocol across different zones. This issue will be included in the standard starting with H.323 version 3. The gatekeeper-to-gatekeeper protocol is likely to use primarily ARQ/ACF and DRQ/DCF messages.

Direct call model

Call setup

In the direct call model, only the RAS messages are routed by the gatekeepers (Fig. 1.20). Now John wants to call his grandmother using a gateway managed by a service provider, Cybercall. The service provider has his own gatekeepers. Therefore John's terminal and the gateway will be located in different zones. John's terminal will register to his own gatekeeper, and the gateway will be regis-tered to the service provider's gatekeeper. When John has become a customer of Cybercall, John's gatekeeper has registered with Cybercall's gatekeeper, and vice versa. Therefore those gatekeepers know about each other.

The admission request is sent by John's terminal to the gatekeeper to which it has registered. This gatekeeper knows that all calls to the PSTN (public switched telephone network) are handled by Cybercall. Therefore it routes the ARQ to the gatekeeper of Cybercall. Because the ARQ comes from a gatekeeper that is regis-tered, Cybercall's gatekeeper will accept it and returns an admission confirm.

We have an additional parameter in this ACF compared to what we have seen already: a token. A token is an optional parameter that consists of a 'bag of bits'. Unless it knows of this specific token, an H.323 entity should simply pass it

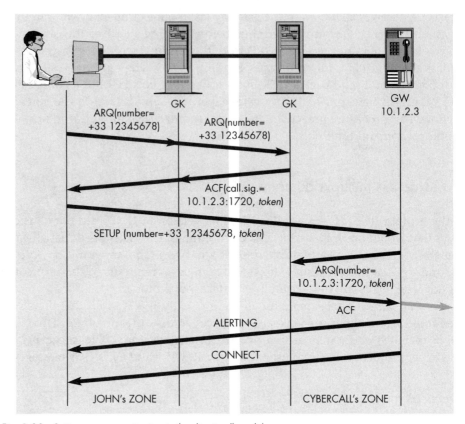

Fig. 1.20 : Setting up communication in the direct call model

along transparently. Here the token serves as a secret which will be copied by John's terminal in the Setup message. Cybercall's gatekeeper has put in this token a digital signature of some important aspects of the call, such as the destination and the current time. When it receives a Setup message including this token, the gateway can verify that the call has been authorized by the gatekeeper.

Here, Cybercall, for security reasons, has not given the gateway enough information to decode the token locally. The gateway will simply pass this token in the ARQ, Cybercall's gatekeeper will check it and return an ACF. When it receives the ACF, the gateway will set up the call on the PSTN side, and send a Connect message to John as soon as Grandma picks up the phone.

John establishes the H.245 control channel to the gateway using the address and port specified by the gateway in the Connect message. Logical channels are established using OpenLogicalChannel messages, and John can talk.

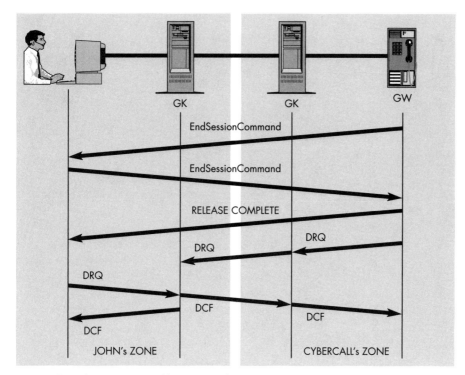

Fig. 1.21 : The EndSessionCommand between gatekeepers

Call tear-down

This time, if Grandma hangs up first, the gateway will send an EndSessionCommand and ReleaseComplete message to John's terminal. The gateway then sends a DRQ message to Cybercall's gatekeeper, which routes the DRQ message to John's gatekeeper. As soon as John's gatekeeper receives a DRQ from John's terminal, it sends an DCF to John's terminal, and another DCF to Cybercall's gatekeeper, which routes it to the gateway (*see* Fig. 1.21).

If John hangs up first, a symmetric procedure occurs, as shown in Fig. 1.22.

Gatekeeper routed model

There are many reasons why Cybercall would like to have more control over John's communication. With the direct model, Cybercall does not know what occurs during the call. If, for instance, Grandma's phone is busy, Cybercall's gatekeeper will see it simply as a very short call. This forces Cybercall to do all accounting at the gateway level, which can lead to a lot of work if the Cybercall domain has dozens of gateways. Also, unless the billing is done at the gateway level, the gate-

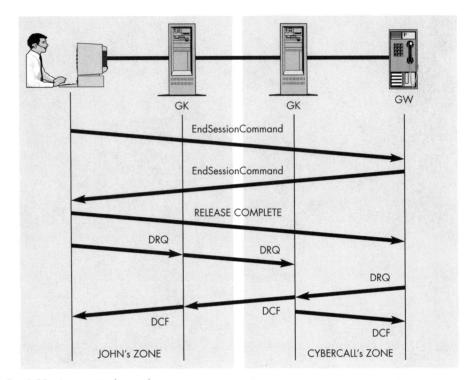

Fig. 1.22 : A symmetrical procedure

keeper knows only the overall bandwidth used by the call, while it might want to bill for each logical channel separately depending on the codec used.

Cybercall may also want to protect its domain using firewalls. We will see later that because H.323 uses dynamic UDP ports, the implementation of such firewalls is difficult. One way to do it if the gatekeeper has access to the Q.931 and H.245 channel is to control packet filters from the gatekeeper. This is impossible to do using the direct model.

These are just a few of the reasons why the gatekeeper routed model – or a mixture of direct and gatekeeper routed model – will be preferred in most situations where the network involves several administrative domains. There is even more pressure to use the gatekeeper routed model as soon as the network provider wants to introduce non-terminal-based services, such as virtual call centers.

Call setup
In this example Cybercall's gatekeeper decides to route the call by putting its own IP address (10.1.2.2) in the ACF call signaling address (Fig. 1.23). John's gatekeeper also decides to route the call by putting its own IP address in the ACF call

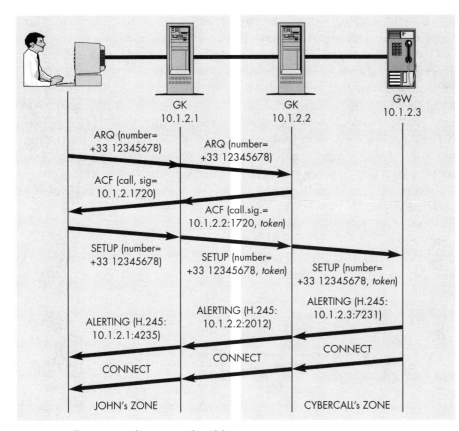

GK
10.1.2.1

GK
10.1.2.2

GW
10.1.2.3

ARQ (number=
+33 12345678)

ARQ (number=
+33 12345678)

ACF (call, sig=
10.1.2.1720)

ACF (call.sig.=
10.1.2.2:1720, *token*)

SETUP (number=
+33 12345678)

SETUP (number=
+33 12345678, *token*)

SETUP (number=
+33 12345678, *token*)

ALERTING (H.245:
10.1.2.3:7231)

ALERTING (H.245:
10.1.2.2:2012)

ALERTING (H.245:
10.1.2.1:4235)

CONNECT

CONNECT

CONNECT

CONNECT

JOHN's ZONE

CYBERCALL's ZONE

Fig. 1.23 : A call using a gatekeeper routed model

signaling address. But John's gatekeeper could also have used the direct model by copying the call signaling address provided in Cybercall's ACF in its own ACF. In this case John's terminal would have sent the Setup message directly to Cybercall's gatekeeper. This would be a call using a mixed model.

You probably remember that one of the most important information elements of the Alerting or Connect message is the H.245 call control channel address that John's terminal must use to establish the call control channel. Here the H.245 channel will also be routed because both Cybercall and John's gatekeepers have put their own IP address in the Call Control transport address field of the Alerting message.

In theory, it is possible to route the Q.931 messages but let the H.245 call control channel be established directly between the endpoints and there will probably be situations in which this will occur. However, H.323 recommends routing the Q.931 and H.245 channels together.

What about the media channels? They could be routed too, but there would be little to gain from doing so because all the significant events of the call are signaled using H.245 or Q.931 messages. An exception could be fax because, as we will see later, the entire T.30 protocol is encapsulated in a media channel, and therefore the gatekeeper needs to have access to the media channel to know how many pages have been transferred. But unless there is a specific need to do so, media channels flow directly between the endpoints, even if the gatekeeper routed model is used. This optimizes media latency, even if the call signaling has to go through many gatekeepers. Routing media flows through the gatekeeper forces the provider to place gatekeepers near the customer premises, and thus ruins the economics of VoIP, which allows the control of all end-points from a single gatekeeper.

Call tear-down

The call tear-down (Fig. 1.24) is similar to the direct model case, except of course that H.245 and Q.931 messages are routed through the gatekeepers.

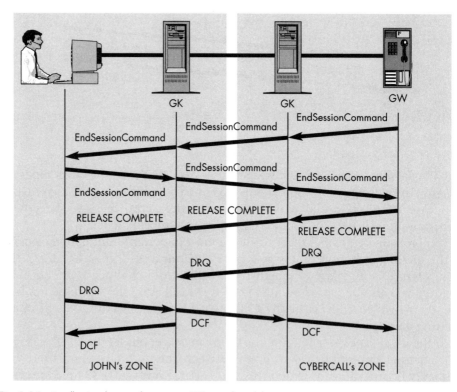

Fig. 1.24 : A call using the tear-down using GK routed model

Other RAS messages – LRQ versus ARQ

H.225 defines more RAS messages to talk to a gatekeeper, which are mostly unused for now in the majority of implementations, except the location request message. There has been a lot of confusion over the respective uses of LRQs and ARQs.

LRQ and ARQ: quotes from H.225
ARQ and LAN access permission
The ARQ is used to request an access to the LAN (local area network). Once the connection is open, the terminal may use a BRQ to request more bandwidth to the LAN when it opens new logical channels.

H.225.0 states: 'As part of the process of opening the channel, before sending the open logical channel acknowledgement the endpoint uses the ARQ/ACF or BRQ/BCF sequence to ensure that sufficient bandwidth is available for the new channel (unless sufficient bandwidth is available from a previous ARQ/ACF or BRQ/BCF sequence).'

Since the ARQ is used to request an access to the LAN, the terminal, once it has sent an ARQ, for a new call is expected to send a Setup. The CRV parameter can be used to link the two messages, e.g. within a gatekeeper routing the call. (H.225 states for the Setup message: ' If an ARQ was previously sent, the CRV used here shall be the same.')

Address translation
The situation is more confusing for the address translation function. The obvious choice is to use the location request message. But when comparing the semantics of the LRQ and the ARQ, it becomes apparent that the ARQ can also serve this purpose. In fact, an ARQ is a superset of an LRQ, requesting not only an address translation but also LAN access. This alleviates the need for terminals to first do an LRQ, then an ARQ, and finally a Setup.

Note that this address translation can be:

- a pure alias to transport address resolution; for instance from an email alias the gatekeeper indicates to which IP address to send the Setup;
- an alias translation if the terminal specifies it can map aliases (canMapAlias parameter of the ARQ); in this case the gatekeeper can also force the terminal to change the destination alias in the Setup.

Conclusion
Usually a terminal needs to do an address resolution just before it sends a Setup. In this case the ARQ can be used to request LAN access as well as an address resolution, and the LRQ is redundant. This is reflected by the fact that H.225 mandates the support of ARQs by H.323 endpoints, whereas the support of LRQs is optional.

Some special terminals might need to perform address translation without originating a call afterwards (I can imagine, for instance, an office mapping application that would try to track where the users are currently logged and publish a map on the web). These terminals should use the LRQ for address resolution.

Overall, the LRQ message is not particularly useful and consideration was even given to removing it for TIPHON-compliant systems.

Usage scenarios

From the remarks made in the previous paragraph, we can expect the following behavior, depending on the value of a parameter called pregrantedARQ that is contained in the last RCF (registration confirm).

No pregranted ARQ

The terminal needs to send an ARQ to the gatekeeper before each call setup. It is illicit to send an LRQ and then a Setup. It is licit to send an LRQ, then an ARQ, then a SETUP, but useless.

Pregranted ARQ

Pregranted ARQs are an excellent way to optimize call setup times. In the pregrantedARQ element of the RCF, the gatekeeper can allow a terminal to:

- initiate a call without first sending an ARQ
- initiate a call without first sending an ARQ, but *only* if it sends the Setup to the gatekeeper
- answer a call without first requesting permission to the gatekeeper
- answer a call without first requesting permission to the gatekeeper *only* if the Setup message comes from the gatekeeper.

Advanced topics

Faster procedures

Call setup time

One of the major weaknesses of H.323v1, which has been constantly pointed out by those who favor the SIP protocol, is the time it takes to actually set up a call (Fig. 1.25). Even in the simple cases, the above procedures involve:

- one message round trip for the ARQ/ACF sequence (except in pregrantedARQ mode)
- one message round trip for the Setup-Connect sequence

- one message round trip for the H.245 capabilities exchange
- one message round trip for the H.245 master slave procedure
- one message round trip for the setup of each logical channel.

This looks bad already, but the real situation is even worse because the Q.931 and H.245 channels use TCP connections which must also be set up.

Each TCP connection needs an extra round trip to synchronize the TCP window sequence numbers. In a WAN environment where each round trip may take several hundred milliseconds, this can lead to unacceptably long setup delays, especially when using the gatekeeper routed call model where a TCP connection needs to be established between each gatekeeper.

Network-generated messages

Network experts discovered another problem after H.323v1 had been standardized. In the switched circuit network there are situations in which a message is played to the caller before it receives a connect:

- when the SCN (switched circuit network) is congested and the call cannot be established, you can get a message saying 'Due to a congestion, your call cannot be connected, please call later'. This message is generated by the network at the local exchange, and because it does not originate from the called endpoint, no connect message is sent;

- in some applications the intelligent network (IN) can also generate network prompts without always finding a connect ISDN message first, for instance for televoting applications: you dial a number and you get back a message saying 'Thank you for voting YES, the current status is 34 per cent YES, 66 per cent NO'.

With H.323v1, it is impossible to send a voice message to the calling party before sending a connect because the media channels are not yet established.

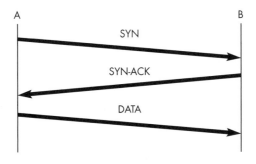

Fig. 1.25 : Setting up a TCP connect

The Fast Connect procedure

The solution to both problems should:

■ enable unidirectional or bi-directional media channels immediately after the Q.931 Setup message.

■ allow a basic bidirectional communication (i.e. audio only) immediately after the Connect message has been received.

■ improve set-up delays.

This is exactly what the Fast Connect procedure is doing. Typically, when calling an IN-based card telephony service, an IVR server requests the card code before sending a Connect because the call is not yet charged. The Connect is sent only after the code has been checked and the destination party has answered the call (*see* Fig. 1.26).

An endpoint which decides to use the Fast Connect will include a new parameter, called fastStart, in the Setup user to user information element. This parameter includes a description of all the media channels that the endpoint is prepared to receive and all the media channels that the endpoint offers to send.

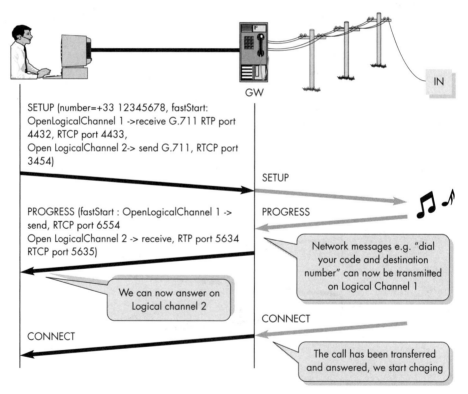

Fig. 1.26 : The Connect procedure, an example of a calling card service

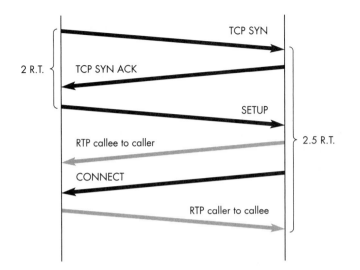

Fig. 1.27 : Evaluating round trips needed to set up a conversation

This description includes the codecs used, the receiving ports, etc. This allows the receipt of network prompts and improves set-up delays (but the TCP setup must also be taken into account to evaluate the number of round trips needed to set up the conversation, as shown in Fig. 1.27).

If the called endpoint cannot or does not want to use the Fast Connect procedure, it will not return the fastStart element in subsequent Q.931 messages. In this case the normal procedure involving H.245 will take place.

If the called endpoint supports Fast Connect, it will return in the Call Proceeding, Progress, Alerting or Connect Q.931 messages a fastStart element selecting among the media offered by the caller.

For example, the Setup message is modified as follows (in bold):

■ protocol discriminator field (08H)

■ call reference value (CRV)

■ a message type (Setup)

■ ...

■ called party number and subaddress

■ calling party number and subaddress

■ the H.323 user to user element which contains the Setup user to user information element in which we find:

 – the protocol identifier;

 – ...

 – the sender's aliases;

 – the destination address;

- the CID and CallID;
- **fastStart** – used only in the Fast Connect procedure, **fastStart** is a sequence of **OpenLogicalChannel** structures. Each **OpenLogicalChannel** structure describes *one* media channel that the caller wants to send (**forwardLogicalChannelParameters** within the **OpenLogicalChannel** structure) or receive (**reverseLogicalChannelParameters**). All proposed **OpenLogicalChannel** structures can be selected simultaneously, unless they share a common **sessionID** value in **H2250LogicalChannelParameters** of the **OpenLogicalChannel** structure, in which case they are considered alternative options for the same channel;
- the **MediaWaitForConnect** boolean.

```
Open LogicalChannel          : :=SEQUENCE
{
        forwardLogicalChannelNumber LogicalChannelNumber,

        forwardLogicalChannelParameter          SEQUENCE
        {
                portNumber   INTERGER   (0,.65535)   OPTIONAL,
                dataType     DataType
                multiplexParameters       CHOICE
                {
                        h2250LogicalChannelParameters       H2250LogicalChannelParameters,
                        none         NULL

                },
                . . . ,
                forwardLogicalChannelDpendancy        LogicalChannelNumber   OPTIONAL
                replacementForLogicalChannelNumber  OPTIONAL

        },


        reverseLogicalChannelParameter          SEQUENCE
        {
                dataType     DataType
                multiplexParameters          CHOICE
                {
                        h2250LogicalChannelParameters   H2250LogicalChannelParameters
                } OPTIONAL,  –– Not present for H.222
                . . . ,
                reverseLogicalChannelDependancy        LogicalChannelNumber   OPTIONAL
                replacementForLogicalChannelNumber  OPTIONAL

        }  OPTIONAL,  –– Not present for uni–directional channel request

        . . . ,
        seperateStack                NetworkAccessParameters   OPTIONAL
        encryptionSync               EncryptionSync  OPTIONAL  –– used only by Master

}
```

Fig. 1.28 : The OpenLogicalChannel sequence

The network can send media to *any* of the receiving channels mentioned in the Setup message of the caller immediately after the calling terminal has sent this message, unless MediaWaitForConnect is true. Therefore, even if the calling terminal plans to use only one of those channels in the regular conversation, it *must* be prepared to receive media on any one of those offered channels.

The calling terminal can select one or more acceptable OpenLogicalChannel structures (*see* Fig. 1.28) within the offered fastStart parameter and return them in a fastStart parameter within an H.225 Call Proceeding, Progress, Alerting, or Connect message. The selected logical channels are considered open after this.

Usually, in a normal ISDN call, the called party does not send media until the Connect message has been received. It is possible to force this usual behavior with the fastStart procedure by setting the MediaWaitForConnect element of the Q.931 Setup to 'true'.

Since the Fast Connect procedure repairs a major flaw of H.323v1 regarding interworking with the SCN, it has been made a core feature in the H.323 profile of the ETSI TIPHON project. Work is still needed on DTMF transmission as H.245 UserInputIndication cannot be used (no H.245 channel is opened). H.245 tunneling might lead to fewer interworking problems in the meantime.

H.245 tunneling

H.323v2 offers another way to improve the call setup time by encapsulating H.245 messages in Q.931 messages, so that only one TCP connection is needed. This method can also solve the issue of network-generated messages, and therefore is a possible replacement for the Fast Connect procedure. It is also an optimization that can apply for all calls that require complex H.245 signaling, such as multipoint conferences.

An endpoint which wants to use H.245 tunneling must set the H.245Tunneling element of the Setup message and all subsequent Q.931 messages to 'true'. A called endpoint also indicates its willingness to accept H.245 tunneling by setting this same element to 'true' in all Q.931 messages.

The calling endpoint encapsulates one or more encoded H.245 messages in the H.245Control element of any Q.931 message. If the called endpoint is also capable of receiving it, all H.245 messages can be exchanged this way and there is no need to open a separate H.245 channel. If the called endpoint has not set the H.245Tunneling to 'true' in the first Q.931 message it sends back (it could be Call Proceeding, Progress, Alerting or Connect), the calling endpoint knows this is not supported and the normal procedure for opening an H.245 channel is followed.

Q.931 messages are modified as shown in bold:

■ protocol discriminator field (08H)
■ call reference value (CRV)

- a message type (Setup, Alerting, etc.)
- …
- called party number and subaddress
- calling party number and subaddress
- the H.323 user to user element now contains:
  - the **H245Tunneling** boolean;
  - **H245Control** – a sequence of octet strings representing encoded H.245 PDUs;
  - the H.323 message body can now be the usual Setup, CallProceeding, Connect, Alerting, UserInformation, ReleaseComplete, Facility or Progress information element, or a new 'null' value called **empty**, which is explained later.

When using H.245 tunneling the Q.931 channel needs to remain open for the duration of the call. If an H.245 message needs to be sent when no Q.931 message is pending, the H.245 message will be encapsulated in a Q.931 Facility message. In this case the Q.931 Facility message is sent, but the H.323 user to user element contains only the H.245Tunneling boolean and the H.245 PDUs encoded in H.245Control. The H.323 message body itself is not the usual Facility user to user information element, but is set to empty.

Such a need to use Facility messages may also occur in the gatekeeper routed model, as shown in Fig. 1.29.

A terminal can signal that it wants to use H.245 tunneling in a fastStart Q.931 message which already contains an OpenLogicalChannels parameter by setting H245Tunneling to 'true'. However, it must not encapsulate H.245 messages in the same Q.931 messages as they would supersede the indications found in the OpenLogicalChannels parameter.

Reverting to normal operation

In some cases a terminal using fastStart and/or H.245 tunneling may need to use a separate control channel in the middle of an established call (for instance, when a terminal that has opened an audio connection in fastStart mode needs to open a new media channel). In this case the terminal can send a Facility message to the other terminal indicating it wishes to establish a separate H.245 channel and proposing a transport address for this. The terminal which receives the Facility message must establish a new TCP connection for the H.245 channel using this transport address. Once the new connection is established, the terminals must stop using the H.245 tunnel.

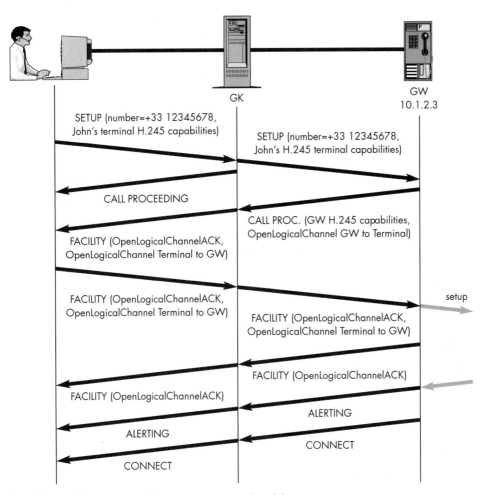

Fig. 1.29 : Facility messages in the gatekeeper routed model

Limited capability terminals

The addition of Fast Connect mode to H.323 has made it possible to manufacture a simpler, yet 'H.323 compliant' terminal. By supporting only H.323 in Fast Connect mode, implementors can avoid implementing most of H.245, and it should be easier to make simple appliances like LAN phones this way.

However, most of the potential of H.323 comes from the conferencing features which are enabled by H.245. Simple H.323 terminals without H.245 will not be able to participate in such conferences. Moreover, DTMF is usually carried using H.245; simple terminals may have to use in-band DTMF coding which is unreliable.

Overall, it seems to be a misunderstanding to consider the features described above as simplifications of H.323. In fact, they were introduced mainly to fix shortcomings in the existing H.323v1 framework regarding call setup times and operation with the SCN.

The TCP slow-start issue

It should be clear by now that the use of TCP causes at least one unnecessary round trip due to the SYN/ACK handshake. In fact, the situation can be worse if the Setup message is larger than the MTU (maximum transmission unit). In this case the sender must send the Setup in two or more TCP segments. The problem is that most TCP implementations are designed to be friendly to the network and follow RFC 2001, which mandates a slow-start procedure. In our case, after sending the first segment, the sender must wait until it has received an acknowledgement before transmitting the next segment. Only then can it increase the window size and send two segments at once.

Because of this, large Setup messages may cause one additional round trip. It is worth trying to limit the size of the Setup message below 576 octets, as this is the minimal IPv4 MTU, but this may not always be possible.

For this reason, among others, there will be a special H.323v3 mode allowing the use of UDP signaling instead of (or simultaneously with) TCP signaling. This will be specified in annex E of the standard.

Conferencing with H.323

The MCU, MC and MP

There are two distinct functions that may be present in any conference. The first is the control function, which decides who is allowed to participate, how new participants are introduced in existing conferences, how the participants synchronize on a common mode of operation, who is allowed to broadcast media, etc. This role is assumed in H.323 by a functional entity called the multipoint controller (MC).

When many people talk in an audio conference, they might simply multicast their audio, and all terminals can do the mixing of individual media streams themselves. In most cases however, individual terminals will have limited capabilities, or it might be impractical to multicast all media streams (especially in the case of video). At some point in the network an entity needs to do the mixing or switching of incoming media streams, and send only the resulting processed outgoing stream to each terminal. In the case of video it can be the image from the last active speaker; in the case of audio each terminal will receive a stream resulting from the addition of all streams from *other* speakers in the conference. In H.323, this functional entity is called the multipoint processor (MP).

A dedicated callable endpoint which contains an MC, and optionally one or more MPs, is called a multipoint control unit. Not only MCUs can have the MC functionality, however, A terminal or gatekeeper with sufficient resources can also have the capability to act as an MC, and may be able to do some media mixing locally. However, the MC functional entity in a terminal or gatekeeper cannot be called directly but will be included in the call when it becomes multiparty.

A conference is called a centralized conference when a central MP is used to mix or switch all media streams for participating terminals. When each terminal sends its media streams to all other participating terminals (in multicast or multi-unicast), it is called a decentralized conference.

Creating or joining a conference

Using an MCU directly

Most of the time, people will decide to create a conference and name it, for instance, *myconference@conferencerooms.com*. Therefore the participants know from the outset that it is going to be a conference call. The easiest way to create such a conference is to call an MCU and send a Setup message with the ConferenceGoal parameter set to 'create' and a globally unique CID. The message may also include the alias of the conference (*myconference@conferencerooms.com*). So far, nothing differs from a regular call.

If the MCU decides to accept the call (this can be based on previous reservation done through a web site), it replies with a Connect. The endpoint and the MCU exchange their TerminalCapabilitySets. Then the master-slave procedure begins, the MCU always wins, and becomes the active MC of the conference. The MCU indicates it is the active MC of the conference by sending an MCLocationIndication to the calling endpoint. It can also assign an 8-bit number to the terminal with a TerminalNumberAssign message (the terminal must copy those 8 bits into the low 8 bits of the SSRC field of all its RTP datagrams). *See* Fig. 1.30.

Inviting people

Once a terminal is in a conference, it may invite others to participate by sending a Setup message to the active MC with a new CRV, the CID of the conference and the ConferenceGoal parameter set to 'invite'. The destination address and the optional destination call signaling address of the Setup message must be those of the terminal invited to join the conference, for instance terminal C.

When it receives this message, the MCU will send a Setup message to terminal C with CID=N and ConferenceGoal=Invite. Terminal C accepts by sending a

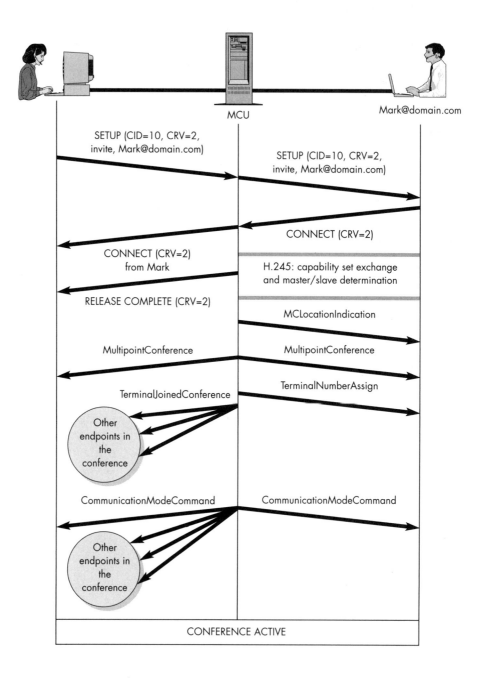

Fig. 1.30 : Setting up a conference

Connect message. At this point the MCU sends a Release Complete to the inviting terminal.

The active MC establishes an H.245 control channel with terminal C using the transport address provided in the Connect. They exchange their TerminalCapabilitySets. The MC signals during the master-slave procedure that it is the active MC and may send an MCLocationIndication message. When this is done, the MC sends a MultipointConference message to the inviting and invited terminals. If there were already other terminals in the call, the MCU will send them a TerminalJoinedConference H.245 message to make them aware of the new entrant.

Because the incoming terminal might have capabilities which are incompatible with the existing media channels in place in the conference, the MCU must send a CommunicationModeCommand to all terminals specifying the new set of transmitting modes for each stream. All media channels that do not conform must be closed.

At this point the MC can begin to send OpenLogicalChannel messages to the endpoints. The endpoints, having received a MultipointConference message, should wait until they receive a CommunicationModeCommand message to open logical channels. All endpoints must send the OpenLogicalChannel messages to the MC.

The MCU can also initiate the invitation, if, for instance, the invitation is not sent from an H.323 terminal but from a web interface of the MCU.

Joining an existing conference
A terminal can easily join an existing conference by sending a Setup message to the MCU with the CID of the conference and ConferenceGoal=Join. If the terminal knows only the alias of the conference, it must provide it and leave the CID set to 0.

Browsing existing conferences
The MCU can provide a list of existing conferences that a terminal could join by sending a ConferenceListChoice H.245 message to a terminal. This can be used, for instance, when an alias that has been used in the Setup message is in fact the name of a group of conferences – *H323support@conferences.com* might be a group name for Q931support, H245support and *RASsupport@conferences.com.*

Ad hoc conferences
When two endpoints (John and Mark) have started a call as a point-to-point call, they still might want to include someone else in the conversation. Someone might call one of the two parties, or they might need to discuss a problem with someone else. In this case the call has not been set up directly using an MCU.

John invites Mary

During the discussion, John and Mark decide to go to the cinema, but they need to ask John's wife, Mary, to choose the movie.

If John and Mark are using the direct call model, either terminal needs to have an MC functionality. In this case the MC will basically behave as the MCU in the Invite example above. If Mark's terminal has an MC, John will send to Mark's terminal a Setup message with a new CRV (not the one used for the point-to-point call between John and Mark), ConferenceGoal=Invite and Mary's alias.

The rest of the procedure is exactly as in the Invite example above.

If neither John nor Mark has an MC capable terminal, they must clear the call and phone Mary again via an MCU – not very user friendly!

If John and Mark are using the gatekeeper routed model, but no terminal has an MC, they can still invite Mary if the gatekeeper has an MC capability. If the gatekeeper belongs to a service provider, it will probably have that capability, and the provider will charge more for conference calls.

In this case the gatekeeper behaves as an MCU in the Invite example above. In some cases the gatekeeper will not have an MC in the same box, but it can easily redirect all conference-related messages to an external MCU entity as it routes all Q.931 and H.245 messages.

Mary calls John

When Mary calls John, she has no reason to know that he is already in a conference, so she sends a regular Setup message.

If John and Mark are using the direct call mode when John's terminal receives the Setup it will probably propose a menu to John asking whether he wants to:

- reject the call
- put the call with Mark on hold and talk to Mary
- include Mary in the call with Mark.

If John or Mark has a terminal with an MC capability, John can choose the third option. For our example we consider that only Mark's terminal has an MC capability.

Mary's terminal will receive a Facility message indicating that the call should be routed to John's terminal (RouteCallToMC) which is the MC capable terminal. This message also indicates the existing CID of the call with Mark. Mary's terminal releases the call with John (Release Complete) and sets up a new call with Mark. Now the Setup message sent by Mary's terminal contains the right CID and ConferenceGoal=Join, and things go on as if Mark was the MCU in the join example above.

If John and Mark are using the gatekeeper routed model, this is similar to the direct call case, except that now the Facility message sent by John's terminal will contain the address of the gatekeeper for call setup.

Conferences and RAS

In most cases terminals will know only the alias of the conference they want to join. Therefore the initial ARQ will contain only the conference alias in the DestinationInfo parameter. The CID parameter will be set to 0, which means it is unknown. The CallIdentifier must be set by the caller as usual.

The gatekeeper will return the Q.931 transport address of the endpoint containing the MC (the MCU, or an endpoint with MC capability) in the ACF.

As soon as the caller knows the exact value of the CID (after receiving a Connect from the endpoint with MC capability), it must inform the gatekeeper using an IRR RAS message. Alternatively the ACF can contain the address of the gatekeeper itself if it has an MC capability.

H.332

The conference model described above is 'tightly coupled', i.e. all the participants maintain a full H.245 control connection with the MCU. This is resource intensive and breaks down when the number of participants increases.

Conferences with a large number of participants tend to be organized with a panel of several speakers (less than ten, typically) and a large audience that listens most of the time and speaks only when requested by the moderator (*see* Fig. 1.31). H.332 describes the electronic equivalent of a panel conference, called a 'loosely coupled conference', and is designed to scale to thousands of participants. H.332 is a mix of a normal tightly coupled conference (used by permanent speakers) and a multicast RTP/RTCP conference (as known on the mBone) for passive listeners.

The RTP/RTCP-only listeners must know which codec is used and other details such as UDP ports. H.332 uses the syntax of the IETF Session Description Protocol (SDP) to encode the value of those parameters. A new SDP type (a=type:H332) is defined to let the RTP listener know that this is an H.332 conference. The information can be conveyed using SAP (IETF session announcement protocol) or a simple file on a web page, or it can be sent by email.

Due to the large number of participants, the tightly coupled conference among panel members is subject to several constraints: the codecs used should remain stable. If a new member forces a new capability negotiation and triggers a change of codecs, a new SDP announcement must be created. Spreading this information using SAP or another mode takes time and most RTP listeners are left out until they have been notified of the new announcement.

The difficult part is to allow the panel to invite a listener to talk, and to let listeners request and be granted the right to become a member of the speakers asking a question. In order to join or be invited by the panel, the RTP listener must also have some H.323 capabilities. Simple RTP/RTCP terminals can only listen. In order to join the panel, a listener must use the regular conference join. They must know the address of the MC which is provided in the SDP session description.

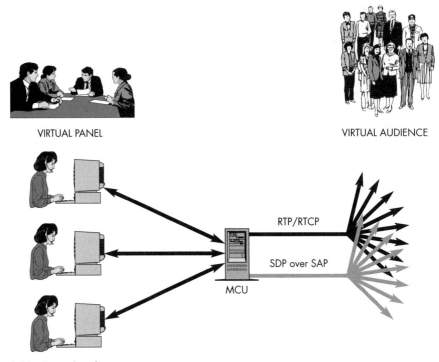

Fig. 1.31 : A panel conference

Similarly, the panel needs to know the callable address of the terminals to be able to invite them to the conference. This is possible because the conference listeners periodically transmit information elements such as their name and email address as RTCP SDES items. A new information element, RTCP SDES item 'H323-CADDR', conveys the H.323 callable address of the terminal. Since bandwidth reserved for RTCP traffic is limited, it takes some time to build a complete list of listeners, and therefore a listener may become callable only some time after it has joined the conference.

Directories and numbering

In the early days of IP telephony (which was not so long ago), one of the major problems was to call someone using a dial-up connection, since the IP address of such users is allocated on demand. Early solutions all used the same scheme: when the IP telephony sofware was started, it immediately contacted a central server on a preconfigured IP address and sent a message with the name of the phone user and the current IP address. There were many implementations, ranging from Microsoft ILS/ULS to solutions running on top of IRC servers.

H.323 makes those solutions obsolete. A terminal implementing RAS properly has to register to a gatekeeper, and the RAS message contains all the necessary information – in particular the current IP address needed to contact the terminal from an alias.

Current solution: contacting an email alias with H.323

The gatekeeper can be asked for the location of the aliases within its zone with an LRQ or an ARQ if a call follows immediately. When trying to reach an alias, the first step is to find the gatekeeper responsible for this alias. A possibility in small environments is to multicast the LRQ until someone answers, but there are obvious scaling issues with this approach.

If the alias used is an email alias, such as *someone@domain.org*, a much better strategy is described in an informational annex of H.225. Much information about a domain name can be found by using the Internet Domain Name System.

The DNS was invented to help track down IP addresses. When your computer needs to talk with another computer named othercomputer.domain.org, it uses the DNS to find the IP address. This involves several steps:

- first the computer asks a well known master server which DNS server has the information about domains ending with .org. In fact, this information is likely to be cached locally, and this step can probably be skipped;
- then the computer queries the appropriate DNS about domain.org, and the reply tells it the IP address of the DNS that stores the information about all names within the domain.org name space;
- finally, the computer approaches this DNS server and obtains the IP address of othercomputer.domain.org.

The DNS holds much more information about the domain, such as the name of the administrator, the address of the mail server for this domain, etc. All this information is stored in 'DNS records'. For example, the DNS record:

Othercomputer IN A 10.0.1.1

means that the computer named othercomputer can be reached at the IP address 10.0.1.1.

The DNS record:

Domain.org IN MX 10 10.0.1.2

means that the mail server (Mail eXchange) for domain.org can be reached at 10.0.1.2.

How can we use this? A special DNS record of type TXT can hold any text. So we can use it to store the location of the gatekeeper handling the alias resolution for the entire domain. The syntax used is:

Domain.org IN TXT **ras [< gk id>@]<domain name >[:<portno>] [<priority>]**

<domain name> can be the name of the host running the GK software or its IP address. The other fields are optional. <portno> specifies a non-standard RAS port, <gk id> can be used if multiple logical GKs are running on the same host and therefore the name of the host cannot be used as the GK ID. Priority can be used if there are multiple gatekeepers in this domain, smaller numbers first. For instance, valid TXT records could be:

ras 10.0.1.3

ras gatekeeper.mydomain.com: 1234 10

Now when trying to call *someone@domain.org*, a computer can first locate the appropriate DNS for domain.org (as explained above), then retrieve all the TXT records for domain.org. If a TXT record contains ras://, the IP address or server name that follows is the name of the gatekeeper for this domain. There can be several RAS records, therefore a zone can be served by several gatekeepers, and a domain can be used by several zones.

Once the gatekeeper has been found, the caller can determine to which transport address to send the Setup by sending a unicast LRQ or an ARQ.

Gaps and future views

A country code for the Internet

If IP telephony becomes a sucessful technology, more and more people will have only an IP phone or IP telephony software running on a computer. So how could they be called from the PSTN (public switched telephone network)?

Obviously the easiest way is first to call a gateway with an interactive voice response system that will ask which person must be called on the IP network – it could ask for an IP address or a subscriber identifier. Companies may even buy a large block of numbers from their carrier and use the called party information element of the ISDN Setup message to find out who is being called and route it to the appropriate IP address.

But all these solutions will be unusable if the number of IP phone users grows. The problem is that no specific numbering resource has been allocated to IP telephony. In 1997, discussions began within ETSI TIPHON about which numbering resource would be most appropriate. Many solutions were proposed:

- a special prefix used in each country. For example, all numbers beginning with 099 would be IP phone numbers and would be routed to a gateway within the country;
- a global service code for IP telephony. An example of such a global service code is 800 for freephone calls. From anywhere in the world, you know that

dialing the international access code + 800 + a number connects you to a free phone service;

■ a global network code. Providers offering service in several countries can request a five-digit network code allocated to them. A satellite phone company could be allocated the network number 99999 and you would reach its subscribers by dialing the international access code + 99999 + the subscriber number;

■ a country code for IP telephony.

The first solution can be implemented easily in each country if the local carrier agrees and if local regulations permit it. This may allow some countries to implement the service more easily, but it has some drawbacks:

■ the prefix chosen will probably be different in each country, and make IP numbers less easily recognizable;

■ when calling an IP phone user from another country, the call would still be routed to the user's country via regular telephone lines, prohibiting the use of IP for international transit.

The other three solutions are technically identical – the difference comes in the ITU rules for allocating each type of global code. IP telephony falls between those rules:

■ it is not a geographic country;

■ it is not a private network;

■ it is not a specific service.

Still, the need is there and a global code has many advantages:

■ IP phone users now have a phone number that can be used, and is identical, worldwide. This is coherent with the global nature of the Internet;

■ the PSTN can easily recognise that this is a call for an IP network. The call can be routed immediately to an IP gateway, and breaks the de facto monopoly of the PSTN for international calls. Without a global code, calls to IP terminals will have to be routed via the PSTN to a home country, and from there be rerouted to IP. Obviously the media path is not optimal in this case.

Although some political discussion is likely to delay the introduction of a country code for VoIP, many standard bodies, including the IETF, are working on the issue. But ITU Study Group 2 holds the final decision (ITU has a draft on the subject called E.IP, which is not yet very advanced). Nevertheless some countries have started to allocate a special prefix for IP telephony – on 14 December 1998, Norway allocated prefix 850 to Telenor Nextel for its VoIP service Interfon PC (*www.totaltele.com/view.asp?ArticleID=20742*).

Meanwhile, several technical proposals have been made to support address resolution for an IP telephony country code. All proposals use a database (flat or hierarchical) to find the home gatekeeper handling the resolution of the phone number into a call signaling address that can be used to send the Setup message.

It was decided not to resolve the number directly into an IP call signaling address because the user's IP address will change often:

- for a dial-up user, a new address will be dynamically allocated each time he connects to the Internet;

- supplementary services based on the gatekeeper may redirect the call to different terminals depending on time-based or other rules.

DNS-based number resolution

This proposal was presented to ETSI TIPHON, and details are available in temporary document 24 of Tiphon 8 (*www.etsi.org/tiphon*). It uses the network part of the IP address as the first part of the phone number. For instance, a user having an IP address allocated from class C 192.190.132.xxx could have +999 192 190 132 678 as a telephone number, where 999 is the country code allocated to IP telephony (only one thing is certain for the moment: 999 cannot be allocated for IP telephony!).

Readers familiar with IP addressing will be surprised by the three final digits, which clearly are outside the 1...254 range. We chose those numbers on purpose because they do not need to respect the IP addressing rules.

According to this proposal, when a gatekeeper routes a call to +999 192 190 132 678, it will decide, from the first digits, that the network part of the phone number is a class C (see the multicast chapter for more details on IP addresses classes). So the part of the number that is an IP network identifier is 192.190.132.

Then the gatekeeper will locate the DNS that has information about that network by doing a Reverse Lookup. During this operation, the IP address is mapped to the DNS name 132.190.192.in-addr.arpa. Once the proper DNS is located, using the regular hierarchical DNS procedure, the gatekeeper asks the DNS server for information on 678.132.190.192.in-addr.arpa. At this stage 678 is just a name for the local DNS server, so there is no need to follow the rules for IP addresses. There should be an SRV (SeRVer) record or a TXT (TeXT) record with the IP address or DNS name of a home gatekeeper.

Once it has obtained this information, the gatekeeper can route the call to the home gatekeeper, or make inquiries to this gatekeeper using an LRQ.

This proposal is typical of Internet technologies: it is clever, simple, and it works right away. However, it has a number of drawbacks that make it unlikely to happen.

1 It is a hierarchical dialing plan. In the past, hierarchically structured address spaces have caused problems:

   ■ number portability is not supported;

   ■ it is impossible to assign blocks of numbers of arbitrary size. Very often, large blocks are assigned to entities which just needed slightly more than the granularity of the small blocks, and this leads to a quick exhaustion of the numbering space.

2 It is unfair. Some US universities have a class A of their own (255*999*999*999 potential phone numbers) and entire countries in Africa have only a class C (999 numbers). This is the unfortunate result of careless past IP address allocation but it is unlikely that people would accept this explanation if given for a similar situation in telephony.

3 It is not centrally managed. It is a clear advantage for the speed of deployment, but it will lead to a problem called third-party dependency. If in the process of the hierarchical DNS resolution one server fails, all numbers that depend on this server for their number resolution will become unreachable. The security issue is even greater. If such a DNS server is compromised, the attacker can do all sorts of interesting things with the numbers that depend on this DNS. Maintaining bulletproof security for thousands of DNS servers managed by hundreds of organizations would be a challenging, if not impossible, task.

Finally, the concept of network classes is obsolete. IP addresses are allocated in blocks of arbitrary size (as long as it is to a power of two). The mechanism of Reverse DNS Lookup can be adapted for classless IP addresses, but most DNS servers do not support it, and very few of those which do support it have been properly configured.

Flat numbering space

The TIPHON ARS (address resolution server) proposal aims at solving the latency and numbering space exhaustion problems of DNS-based solutions. Other design goals for ARS were:

■ optimize the cache efficiency at the client level and reduce latency. An efficient cache scheme is easy to imagine for local IP clients; for national gateways, however, it is not as obviously efficient because the requests will not be as focused and repetitive;

■ limit the workload of the root ARS servers and have a scalable, but not hierarchical, architecture;

■ allow the reuse of the ARS servers for other technologies besides H.323 (e.g. voice over ATM). This should ease the attribution of a global service code because it could be shared among several technologies.

The first goal leads to prefixes rather than individual numbers being stored in the ARS (although individual numbers are still allowed). So a request such as

'Which home gatekeeper handles call management for phone number 1234567890?'

will be answered by the ARS by

'All numbers of the form 12345x are handled by home gatekeeper 190.193.3.56'

This way the inquirer can put the answer in cache and will not need to ask the ARS to resolve, say, 1234576767.

The second goal is not straightforward because it is necessary to reduce the number of hierarchy levels in the ARS framework (unlike DNS) to reduce the latency of the resolution. This can be achieved with two strategies:

■ store only large blocks at the root ARS level to reduce the number of records. This is desirable but, since IP telephony may lead small corporations or even individuals to maintain their own home gatekeeper, will probably not be possible;

■ distribute the data among many root ARSs using a hash of the requested phone number. This hash function takes a number string as input and yields a result between 1 and N, where N is the number of servers. This solution is linearly scalable with the number of ARS servers. However, the number of root ARS servers must be kept at a manageable level.

The compromise chosen for the ARS proposal is to allow the storage of blocks of up to six digits and base the hashing on the first six digits. Hashing on six digits (using an algorithm similar to the one specified in PIM sparse mode RFC) should provide a reasonably homogeneous spreading of data among the root ARSs, up to a few hundred ARSs (100 is probably the upper limit from a manageability point of view). To resolve the phone number 123456781234 to a home GK, for example, the client chooses the appropriate ARS by hashing 123456.

The objective of the third goal is met by introducing resource type identifiers in the ARS, so that other resources besides H.323 GK could be stored.

Each record in the ARS server contains the following information:

■ number – the Internet phone number

■ type of resource – 1: H.323 home gatekeeper, 2: pointer to ARS, 3: SIP server

■ type of address – 1: Ipv4 address, 2: Ipv6 address, 3: DNS name

■ resource address – for type of resource = 1: the home gatekeeper IP address or DNS name, depending on type of address field

- time to live – length of time during which the information can be cached (1 to 2^16 minutes=45 days)
- authentication type – 1: keyed MD5
- authentication data – MD5 key for authentication type 1
- administrative owner – string [1...32].

The ARS was nothing more than a technology proposal at the time (*see* Fig. 1.32). It was useful to prove that centralized databases could be scalable and that hierarchical numbering schemes could be avoided. Some of the framework proposals brought to ETSI TIPHON and the ITU have proposed using a central database, referring to this scheme to demonstrate the scalability of the design.

Even if the distribution concept is kept, the original protocol proposed to access the ARS database will probably be changed and adapted to the needs of the framework that will ultimately be adopted. The speed of deploying such a solution is not a problem, but the decision of who will allocate numbers and administer the database has many political implications that will impede the adoption of such a global number resolution scheme until an agreement is reached at ITU.

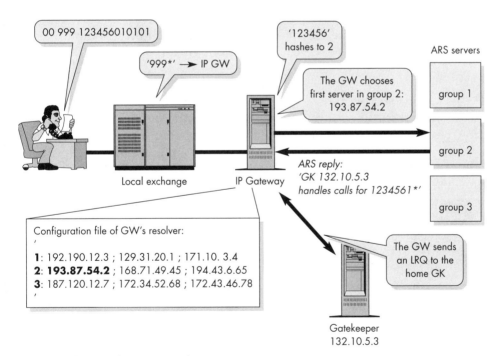

Fig. 1.32 : Illustrating the ARS proposal

UPT

The ITU already has a framework for a service called UPT (universal personal telephony), which is based on a special access code, and has many similarities with the solutions presented above. UPT calls are routed to a 'serving exchange' which resolves the original number into an E.164 number. UPT includes several models:

- model 3a is a flat numbering scheme behind access code +878;
- model 3b is a numbering scheme behind access code +878 that sub-structures the numbering space with country codes.

These models are very close to the ETSI TIPHON proposals; the only difference is that the 'serving exchange' of ETSI TIPHON (the ARS, or DNS system) returns an indication of the telephony technology to use (H.323, SIP and so on) instead of assuming it is a PSTN device. The servicing exchange also returns the address of the relevant home call agent (ARS, the IP address of a gatekeeper, DNS) instead of assuming a particular user location mechanism. Extending the existing UPT 3a model to allow the serving exchange to return a technology identifier (ISDN, H.323, voice over ATM, etc.) and a home call agent would fit all the requirements set by ETSI TIPHON.

The reader will not be surprised to learn that UPT 3a faces problems similar to the IP country code requests. There is no agreement on how to administer the flat space, and the many political implications are far more complex to solve than all the technical problems.

Dialing plan distribution

The previous discussions on the country code for IP telephony apply to reaching an IP terminal with its own phone number allocated from an E.164 resource. Another interesting problem is how to choose among several possibilities to route a call to a regular PSTN number or an H.323 alias. Many IP telephony providers will offer outgoing gateways to call regular phones, or there could be several transit IP neworks on offer to reach a particular H.323 alias.

A gatekeeper needs to have reachability information and additional data (prices, quality of service levels, etc.) to be able to make an intelligent decision.

The goal of H.323 annex G ('Communications between administrative domains'), scheduled for approval in 1999, is to specify how gatekeepers exchange this type of information across administrative domains.

H.323 security: H.235

H.235 aims to provide privacy (no eavesdropping) and authentication (ensuring that people really are who they claim to be) to all protocols using H.245, including H.323 communications. Because H.323 can be used on the open Internet, some say it is less secure than regular telephony. In fact, even without H.235, it is more difficult to listen to an H.323 phone call than to wiretap a phone line because you need to implement the codec algorithm.

With H.235, IP telephony becomes *much* more secure than regular telephony. It becomes impossible, even for someone having free access to the IP network, to listen to any conversation that has been secured by H.235, and it even allows the caller to hide the destination number they are trying to reach.

A short introduction to cryptography

In this chapter we have tried to minimize references to complex notions of algebra, but unfortunately we cannot avoid it altogether. It is possible to read H.235 by considering each encryption function as a black box, but many parameters, random numbers here and there, remain obscure. We have chosen to describe the cryptographic algorithms used by H.235 in a simple way, but this does not mean they are simple. The real complexity of cryptography is in details. How do you choose a random number? How do you calculate a large prime? This chapter will probably seem crude to cryptography experts, but we hope it will help those who simply want an overview.

Common terms

Cryptography is a set of techniques and mathematical algorithms which fulfill one or several of the following needs:

- privacy: the need to keep the content of a document unknown to anybody except a controlled set of individuals
- authentication: the need to check and verify identities, and attribute with certainty a document to an author
- integrity: the need to preserve the original content of a document from any modification or falsification.

Cryptographic techniques

Two main techniques are in use today:

- symmetric cryptography, or secret key cryptography, is probably as old as civilization – Caesar was using it to send messages to Rome;
- asymmetric cryptography, or public key cryptography, is much more complex and is based on elaborate mathematical algorithms.

Secret key cryptography
Simple algorithms

Secret key cryptography relies on a shared secret between the sender of a message and the receiver. The shared secret can be an algorithm used to encode the message (e.g. a permutation of letters) or a 'key' used as a parameter in a well known algorithm.

Simple algorithms such as letter permutation are weak unless the permutation changes frequently – a message can usually be cracked by examining about 40 letters of the cryptogram when a fixed permutation is used.

A refinement of this algorithm, called one-time pad, was described by Vernam in 1926. If a message is encrypted by adding a random key of the same length (for instance doing an exclusive OR (XOR) with a random bitstream), the cryptogram contains absolutely no information for anyone not knowing the random key. Nothing can distinguish it from a random message. In other words, the security of this system is perfect. A pseudo-random string can be used instead, but then the security of the system depends on the quality of the pseudo-random generator.

One-time pad has, however, a serious drawback: the need to send in advance an extremely long random key to the recipient of the message in a secure way. The advent of CD-ROM has made it relatively easy, and this system is still used for military or diplomatic communications.

DES

The most widely used secret key algorithm is DES (data encryption standard). In 1971 the US Commerce Department asked for a secure, yet easily implementable, encryption algorithm. They requested a publishable algorithm (i.e. the security could not rely on the fact that the algorithm was unknown). It was not until 1974 that an appropriate proposal was submitted: IBM's Lucifer algorithm. This was modified and eventually resulted in the algorithm which was standardized in 1976 as DES.

DES is a block algorithm which can code a message of 64 bits into a cryptogram of 64 bits using a 56-bit key (the actual key has 64 digits, but eight are used just for error detection). The current standard is Federal Information Processing Standards Publication 46-2 (FIPS PUB 46-2) of 1993.

IBM grants free licenses for devices using DES under certain conditions.

Coding 64 bits is not terribly useful, and an additional standard (FIPS PUB 81) describes how to extend the use of DES to data of arbitrary size:

■ ECB (electronic code book) is the direct application of DES on a message split in 64-bit chunks using the same key repeatedly. It is not very secure because similar sequences in the initial message will also appear in the coded message, leading to potential attack;

- CBC (cipher block chaining) avoids this weakness of ECB by using the result of the encryption of a block 'n' to XOR with block 'n+1' before encrypting it. A transmission error on one block of a CBC encoded file will prevent the proper decoding of this block and the next one;

- CFB (cipher feedback) is more appropriate to code short sequences of less than 64 bits;

- OFB (output feedback) uses DES to generate a pseudo random bit sequence which is added to the message to be encoded. OFB can in theory code small messages of less than 64 bits but is considered more secure if coding 64-bit messages. It is not subject to error propagation and for this reason is quite appropriate for coding audio or video (the coding used in the GSM cellular standard is derived from OFB).

Because CBC, CFB and OFB all use chaining, the sender and the receiver must be given a common initialization vector.

When using H.235, the key is carried in the EncryptionSync parameter. H.235 also describes how to construct an initialization vector for CBC, CFB and OFB.

With the power of computers increasing all the time, the safety provided by DES has been questioned. Triple DES simply chains three individual DES blocks using different keys, which raises the complexity of the algorithm from a 2^{57} equivalent codebook to 2^{112}. The justification for three stages instead of two is quite involved, but in short it has been proved that using just two stages does not increase the security of basic DES.

There are many other efficient algorithms using a shared secret key:

- RC2 is coding blocks of 64 bits with a key of 40, 56 or 128 bits;

- RC4 is flow oriented and uses a 40 or 128-bit key.

These algorithms are favored by many US companies as they seem to be easier to export than DES-based solutions.

Asymmetric cryptography

Asymmetric cryptography is based on a pragmatic way to consider the security of information: a piece of information is secure not only when you don't know how to extract the information, it is also secure when you do know how to extract the information but you cannot practically do so because it would require too much time to run the extraction algorithm, even for the fastest computer.

One-way functions

Asymmetric cryptography uses many so-called 'one-way' functions. A function F is a one-way function when it is extremely difficult to find x knowing F(x). The idea is that if we have such a function mapping a set of messages M to another set of messages C, it is possible to code a message m from M by using F(m) = c as a cryptogram.

The following function is 'one-way':

$$Z/pZ \dashrightarrow Z/pZ$$

$$x \dashrightarrow q^x \bmod p$$

where p is a very large prime number (typically with 100 digits). It is possible to demonstrate that in this case there is at least one number q that is 'primitive', that is to say that for any element E of Z/pZ it is possible to find an element x such as $q^x = E$. If q is chosen to be primitive, there is a one-to-one mapping between the initial message m and the cryptogram F(m). There are classic methods to find a primitive element of Z/pZ when p has been fabricated to have some 'good' properties.

In theory, it is possible to find the initial message from the cryptogram by calculating F(x) for each possible x and comparing the result with the cryptogram, but there are about 10^{100} possible values for x and each calculation is very costly. Just imagine how long it takes to calculate $12343323223^{654654654654}$. Even being smart and trying to optimize the calculation, for instance trying to calculate $(((((q^2)^2)^2)^2)^2)^2$, there will still be about $\log(^{654654654654})$ multiplications.

You might think of using the inverse function, but we do not know to invert this function efficiently. There is no other way than to try each possible solution until a match is found.

A straightforward application of one-way functions is password storage. Instead of storing the clear form of a password p, we store F(p) on the server. This way the password file cannot be used to find the original passwords. When a user logs on with a password p', the system can simply check the validity of the password by verifying that F(p') equals the stored value F(p).

How to negotiate a shared secret with the Diffie–Hellman algorithm

This algorithm allows two people, say Bob and Mary, to negotiate a common secret over a public link. First Bob and Mary need to agree on a large prime p and a number q. It is not a problem if other people know their choices as well. Then:

1   Bob chooses secretly an element of Z/pZ: a.
    Mary chooses secretly an element of Z/pZ: b.

2   Bob sends $q^a \bmod p$ to Mary.
    Mary sends $q^b \bmod p$ to Bob.

3   Bob and Mary choose $S = q^{ab} \bmod p$ as a common secret. They both can calculate it easily because $(q^a \bmod p)^b = q^{ab} \bmod p = q^{ba} \bmod p = (q^{ba} \bmod p)^a$.

There is no practical algorithm for computing discrete logarithms modulo a very prime number; it is not feasible to solve $q^x \bmod p$. Therefore it is not possible to calculate S knowing only q^a or q^b.

There is no known way to calculate S knowing only q^a or q^b. Bob and Mary have managed to negotiate a common secret on a public link, and can use any symmetric cryptography method to exchange messages.

Public key encryption with the El Gamal algorithm

Again we use the discrete logarithm function F: $x \rightarrow q^x$ mod p, in which q and p are known to both the sender and the receiver and possibly other people as well.

This public key encryption system was authored by El Gamal. The recipient A has a public key $P_a = F(a)$ built from his secret a. B wants to send a secret message to A, and of course B wants to be sure that only A can decipher the message. For simplicity, let us assume for a moment that the message is a number in Z/pZ. B chooses a random number k and sends q^k mod p and $M*P_a^k$ mod p to A. Note that in this system the cryptogram is twice as long as the original message.

Anyone intercepting the message needs to know the value P_a^k in order to find M. P_a is widely known, so they just need to know k. But as we have seen above, it would take an enormous number of calculations to find k from q^k if p is large enough. So, unless a government agency with a large budget is really willing to know M, B can be pretty safe.

For A, it is easy to find M from the information sent by B. We know that $Pa^k = (q^a)^k = (q^k)^a$. A knows q^k and a, so can easily calculate the value of Pa^k , and deduces M immediately.

Public key encryption is Processor intensive, and should never be used when not strictly necessary. It is much more efficient to negotiate a shared secret (using for instance the DH algorithm) and then use a secret key algorithm such as DES.

RSA

RSA is based on the difficulty of decomposing a large number into its prime factors when some of these factors are very large primes. The principle is to encrypt a message m using m^e mod n as the cryptogram. e is a prime, for instance e = 3. n is the *public key* of the recipient of the message. For instance, $C(7) = 7^3$ mod 15 = 343 mod 15 = 13.

The public key n is not a random number but the product of two large primes p and q. In our oversimplified example n = p*q = 3*5. Both p and q are kept secret. In order to decipher the message, the recipient seeks a number d with the following property: $m^{ed} = m$. It is equivalent to say that $m^{(ed-1)} = 1$ mod m.

If gcd(m,n) = 1 we know from the Fermat theorem that $m^{\phi(n)} = 1$ mod m, where $\phi(n)$ is the cardinal of the set of numbers having no common divisors with n. When n is a product of primes it is easy to calculate $\phi(n) = (p-1)*(q-1)$. Of course there could be cases where gcd(m,n)≠1, but the probability – (p+q-1)/pq – is negligible for large primes. Calculating $\phi(n)$ is straightforward when you know p and q, but if you know only the public key n = pq, you cannot find p and q in a reasonable time.

So in our example the recipient seeks d such as ed = 1 mod $\phi(n)$, with $\phi(n)$ = (p-1)(q-1) = 8. The problem is reduced to finding d and k in 3d+k8 = 1. We know that a solution can be found with the Euclidean algorithm because gcd(3,8) = 1 since e = 3 is a prime. Here the solution is d = 11 (3*11–8*4 = 1).

d = 11 is the *private key* of the recipient and can be used to decipher the message. $M = C^d \bmod n = 13^{11} \bmod 15 = 1792160394037 \bmod 15 = 7$.

Note that the roles of the private key d and the public key e are symmetric – it is possible to encrypt a message using the private key, in which case it can be decrypted with the public key. This is used for digital signatures.

Digital signatures

There are many ways to cryptographically sign a document. In this paragraph we present only one of these methods, based on the ability to cipher with a private key and decipher with a public key in RSA algorithm, as shown in Fig. 1.33.

First a hash of the document to be signed is calculated. A hash is a function that takes a long document as input and produces a small string as output. If the initial document changes slightly (for instance only one bit changes), a good hash function should lead to a completely different result. One of the most popular hash algorithms is called MD5 (message digest 5).

The result of the hash function is then encrypted with the private key of the person who signs the document – it becomes the signature. It is easy to check if a document is original (has not been modified since the signature):

- first a hash of the document is calculated with the same algorithm;
- then the signature is deciphered using the public key of the alleged author;
- finally both digests are compared. If the document has been modified in any way since the signature, they will differ.

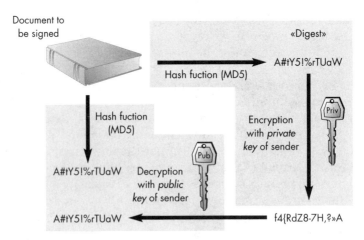

Fig. 1.33 : Digital signature

Certificates

Digital signatures are useful, but only if you are sure that the public key the receivers will use to check the authenticity of the message has not been faked. The public key can be sent using a secure method, but this is not very practical. Certificates are a much more efficient way to ensure that a public key is not fake.

Certificates usually contain the public key of the presenter, along with some identity information (name and address, corporation name, etc.) and a validity period. All the information contained in the certificate is digitally signed by an authority – someone owning a widely known public key (so widely known that no one can fake it. It can be included by default in the operating system, or configured by an administrator). When the authority signs a message with its private key, everyone can verify the signature using the public key. If the authority is known to sign only verified information (this is very important), then a document which it has signed can be trusted.

Anyone can present the certificate of another person. One further step is needed in order to check that the person who presents the certificate is the right one, i.e. the person owning the private key corresponding to the public key contained in the certificate. The presenter of the certificate cannot simply show his private key.

There are a number of ways to do this. You can encrypt a random string with the public key, send it to the presenter of the certificate and ask him to decrypt it. If the presenter of the certificate has managed to decrypt the string, he has access to the private key and is the owner of the certificate.

If there was only one root authority R, it would be difficult to handle the workload associated with checking the identity of people or organizations requesting a digital certificate. Having many root authorities is also problematic however, as each time the new authority faces the task of making its public key widely known. Go to Microsoft or Netscape and ask that they include it in the default configuration of their browsers and just wait for the response. . .

In fact, it is quite easy for a root authority to delegate this task to intermediary authorized agencies. The root authority creates certificates for each intermediary agency by signing a document containing their public key, name, and possibly other elements. Then an intermediary authority A, when requested to create a certificate by signing a message M which contains the name of the customer, his public key, etc., just signs this message with its public key A. The signed document is returned to the client, *with the certificate of the intermediary authority A signed by R. See* Fig. 1.34.

How does it work? When someone needs to verify the validity of M, he first checks that the signature of the document by A is valid. He can do this because the public key of A is included in the certificate of the intermediary authority A signed by R. But the public key of A is not well known, it could merely be an untrusted local agency. So it is also necessary to check that the certificate of the

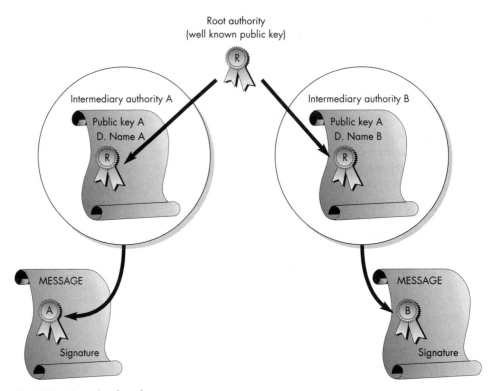

Fig. 1.34 : Hierarchy of certificates

intermediary authority A has been properly signed by R, certifying that A can be trusted. This is easy because the public key of R is well known.

Securing H.323 with H.235

During the ITU meetings that led to H.235, it was felt that H.323 phone users would not want anyone on the network to listen to their conversations, and the initial focus was on securing the media channels. But it soon became clear that above all they would want no charge for calls they did not make, and would want to be sure that no one was monitoring the phone numbers they were calling. Also, the providers would want to authorize calls when they were set up, not when media or control channels were established. So the call signaling channel also had to be authenticated and secured.

The keys encrypting the media channels are determined using OpenLogicalChannel messages. If the H.245 channel itself is secure, the implementation need not worry about ways to secure the parameters within the

OpenLogicalChannel message. This is the main motivation for securing the H.245 channel, but there are other important aspects such as protecting the DTMF information carried in H.245 UserInputIndication messages which may contain sensitive credit card data or passwords.

In the context of H.235, any element in the network which needs to know the contents of the H.225 or H.245 messages needs to be trusted by the communicating endpoints because it will have access to all confidential information elements: DTMF digits, encryption keys of the media channels, etc. These elements include the gatekeepers in the gatekeeper routed model, the MCUs and gateways otherwise.

Tools

Authentication procedures
Authentication can be done at call setup time, using TLS (transport layer security) for instance, or while securing the H.245 channel. For authentication schemes which do not use certificates, H.235 allows challenge response exchange. However, the communicating terminals much know a shared secret to do this, and H.235 does not specify how this shared secret has been obtained (during the subscription phase to a service, or otherwise).

When a certificate is used, H.235 does not describe the contents of the certificates, but provides ways to exchange certificates and verify the identities of the presenters.

Tokens
Tokens are generally parameters transmitted within H.323 messages that are opaque to H.323 itself but can be used by higher level protocols. H.235 uses two types of tokens:

■ a ClearToken is an ASN-1 sequence of optional parameters such as timestamp, password, Diffie-Hellman parameters, challenge, random number, certificate, generalID;

■ a CryptoToken contains an object identifier of the encrypted token, followed by a crypto algorithm identifier, some parameters used by the algorithm (e.g. initialization vector), and the cryptographic data itself. CryptoTokens can be used to convey hidden tokens, signed tokens or hash values. The algorithm needs a key of a specific size N. For symmetric key algorithms the key is derived from a secret shared between the communicating parties. If the secret is shorter than the required key, the secret is simply padded with zeros; if it is longer than the key, the secret is split into blocks of size N octets (or less for the last chunk) which are XORed. The resulting value is used as the key.

Identity verification methods

We suppose that terminals A and B have first exchanged their identities in clear form, then three methods can be used to verify the identities:

- *symmetric encryption*: each terminal sends to the other a cryptotoken containing a timestamp and the identity of the other party, encrypted with a key derived from the shared secret with the following simple rule – if the key must be larger than the password, then the key is simply the password padded with zeros; if the key must be smaller than the password (say size S), the password is split into chunks of size S which are XORed to form the key;

- *hashing*: each terminal sends to the other the result of a hash function applied to the timestamp, the identity of the other party, and the password;

- *certificates and signatures*: each terminal returns to the other a token containing a timestamp, the timestamp and identity of the other party signed with the private key, and optionally a certificate to authenticate the corresponding public key.

In all methods, the timestamp prevents replay attacks.

Generating a shared secret with Diffie-Hellman

If the communicating endpoints do not share a secret, they must create a common one, beginning with a communication that someone can potentially intercept.

The Diffie-Hellman key negotiation (described on p. 68) can be used within H.235 (*see* Fig. 1.35).

The DhA parameter contains p, q and q^a, the DhB parameter contains p, q and q^b. The random value passed in B's reply is used for XORing parameters for further exchanges to prevent replay attacks. The CryptoToken is optional and can be used to digitally sign some parameters in order to prove the identity of the sender.

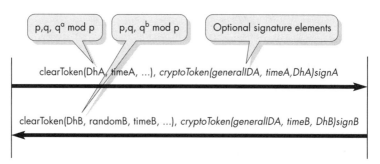

Fig. 1.35 : The Diffie-Hellman key negotiation

Securing RAS

RAS messages are exchanged between an endpoint and a gatekeeper prior to any other communication. H.235 does not provide a way to ensure privacy on the RAS link, but it provides authentication. There are two modes of operation depending on whether the GK and the endpoint share a secret. Two parameters are present in the GRQ that ensure the use of the right mode and algorithms: authenticationcapability indicates the authentication mechanism that can be used, and algorithmOIDs contains the list of algorithms supported (DES CBC, DES ECB, RC2 ...).

If there is no previous relationship and no shared secret between the GK and the endpoint, they need to negotiate one. For this purpose a Diffie-Hellman negotiation takes place during the GRQ, GCF (gatekeeper request, gatekeeper confirm) phase using a ClearToken to convey the DHset of parameters needed by Diffie-Hellman. After this, the GK and the endpoint share a common secret, which can be used to authenticate any subsequent RAS messages between them, in particular the RRQ and URQ. This is done by including in those messages a CryptoToken (encrypted using the DH secret) containing an XORed combination of the GatekeeperIdentifier, the sequence number of the request, and the last random value received from the GK (in the RCF or an xCF message). The key used to code the CryptoToken is derived from the Diffie-Hellman secret as described above. The GK provides new random values in each xCF in a ClearToken.

When the gatekeeper and the endpoint share a common secret, defined at subscription time, the following procedure can be used:

- the terminal sends a GRQ with authenticationcapability set to pwdSymEnc (other modes can be used besides pwdSymEnc, such as hash-based or certificate-based authentication, with a similar procedure) and a choice of algorithms in algorithmOIDs;

- the GK replies with a GCF containing a ClearToken with a challenge string and a timestamp to prevent replay attacks, authenticationmode set to pwdSymEnc and algorithmOID set to the chosen algorithm, for instance 56-bit DES in CBC mode;

- at this point the endpoint may have received more than one answer from several gatekeepers. It chooses one gatekeeper and registers by sending an RRQ. This RRQ should contain a CryptoToken (using the algorithm chosen by the GK, here 56-bit DES CBC) with the encrypted challenge (or a hash value or certificates). The gatekeeper can check the validity of this answer by encrypting the challenge locally with the key associated with the endpoint alias (known from the GRQ) and comparing the result with the endpoint-provided encrypted challenge;

■ after this other RAS messages can be authenticated by including a CryptoToken with the XORed combination of the GatekeeperIdentifier, sequence number and GK-provided random value.

Using one of these methods, the gatekeeper can authenticate the messages of each terminal in its zone.

Securing the call signaling channel (H.225)

The call signaling channel can be secured using TLS or IPSEC. Authentication between the communicating terminals can be done at this stage. An endpoint knows that it needs to secure a channel using TLS if it receives the call on port 1300. In the Setup, the caller will indicate which security schemes it supports for the H.245 channel in the h245SecurityCapability information element. The callee chooses one in the h245SecurityMode information element of the Connect message. If no common security mode can be found, the callee can release the call with the reason code set to SecurityDenied.

h245SecurityCapability includes a specific object identifier for each cryptographic algorithm, i.e. 56-bit DES CBC and 56-bit DES OFB each have their own identifier.

Securing the call control channel (H.245) and the media channels

The method used to secure the H.245 channel is negotiated in the call signaling channel in the initial setup procedure. The necessary messages needed to secure the H.245 channel are exchanged before any other H.245 message. Different methods can be used to initiate the secure channel, depending on whether the communicating endpoints share a secret or not.

Media channels

Once the H.245 channel is secured, the terminals need to know which security modes can be used for the media channels. This is part of the capabilities exchange – terminals can signal that they support GSM (global system for mobile communications) capability and/or encrypted GSM capability. A new capability has to be defined for each combination of codec and encryption mode. Since encryption algorithms can use a significant portion of the CPU, it is possible to signal capabilities such as (plain GSM + H.263 video) or (Triple DES encrypted GSM).

If the H.245 channel must not be encrypted for some reason, H.235 has provisions to open a separate specific logical channel of type h235Control to negotiate key parameters for the logical channels.

When a new logical channel is opened, the security mode is specified (chosen by the source) and the key that will be used for logical channel encryption is *provided by the master* either in the OpenLogicalChannel or in the OpenLogicalChannelAck using the encryptionSync field. The key is associated with a dynamic payload type, so a receiver which has just been given a new key in the encryptionSync field will know it must use it as soon as the payload type of the RTP packets it receives matches the payload type associated with the key.

The key can be refreshed afterwards using dedicated H.245 commands – EncryptionUpdateRequest and EncryptionUpdate. The key negotiation can be inherently secure using certificate exchange, or can be secured by securing first the H.245 channel.

For multipoint communication, the secured H.245 channel is established with the MCU, and therefore the MCU must be trusted. New endpoints arriving in the conference can retrieve other endpoints' certificates, through ConferenceRequest/ConferenceResponse commands. However, they must trust the MCU for checking whether the endpoints actually own those certificates.

As mentioned in the RTP chapter, many popular algorithms such as DES ECB or CBC are block oriented. They are designed to code data aligned on the block size (64 bits for DES). The most simple way to cope with this is the RTP padding method described in the RTP RFC; when it is used, the P bit of the RTP header is set.

However, there are other techniques that can be used with DES. In addition to regular RTP padding, H.325 mandates that all implementations support Ciphertext Stealing for ECB and CBC; zero pad for CFB and OFB. These techniques are modifications of the regular ECB/CBC/CFB/OFB chain-coding process for the incomplete data block and its predecessor, leading to a cryptogram exactly as long as the original message. When the payload length is not a multiple of the block size, and the P bit is not set, the decoder must assume that one of these methods is used.

In all cases, when an initialization vector is needed, it is constructed from picking as many octets as required from the concatenated sequence number and timestamp octets, repeated if necessary. If the master decides to update the key (using the H.245 EncryptionSync message), the payload type of the RTP stream must change for the RTP packets that use the new key.

Media streams

Codecs

We have seen already that audio and video data streams were carried over RTP. So far we have not described how the analogue signals were transformed into data. This is the purpose of codecs. This section provides a high-level overview of some of the most popular voice and video coding technologies, sufficient in most cases to understand H.323, SIP or MGCP. For more details, *see* Chapter Seven.

What is a good codec?

When the IMTC tried to choose a default low bitrate codec, they faced a difficult issue because there was no common understanding of what was a good codec. What follows is a set of the criteria that must be taken into consideration in evaluating a voice codec.

Bandwidth usage

The bitrate of available narrowband codecs today ranges from 1.2 kbits/s to 64 kbits/s, with an inevitable effect on the quality of restituted voice. This is usually measured as MOS (mean opinion score) marks. Mean opinion scores for a particular codec are the average mark given by a panel of auditors listening to several recorded samples (voice, music, voice with background noise) and they range from 1 to 5:

- from 4 to 5 the quality is 'high', i.e. similar or better than the experience we have in an ISDN phone call;
- from 3.5 to 4 is the range of 'toll quality'. This is similar to what is obtained with the G.726 codec (32 kbit/s ADPCM) which is commonly taken as the reference for 'toll quality' and is what we experience on most phone calls. Mobile phone calls are usually just below toll quality;
- from 3.0 to 3.5 the communication is still good, but the voice degradation is already easily audible;
- from 2.5 to 3 the communication is still possible, but requires much more attention. This is the range of 'military quality' voice.

There is a trade-off between voice quality and bandwidth used. With current technology, toll quality cannot be obtained below 5 kbit/s.

Silence compression (VAD, CNG, DTX)

During a conversation, we talk on average only 35 per cent of the time. Therefore silence compression or suppression is an important feature. In a point-to-point call it saves about 50 per cent of the bandwidth, but in decentralized multicast conferences the activity rate of each speaker drops and the savings are even greater. It would not be reasonable to do a multicast conference with more than half a dozen participants without silence suppression.

Silence compression includes three major components:

- VAD (voice activity detector) is responsible for determining when the user is talking and when he is silent. It should be very responsive (otherwise the first word may get lost, and useless silence might be included at the end of sentences), without being triggered by background noise. Voice activity detection evaluates the energy of the incoming samples and activates the media channel if this energy is above a minimum. Similarly, when the energy falls below a threshold for some time, the media channel is muted.

If the VAD module dropped all samples until the mean energy of the incoming samples reached the threshold, the beginning of the active speech period would be clipped. Therefore VAD implementations require some lookahead, i.e. they retain in memory a few milliseconds worth of samples to start the media channel activation before the active speech period. This usually adds some delay to the overall coding latency, but some tricks can be used, depending on the coder used.

The quality of the implementation is important – good VAD should require a minimal lookahead and still avoid voice clipping, and have a configurable hangover period (150 ms is usually fine, but some languages, such as Chinese, require different settings). VAD is also useful to save battery-powered devices, stopping the transmitter during periods of no activity. Moreover, less complexity on the DSP means less power consumption.

■ DTX (discontinuous transmission) is the ability of a codec to stop transmitting frames when the VAD has detected a silence period. If the transmission is stopped completely, it should set the marker bit of the first RTP packet after the silence period. Some advanced codecs will not stop transmission completely, but instead switch to a silence mode in which they use much less bandwidth and send just the bare minimum parameters (intensity, etc.) in order to allow the receiver to regenerate the background noise;

■ CNG (comfort noise generator) is used to recreate some sort of background noise. When the caller isn't talking, there is silence on the line, so when the VAD detects a silence period it should be enough to switch off the loudspeaker completely. In fact, this approach is wrong. Movie producers go to great lengths to recreate the proper background noise for 'silent' sequences. The same applies for phone calls. If the loudspeaker is turned off completely, street traffic and other background noise that could be overheard while the caller was talking suddenly stops. The called party gets the impression that the line has been dropped and will usually ask if the caller is still there.

CNG helps to avoid this. With the most primitive codecs that simply stop transmission, it will use some random noise with a level deduced from the minimal levels recorded during active speech periods. More advanced codecs such as G.723.1 (annex A) or G.729 (annex B) have options to send enough information to allow the remote decoder to regenerate ambient noise close to the original background noise.

Intellectual property

End users do not care about this, but manufacturers have to pay royalties to be allowed to use some codecs in their products. For some hardware products where the margin is very low, this can be a major issue. Another common situation is that some manufacturers want to sell some back-end server applications, while distributing clients for free. If the client includes a codec, intellectual property again becomes a major choice factor.

Lookahead and frame size

Most narrowband codecs compress voice in chunks called frames, and need to know a little about the samples immediately following the samples they are currently encoding (this is called lookahead).

There has been a lot of discussion (especially at the IMTC when they tried to choose a low bitrate codec) on the influence of the frame size on the quality of the codec. This is because the minimal delay introduced by a coding/decoding sequence is the frame length plus the lookahead size. This is also called the algorithmic delay. In reality DSPs (digital signal processors) do not have an infinite power and most of the time it is reliable to estimate that the real delay introduced is twice or three times the frame length plus the overhead (some authors improperly call this the algorithmic delay, although it is merely an estimation linked to the limited DSP power).

Thus codecs with a small frame length are better than those with longer frame length as far as delay is concerned. That is, if each frame is sent immediately on the network ... This is where it becomes tricky because each RTP packet has an IP header of 20 octets, a UDP header of 8 octets, and an RTP header of 12 octets. For a codec with a frame length of 30 ms, sending each frame separately on the network would introduce a 10.6 kbit/s overhead – much more than the actual bitrate of most narrowband codecs. (Note that on point-to-point links using Point to Point Protocol (PPP), it is possible to use PPP compression and to reduce the overhead of PPP+IP+UDP+RTP to only 2 bytes.)

Therefore most implementations choose to send multiple frames per packet, and the real frame length to take into account is in fact the sum of all frames stacked in a single IP packet. This is limited by echo and interactivity issues (see this chapter), and a common choice is to send up to 120 ms of encoded voice in each IP packet.

So for most implementations, the smaller the frame size, the more frames in an IP packet, and there is no influence on delay. Overall it is even better to use codecs which have been designed for the longest frame length (limited by the acceptable delay), since this allows even more efficient coding techniques – the longer you observe a phenomenon, the better you can model it.

The end of the story is that in most cases, the frame size is not so important for IP video conferences when bandwidth is a concern. The exception is high-quality, high-bandwidth conferences.

Resilience to loss
Packet loss is a fact of life in IP networks. Since packets carry codec frames, this in turn causes codec frame loss. However, packet loss and frame loss are not directly correlated; many techniques such as FEC (forward error correction) can be used to lower the frame loss rate associated with a given packet loss rate. These techniques spread redundant information over several packets so that the frame information can be recovered even if some packets are lost.

However, the use of redundancy to recover from packet loss is tricky. To understand why, consider what some manufacturers could do (and have done):

- you prepare a big show to compare your product and the product of a competitor. You advertise that you can resist a 50 per cent packet loss without any consequence on the voice quality;
- you simulate the packet loss by losing one packet out of two;
- you put in your RTP packet 'N' the frames 'N' and 'N–1'.

Your product can recover all the frames because one packet out of two is lost. The competitor can emit only a few crackles. The customer is convinced.

The only problem is that packet loss on the Internet is not so neat. Packet loss occurs in a correlated way, and you are much more likely to lose several packets in a row than exactly one packet out of two. So in reality this simple RTP redundancy scheme will be close to useless in real conditions – and still adds a 50 per cent overhead.

The effect of frame erasure on codecs is a case by case issue. If you lose N samples from a G.711 codec, this will result in a gap of N*125µs at the receiving end. If you lose just one frame from a very advanced codec, it may spoil much more than the duration of this frame because the decoder will need some time to resynchronize with the coder. For a frame of 20 ms or so, this may result in a very audible crack of 150 ms.

Codecs such as G.723.1 are designed to cope relatively well with an uncorrelated frame erasure of up to 3 per cent, but after this the quality drops rapidly. The effect of correlated loss is not yet fully evaluated.

Apart from the built-in features of the codec itself, it is possible to reduce the frame loss associated with the packet loss through several techniques.

FEC-style redundancy (Fig. 1.36) can be used to recover from serious packet loss conditions, but it has a significant impact on delay. If you choose to repeat the same G.723.1 frame in four consecutive IP packets in order to be able to recover from the loss of three consecutive packets, the decoder needs to maintain a buffer of four IP packets and this ruins the delay factor.

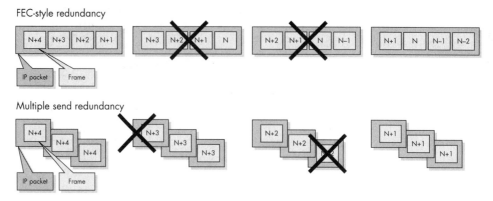

Fig. 1.36 : FEC-style redundancy

It is also possible to send several copies of each frame immediately. But if one packet gets lost, all the copies are likely to arrive at the same congested router at around the same time, and might get lost as well.

Some understanding of the different types of congestion is also important to decide whether redundancy is useful, and which type to use. The network can lose packets because a link is congested, or because a router has to route too many small packets per second. If a link is congested, then any type of redundancy will add to the congestion and increase the overall loss percentage of IP packets. But still the frame loss rate of the communicating devices that use the FEC redundancy will be reduced.

Say we have congestion on a 2 Mbit/s line. It receives 2.2 Mbit/s and the average loss rate is .2/2.2 = 9 per cent. Part of this is someone using a codec that produces a 100 kbit/s stream. The software detects a high loss and decides to use the FEC scheme described above. Now that same application produces a 400 kbit/s stream. The 2 Mbit/s line receives 2.5 Mbit/s and the packet loss rate is increased to 20 per cent for all the users of the link.

But still if we assume the congested link never causes the loss of four packets in a row (on average one packet out of five is dropped), then the software will recover from *all* loss. However, this is *very bad* behavior because it is most unfair to the other users. The next generation IP networks will probably include advanced techniques such as Random Early Detection (RED) that will detect the greedy user and drop most of his packets.

If the congestion is due to an overrun router, FEC-style redundancy is not such a bad thing. It increases the size of packets but does not increase the average number of packets that the router has to forward per second. In this case increasing the size of the packets will not add to the congestion. The other type of redundancy (multiple simultaneous sending) will increase the number of packets through the router and will not work well.

Layered coding

There are several situations in which the current codecs are not well suited. If you want to broadcast the same event to several listeners (H.332 type of conference), some of them will want a high-quality reception (either because they have paid for it or because they have large IP pipes) and others will be able to receive only a lower quality. You could send a customized data stream to each listener, but this is not practical for a large audience. The best option is to multicast the data stream to all listeners (for more information on multicast, refer to the multicast section). With current codecs the complete information is included in one data stream. If it is multicast, all participants will receive the same amount of data, so you usually have to limit the data rate to the reception capability of the least capable receiver.

While most codecs are still at the experimental stage, some can produce several data streams simultaneously, one with the core information needed to have a 'military quality' reception, and the others with more information as needed to rebuild a higher fidelity sound or image. A crude example for video would be to send the black and white information on one channel and the color (chrominance) information on another.

Now each part of the data stream can be multicast using different group addresses, so that listeners can choose to receive just the core level or the other layers as well. In a pay-for-quality scheme, you would encrypt the higher layers (this way you could have a free low-quality preview, and later have the broadcast quality image only if you pay).

Layered codecs are also useful for when it comes to redundancy – the sender can choose to use a redundancy scheme for the core layer so that the transmission remains understandable at all times for everyone, but leave the other layers without protection.

H.323v2 was approved with a specific annex on layered video coding – annex B: procedures for layered video codecs.

Fixed point or floating point

We first need to say a few words about digital signal processors (DSPs). These are processors that have been optimized for operations frequently encountered in signal processing algorithms. One such operation is (a*b)+previous result: one multiplication and addition. In a conventional processor, this operation would require multiple processor instructions, and would be executed in several clock cycles. A DSP will do it in one instruction, and a single clock cycle. Another example is codebook searches which are frequently used by vocoders (a coder optimized for voice).

Some conventional processors also have extensions to accelerate signal processing algorithms. MMX processors can execute a single instruction simultaneously on several operands as long as they can be contained in a 32-bit register. Video algorithms can be accelerated by processing four pixels (8 bits each) simultaneously.

There are two types of DSP: floating-point DSPs which are capable of operating on floating-point numbers, and fixed-point DSP. Fixed-point DSP operands are represented as a mantissa n and a power p of 2 (e.g. 12345678*2^5), but the DSP can operate on two operands only if the power of 2 is the same on the two operands. They are less powerful, but also less expensive, and chosen by many designers for products sold in large quantities.

Some codecs have been specified with only fixed-point C code. However, many implementations will run on processors or DSPs which are capable of floating-point operation, and developers must produce their own version of floating-point C code for the algorithm. This often results in interoperability problems between floating-point versions. Therefore it is a good thing if the codec has also been specified in floating-point C code, especially if the code has to run on PCs.

ITU

Choosing a codec at ITU

The choice of a codec at ITU WP 3 is typically a long process, due to the stringent requirements of ITU experts.

Before a codec is chosen, the ITU evaluates the MOS scores and usually requires a quality equivalent or better than G.726 ('toll quality'). The ITU checks that this quality is constant, for a man or a woman, and in several languages. The ability to take into account background noise and recreate it correctly is also evaluated. The ITU pays special attention to the degradation of voice quality in tandem operation (several successive coding/decoding processes) since this is a situation that is likely to occur in international phone calls. Other important features that are checked are the ability to pass DTMF signals transparently, and the ability to transcode the coded signal into other ITU standard coders easily. Last but not least, if the codec has to be used over a non-reliable medium (a radio link, a frame-relay virtual circuit), the ITU checks that the quality remains acceptable if there is some frame loss.

After checking all those parameters, it frequently occurs that no single proposal passes the test. Therefore many ITU codecs are the combination of the most advanced technologies found in several different proposals. This leads to state-of-the-art choices but, as we will see, is also a nightmare for anyone who needs to keep track of intellectual property.

Audio codecs

G.711 (approved in 1965)

G.711 is the grandfather of digital audio codecs. It is a simple way to digitize the analogue data by using a semi-logarithmic scale. This is called companded PCM (pulse code modulation), and it serves to increase the resolution for small signals, while large signals are treated proportionally – operating as the human ear does. Two different types of scales are in use in Europe and the US respectively, the A-Law scale and the μ-Law scale, which differ only in the choice of some constants. G.711 is used in ISDN and on most digital telephone backbones.

A G.711 encoded audio stream is a 64 kbit/s bitstream where each sample is encoded as an octet, therefore the 'frame' length is only 125 μs. (Note that H225 stipulates that, by convention, a G.711 frame is in fact 8 125 μs samples, or 1 ms.)

Many sound cards are able to record directly in G.711 format. However, in some cases it is better to record using CD-quality, which samples at 44.1 kHz (one 16-bit sample each 23 μs), especially if echo-cancellation algorithms are used, since the full performance of some echo cancellation algorithms cannot be achieved with the lower resolution of G.711 samples.

The typical MOS score of G.711 is 4.2.

G.722

Although G.711 has a very good quality, some of the voice spectrum (above 4 kHz) is still cut. G.722 provides a higher quality digital coding of 7 kHz of audio spectrum (this is called a wideband coder) at only 48, 56 or 64 kbit/s, using about 10 DSP MIPS (Million Instructions per Second). This is an 'embedded' coder, which means that the rate can freely switch between 48, 56 and 64 kbit/s without notifying the decoder.

This coder is good for all professional conversational voice applications (the algorithmic delay is only 1.5 ms), but musical applications are not recommended.

The ITU is working on another (0–7 kHz) coder at a bitrate of 32 and 16 kbit/s. It should have the same quality as G.722 at only 32 kbit/s. Two modes are being studied, one with an algorithmic delay of 10 ms, the other with an algorithmic delay of 20 ms but less complex.

G.723.1 (approved in November 1995)

The IMTC VoIP forum has chosen the G.723.1 codec as the baseline codec for narrowband H.323 communications.

Technology

G.723.1 uses a frame length of 30 ms and needs a lookahead of 7.5 ms. It has two modes of operation, one at 6.4 kbit/s (each frame requires 189 bits which are aligned to 24 octets) and one at 5.3 kbit/s (each frame requires 158 bits which are aligned to 20 octets). The mode of operation can change dynamically at each frame. Both modes of operation are mandatory in any implementation.

The higher bitrate mode uses MP-MLQ (multipulse-maximum likelihood quantization) to model the voice signal, while the lower bitrate mode uses ACELP (algebraic-code-excited linear prediction).

G.723.1 achieves a MOS score of 3.7 in 5.3 kbit/s mode, 3.9 in 6.4 kbit/s mode. A comparison of the performance of G.723.1 (6.4 kbps) and ADPCM released by the Bell Labs in March 1994 is shown in Table 1.5.

Table 1.5 : A comparison of the performance of G.723.1 and ADPCM

	G.723.1, 6.4 kbps	G.723 32 kbps
Clear channel, no errors or frame erasure	3.901	3.781
3% frame erasure	3.432	—
Tandeming of two codecs	3.409	3.491

The main effect of frame erasures is to desynchronize the coder and the decoder, and they may need many more frames to resynchronize. G.723.1 is specified in both fixed-point (it needs about 16 MIPS on a fixed-point DSP) and floating-point C code (running on a Pentium 100, it takes about 35–40 per cent of the processor).

Silence compression

G.723.1 has a voice activity detection, discontinuous transmission, comfort noise generation capability defined in annex A of the recommendation. The silence is coded in very small four-octet frames at a rate of 1.1 kbit/s. If the silence information does not need to be updated, the transmission stops completely.

Intellectual property

G.723.1 is one of the codecs that resulted from many contributions and therefore uses technology patented from several sources. About 18 patents apply to it, from eight companies. The main licensing consortium groups holding the patents are AudioCodes, DSP Group, FT/CNET and Université de Sherbrooke (USH, Canada). Licenses for these rights can be obtained from each of these companies but are mainly managed by DSP group and Sipro Lab Telecom. Other patents are held by AT&T (1), Lucent (3), NTT (3) and Cisco (1, formerly held by British Technology Group and VoiceCraft), Nokia Mobile Phone (1, formerly held by VoiceCraft). Claims have also been made by Siemens, Robert Bosch and CSELT.

The source code is copyrighted by four companies.

There are typically several licensing agreements for this codec (the details vary from company to company), depending on whether the application is for a single or for multiple users, whether it is going to be a paying or free application, and depending on the volume licensed. The exact prices have to be negotiated with both patent owners and implementers, but some data can be gathered from conferences and newsgroups, *although they must be taken with great care.* (This pricing is only related to the rights of the Pool of companies – FT, USH, Audiocodecs, DSP Group. This pricing is not public and is subject to frequent changes. Changes can be anticipated for the near future.) Some indications for the intellectual rights of G.723.1 are:

- a license for a mono-user client is said to be worth around $50000 one-time plus $0.8 per unit;
- a license for a server is said to be about $20000 plus $5 per port;
- a license for unlimited distribution of a single-user application is about $120 000.

Then, unless you do your own implementation (not recommended), be prepared to approximately double the previous fees to license a well optimized implementation.

Consider this quote from a company trying to license those codecs, picked from a mailing list:

'We have been trying to negotiate licensing arrangements with the patent holders for more than six months. As of today, we have received terms and conditions from six of the holders, and little to no response from the rest. The costs proposed by the first six strongly imply a substantial initial investment, and a per port cost in excess of $20.00. Our concern, however, extends far beyond the cost. The Internet's success is due to its readily available standards and lack of non-essential rules and constraints. The time requirements and logistics of establishing contact with 12 parties and negotiating licensing are significant barriers to growth in the industry. The legal risks associated with not doing so are an impediment to the rapid evolution of the industry.'

The reality is not quite so bad, and the investments put behind the technology of standardized codecs such as G.723.1 indeed justify a fee, but which fee is reasonable? This question is the real fuel behind the so-called 'codec wars' that periodically emerge in the VoIP standard bodies.

G.726 (approved in 1990)

G.726 uses an ADPCM technique to encode a G.711 bitstream in words of two, three or four bits, resulting in available bitrates of 16, 24, 32 or 40 kbit/s. G.726 at 32 kbit/s achieves a MOS score of 4.3 and is often taken as the reference for toll quality. It requires about 10 DSP MIPS of processing power (full duplex), or 30 per cent of a Pentium 100. The 'frames' are 125 μs long and there is no lookahead. There is an embedded version known as G.727.

G.728 (approved in 1992–94)

G.728 uses an LD-CELP (low-delay, code-excited linear prediction) coding technique and achieves MOS scores similar to those obtained by G.726 with a bitrate of only 16 kbit/s. Compared to PCM or ADPCM techniques, CELP is a coder optimized for voice. Those coders specifically model voice sounds and work by comparing the waveform to encode with a set of waveform models (linear predictive codebook) and finding the best match. Then only the index of this best match and parameters such as voice pitch are transmitted.

Fax and low bitrate modem transmission succeed with G.728 compression. G.728 is used for H.320 video conferencing.

G.728 takes approximately the power of a P100 and 2 kbytes of RAM to implement. It has a low delay (between 625 μs and 2.5 ms, depending on the source).

G.729
Technology
G.729 is very popular for voice over frame-relay applications and V.70 voice and data modems. It uses a CS-ACELP (conjugate structure, algebraic-code-excited linear prediction) coding technique. G.729 produces 80-bit frames encoding 10 ms of speech at a rate of 8 kbit/s. It needs a lookahead of 5 ms. It achieves MOS scores around 4.0. G.729 annex C specifies a reference floating-point C code for the codec.

There are two versions of G.729:

■ G.729 (approved in December 1996): it requires about 20 MIPS for coding, and 3 MIPS for decoding. The frame size is 10 ms and the lookahead is 5 ms.

■ G.729 A (approved in November 1995): Annex A is a reduced-complexity version of the original G.729. It requires about 10.5 MIPS for coding and 2 MIPS for decoding (about 30 per cent less than G.723.1).

Silence compression
Annexes A and B of G.729 define VAD, CNG and DTX schemes for G.729. The frames sent to update the background noise description are 15 bits long and are sent only if the description of the background noise changes.

Licenses
Both G.729 and G.729A are the result of about 20 patents belonging to nine companies – AT&T, CSELT, France Telecom, Lucent, Université de Sherbrooke (USH, Canada), NEC, Nokia NTT and Cisco. NTT, France Telecom and USH have formed a licensing consortium, the G.729 Consortium. Licenses for these patents of the G.729 Consortium can be obtained from Sipro Lab Telecom, as well as licenses for AT&T's patents which are not included in this consortium.

The source code is copyrighted by five companies.

As with G.723, several options exist to license this codec. The main difference between G.723.1 and G.729 is that there is no specific price for server-type applications for G.729. The pricing schedule for G.729 is public and will not be subject to great changes. Here is an extract of the current price list (details and updates can be obtained from the Lab's web site, at http://www.sipro.com/licensing/G729pool.htm)

Pricing scheme for G.729 (combined with G.729 Annex A).

Option 1 – Royalty Based

■ Initial Fee $15,000
■ Cumulative unit royalty per channel per licensed product sold

Table 1.6 : Option 1

Number of channels	Unit Royalty in $
<100K	1.45
100–500K	1.30
500K–1M	1.00
1–3M	0.80
3–5M	0.70
5–10M	0.50
>10M	0.30

■ Royalty Cap

Introduced of a cap (maximum amount paid) fixed at:

a. For manufacturers of end-products: $1,93M
b. For chipsets manufacturers: $6,68M

■ Mimimum Annual Royalty (after first year) $7,500

Option 2 – Pre-paid Option

Table 1.7 : Option 2

Maximum number of channels sold	Pre-paid license fee G.729 in $	Pre-paid unit (channel) * royalty G.729 in $
200K	217K	1.09
500K	476K	0.95
1M	767K	0.77
3M	1,668M	0.56
5M	2,299M	0.46
10M	3,34M	0.33
15M	4,09M	0.27

Future coders

ITU is working on new coders:

■ a wideband coder (0–7kHz) at a rate of about 16 kbit/s. The latest proposals did not meet ITU requirements and ITU has reopened the competition for this coder;

■ a 4 kbit/s coder. The latest proposals also fall short of ITU requirements and ITU will review additional proposals in 1999. A decision is scheduled for the beginning of 2001.

Video codecs

Representation of colors

The representation of colors is derived from the fact that any color can be generated from three primaries. From a painter's point of view, the three primaries are red, yellow and blue. These are called subtractive primaries because any color can be generated from a white beam passed through a sequence of red, yellow and blue filters. When a painter puts a layer of yellow paint on a sheet of paper, this acts as a filter that lets most of the yellow component of the white light be reflected, but filters out most of the other colors.

But video monitors use additive primaries: red, green and blue. By mixing three beams of red, blue and green light with various intensities, it is possible to generate any color. Therefore any color can be represented by its barycentric coordinates (representing relative intensities) in a triangle with a primary at each edge. The weight of each color ranges usually from 0 to 255 in the RGB format: each pixel is described with 8 bits for each color weight, which leads to 24 bits per pixel.

Another common representation is to use luminance (brightness represented by the letter Y) and chrominance (hue represented by U and V, or Cr and Cb). Several conventions exist for this conversion (JFIF for JPEG, CCIR 601 for H.261 and MPEG). The conversion between an RGB format and a YUV format according to JFIF is:

$$\begin{pmatrix} Y \\ U \\ V \end{pmatrix} = \begin{pmatrix} 0.299 & 0.587 & 0.114 \\ -0.1687 & -0.3313 & 0.5 \\ 0.5 & -0.4187 & -0.0813 \end{pmatrix} \begin{pmatrix} R \\ G \\ B \end{pmatrix}$$

Y, U and V range is from 0 to 255 (U and V are often shifted to take values between –128 and + 127). For CCIR this range is from 16 to 235.

Experiments have shown that most of the relevant information for the human eye is encoded in the luminance parameter. Because of this, U and V values can be sampled with a reduced frequency without inducing significant loss in the quality of the image. Typically U and V will be sampled only for a group of 4 pixels. Coding an image this way already leads to a 2:1 compression (instead of 24 bits per pixel, we now have 8 bits for Y, and (8+8)/4 pixels for U and V).

Image formats

Several image formats are commonly used by video codecs. CIF, the common intermediary format, defines a 352*288 image. This size has been chosen because it can be sampled relatively easily from both the 525 and 625 lines video formats and approaches the popular 4/3 length/width ratio.

Although the resolution of CIF is already below television quality, it is still relatively difficult to transmit over low bandwidth lines, even with efficient coding schemes such as H.261 and H.263. For this reason two other formats with lower resolutions have been defined. At half the resolution in both dimensions, Quarter CIF (QCIF) is for 176*144 images, and SQCIF is only 128*96. For professional video applications, CIF is clearly insufficient, and images can be coded using 4CIF (704*576) or 16CIF (1408*1152) resolution. *See* Table 1.8.

Table 1.8 : Image formats

| Picture format | Luminance pixels | lines | Uncompressed bitrate (Mb/s) | | | |
| | | | 10 frames/s | | 30 frames/s | |
			Gray	Color	Gray	Color
SQCIF	128	96	1.0	1.5	3.0	4.4
QCIF	176	144	2.0	3.0	6.1	9.1
CIF	352	288	8.1	12.2	24.3	36.5
4CIF	704	576	32.4	48.7	97.3	146.0
16CIF	1408	1152	129.8	194.6	389.3	583.9

Gray images are obtained by transmitting only the Y luminance component
Color images are obtained by transmitting also the U, V chrominance components sampled at half the resolution

H.261

H.261 is a video codec used in H.320 video conferencing to encode the image over several 64 kbit/s ISDN connections, but in H.323 the bitstream is encoded in a single RTP logical channel. The H.261 codec is intended for compressed bitrates between 40 kbit/s and 2 Mbit/s. The source image is normally 30 (29.97) frames per second, but the bitrate can be reduced by transmitting only one frame out of two, three or four. The following image formats can be encoded by H.261:

SQCIF	128*96	Optional
QCIF	176*144	Required
CIF	352*288	Optional

The 4CIF and 16CIF formats are not available.

The H.261 coding process involves several steps. After an initial YUV coding of the original image using CCIR parameters, as described above, each frame can be coded as an intraframe (I-frame) or interframe (P-frame). The 'intra' method codes frames using only a local compression method, while the 'inter' method codes a frame relatively to the adjacent frames. The inter method is much more efficient, but leads to error accumulation, so it is necessary to send intraframes from time to time (Fig. 1.37).

I-frames use a coding similar to the one used by JPEG: DCT (discrete cosine transform), quantization, run-length encoding and entropy encoding (Fig. 1.38).

For P-frames compression uses the following steps:

■ motion detection: comparison of the image to be coded with the last coded image trying to find parts of the image that have simply moved. This results in a 352*288 (for CIF) representation of the difference between the two images;

■ coding of the difference-image using DCT transform and run-length encoding;

■ entropy encoding to further reduce the image size.

Motion detection

The second stage of the H.261 coding process is based on the fact that most images in a video sequence are strongly related. If the camera angle changes, all pixels will simply shift from one image to another. If an object moves in the scene, most of the pixels representing the object in a frame can be copied from the preceding frame with a shift.

For the motion detection stage, the image is divided into 8*8 luminance pixel blocks. The same surface is coded with only 4*4 chrominance pixels for each chrominance plane. Four luminance blocks are grouped with two chrominance blocks (one for U, one for V) in a macroblock. For each macroblock of the image to be encoded, the algorithm tries to determine whether it is a translated macroblock block of the previous image. The search is done in a vicinity area of ±15 pixels and considers only the luminance elements.

The difference between the original macroblock of the n+1 frame and each translated block of the n frame in the search area is the absolute values of the pixel-to-pixel luminance difference throughout the block. The translation vector of the best match is considered the motion-compensation vector for that macroblock.

The difference between the translated macroblock and the original block is called the motion compensation macroblock. *See* Fig. 1.39.

If the image has changed completely (e.g. a new sequence in a movie), interframe coding is not optimal. Therefore the H.261 coding process must decide at each frame which coding is better for the macroblock: intra or interframe. The

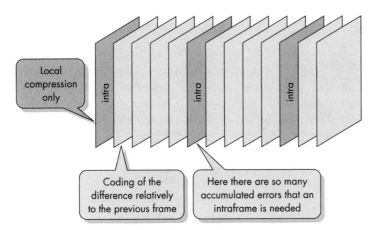

Fig. 1.37 : Intraframes and interframes

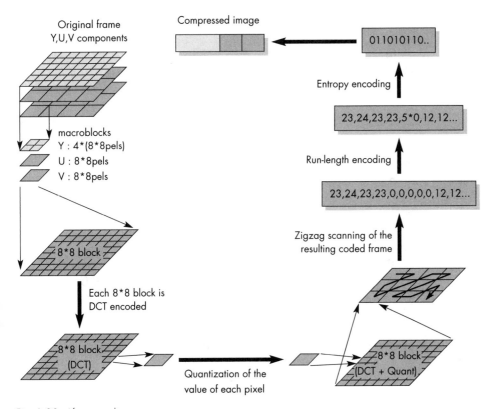

Fig. 1.38 : I-frame coding

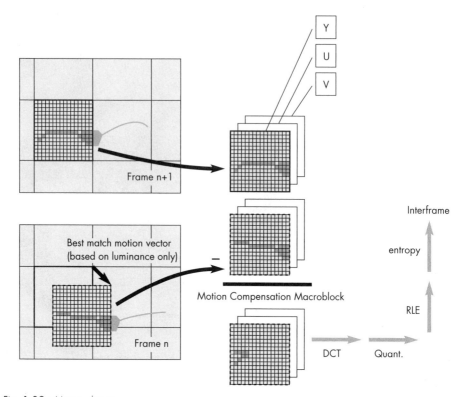

Fig. 1.39 : Motion detection

decision is based on the energy and variance of the original macroblock and the motion-compensated macroblock.

DCT transform

The pixel values of the image difference obtained at the previous stage vary slowly within a macroblock. We take such a macroblock and repeat it in two dimensions so that we obtain a periodic function (Fig. 1.40). Such functions can be reproduced efficiently with just a few coefficients of their Fourier transform.

This transformation is called a bidimensional DCT. The formula used by H.261 to calculate the DCT of an 8*8 block is:

$$F(u,v) = \frac{1}{4}C(u)C(v) \sum_{i=0}^{7}\sum_{j=0}^{7} f(i,j)\cos\left((2i+1)u\frac{\pi}{16}\right)\cos\left((2j+1)v\frac{\pi}{16}\right)$$

where

$$\begin{cases} C(0) = 1/\sqrt{2} \\ C(x \neq 0) = 1 \end{cases}$$

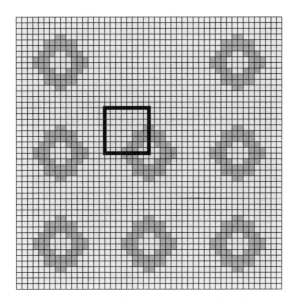

Fig. 1.40 : A macroblock

The DCT is a 'frequency' representation of the original image. The coefficient in the upper left corner is the mean value of the image. Values in higher row positions represent higher vertical frequencies and values in higher column positions represent higher horizontal frequencies. The DCT is interesting because most high-frequency coefficients are usually near 0.

At the decoder side, the inverse of the DCT is obtained with

$$f(i,j) = \frac{1}{4} \sum_{u=0}^{7} \sum_{v=0}^{7} C(u)C(v)F(u,v)\cos\left((2i+1)\,u\frac{\pi}{16}\right)\cos\left((2j+1)v\frac{\pi}{16}\right)$$

Quantization

So far the representation of the image that we have is still exact. We could obtain the exact original image by reversing the DCT and adding the resulting block to the shifted block of the previous frames. Quantization is the 'lossy' stage in H.261. It consists in expressing each $F(U,V)$ value in coarser units, so that the absolute value to be coded decreases and the number of zeros increases. This is done using standard quantization functions. One is used for the constant component (DC) coefficient, and another one is selected for a macroblock. Depending on the amount of loss that can be tolerated, the coder can choose fine or very coarse functions.

Zigzag scanning and entropy coding

Once the DCT coefficients are quantized, they are rearranged in a chain with the DC coefficient first, then as shown in Fig. 1.41.

This concentrates most non-zero values at the beginning of the chain. Because there are long series of consecutive zeros, the chain is then run-length encoded. This uses an escape code for the most frequently occurring sequences of zeros followed by a non-zero coefficient, and variable escape codes for other less frequently occurring combinations.

This chain can be further compressed using entropy coding similar to a Huffman coder. This creates smaller code words for frequently occurring symbols. The Huffman coding first sorts the values to be encoded according to frequency of appearance, then constructs a tree by aggregating the two least frequent values in a branch, and repeating the process with the two values/branches with smallest occurrence values (counting the occurrence of a branch as the sum of the occurrences of its leaf nodes). Once the tree is complete, a 1 digit is assigned to each left side of any two branches, and a 0 digit to each right side. Any value can be identified by its position in the tree as described by the sequence of digits encountered when progressing from the root of the tree to the value.

The output of the H.261 encoder consists of the entropy-encoded DCT values. This bit stream can be easily decoded once the decoder has received the Huffman tree. In the case of H.261, the tree calculation is not done in real time; the recommendation itself provides codes for the most frequently occurring combinations.

Output format

The H.261 bitstream is organized in GOBs (group of blocks) of 33 macroblocks (each encoding 16*16 luminance pixels and 8*8 U and V pixels). A PAL (phase-

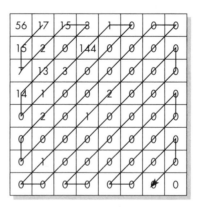

Fig. 1.41 : Zigzag scanning

alternation-line video format) CIF image has 12 GOBS, a PAL QCIF image has 3 GOBS. A CIF picture cannot be larger than 256 kbit/s, and a QCIF picture cannot be larger than 64 kbit/s.

The output bitstream will consist of an alternance of intercoded macroblocks and intracoded macroblocks. The receiver can force the use of intra coding to recover from cumulative or transmission errors. Otherwise a macroblock should be updated in intra mode at least once for every 132 transmissions to compensate for error accumulation.

Conclusion

This description of H.261 has not made us video experts, but it is enough to allow a network expert to understand the nature of video traffic. The most important conclusion is that video traffic using H.261-style coding (this is also valid for H.263 and MPEG) is extremely sporadic or 'bursty'. The typical network load profile is shown in Fig. 1.42.

Microsoft Netmeeting, for instance, sends an intraframe every 15 seconds. A video-conferencing MCU will send an intraframe for all macroblocks each time the speaker, and therefore the image, changes ('videofastupdate'). In other circumstances most implementations will not send all intra mac-roblocks simultaneously, in order to avoid sending giant traffic peaks through the network.

Another important conclusion is that H.261 specifies only a decoder. In fact, a very bad implementation could choose to use only intraframes if it was not capa-ble of doing motion vector searches for interframes, and still be H.261 compliant. This explains why all video boards and all video-conferencing software are not equal, even if they all claim they are using H.261 or H.263. A network engineer should always try to measure the actual bandwidth used by these devices.

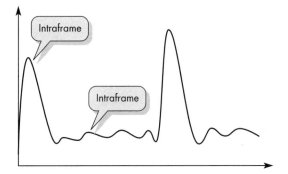

Fig. 1.42 : Typical network load profile for H.261

H.263

Several image formats can be encoded with H.323, as shown in Table 1.9.

Table 1.9 : Image formats encoded with H.323

SQCIF	128*96	Required
QCIF	176*144	Required
CIF	352*288	Optional
4CIF	704*576	Optional
16CIF	1408*1152	Optional

H.263 was designed for low-bitrate communications, as low as 20 kbit/s. The coding algorithm of H.263 is similar to that used by H.261, but with some changes to improve performance and error recovery. H.263 is more recent, more flexible and about 50 per cent more bitrate effective than H.261 for the same level of quality, and should replace it in most applications. The main differences between H.261 and H.263 are:

- half-pixel precision is used for motion compensation whereas H.261 used full pixel precision and a loop filter. This accounts for much of the improved efficiency;

- some parts of the hierarchical structure of the datastream are now optional, so the codec can be configured for a lower data rate or better error recovery;

- there are now four optional negotiable options to improve performance: unrestricted motion vectors, syntax-based arithmetic coding, advance prediction, and forward and backward frame prediction similar to MPEG called P-B frames. Backward frames are added to allow motion vectors to refer not only to past frames but also to future frames, for instance when a partly hidden object becomes visible in a future frame;

- H.263 supports five resolutions. In addition to QCIF and CIF that were supported by H.261 there is SQCIF, 4CIF and 16CIF. SQCIF is approximately half the resolution of QCIF, while 4CIF and 16CIF are four and sixteen times the resolution of CIF respectively. The support of 4CIF and 16CIF means the codec can compete with other higher bitrate video coding standards such as the MPEG standards.

With these improvements, H.263 is a good challenger to MPEG-1 and MPEG-2 for low resolutions and low bitrates. They have similar features (B frames in MPEG, P-B frames for H.263 which are as good for moderate movements). MPEG has more flexibility, but flexibility means overhead. H.263 even has some options not found in MPEG, such as motion vectors outside the picture and syntax-based arithmetic coding. For video-conferencing applications, with little movement and a strong bandwidth constraint, H.263 is a very good choice.

ETSI SMG

The ETSI SMG11 (European Standards Telecom Institute Special Mobile Group) standardized the speech codecs shown in Table 1.10:

Table 1.10 : ETSI SMG11 standardized speech codecs

Codec	MOS in clean conditions	Vehicle noise	Street noise
GSM FR	3.71	3.83	3.92
GSM HR	3.85	4.45	3.56
GSM EFR	4.43	4.25	4.18
Reference with no coding	4.61	4.42	4.35

Source: TR 06.85 v2.0.0 (1998)

GSM full rate (1987)
GSM full rate, also called GSM 06.10, is perhaps the most well known codec in use today, and runs daily in millions of 'GSM' cellular phones. It provides a good quality and robust operation in the presence of background noise. It uses a RPE-LTP technique to encode voice in frames of 20 ms at a rate of 13 kbit/s. It needs no lookahead. GSM-FR achieves MOS scores slightly below toll quality. It is not extremely complex and requires about 4.5 MIPS and less than 1 kbyte of RAM.

The GSM full-rate patent is held by Philips and the license is free for applications on mobiles.

GSM half rate (1994)
Also called GSM 06.20, this coder aims at using less bandwidth while preserving the same or slightly lower speech quality as GSM-FR. This codec uses VSELP and encodes speech at a rate of 5.6 kbit/s. The frames are 20 ms long and there is a lookahead of 4.4 ms. It needs approximately 30 MIPS and 4 kbytes of RAM.

The patent is also held by Philips; ATT patents on CELP (code excited linear predictive codec) and NTT patents on LSP (Line Spectrum Pair) may apply.

GSM enhanced full rate (1995)
This high-quality coder exceeds the G.726 'wireline reference' in clear channel conditions and in background noise. It is also called GSM 06.60. It was selected as the base coder for the PCS 1900 cellular phone service in the US, and was

standardized by TIA in 1996. This codec uses a CD-ACELP technique and encodes 20 ms frames at a rate of 12.2 kbps. Optional VAD/DTX functions with comfort noise generation have been defined and there is an example implementation for error concealment.

AT&T patents for CELP and NTT patents for LSP may apply.

Other proprietary codecs

Lucent/Elemedia SX7003P

Another popular codec used in Lucent hardware and licensed to other manufacturers, this codec has a frame size of 15 ms, which contains four control octets and 14 data octets. Silence frames have 2 octets of data. If two frames are packed in each packet (overhead of 40 bytes), this leads to a bitrate of 20.3 kbit/s during voice activity periods, and only 13.6 kbit/s during silence periods.

RT24 (Voxware)

One of the ultra-low bitrate coders, unfortunately spoiled by the IP overhead, RT24 has a bitrate of 2400 bps, and achieves a MOS of 3.2. It has a frame size of 22.5 ms (54 bits) which results in a measured bandwidth of 16.6/9.5/7.1/6 kbps with one/two/three/four frames per IP packet.

DTMF

Strictly speaking, the DTMF tones that are generated by a touchtone telephone when you press a key are part of the media stream. They are just another sound transmitted by the telephone. In the switched circuit network, this sound is digitized by the G.711 codec as part of the media stream and played back at the receiving end of the line. This does not cause any problem because G.711 does not assume that the signal is voice.

But some narrowband codecs which achieve much higher compression rates do assume that the signal is voice. Others do not but distort it in such a way that the pure frequencies composing the DTMF tone cannot be correctly recognized when the signal is regenerated. DTMF will not get through those codecs.

Whenever a communication involves an IVR (interactive voice response) system, it is important to be able to transmit the DTMF tones correctly. In most cases the IVR system simply asks a question and waits for a DTMF input; it wants to ascertain which key has been pressed, and the exact duration and timing of the tone is not so important. In other cases the IVR system will need more accuracy in the timing, for instance when the system reads a list and asks you to press * when you hear something of interest.

In order to interact properly with those IVR systems, it was necessary to develop procedures to handle DTMF. There are two ways to do this:

■ a mandatory method is available. A special H.245 message, UserInputIndication, can carry all numeric characters, plus * and #. It has the advantage of using a reliable TCP connection, and cannot be lost. But because TCP will try to retransmit the packet if it has been lost in the network, information might get delayed and get to the receiver too late;

■ a non-standard method has been proposed in the VoIP forum, and may be used in H.323v3 terminals when the fastStart procedure is used and no H.245 channel is available. A special RTP logical channel can be opened to carry the RTP DTMF payload, which is formatted as:

R (3)	Digit (5)	R (2)	Volume (6)	Duration (16)

– the first 3 bits are reserved (R) and should be set to zero for now;
– digit (5 bits): the DTMF digits are encoded as follows:

DTMF digit	Encoding
0	00000 (0)
.	.
.	.
9	01001 (9)
*	01010 (10)
#	01011 (11)
A	01100 (12)
B	01101 (13)
C	01110 (14)
D	01111 (15)
Flash	10000 (16)

– the next two bits are also reserved and should be set to zero;
– volume (6 bits): This is a value in negative dBm0. For example, the value 20 denotes a volume of –20 dBm0. The possible range is between 0 and –63dBm0, but values lower than –55dBm0 should be rejected;
– duration (16 bits): The unit used is the same as the unit used for the timestamp. If the separate logical channel is opened, the sampling rate will be considered to be 8000 Hz, therefore this field is large enough for DTMF tones of up to eight seconds. A DTMF tone should always be longer than 40 ms in order to be properly recognized by in-band detectors.

It is possible to insert a DTMF RTP packet in the same logical channel as voice. In this case the payload type should be formed as follows to avoid confusion with dynamic or fixed RTP PT (these should be less than 128):

« chosen voice PT: e.g. 8 » + « DTMF PT » + 128

This PT should be used in the OpenLogicalChannel. If the remote terminal does not understand this meta-type, it means it does not support this method.

In any case, a terminal should use one method or the other, depending on the choice of the manufacturer. Overall, it seems that the first method is preferred, since in many situations the playback buffers are large enough to allow for one TCP retransmission in cases where the round trip time on the network between the endpoints is not too large. However, for international calls with large round trip times and time-sensitive IVR systems, it might prove necessary to use the second method.

Gateways should be extremely careful to mute in-band DTMF and convert it to an H.245 UserInputIndication or a special RTP payload type, since simultaneous transmission of in-band DTMF and the special H.245 or RTP messages might cause the egress gateway to first render the RTP DTMF packet or H.245 UserInputIndication and then transmit the DTMF tone contained in the audio stream, duplicating the original tone.

There is even more than DTMF – for instance, users can use other control signals, such as Hook-Flash, which in some situations should also be carried across the network. So far there is no standard solution for this outside the VoIP forum RTP DTMF payload type.

Fax

A short primer on G3 fax technology

The purpose of facsimile transmission is to transmit one or several pages of a document across the telephone network. The first fax systems used Group 1 or Group 2 technologies, which scanned the document line by line and converted each line in black or white pixels. The data was then transmitted without compression over the phone line at the rate of three lines per second for Group 1 and six lines per second for Group 3.

Because this took over three minutes for an A4 document (1145 lines of 1728 bits) even in the best case, Group 3 technology was introduced. Group 3 faxes use a more efficient image coding mechanism known as Modified Huffman coding (MH). MH coding relies on the fact that each line is composed of large sequences of white pixels, and large sequences of black pixels. Instead of sending data for each pixel, MH coding sends a short code for the sequence. Now the

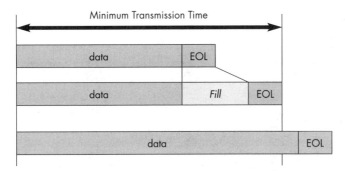

Fig. 1.43 : Transmission of a single line

transmission time depends on the document, but is usually much shorter than three minutes. No wonder Group 3 faxes today dominate the fax market.

With the advent of ISDN, Group 4 faxes have been introduced. The main difference to Group 3 is that ISDN can transmit raw data, so Group 4 technology need not care about the many hacks that are needed to carry data over an analogue line. However, G4 has not succeeded in gaining a significant market share, and the probability of having a G4 fax talking to another G4 fax is so low that this case has not so far been considered in SG16 of the ITU.

Behind a fax, there is most of the time a physical printer. Because of the compression, it is possible to transmit a single line very quickly if the line is simple, so quickly that the receiving fax may not have enough time to print it. Of course, the fax could buffer it in its memory, but most faxes are simple appliances with little memory. Therefore G3 has a minimum transmission time (MTT). If a line does not contain enough compressed data to take more than MTT to be transmitted, a filling sequence of zeros will be added before the end of line sequence (FOL), as shown in Fig. 1.43.

The transmission of a page is quite simple as shown in Fig. 1.44. Each line is transmitted in sequence, separated by an EOL, and the whole page is terminated by six consecutive EOLs, which means the fax has to return to command mode (RTC).

Figure 1.45 illustrates a typical fax transmission. The calling fax dials the number, then sends a special sequence called CNG, which consists of a repetition of 1100 Hz tones sent for 0.5 seconds separated with three seconds of silence. Faxes manufactured before 1993 may not send this tone. When an incoming connection arrives on the receiving fax, it sends a special tone called CED for three seconds. After a short pause, the receiving fax begins to send commands. It uses a V.21 modulation – quite slow at 300 bps – to transmit synchronizing flags for one second (called a preamble), then may transmit some non-standardized data (NSF) and its local identity (CSI), then must transmit its capabilities (DIS).

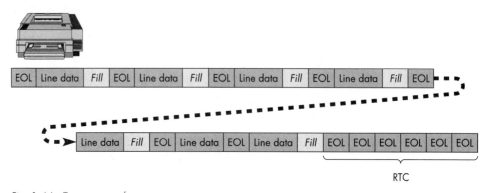

Fig. 1.44 : Transmission of a page

Each of these data elements is an HDLC frame which consists of:

- a starting flag (7Eh)
- an address field (always set to FFh)
- a command field which is set to C8h for a final frame, C0h otherwise,
- a fax control field (FCF): 02h for CSI, 01h for DIS, etc.
- a variable length fax information field (FIF)
- a checksum (FCS).

Transmitting NSF, CSI and DIS may take up to two-and-a-half seconds. The sending fax selects a mode of transmission (DCS) and replies sending its own capabilities and its identity (TSI).

At this moment the receiving fax is ready, so the sending fax begins the actual transmission phase which will use a faster modulation scheme, such as V.27ter (4800 bit/s) or V.29 (9600 bits/s). This requires a training phase that is used by the receiving side to compensate phase distortions and other issues. At the end of the training phase the sending fax sends only zeros for 1.5 seconds (called Training check, TCF). If the called fax receives this sequence correctly it considers the training phase successful and sends a CFR command to let the transmitting fax know this. After another training sequence, the sending fax transmits the actual page data as formatted above. This takes approximately 30 seconds in V.29 mode and one minute in V.27ter mode.

When this is finished, the modem can send an MPS message to send another page or an EOP (end of procedure message) when it has transmitted the last page. The receiving fax acknowledges it with an MCF (which means that the image data has been correctly received) and the sending fax sends a disconnection message DCN.

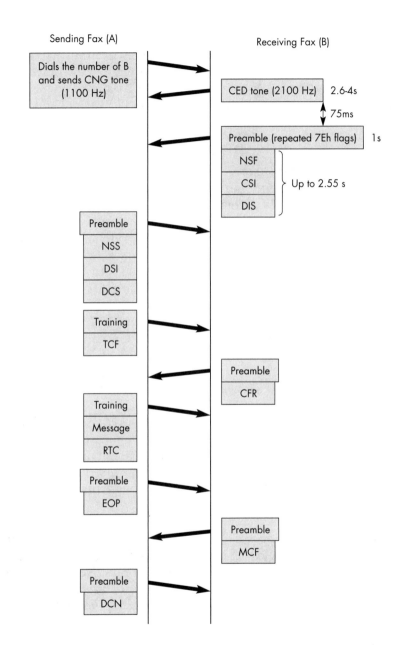

Fig. 1.45 : A typical transmission

Error conditions

If the training is not successful, the receiving fax can send an FTT command to ask for another try at a lower speed. If an error is present in a line, the receiving fax will find it by counting how many pixels are present in the decoded line if there are not exactly 1728 (A4 format). The line is ignored or copied from the previous line, at the choice of the manufacturer. At any moment a fax can request the retransmission of a command by sending a CRP command.

Fax transmission over IP (T.38 and T.37)

Store&forward and the challenge of real-time fax

Sending faxes over the Internet is not something new. Many companies have been offering this service, called store&forward fax. The idea is simple. If a computer (A) receives a fax, the actual fax data is a set of bitmaps representing the document. This bitmap is a file that can be transmitted to another computer (B) closer to the destination. Once this computer has received the file, it simply needs to dial the receiving fax machine and emulate a fax to send the bitmap.

This technique is also used for bulk faxing. The original document is faxed once to a computer, which is then provided with a list of fax telephone numbers and sends a copy of this fax to each of them. The store&forward fax transmission is standardized at ITU in recommendation T.37, but since this book focuses on real-time applications, we chose to put the emphasis on the real-time standard, T.38.

The problem with this store&forward fax technology is that many faxes give a feedback on the transmission of the document. Usually they keep the result code in memory and they can print it on demand. Many people tend to rely on these transmission reports. For fax-to-fax transmission this is indeed a confirmation that the fax has been correctly received, with a timestamp and the identity of the receiving fax machine. When using store&forward, this report is only a confirmation that the fax has been sent because the receiving machine is in fact computer A.

When it receives the file containing the document, computer B will dial the number indicated, but the fax can be busy, or even worse, it can be a wrong number, or a wrong fax. So any company providing a store&forward service needs to provide the sender with feedback via email or fax. Now when it receives a negative acknowledgement the sender has to believe that it is indeed a problem with the receiving fax, not the provider. This leads to potential conflicts and increases the cost of providing the service.

It is much easier for a service provider to be completely transparent in the transmission. More precisely, the success report received by the originating fax machine should appear as a success report from the distant fax machine. Such a service is called real-time fax.

Real-time fax is much more complex than store&forward fax. There are many timers in the T.30 protocol. Once computers A and B have both picked up the line and recognized that the call is a fax, they have only a limited time to relay fax commands. During the call, when the fax machine on the A side has sent a command, it expects a reply within three seconds, so during this limited time A must send the command to B over the Internet, B must send it to the receiving fax machine, receive the reply and forward it to A.

Fortunately, the ITU had a human operator in mind when setting the value of these timers, so they are all expressed in seconds. Moreover, as we have seen, there are many procedures to recover from error conditions which can be used to 'spoof' the sending fax and get it to wait a little longer if necessary. These techniques are quite difficult to implement reliably with all brands of faxes, but some manufacturers have announced they can transmit real-time faxes over IP networks with a round trip latency of up to two seconds.

Many carriers have been tempted to do IP trunking without telling their customers. With H.323 gateways having T1 or E1 interfaces, this is quite feasible – except that when a subscriber tries to send a fax, and this IP trunk happens to be in between, it will fail. Of course, it is always possible to tell those subscribers not to use their faxes, or to dial a special prefix for faxes, but this significantly complicates their lives.

Real-time fax is the only appropriate answer to these issues. Gateways which are able to dynamically recognize a fax call (e.g. by constantly checking the 2100 Hz frequency of the CNG tone) will allow transparent IP trunking.

T.38 (formerly T.iFax2)

IFT

T.38 is the approach of ITU Study Group 16 to the problem of real-time fax. Its title is 'Procedures for real-time Group 3 facsimile communication between terminals using IP networks'. This recommendation will allow fax transmission between faxes via gateways over an IP network, between faxes and computers connected on the Internet, or even between computers (this one may not seem useful, but in some cases the receiving computer will be identified by an H.323 alias or even a phone number, and you may not know this is a computer). The usage of the T.38 protocol within the framework of H.323 is defined in H.323 annex D which is currently determined (i.e. the ITU draft is stable). This will be a feature of H.323v3.

T.38 uses a special protocol called IFT. IFT packets (Fig. 1.46) can be carried over TCP, but can also be transported over UDP using a forward error correction mechanism. According to H.323 annex D, an H.323 terminal with T.38 capabilities has to support IFT over TCP – IFT over UDP is optional.

The purpose of IFT is to carry messages between two gateways or PCs. These messages contain a type field, and data field, both encoded using ASN1. In the current state of the specification the type can be:

- T30_indicator: the value of this indicator gives information on received CED and CNG tones, V.21 preambles and V.27, V.29 and V.17 modulation trainings;
- T30_data: the value of this indicator tells over which transport (V.21, V.17 or v.29) the data part of the message has been received;
- T30_disconnect: used to disconnect the session normally or after a failure, the value describes the error code (normal, communication failure, etc.).

The data part of the message contains T.30 control messages as well as the image data. This data element is organized in fields which themselves contain a field type and field data. Examples are:

- type HDLC data: the data part of the field contains one or part of an HDLC data frame, not including the checksum (FCS). This is coded as an ASN-1 octet;
- type FCS OK: indicates that an HDLC frame is finished and the FCS has been checked. There are still other HDLC frames after an FCS OK;
- type FCS OK-sig-end: same as FCS OK, except that this is the last HDLC frame;
- T4-non-ECM: the data part contains the actual image data including filling and RTC.

IFP over TCP or UDP
These IFP messages can be carried as a TCP payload or can be encapsulated in UDP.

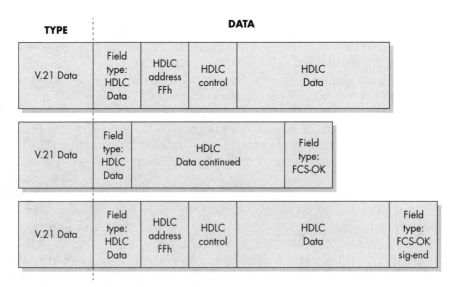

Fig. 1.46 : IFP packets

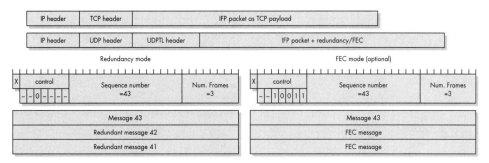

Fig. 1.47 : IFP packets over TCP or UDP

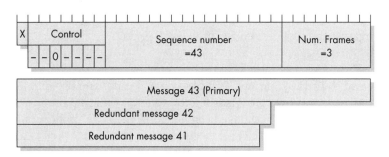

Fig. 1.48 : Redundancy mode

An additional transport layer has to be used on top of UDP to make the delivery of IFP packets more reliable. This layer is formatted as shown in Fig. 1.47. The payload part contains one or more IFP messages, and the sequence number that appears in the header is the sequence number of the first IFP message in the payload, which is also called the primary message. The first message sent by a gateway should have a sequence number of 0.

After this primary message other messages are inserted for error/loss recovery purposes, using two modes: the redundancy mode and the FEC (forward error correction) mode. The control part indicates whether the secondary messages are redundancy messages (bit 3 set to 0) or FEC messages (bit 3 set to 1).

In redundancy mode (Fig. 1.48), copies of previous IFP messages are simply copied after the primary message. The number of copies is the number of frames minus one. By adding n copies in the message, the transmission is protected against loss of up to n consecutive packets. A gateway is not required to transmit redundancy packets, and receiving gateways which do not support them may simply ignore the presence of redundancy packets.

FEC mode is more complex. Each FEC message is the result of a bit per bit XOR performed on n primary IFP messages. Before performing the XOR, shorter messages are right-padded with zeros, so the resulting FEC message is as long as the

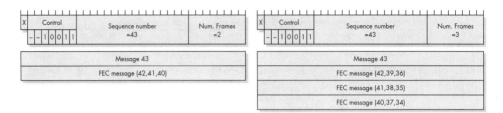

Fig. 1.49 : FEC mode

longest of the n primary messages. The value of n is indicated in the four last digits of the control field – 3 in our example. When several FEC messages are added, as in the left part of Fig. 1.49, the primary messages used for each FEC message are interleaved. When n FEC messages are added, the transmission is protected against the loss of n consecutive UDP packets.

T.38 and H.323

T.38 is referred to in H.323 annex D. Annex D mandates the use of IFP transport over TCP, but transport over UDP is still allowed as an optional mode. These capabilities (T38-TCP and T38-UDP) have been added in the DataApplicationCapability of DataProtocolCapability of H.245.

IFP is transmitted over two logical channels (sender to receiver and vice versa). When using TCP as a transport layer, it is not yet clear whether the preferred transmission method would be to use a tunnel in Q.931 or a new TCP connection.

Supplementary services using H.450

A set of supplementary services has been defined in H.450.1, H.450.2 and H.450.3:

■ H.450.1 defines the 'generic functional protocol for the support of supplementary services in H.323';

■ H.450.2 describes 'call transfer supplementary services for H.323'.

H.450 is the standard, and someone will probably end up using it. However, much of the functionality it implements can readily be achieved using the GK routed model and a web interface with the end user, or with an MCU. H.450 is cleaner (multiple call diversion is handled, the control protocol is well defined and standardized), but no manufacturer is going to implement it before all the niceties that can be achieved with the MCU and the gatekeeper have been thoroughly exploited – and before at least one major client manufacturer supports it.

H.450.1

This recommendation defines a generic protocol based on application protocol data units (APDUs) carried in the call signaling messages (Alerting, Call Proceeding, Connect, Setup, Release Complete, Progress) or in Facility messages.

H.450.1 can be used to convey call-related instructions (e.g. redirecting a call) or call-independent instructions (e.g. program call screening). In the latter case, a special Setup message with specific bearer capability and conferenceGoal information elements is used.

H.450.1 APDUs have the following structure:

■ optional network facility extension (NFE) with the source entity type (endpoint or anyEntity) and address, and the destination entity type and address;

■ a description of what to do with unrecognized messages (discard, clear call, etc.);

■ a structure with the actual operation invoked.

The NFE part of the APDU provides a way to route supplementary service messages. The network entity receiving a Setup message with an H.450.1 APDU may not be the intended recipient of the instructions contained in the APDU. It may have to relay it, or choose to intercept it in the case of a gatekeeper.

Both H.450.2 and H.450.3 are built on top of H.450.1.

H.450.2: call transfer

This recommendation provides a way to transfer calls between H.323 endpoints once the initial call is established (the callee has answered).

Call transfer between H.450.2 aware endpoints

This scenario is an example of a call transfer between endpoints (Fig. 1.50). The call could be routed through a gatekeeper, but the gatekeeper would simply relay all H.450.2 APDUs:

■ user B calls user A (the transferring user). This is the primary call;

■ user A answers the call and uses H.450.2 to transfer the call to user C. A may previously have established a separate call (secondary call) with user C to announce the transfer. If this secondary call exists, endpoint A notifies C of the pending call transfer, and C returns a temporary identifier for this secondary call if it can participate in the transfer. Otherwise the attempt aborts here;

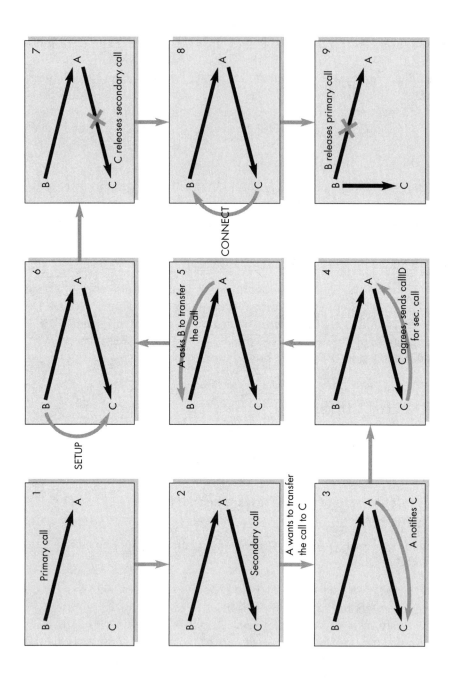

Fig. 1.50 : A call transfer with consultation between endpoints

- the endpoint A sends a H.450.2 request to user B to call C (if there is an A–C secondary call, the temporary identifier is mentioned). The endpoint may handle this directly if it is H.450.2 capable, or B's gatekeeper may choose to do it;

- when the new call request initiated by B arrives at C, C releases the secondary call if it existed. Then if C answers the call, the primary call is also released. B and C can talk.

In this scenario, A could have called B in the first place, the next steps of the call transfer would remain the same. The invoke and result APDUs are carried in normal Q.931 messages whenever possible, or in Facility messages otherwise, as shown in Fig. 1.51.

Note: H.323 mentions another simple way to support call transfer. An endpoint can send a Facility message with the address of the transferred to endpoint. When it receives such a Facility message, a terminal should release the current call, and restart a new call to the address specified in the Facility message. This is an easy way of transferring a call without consultation, but to our knowledge only very few endpoints and gateways support it. However, even fewer endpoints support H.450.2.

Transfer using the gatekeeper

H.450.2 is not very easy to implement. Figure 1.51 describes only the normal case, but it would become much more complex if it took into account the many options of H.450.2 and the error conditions. Because of this complexity, many H.323 endpoints such as standalone IP phones with stringent memory constraints may not implement H.450.2.

However, in the section on H.450.1 we emphasized the fact that all H.450 APDUs could be routed (using the origin and destination addresses found in the NFE) or intercepted by a gatekeeper. Therefore, if the terminals involved in the primary call were using the gatekeeper routed model (all Q.931 and H.245 messages get relayed by a GK), the intermediary gatekeeper could intercept and act upon H.450.2 APDUs. This allows the use of H.450.2 even if only terminal A is H.450.2 aware. Terminal A could be a sophisticated secretary terminal, while endpoints B and C could be ordinary simple IP phones. If we go one step further, endpoint A could be a simple IP phone also, but the gatekeeper would have a web interface allowing the user of terminal A to ask the gatekeeper to initiate the call transfer.

The task of the gatekeeper is more complex than what we have seen before. In the previous case endpoint B initiated a *new* call to terminal C, and the normal H.323 procedure was used. Now the gatekeeper must find a way to cause endpoint B (connected to A) to transfer its media channels to C without ever

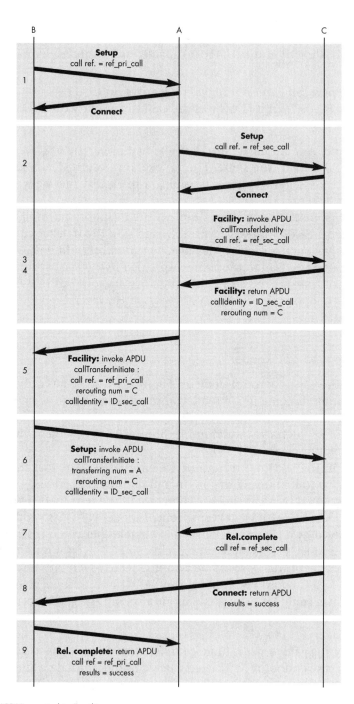

Fig. 1.51 : APDUs carried in Facility messages

releasing the call. Fortunately, this operation, called third party rerouting, has been taken into account in H.323, and is carried out as follows:

■ as soon as it knows it needs to transfer the call to C, the gatekeeper calls end-point C – it sends a Setup and receives a Connect. If it receives a Release Complete (busy terminal), it aborts the operation;

■ the gatekeeper sends an empty terminal capability set to endpoint B, end-point A and endpoint C. This is possible because it relays the H.245 messages between A and B and therefore can 'insert' messages. The empty capability sets indicate that the remote terminal has no receive capabilities and, logically, this causes terminals A and B to close all active logical channels. Terminal C will also not attempt to open a logical channel to the gatekeeper;

■ the gatekeeper can close the connection with A now (H.245 end session command and Q.931 release complete) or wait until the transfer is completed;

■ during the H.245 channel establishment with C, the gatekeeper has received the capability set of terminal C, and now forwards it to terminal B. This will cause terminal B to restart the H.245 state machine just after the capability set exchange, and B will start a master/slave determination exchange;

■ then B sends an OpenLogicalChannel command over the H.245 channel, the gatekeeper relays it to terminal C. The OpenLogicalChannelAck contains the RTP/RTCP addresses of terminal C, so B will now establish the logical channels with C;

■ C also opens logical channels with B, and this completes the transfer.

If the endpoints are H.450.2 aware, the gatekeeper can still perform the call redirection. In this case H.450.2 APDUs are used to notify the endpoints of the progress of the call transfer, e.g. a Facility message with a CallTransferComplete invoke APDU to endpoint B to inform endpoint B that it has been transferred to C.

Blind transfer, secure transfer, transfer with consultation

To sum up, here is how an H.450.2 aware terminal can perform the classic types of call transfer:

■ *blind transfer.* In this type of transfer, A does not want to check if C is reachable before disconnecting from B. As A and B are still in an active call, A sends a facility message to B – the FacilityReason field is of type CallTransfer and contains a CallTransferInvoke (CallTransferInitiate) invoke APDU informing B of the address of C. Then A terminates its conversation with B using the regular H.323 procedure. When it receives the Facility message, B initiates a call with C;

- *secure transfer.* Now if B cannot connect to C, A wants to remain in conversation with B. A sends the CallTransferInvoke to B but does not disconnect from B immediately. Instead, it waits until it receives the Facility message from B with the result of the call transfer (CallTransferResult = success or failure). Depending on the result, A terminates the conversation with B (B might also send the Release Complete) or keeps it active;

- *transfer with consultation.* Now A might be a secretary and needs to check if C is available or in a meeting. In a regular phone system, A can put B on hold. But for some reason the Q.931 message hold is forbidden in H.323. So A can simply stop sending media to B (or send prerecorded music). Another solution will be to use the new H.450.Hold supplementary service, which is being defined at the ITU. Now A establishes a new call with C. Once A has been allowed to perform the transfer, A can use either the blind transfer or the secure transfer procedure. The procedure shown in Fig. 1.51 is a transfer with consultation using secure transfer after the consultation.

H.450.3: call diversion

This recommendation provides a way to redirect calls between H.323 endpoints before the call is established. This includes call forwarding on busy, call forwarding on no reply, call forwarding unconditional, and call deflection. The diversion might be performed by a gatekeeper, or by the endpoint itself. H.450.3 enables the number of successive call diversions to be controlled/limited.

When activating the call forwarding unconditional (CFU) supplementary service for a particular address A, a user can still originate calls, but all calls to A will be redirected to another address. The user can activate/deactivate this service directly on the endpoint associated with A, or remotely on a gatekeeper. H.450.3 also provides ways to interrogate an entity to find out whether the supplementary service is activated or not, and for which addresses. The user receiving the diverted call is notified that the call has been diverted, and also where the last diversion point was. The calling user also has the option of be notified that the call has been diverted, with or without the new call destination address.

When activating the call forwarding on busy service, the same operations as in CFU will occur if the user's line is busy. There might also be more specific conditions (diversion if more than N calls are waiting, etc.).

The call forward on no reply is similar, but occurs if the called user opting for this supplementary service has not answered after a programmable time.

The call deflection supplementary service can be invoked by a called user dynamically before the user answers a call. It causes the call to be diverted to the address entered by the called user.

Because the call diversion occurs before capability negotiation and media channel activation, it is very easy to perform. The simplest way is to use a gatekeeper
to perform call diversion. If a call diversion supplementary service has been activated for an address, the gatekeeper will force the incoming calls to this address to
be routed through the gatekeeper. This is done in the ARQ/ACF exchange by
putting the gatekeeper's call signaling address in the ACF. Then the gatekeeper
can 'play' with the Setup message. For call forwarding unconditional it can
simply change the called party information element of the Setup message and forward it to the new destination. For call forward on busy it will first forward the
Setup to the original destination address, then if it receives a Release Complete
(cause busy), send a new modified Setup to the next destination.

The only difficulty with all these supplementary services is the signaling
needed to program or invoke them. For instance, the call deflection needs to be
triggered by the called endpoint – this is done using the CallRerouting invoke
APDU. Even this simple task requires many information elements:

- the reroutingReason, if needed
- the new calledAddress to use for the redirected call
- a diversionCounter that is useful to avoid loops
- the lastReroutingNr with the address of the last endpoint that performed the
  rerouting
- subscriptionOptions: Does the terminal want to inform the calling party?
- the original callingNumber (note that the 'number' here can be any H.323
  address)
- more textual information in fields such as callingInfo, redirectingInfo, etc.

At this stage we can only guess about what will be implemented in the near
future, but there is no doubt that IP telephony in the corporate environment will
make heavy use of supplementary services. What's more, these services will probably become the main differentiating factor between various brands of IP
terminals and gatekeeper products.

My guess is that a lot can be done already with the ubiquitous web interface for user interaction: if you have a web phone and you want to program
call forward on busy, this can be done in a few mouse clicks. With a little
imagination it is even possible to let the user customize his call control with
much more flexibility with a web interface: something like 'if-my-boss-is-call-
ing-then-use-that-loud-ring-tone-otherwise-go-to-the-answering-machine, or
if-it's-my-banker-calling-again-to-say-my-account-is-low-then-sound-as-if-I-
wasn't-here …'

It seems that only call deflection needs a specific standard message to be sent
between the IP phone and the gatekeeper. So if only a part of H.450.3 is to be

implemented soon it will probably be the CallRerouting part and related messages. However, most manufacturers are likely to avoid having to implement the H.450.1 framework just for this and will probably go for proprietary messages.

An advantage of using H.450.3 over a web interface is that it offers a well defined interface that could be used by programmers to remotely control the call deflection supplementary services on a gatekeeper. At first, most gatekeepers will probably offer a CORBA or DCOM interface to do this, but it will lead to many proprietary interfaces. At present it is difficult to say whether the H.450.3 protocol will emerge as the standard way to control call diversion supplementary services, or whether other methods will be preferred.

The future of H.450

H.450 still lacks many of the features needed in a complete business phone system, such as the ability to put someone on hold, park and retrieve calls, etc. A number of extensions have been proposed to add these functionalities in H.450:

- H.450.4 hold supplementary service
- H.450.5 call park and call pickup supplementary service
- H.450.6 implements the call waiting supplementary service
- H.450.7 implements the message waiting indication (MWI)
- H.450.8 implements identification services.

These extensions will probably be approved in 1999.

Future work on H.323

Work on H.323v3 is ongoing. As well as the features mentioned above, several additions are being discussed:

- annex E, 'Call connection over UDP', should address one of the major weaknesses of H.323 in high-volume applications, due to the limitation of the number of TCP connections that can be opened on several operating systems. This annex is currently determined (i.e. the ITU draft is stable). It also reduces the number of round trips needed to establish a connection. From callee to caller fastStart establishes a connection in two round trips; the UDP method reduces it to one. From caller to callee we go down from 2.5 round trips to 1.5. TCP-based signaling also has some drawbacks:
  - when a segment of data sent over TCP is lost, TCP takes a long time to detect this loss, and this may affect the average call setup time on congested networks;

- when a long PDU is sent and needs more than one TCP segment, TCP will wait to have received an ACK for segment 1 before sending segments 2 and 3. This in fact means more round trips;
- in the case of failures, it is easier to reroute a UDP data stream than a TCP data stream;

■ annex F, 'Single use audio device', will describe streamlined H.323 implementations for simple audio-only telephones, and possibly text conversation terminals and fax devices;

■ H.341 will define a Management Information Base (MIB) for all H.323 entities, to be used with Simple Network Management Protocol (SNMP) v2. At the RTP/RTCP level, the IETF MIB will be used;

■ annex G, 'Communication between administrative domains', will allow several providers to interconnect their H.323 domains and exchange administrative and routing information.

The ITU SG 16 will also take into account related proposals at the IETF (Internet engineering task force) from the MMUSIC (multiparty multimedia session control) working group, the IPTEL (IP telephony) working group, the PINT (PSTN-Internet interworking) working group, the AVT (audio-visual transport) working group, and the SS7 and E.164 working groups.

The Session Initiation Protocol (SIP)

The origin and purpose of SIP

SIP is defined in RFC 2543 (March 99) of the MMUSIC (Multiparty Multimedia Session Control) working group of the IETF.

The MMUSIC working group is focused on loosely coupled conferences as they exist today on the MBONE (*see Chapter eight for additional details on the MBONE*) and is working on a complete framework based on the following protocols:

- The Session Description Protocol (SDP) and the Session Announcement Protocol (SAP);
- The Real-Time Stream protocol (RTSP) to control real-time data servers;
- The Simple Conference Control Protocol (SCCP) for tightly coupled conferences. This work has just begun with the definition of a message bus between conferencing systems;
- SIP.

So far only SIP, RTSP and SDP have become requests for comments (RFCs).

These protocols complement existing IETF protocols, such as RTP from the AVT (Audio/Video transport) working group for the transfer of isochronous data, or RSVP from the INTSERV (integrated services) working group for bandwidth allocation.

Overview of a simple SIP call

Successful call to an IP address directly

Here we assume that the initiator of the call knows the IP address of the called endpoint (we will see later that there are many other types of SIP addresses). The caller might be calling the following SIP address:

sip: *john@192.190.132.31*

SIP entities communicate using 'transactions'. SIP calls a transaction a request (e.g. the Invite request below) and the response(s) it triggers (200 OK in our example) up to a final response (see the definition below, all 2xx, 3xx, 4xx, 5xx and 6xx responses are final). The initiator of a SIP request is called a SIP client, and the responding entity is called a SIP server. The messages exchanged during a transaction share a common Cseq number, with one exception: the ACK message uses the same Cseq as the transaction to which it applies but is a transaction of its own.

The first step is to open a signaling connection between the calling and the called endpoint. SIP endpoints can use UDP or TCP signaling – the message syntax is independent of the transport protocol being used. When using TCP, the same connection can be used for all SIP requests and responses (*not* for the media data), or a new TCP connection can be used for each transaction. If UDP is used, the address and port to use for the answers to SIP requests are contained in the 'via' header parameter of the SIP request. Replies must not be sent to the IP address of the client. If no port is specified in the SIP address, the connection is made to port 5060 for both TCP and UDP.

A SIP client calls another SIP endpoint by sending an Invite request message (Fig. 2.1). The Invite message normally contains enough information to allow the called terminal to immediately establish the requested media connection to the calling endpoint. This information includes the media capabilities that the calling endpoint can receive (and send: coder capabilities are assumed to be both sending or receiving in SIP, unless the SDP parameters 'sendonly' or 'reconly' are used), and the transport address where the calling endpoint expects the called endpoint to send this media data. Most endpoints will be able to receive many different encodings for each media type. The particular encoding chosen by the sender appears as part of the RTP header.

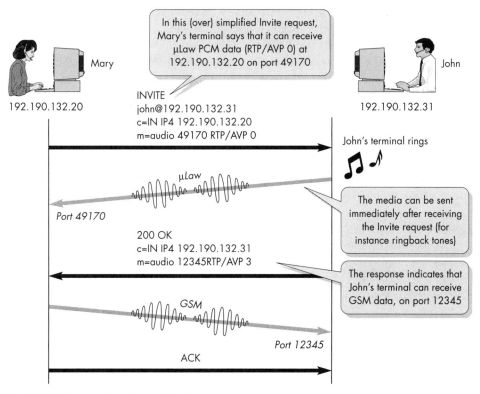

Fig. 2.1: Making a call to a known IP address

The called endpoint needs to indicate that it is accepting the request. This is the purpose of the OK response message. Since the request was an invitation, the OK response also contains the media capabilities of the called endpoint, and where it is expecting to receive the media data. The caller needs to acknowledge that it has properly received the response of the called endpoint (remember we might be using UDP) with the ACK message.

From this simple example, we can see that SIP is very efficient – the callee to caller media channel can be set in one round trip, and the caller to callee media channel can be set up in one-and-a-half round trips. This is much better than the many round trips needed by the bootstrap nature of H.323v1 (H.323v2 is as efficient as SIP if fastStart call setup is used).

Codec negotiation

In the previous call, Mary's terminal offered to receive an audio channel encoded in PCM. This may not be acceptable for John's terminal, either because John does not have enough bandwidth available (PCM requires 64 kbit/s, plus the RTP/UDP/IP/PPP overhead) or because John's terminal does not have a PCM μ-Law coder. In this case John's terminal will reply with a 606 Not Acceptable reply, and eventually list the set of coders that it can use. With this information, Mary's terminal can either send a new Invite request, with the same call identifier, advertising the proper code (but if it had such capability, it could have sent it as a choice in the first Invite request) or re-initiate a call through a transcoding proxy. *See* Fig. 2.2.

The voice over IP forum agreed on a default coder to use for low bitrate voice, G.723.1, in order to keep the probability of such incompatibility to a minimum in H323. No such recommendation exists for SIP, but most terminals seem to be able to receive PCM A-Law and μ-Law, and GSM.

SIP does not have a notion of logical channels (as defined in H.323). When a client offers to receive several types of media on several UDP or TCP ports, it must be prepared to immediately receive media on any of those ports. However, the called terminal may choose to send data on some ports only (e.g. it does not have video capabilities and sends audio only). Nothing in the signaling tells the client whether a port is going to be active or not. In general, this is not really a problem as most endpoints can keep listening to unused ports without significant performance impact. In some cases, however, SIP entities need to maintain many media channels and have to reuse UDP ports as efficiently as possible – this is the case for large gateways or centralized media resources. Those entities may have to multiplex several media channels on a single port, or close idle ports based on heuristics, for instance after a time-out period with no activity.

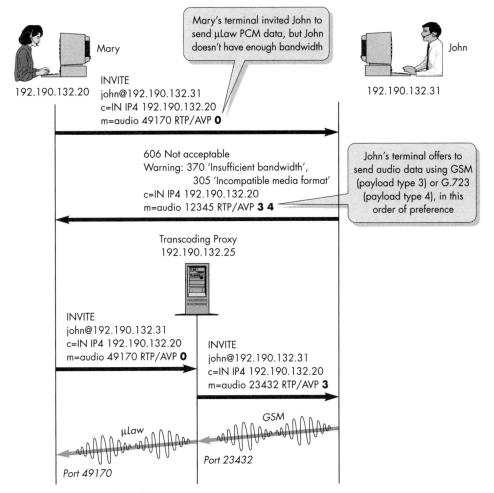

Fig. 2.2 : Negotiating the call setup

Terminating a call

The above example is a simple and successful call setup. Here we look at the complete call signaling, including the call termination by John (Fig. 2.3). If Mary had terminated the call, she would have sent the BYE request, and the From and To fields would be reversed. The media flows are not shown, but the signaling messages include all mandatory headers.

Some SIP headers have abbreviated forms that can help in keeping the total size of a message below the MTU. In this example John's terminal is using the abbreviated form.

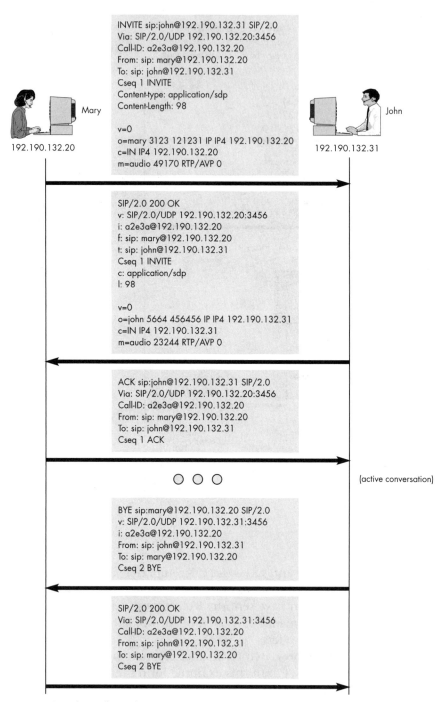

```
INVITE sip:john@192.190.132.31 SIP/2.0
Via: SIP/2.0/UDP 192.190.132.20:3456
Call-ID: a2e3a@192.190.132.20
From: sip: mary@192.190.132.20
To: sip: john@192.190.132.31
Cseq 1 INVITE
Content-type: application/sdp
Content-Length: 98

v=0
o=mary 3123 121231 IP IP4 192.190.132.20
c=IN IP4 192.190.132.20
m=audio 49170 RTP/AVP 0
```

Mary
192.190.132.20

John
192.190.132.31

```
SIP/2.0 200 OK
v: SIP/2.0/UDP 192.190.132.20:3456
i: a2e3a@192.190.132.20
f: sip: mary@192.190.132.20
t: sip: john@192.190.132.31
Cseq 1 INVITE
c: application/sdp
l: 98

v=0
o=john 5664 456456 IP IP4 192.190.132.31
c=IN IP4 192.190.132.31
m=audio 23244 RTP/AVP 0
```

```
ACK sip:john@192.190.132.31 SIP/2.0
Via: SIP/2.0/UDP 192.190.132.20:3456
Call-ID: a2e3a@192.190.132.20
From: sip: mary@192.190.132.20
To: sip: john@192.190.132.31
Cseq 1 ACK
```

○ ○ ○   (active conversation)

```
BYE sip:mary@192.190.132.20 SIP/2.0
v: SIP/2.0/UDP 192.190.132.31:3456
i: a2e3a@192.190.132.20
From: sip: john@192.190.132.31
To: sip: mary@192.190.132.20
Cseq 2 BYE
```

```
SIP/2.0 200 OK
Via: SIP/2.0/UDP 192.190.132.31:3456
Call-ID: a2e3a@192.190.132.20
From: sip: john@192.190.132.31
To: sip: mary@192.190.132.20
Cseq 2 BYE
```

Fig. 2.3 : Complete call signaling

Rejecting a call

John can be unable to receive a call from Mary for a number of reasons. He may not be there or may be unwilling to answer, or he may be in another conversation. These conditions can be expressed in the reply message. SIP provides codes for the usual conditions, but also defines more sophisticated replies, such as 'gone', 'payment required' or 'forbidden'.

A simple 'busy here' reply (Fig. 2.4) tells Mary that John cannot be reached at this location (but she might try to reach another location, such as John's mobile phone through a gateway, or a voice mail). Another reply, '600 busy everywhere', will tell her that John cannot be reached at any location at this moment.

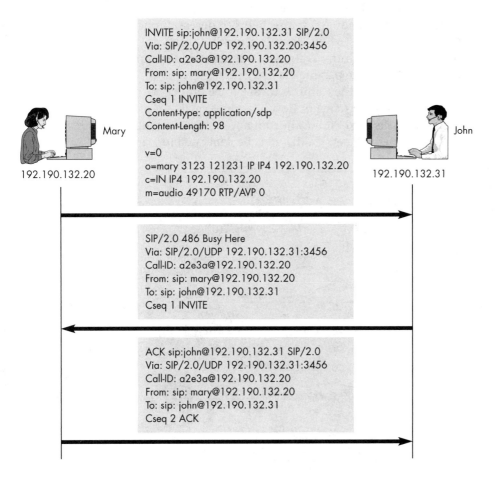

Fig. 2.4 : The 'busy here' reply

SIP messages

SIP messages are encoded using HTTP/1.1 message syntax (RFC 2068). The character set is ISO 10646 with UTF-8 encoding (RFC 2279). Lines are terminated with CRLF (carriage return, line feed), but receivers should be able to handle CR or LF as well.

There are two types of SIP messages: Requests and Responses. They share a common format, shown in Fig. 2.5 (where SP is an abbreviation for 'single space').

Some of the header fields are present in both requests and answers. They are part of the 'general header':

■ *Call-ID* (e.g. 'CallID: f81d4fae-7dec-11d0-a765-00a0c91e6bf6@foo.bar.com'). The CallID parameter serves many purposes. In Register and Options requests it serves to match requests with the corresponding responses. For the Invite and Registration requests it also helps to detect duplicates (duplicate invite requests can occur when there is a forking proxy in the path). Successive Invite requests with the same CallID but different parameters can be used to dynamically change parameters in a conference.

The first part of the CallID is meant to be unique within each host, and the last part, a domain name or host IP address, makes it globally unique (in case an IP address is used, it must be routable, i.e. private addresses such as 10.x.x.x cannot be used). A new CallID must be generated for each call;

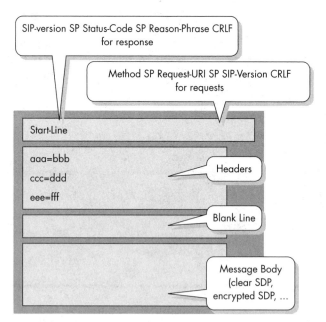

Fig. 2.5 : The SIP message format

- *Cseq* (e.g. Cseq: 1234 Invite). Every request has to have a Cseq header field, which is composed of an unsigned sequence number and the method name. Within a call, the sequence number is incremented at each new request (unless the request is a retransmission of a strictly identical previous request), and starts at a random value. The only exceptions are the ACK and Cancel requests which keep the Cseq number of the acknowledged reply (for ACK) or the cancelled request (for Cancel). The server must copy the Cseq value of the request in the corresponding replies. *See* Fig. 2.6.

- *From* (e.g. From: 'MyDisplayName'<sip:myaccount@company.com>). This field must be present in all requests and responses. It contains an optional display name and the address of the originator of the request. Optional tags can be appended. Note that the 'from' field contained in SIP replies is simply copied from the request and therefore does not designate the originator of the reply;

- *To* (e.g. To: Helpdesk <sip:helpdesk@company.com>;tag=287447). This field must be present in all requests and responses and indicates the intended destination of a request. It is simply copied in responses. The tag is used mainly when a single SIP Uniform Resource Identifier (URI) designates several possible endpoints (as in the case of a helpdesk.) In this case a random tag is appended in the replies to allow a client to distinguish replies from individual endpoints;

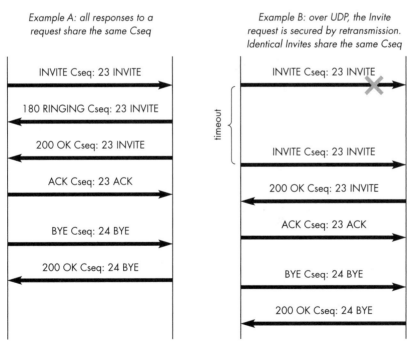

Fig. 2.6 : Cseq usage

■ *Via* (e.g. Via: SIP/2.0/UDP PXY1.provider.com; received 10.0.0.3). The Via field is used to record the route of a request, in order to allow intermediary SIP servers to forward the replies along the same path. *See* Fig. 2.7.

   In order to achieve this, each proxy adds a new Via field with its own address to the list of existing Via fields. The request receiver can add optional parameters, for instance to indicate that it received the request from an address that is not the address contained in the previous hop's Via field. Using this information, a proxy can forward the replies to the original sender, even if there is a network address translation device in the path. In the above example, the call center uses only private addresses (10.x.x.x), and is connected to the Internet through a router doing network address translation. When it receives the Invite request from proxy PXY1, the request's source IP address is not 192.9.5.3, but has been changed by the NAT device to 10.0.0.3. So the Automatic Call Distribution (ACD) system records this information in a 'received' parameter. On receiving the reply for this query, it will know that it must forward the request to 10.0.0.3, not the address of PXY1@provider.com. This mechanism also works when sending a request out of an IP domain using non-routable addresses.

   This example also shows how multicast has been taken into account. When a maddr parameter is present in a Via field, the reply is forwarded in multicast using the maddr address (and the ttl value stored in the ttl parameter).

   The Via header field is one of the most powerful features of SIP, and shows that SIP has been designed with IP networking issues in mind;

■ *Encryption* (e.g. Encryption: PGP version=2.6.2,encoding=ascii). This header field specifies that the message body, and possibly some message headers, have been encrypted. For more detail see the security section further on.

Some header fields apply directly to the message body and are part of the 'entity header':

■ *Content-Type* (e.g. Content-Type: application/sdp). This describes the media type of the content of the message body. In the example, the message body contains a session description using the IETF SDP protocol. Another example is text/html;

■ *Content-length*. The number of octets of the message body.

SIP requests

SIP requests (Fig. 2.8) are sent from the client terminal to the server terminal. There are various methods for doing this:

■ *ACK*. An ACK request is sent by a client to confirm that it has received a final response from a server, such as 200 OK;

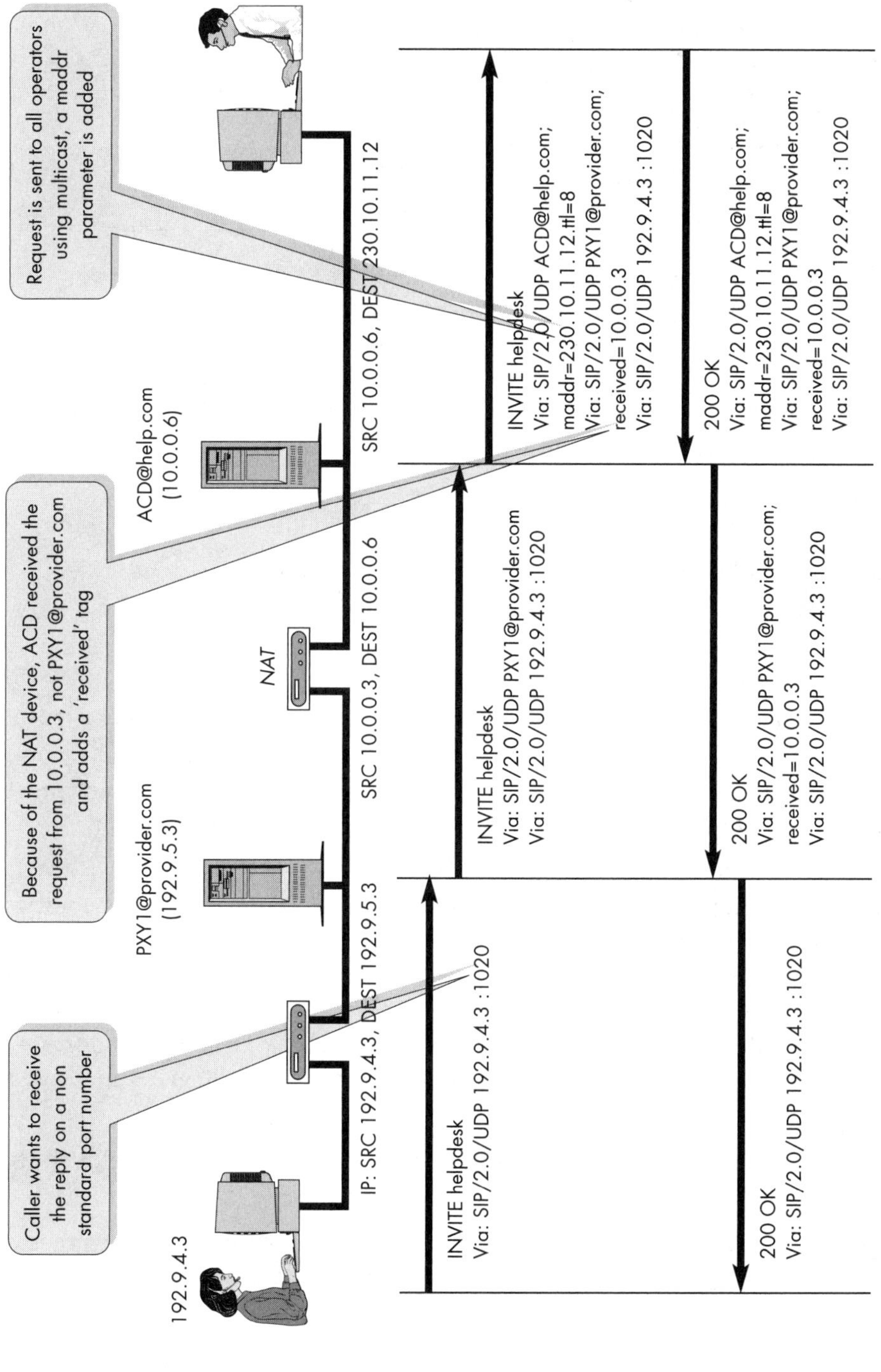

Fig. 2.7 : The Via field

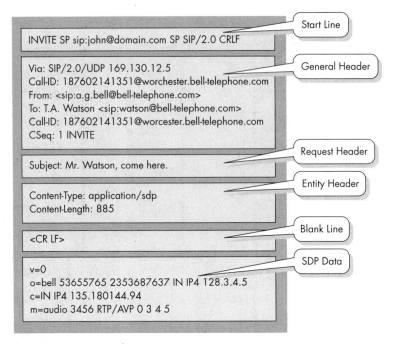

Fig. 2.8 : The SIP Request message format

- *BYE.* A BYE request is sent either by the calling agent or by the caller agent to abort a call;
- *Cancel.* A Cancel request can be sent to abort a request that was sent previously as long as the server has not yet sent a final response;
- *Invite.* The Invite request is used to initiate a call;
- *Options.* A client sends an Option request to a server to learn its capabilities. The server will send back a list of the methods it supports. In some cases it may also reply with the capability set of the user mentioned in the URL (uniform resource locator), and how it would have responded to an invitation;
- *Register.* Clients can register their current location (one or more addresses) with the Register request. A SIP server that can accept a Register message is called a registrar.

In addition to the fields of the general header, requests can carry fields in the request header:

- *Accept* (e.g. Accept: application/sdp, text/html). This optional header indicates what media types are acceptable in the response. The syntax is specified in RFC 1288;

- *Accept-Language* (e.g. Accept-Language: fr, en-gb;q=0.8, en;q=0.7). This indicates the preferred languages of the caller. The syntax is specified in RFC 1288;

- *Expires* – Invite and Register – (e.g. Expires: Thu, 01 Dec 2000 16:00:00 GMT *or* Expires: 5 in seconds). For a Register message, this header field indicates for how long the registration will be valid. The registrar can shorten the desired value in its reply. For an Invite message, this can be used to limit the duration of searches;

- *Priority* (e.g. Priority: emergency). The values are those of RFC 2076, plus 'emergency';

- *Record-Route* – also a response header field – (e.g. Record-Route: sip:acd.support.com;maddr=192.190.123.234,sip:billing.netcentrex.net;maddr=192.194.126.23). Some proxies may add/update this header field if they want to be on the path of all signaling messages. In the example the request has traversed a billing proxy, then an ACD. Such entities need to monitor the state of calls in order to work properly. For example, the billing server might control a firewall to enforce the billing policy;

- *Subject* (e.g. Subject: 'Conference call on the SIP chapter'). This is free text that should give some information on the nature of the call.

SIP responses

A SIP server responds to a SIP request with one or more SIP responses. Most responses (2xx, 3xx, 4xx, 5xx and 6xx) are 'final responses' and terminate the SIP transaction. The 1xx responses are 'provisional' and do not terminate the SIP transaction.

The first line of a SIP response always contains a status code and a human readable reason phrase. Most of the header section is copied from the original request message. Depending on the status code, there may be additional header fields, and the response data part may be empty, or it may contain SDP data or explanatory text. *See* Fig. 2.9.

So far six categories of status codes have been defined, depending on the first digit as shown in Table 2.1.

This classification makes it easier to add new status codes. When an old terminal does not understand a new CXX code, it should treat it as a C00 code. Therefore even old terminals will be able to react 'intelligently' when facing unknown status codes. These terminals can also give some additional information to the user if a reason phrase is present.

Table 2.1 : The six categories of status codes

1xx	Informational		Request received, continuing to process the request
		100	Trying
		180	Ringing
		181	Call is being forwarded
		182	Queued
2xx	Success		The action was successfully received, understood, and accepted
		200	OK
3xx	Redirection		Further action must be taken in order to complete the request
		300	Multiple choices
		301	Moved permanently
		302	Moved temporarily
		380	Alternative service
4xx	Client error		The request contains bad syntax or cannot be fulfilled at this server
		400	Bad request
		401	Unauthorized
		402	Payment required
		403	Forbidden
		404	Not found
		405	Method not allowed
		406	Not acceptable
		407	Proxy authentication required
		408	Request timeout
		409	Conflict
		410	Gone
		411	Length required
		413	Request message body too large
		414	Request-URI too large
		415	Unsupported media type
		420	Bad extension
		480	Temporarily not available
		481	Call leg/transaction does not exist
		482	Loop detected
		483	Too many hops
		484	Address incomplete
		485	Ambiguous
5xx	Server error		The request contains bad syntax or cannot be fulfilled at this server
		500	Internal server error
		501	Not implemented
		502	Bad gateway
		503	Service unavailable
		504	Gateway timeout
		505	SIP version not supported
6xx	Global failure		The request is invalid at any server
		600	Busy everywhere
		603	Decline
		604	Does not exist anywhere
		606	Not acceptable

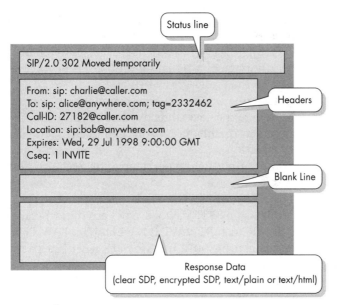

Fig. 2.9 : The SIP response format

Session description syntax, SDP

SIP uses the session description protocol (SDP) specified in RFC 2237. SDP is also a product of the MMUSIC working group, and is heavily used today in the context of the MBONE, the multicast enabled overlay network of the Internet.

In order to be able to receive an MBONE session, a receiver needs to know:

■ which multicast address is going to be used by the session
■ what will be the UDP destination port
■ the audio and/or video coders that will be used (GSM, H.261, etc.)
■ some information on the session (name, short description)
■ contact information
■ activity schedule.

The primary purpose of SDP is to define a standard syntax for this type of information.

The SDP session description can be conveyed using a variety of transport methods, depending on the context:

■ the session announcement protocol (SAP) on the MBONE
■ the real-time streaming protocol (RTSP) for streaming applications
■ SIP to set up point-to-point and multipoint communications.

SDP is a human readable protocol, consisting of several <type>=<value> lines terminated by CRLF. The field names and attributes use US-ASCII characters, but free text fields can be localized since SDP uses the complete ISO 10646 character set. This philosophy, as opposed to a binary encoding like ASN-1 PER, facilitates programming and debugging at the expense of a greater bandwidth usage. However, the bandwidth usage of a signaling protocol is negligible compared to the actual media flows, so the trade-off is very good.

The session description is structured in one section which applies to the whole session (starting with v= ...), and several media description sections (each starting with (m= ...). Parameters in the media sections can override the default parameters of the session level section.

Table 2.2 describes the various field types defined by RFC 2237 for each section.

Dynamic and static payload types

Under a particular profile, some RTP payload types are static: i.e. their meaning is fully defined in the profile (e.g. RTP/AVP 0 is 64 kbit/s μ-LAW PCM). Other RTP payload types have a meaning only in association with a particular session described in SDP. These are dynamic payload types. The SDP RFC gives the example of the 16-bit linear encoded stereo audio sampled at 16 kHz. There is no payload type defined that would exactly correspond to this. Instead we will be using an arbitrary unused number for the payload type, say 98 (m=video 49232 RTP/AVP 98), and will describe the format of the transported data in SDP:

a=rtpmap:98 L16/16000/2

The format is a=rtpmap:<payload type> <encoding name>/<clock rate>[/<encoding parameters>], which in our case translates to 16 linear, 16 000 Hz sampling, two channels.

By extension, the term 'dynamic payload type' applies to any RTP stream for which the media encoding characteristics are conveyed out of band (for instance through an H.245 OpenLogicalChannel message).

Advanced services with SIP

Without any extensions SIP allows many call-handling features – most of the common telephony services can be implemented with SIP registrars, proxies and redirect servers.

SIP entities

Registrar

A registrar is a server that accepts Register requests. The same server may also implement other SIP functions (e.g. serve as a proxy). Registrars are needed to keep track of the current location of a user. The IP address of a user may change under a number of situations – connection via an ISP providing dynamic addresses, connection on a LAN that provides addresses via DHCP, or a roaming user. In order to be able to reach this user from his SIP address, an entity in the SIP network needs to maintain the mapping between SIP addresses and IP addresses. This is the purpose of the registrar.

In order to facilitate user mobility and avoid manual configuration as much as possible, SIP defines a well known 'all SIP servers' address (sip.mcast.net: 224.0.1.75). A client can register his current IP address with a multicast register message (Fig. 2.10). For some reason SIP restricts the TTL (time to live) of this message to one, limiting the discovery method to the local subnet.

This feature is roughly equivalent to the gatekeeper discovery method described in H.323. However, in H.323, the gatekeepers that are willing to handle the request can reply, allowing the client to select the appropriate gatekeeper and contact it directly later on. At present, SIP servers cannot reply to a multicast Register message, therefore the client does not have a chance to learn the address of the appropriate SIP server, or even to know if there is a SIP server that accepted the registration.

The registrar can also be contacted by unicast if the address of the registrar is known. In this case the procedure is the same as for any other SIP request.

The registered state is not permanent. If not refreshed, it will 'time out' after one hour by default (this default value can change as specified in the 'expires' header field). In order to maintain the registration, a terminal needs to refresh it periodically. If the terminal (or the user) moves and wants to modify the parameters of the registration, he can cancel an existing registration by sending a contact value of '*' and send a new registration (Fig. 2.11).

Proxy

A proxy server acts as a server on one side (receiving requests) and as a client on the other side (possibly sending requests) (Fig. 2.12). A proxy can forward a request without any change to its final destination, or change some parameters before passing on the request. It can even decide to send a locally generated reply.

The Via and Record Route headers

A request from A to B can be routed through several proxies. It is desirable to force the response(s) to such a request to follow the same route back. For instance, a proxy might be billing the call, or controlling a firewall, and needs to have access to all the information regarding the call.

When a TCP connection is used for a SIP transaction, this is not generally an issue – the reply to a request automatically gets back to the other end of the TCP 'pipe' because TCP maintains a context throughout the connection. On the other hand, when UDP is used some information must be present in the request datagram in order to allow the receiver to know where to send the reply.

Table 2.2 : Field types described by RFC 2237

Session level field type	Sub-section level field type	Usage	Format and example	
v=		protocol version	v=0	M
o=		owner/creator and session identifier	o=<username> <session id> <version> <network type> <address type> <address> o=mhandley 2890844526 2890842807 IN IP4 126.16.64.4	M
s=		session name	s=<session name> s=SDP Seminar	M
i=		session information	i=<free text session description> i=A Seminar on the session description protocol	O
u=		URI of description	u=<Universal Resource Identifier> u=http://www.cs.ucl.ac.uk/staff/M.Handley/ sdp.03.ps	O
e=		email address	e=<email address> (Optional free Text) or e=<Optional free Text> "<"email address">" e=mjh@isi.edu (Mark Handley) e= Mark Handley <mjh@isi.edu>	O
p=		phone number	p=<phone number> (Optional free Text) or p=<Optional free Text> "<"phone number">" p=+44-171-380-7777	O
c=		connection information – not required if included in all media	c=<network type> <address type> <connection address> TTL must be included for multicast sessions. c=IN IP4 224.2.17.12/127 c=IN IP4 224.2.1.1/127	O
b=		bandwidth information	b=<modifier (CT Conference Total l AS Application-Specific Maximum>:<bandwidth-value in kilobits/s> b=CT:120	O
One or more time description sections	t=	time the session is active	t=<start time> <stop time>, using decimal NTP in seconds t=2873397496 2873404696	M
	r=	zero or more repeat times	r=<repeat interval> <active duration> <list of offsets from start-time>, by default in seconds r=604800 3600 0 90000 means that the repeat interval is 1 week (604800 seconds), active for one hour (3600 seconds) after each offset from the start time T. Offsets are here 0 seconds and 90000 seconds (25 hours). I.E, if *** represents active periods and — idle periods:	O

Table 2.2 : *continued*

Session level field type	Sub-section level field type	Usage	Format and example	
			T***T+1h–T+25h***T+26h— T+1week****T+1week+1h—T+1Week+25h*** ... The repetition is valid until the stop time. Unit modifiers can be used for compactness, and the previous record can also be written as follows: r=7d 1h 0 25h	
z=		time zone adjustments		O
k=		encryption key	k=<method>:<encryption key> or k=<method>	O
a=		zero or more session attribute lines	a=<attribute> or a=<attribute>:<value> a=recvonly	O
Zero or more media descriptions	m=	media name and transport address	m=<media> <port> <transport> <format list> m=audio 49170 RTP/AVP 0 3 means that the media is audio, can be received on port 49170 (RTP only uses even ports, the next odd port ring being used by RTCP). The transport is protocol RTP/AVT (IETF's realtime transport protocol using the audio/video profile carried over UDP), and the format is media payload types 0 or 1 of the AVT profile (0 is μ-law PCM coded single channel audio sampled at 8KHz, 3 is GSM) Other RTP profiles would be coded after the slash, e.g. a hypothetical profile XXX would appear as RTP/XXX.	M
	i=	media title		O
	c=	connection information – optional if included at session level		
	b=	bandwidth information		O
	k=	encryption key		O
	a=	zero or more media attribute lines		O

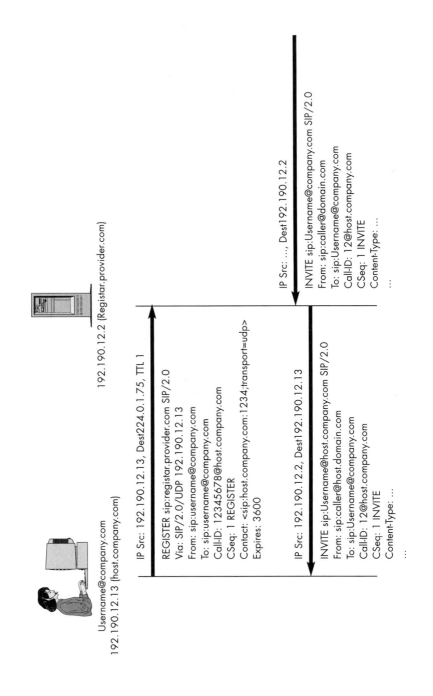

Fig. 2.10 : Multicast registration

Username@company.com

192.190.12.14 (host2.company.com)

192.190.12.2 (Registar.provider.com)

IP Src: 192.190.12.14, Dest 224.0.1.75, TTL 1

REGISTER sip:registar.provider.com SIP/2.0
Via: SIP/2.0/UDP 192.190.12.14
From: sip:username@company.com
To: sip:username@company.com
Call-ID: 87654321@host2.company.com
CSeq: 1 REGISTER
Contact: *
Expires: 0

IP Src: 192.190.12.14, Dest224.0.1.75, TTL 1

REGISTER sip:registar.provider.com SIP/2.0
Via: SIP/2.0/UDP 192.190.12.14
From: sip:username@company.com
To: sip:username@company.com
Call-ID: 43454345@host2.company.com
CSeq: 1 REGISTER
Contact: <sip:host2@company.com:4321>

IP Src: 192.190.12.2, Dest192.190.12.14 port 4321

INVITE sip:Username@host.company.com SIP/2.0
From: sip:caller@domain.com
To: sip:Username@host2.company.com
Call-ID: 34@host2.company.com
CSeq: 1 INVITE
Content-Type: ...

IP Src: ..., Dest192.190.12.2

INVITE sip:Username@company.com SIP/2.0
From: sip:caller@domain.com
To: sip:Username@company.com
Call-ID: 34@host.company.com
CSeq: 1 INVITE
Content-Type: ...
...

Fig. 2.11 : Registration charge

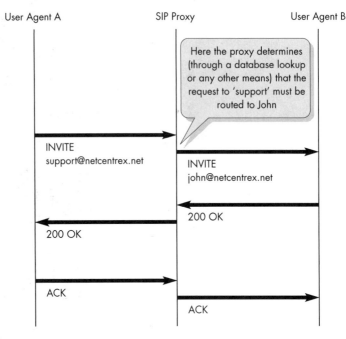

Fig. 2.12 : A proxy server

Since SIP is protocol independent, all SIP requests and replies contain Via headers for this purpose. This helps to avoid routing loops (each proxy checks whether it is already in the Via list). Each time a SIP proxy forwards a request, it appends its name to the list of forwarding proxies recorded in the Via headers. When a proxy forwards a reply, it reverses the process and removes its name from the list. Additional details on the use of Via messages can be found in the messages section further on.

If not only the requests and replies but also all requests must be routed along the same path, the Via header is not sufficient and proxies must use the Record Route header. This is because SIP clients can add a Contact header field that allows servers to send them requests (e.g. BYE requests) directly, and therefore proxies are not guaranteed to be on the path of all requests. When proxies update the Record Route header, they insert their SIP URL, with a maddr parameter, in the first position of the list.

When SIP proxies are used to route the signaling messages, the call model is similar to the H.323 gatekeeper routed call model, except that the SIP messages contain enough information to allow stateless proxies to be built (however, not all functionalities can be implemented on a stateless proxy – accounting/billing proxies, for example, would need to keep track of all messages and communication states to check the coherence of the signaling).

Forking proxy

Forking proxies can duplicate a request and send copies of it to several hosts, enabling them to be used to try to contact several endpoints belonging to the same person. They are not transparent and filter some replies before forwarding them back to the client. The complete pseudo-code of a forking proxy is described in the SIP draft.

Forking proxies may cause some hosts to receive duplicates of the same request with the same CallID, but they must reply to each request.

Redirect server

A redirect server responds to an Invite request with a 3xx reply (or rejects the call with a client error or server error).

■ The 300 multiple choices reply can be used when the SIP URL of the request can be contacted at several alternative addresses. The choices are listed as contact fields. For example the returned contact field could be: Contact: sip:John_gsm@company.com,sip:John_home@family.org;

■ The 301 moved permanently reply indicates that the SIP URL of the request can no longer be contacted at this location. The client should try to contact the new location given by the Contact header field of the reply. This change is permanent and can be memorized by the client. The Contact header can also mention several possible destinations;

■ The 302 moved temporarily reply redirects the client to a new location, as above, but for a limited duration, as indicated by the Expires field;

■ The 380 alternative service reply is more complex, and may seem a little redundant with the previous replies. In addition to providing a new destination in the Contact field, the reply can also contain a session description in the message body that represents the sending capacities of the new destination. The caller is expected to send an Invite request to this new destination, and offer in its SDP session description the appropriate capabilities (a copy of the SDP parameters of the 380 reply, except for the receiving RTP ports).

Other replies (303, 305) were defined in early SIP drafts, but have become obsolete.

A redirect server can be used in conjunction with a registrar to redirect calls to the current location(s) of the caller. It can also act as a primitive form of call distribution system, as shown in Fig. 2.13.

A redirect server can be a useful tool to improve the scalability of call distribution or call agent servers. Inserted as a front end, it can distribute calls among a pool of secondary servers, achieving load balancing. This is permitted by the maddr parameter of the Contact field:

<sip:originaladdress@callcenter.com:9999;maddr=sophisticatedACD3.callcenter.com>

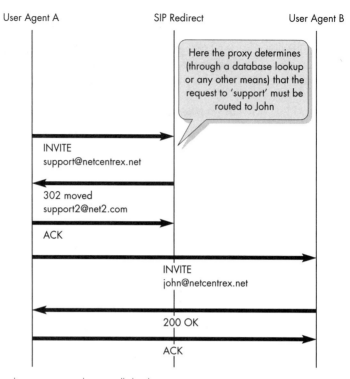

Fig. 2.13 : A redirect server used as a call distribution system

By returning this, the redirect server indicates that the caller should send an Invite with the same destination (*originaladdress@callcenter.com*), but send it to the third ACD server of the pool (ACD3.callcenter.com). The maddr parameter instructs the caller to bypass the normal procedure to find the appropriate SIP server from the domain part of the URL, and to use the domain name provided instead.

The redirect server functionality is similar to the role played by the H.323 gatekeeper when using the direct call model.

User location and mobility

Locating users: SIP addresses

SIP addresses are called uniform resource locators. URLs are really names (with the exception of SIP addresses using an IP host address, as the address used in our simple call example); they do not refer to the transport address to be called but to an abstract entity which can be a user or a multimedia server. The SIP draft specifies that the general format of SIP URLs is *user@host*. In fact, the host part can also be a domain name. Optionally a SIP URL may contain a port number. *See* Table 2.3.

Table 2.3 : Valid SIP URLs

John@netcentrex.net:1234	Vanilla SIP URL ...
Userdomain.com	No user part, default port will be 5060
support@company.fr:2345;transport=UDP	Wants to be contacted using UDP
192.190.234.3:8001	Contact the server at this IP address
support@netcentrex.net;maddr=239.255.255.1; ttl=32	Override normal host name to transport address mechanism: use multicast to 239.255.255.1 with a TTL of 32 instead
+33-231759329@cybercall.com;user=phone	Global phone number
0231759329;isub=10;postd=w11p11@ cybercall.com;user=phone	Local phone number with ISDN subaddress, wait for dial tone, then dial 11 (pause) 11 using DTMF
ACD@netcentrex.net?priority=high& customercode=1234	Using proprietary extension headers to control priority in an ACD system...
Newcomer@reg.usergroup.com; METHOD =REGISTER	Previous URLs would trigger a SIP Invite request, this one initiates a registration to the registrar of usergroup: reg.usergroup.com

In many cases the SIP address of a user will be the same as his email address. Most of the extensions (headers, maddr, etc.) are not allowed in the To, From parameters of SIP requests and responses, but can be used in the Contact parameters.

SIP defines a way to locate the physical endpoint from a name (also called SIP URL). This is done in two stages:

■ First the SIP URL allows the calling endpoint to locate a SIP server. This SIP server will be the destination of the initial Invite message. The SIP server can be the final destination of the call; if not it is supposed to know the transport address of the called endpoint;

■ If the SIP server is not the final destination of the call, it will redirect the Invite request to the called endpoint. This can be done either by instructing the called endpoint to send a new Invite request to another location using the 302 moved reply, or by transparently relaying the Invite message to the appropriate transport address. The first model is similar to the H.323 direct call model, the second to the H.323 gatekeeper routed call model.

In order to locate the SIP server, a SIP terminal will use DNS (Fig. 2.14). A SIP URL domain name must have an SRV record, an MX record, a CNAME or an A record.

First the terminal will retrieve the SRV resource records for the considered domain name. Then it will keep only the records of type 'sip.udp' or 'sip.tcp'. If

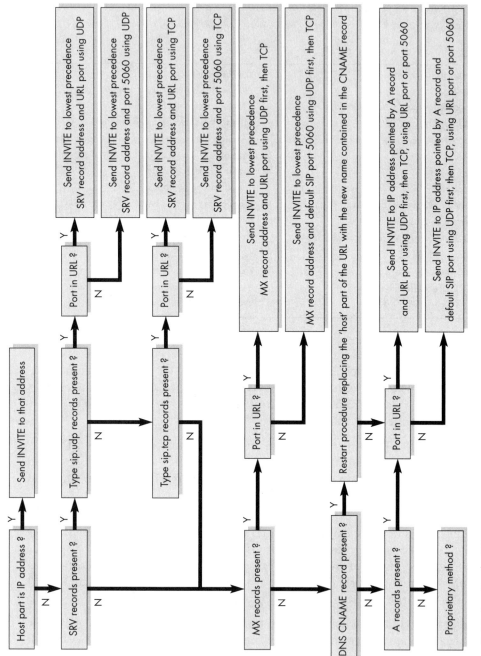

Fig. 2.14 : Locating the SIP server

there is a 'sip.udp' record, the terminal will contact the SIP server using UDP at the specified transport address. It will use the port specified in the SIP URL or default to the port specified in the 'sip.udp' record. If there is a 'sip.tcp' record, the same method will be used, but over TCP. If no SRV record is found, the terminal will try to retrieve the IP address of a SIP server by looking at the MX records first (normally used to point to a mail server), then CNAME records (pointing to an alias), and finally an A record (pointing to an IP address).

Pointing to a SIP server instead of the called endpoint directly allows the called endpoint to move (the transport address changes), while allowing some caching. If the address of the called endpoint is stored directly in DNS, there can be a lot of trouble with DNS caching. Normally all DNS records can be cached by the DNS resolver. The cached record expires after TTL seconds. The value of the TTL is stored in the DNS record. Therefore when the terminal moves, the caller could still have a wrong address in the DNS resolver cache, and the call would fail. The only solution is to set the TTL to zero and update the primary DNS record as the terminal moves – not very easy, and not cache friendly.

On the other hand, the SIP server is unlikely to move very often, and storing its address in a DNS SRV, MX or A record does not cause any trouble. The SIP server is notified of the current location of the called terminal, and can redirect the Invite request to the appropriate location.

Call agents

A call agent is a service that handles incoming and/or outgoing calls on behalf of a user. In traditional telephony this type of function is performed by the intelligent network infrastructure of the operator, or by the Private Branch Exchange (PBX) of the company. The concept of call agent was introduced in the IP telephony area in Scott Petrack's description of a call management agent (CMA).

A call agent can perform the following tasks:

■ try to find the user by redirecting the call setup messages (SIP Invite or H.323 Setup) to the proper location, or several possible locations simultaneously

■ implement call redirection rules such as call forward on busy, call forward on no answer, call forward unconditional

■ implement call filtering with origin/time-dependent rules

■ record unsuccessful call attempts for future reference

■ perform any other call management task on behalf of the user.

All these functions can be performed by the SIP proxy. Simple call redirection and filtering features (call forward unconditional, origin/time-dependent filtering) can also be implemented on a SIP redirect server. The SIP proxy server offers the most flexibility because it can choose to relay all the call signaling, and therefore monitor and control all aspects of the call. In order to be able to use those services, the user must force all incoming call attempts to go through the appropriate SIP proxy. The best way to do this is to configure the DNS SRV record to point to the proxy server.

Figure 2.15 shows a call forward on no answer. Note that if John is not logged on at desk1 and the proxy also acts as a registrar, the redirection can be immediate if John's registration has timed out.

The call agent can also be a functionality of the end-user software, but this is usually less practical than using a separate centralized proxy server because the end-user workstation can be switched off at any time and may have a dynamic IP address.

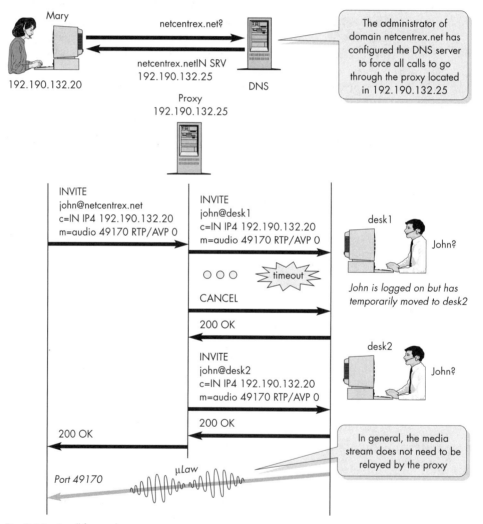

Fig. 2.15 : A call forward on no answer

By accessing the database of a registrar, a SIP proxy can solve most user mobility/address change issues if the end-user terminals are configured to use dynamic (i.e. non-permanent) registrations. For instance, each time a user connects to the Internet via an ISP, he gets a new IP address. But if his SIP software registers this new IP address, the proxy will be able to relay all calls to the new IP address.

Directed pickup and other advanced services

Some PBXs allow sophisticated services such as predictive dialing (outgoing call automation from a database for polling services), directed pickup (the ability to answer a call ringing at another extension from a local terminal) or automatic call distribution with parking (distribution of incoming calls with a queue).

The original SIP draft misses some protocol elements to support some of these services, and lacks detailed explanations on how to implement them. Another work in progress (draft-ietf-mmusic-sip-cc-00.txt SIP Call Control Services) defines a set of extensions to the basic protocol ('org.ietf.sip.call'). Not all SIP entities will support these extensions, and therefore a client that plans to use them should include a Require field for 'org.ietf.sip.call'. This draft is still in its early stages and so far contains:

- a list of advanced telephony services and guidelines on how to provide them with SIP. It is a sort of 'wish list' that will probably evolve into an implementation guide;
- extensions (and replace header fields) that allow a client to instruct a server to send an Invite or a BYE to a third party. This allows a client to set and clear fully meshed conferences, and facilitates the implementation of predictive dialing application;
- extensions to the location header to better describe the destination, e.g. the service tag allows the location to be identified as a fax, an IP phone, a PSTN or ISDN phone, or a pager.

Multiparty conferencing

SIP can be used to establish multipoint conferences (remember this protocol comes from the MMUSIC group). However, SIP does not provide any form of floor control for the moment.

Multicast conferencing

A multicast conference is one in which the media streams are sent using multicast (for more details on multicast, see the multicast chapter). The signaling related to this conference can be sent using multi-unicast or multicast (*see* Fig. 2.16).

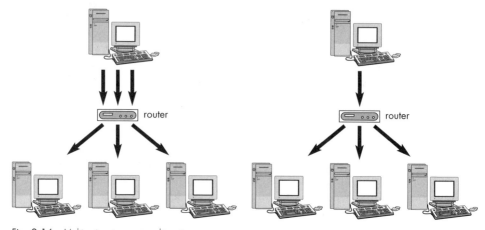

Fig. 2.16 : Multi-unicast versus multicast

In the case of multi-unicast signaling, there is no significant difference to the point-to-point case, except that the SDP session descriptions indicate multicast addresses.

When multicast signaling is used to establish multiparty conferences, the SIP requests are carried using UDP since this is the only transport protocol that can be multicast over IP. Multicast requests are expected to be used mostly to set up conference calls, and therefore the destination URL will generally be a conference name rather than an individual. However, it is also possible to use a multicast request with the URL of an individual, e.g. for multicast searches. The replies to a SIP request are then sent back to the sending UDP port on the same multicast address. In order to reduce network traffic and avoid a possible storm of synchronized replies, there are some modifications compared to the multi-unicast invitation procedure, including:

■ 2xx are not sent

■ 6xx replies are sent only if the destination URL matches the name of a user on the host (i.e. the request is a multicast search rather than an invitation to a multiparty conference)

■ replies are sent after a 0–1 second random delay.

If all Invite messages are sent from a central entity in unicast, this entity can provide a basic form of floor control by sending new Invite messages with the 'c' parameter set to null '0.0.0.0' to mute an endpoint (this usage of SDP is a convention described in the SIP draft) and re-invite it later (non-null 'c' parameter) when it is allowed to take part in the conference.

SIP natively supports layered encodings. This class of coders encode the media information using several simultaneous data streams. One stream contains basic information (just enough to render a low quality signal), and the other streams include additional information that can be used to reconstruct the signal with a higher quality, e.g. a video coder could send intra frames on one channel, and delta frames on another. Therefore a receiver can choose the best bandwidth/ quality trade-off by opting to receive one, two or more data streams. This is particularly suited for multicast conferences, allowing all receivers to tune the reception to their best settings, while preventing the sender from having to send customized data streams for each receiver. SDP describes a layered encoded stream as:

c=<base multicast address>/<ttl>/<number of addresses>

For instance: c=IN IP4 224.2.1.1/127/3. The multicast addresses used need to be contiguous (224.2.1.1, 224.2.1.2, 224.2.1.3).

Multi-unicast conferencing

The support of SIP for multi-unicast conferences is limited. A central entity can be set up to act as an MCU to either mix or switch the incoming media streams (*see* Fig. 2.17). The only way to support proper media switching today would be to send a SIP Invite with the SDP 'c' parameter set to zero (0.0.0.0) since this will signal the sender to stop transmission ('mute'), and re-activate transmission when the speaker becomes active again (this should start with an intraframe) by sending a non-null 'c' parameter.

This is still not trivial because H.26x video coders send full frames only from time to time, and deltas in between. Most of the time, the instant at which a par-

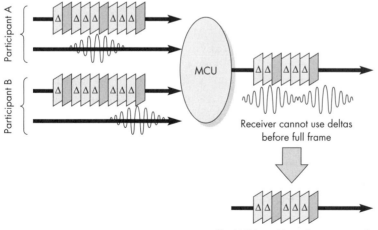

Fig. 2.17 : A too simple switching MCU

ticipant decides to speak will not coincide with the sending of a full frame. Therefore if the MCU simply copies the incoming video stream to the output stream, the receivers will have to wait for the next full frame to get an image. So the MCU would have to completely recode the stream in order to be able to send a full frame when the video switches. In practice, this would be CPU hungry and very inefficient.

In a similar case, H.323 can mute the video stream of non-active speakers, and request a full frame when it switches to an active speaker (VideoFastUpdate message). SIP provides no specific signaling for this, but an RTCP full intra request (FIR) packet could serve the purpose.

Ad hoc conferencing

SIP provides a simple and elegant way to switch from an existing point-to-point call (A-B) to a multiparty conference (A-B-C-). The person (e.g. A) who wants to invite a new participant into the conference sends an Invite message to the other party (B) and the new participant (C) with the parameters for the new session (i.e. a multicast address and eventually new coders instead of a unicast address) but keeps the old CallID. Keeping the same CallID tells B that this is not a new call, but new parameters for the existing call. This method can also be used to change parameters in an existing session.

Configuring network-based call handling

Call-handling features can be installed on a proxy/registrar simply by using Register messages. For instance a user who wishes to temporarily redirect his phone line to another extension just sends a Register request with his name (or regular extension) in the To header field, and the new extension in the Contact header field, with the appropriate Expires value. This is roughly equivalent to the service offered by H.450.3.

More sophisticated call-handling features (i.e. call agent) are outside the scope of SIP, and will probably be configured using other protocols, such as HTTP. SIP endpoints are likely to be multimedia PCs, and the web browser is a perfect interface to customize the behavior of a sophisticated proxy.

Billing SIP calls

By definition, all participants invited by a common source are in the same SIP 'call'. This call is identified by a globally unique CallID. With this definition, a

multi-party conference (known as multimedia session in SIP terms) can be composed of several SIP calls – each user that has called the multipoint controller
directly has a unique CallID.

Within a call, each leg can be identified by a combination of the To, From and
CallID fields. All legs can be grouped into a common multimedia session using
the session description.

In the PSTN, a call is usually paid for by the person who initiates it. A proxy
relaying all signaling from a user terminal can create appropriate accounting
records by logging the Invite, Cancel and BYE requests, as well as the replies. The
duration of each leg can be derived from the first accepted Invite request up to
the first BYE request.

In order to force the user to go through the proxy, a convenient way, as
described in Fig. 2.18, is to control a firewall in the network from the proxy. This
prevents the user from trying to bypass the call-accounting feature of the proxy.

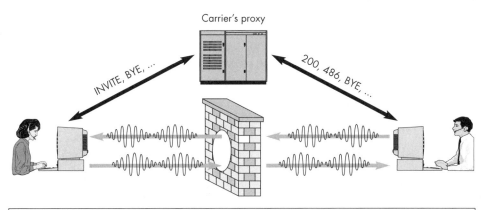

Call-ID	From	To	Operation	timestamp
4321@192.190.12.32	Mary@domain1	John@domain2	INVITE	11/11/1998 11:11:11
4321@192.190.12.32	Mary@domain1	John@domain2	200	11/11/1998 11:11:30
4321@192.190.12.32	Mary@domain1	John@domain2	BYE	11/11/1998 11:21:12
4321@192.190.12.32	Mary@domain1	Mark@domain3	INVITE	11/11/1998 11:14:13
4321@192.190.12.32	Mary@domain1	Mark@domain3	200	11/11/1998 11:14:40
4321@192.190.12.32	Mary@domain1	Mark@domain3	BYE	11/11/1998 11:21:12
4321@192.190.12.32	Mary@domain1	July@domain3	INVITE	11/11/1998 11:14:13
4321@192.190.12.32	Mary@domain1	July@domain3	486	11/11/1998 11:14:40
4444@192.190.12.32	Mary@domain1	Dilan@domain4	INVITE	11/11/1998 15:25:25
4444@192.190.12.32	Mary@domain1	Dilan@domain4	200	11/11/1998 15:25:40
4444@192.190.12.32	Mary@domain1	Dilan@domain4	BYE	11/11/1998 15:31:43

Fig. 2.18 : Proxy call accounting

SIP security

Media security

Media encryption is specified by SDP. The k parameter of SDP stores the security algorithm in use as well as the key. The following formats are defined in RFC 2327 (SDP):

■ k=clear:<encryption key>

This format refers to the encryption algorithms described in RFC 1890 ('RTP profile for audio and video conferences with minima! control', RFC 1890, January 1996). RFC 1890 first describes how to extract a key from a pass phrase in a standard way. The pass phrase is put in a canonical form (leading and trailing white spaces removed, characters put to lower case, etc.), then hashed into 16 octets by the MD5 algorithm. Keys shorter than 128 bits are formed by truncating the MD5 digest. The keys are extracted in order for algorithms that need more than one (e.g. three keys for triple DES).

The name of the algorithm in use is inserted before the key and separated from it with a single slash. Standard identifiers for the most common algorithms can be found in RFC1423: 'DES-CBC', 'DES-ECB'; the default is DES-CBC. RFC 1423 also describes how to store additional parameters needed for the particular algorithms, such as the 64-bit initialization vector of DES-CBC, e.g.:

k=clear:DES-CBC/aZ25rYg7/12eR5t6y

■ k=base64:<encoded encryption key>

The format is the same as above, but base64 is encoded to hide characters not allowed by SDP.

■ k=prompt

Prompt the user for a key. The default algorithm is DES-CBC

Message exchange security

If the media encryption key must be protected, the SDP requests and replies must be encrypted. There are many other reasons for protecting the SIP messages, such as hiding the origin or destination of calls and the related information fields (Subject, etc.). SIP messages can also be authenticated, which is useful not only to prevent call spoofing but also for accounting and billing.

SIP messages can be encrypted hop by hop, for instance using IPSEC (the security framework defined by the IP SECurity protocol working group of IETF). SIP also describes an end-to-end encryption strategy based on a shared secret key between the sender and the receiver, or on a public key mechanism. If a common secret key is used, the receiver of the message is able to decrypt a message encrypted by the sender. If a public key scheme is used, the sender encrypts the message using the public key of the receiver. This encryption can be performed by the sender of the request or by an intermediary security proxy.

Requests

The request line and unencrypted headers are sent first and must include an Encryption header field that indicates the encryption method in use, e.g. Encryption: PGP version=2.6.2,encoding=ascii. The encrypted part begins after the first empty line (CRLF of the previous line immediately followed by CRLF). Fig. 2.19, taken from the SIP draft, is an example.

If only the message body has to be encrypted, an extra empty line must be inserted in the body before encryption to prevent the receiver from mixing up the message body data with encrypted headers.

There are specific issues with the Via header because it is used by proxies to route the request back to the source. The SIP draft describes how to replace the sensitive Via information with an index that serves the same purpose without disclosing sensitive data.

Replies

The sender of the request should also indicate what key must be used to encrypt the reply. A SIP server receiving an encrypted request should not, in its reply, send in clear form any field that was previously encrypted.

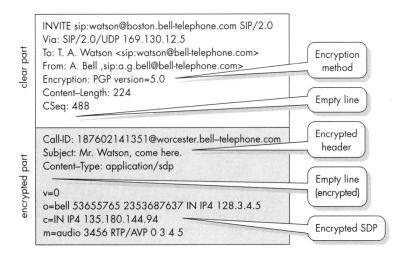

Fig. 2.19 : Encryption in a request

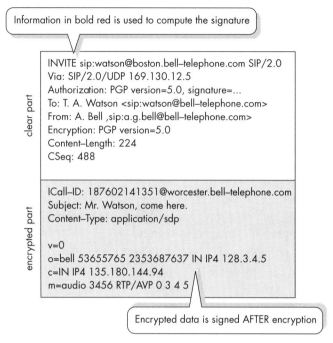

Fig. 2.20 : Authentication through the Authorization header field

Authentication

SIP requests and replies can be authenticated using a digital signature. The Authorization header field is used for this purpose (*see* Fig. 2.20). It contains the signature of:

■ the first line (request line or status line)

■ all headers following the Authorization header

■ the message body.

This semantic allows the exclusion of some variable fields (such as the Via field) from the signed data.

SIP firewalls

SIP terminals can be configured to send all their requests to a SIP proxy server, instead of trying to reach the appropriate SIP server by using the DNS records. Native support for NAT by SIP entities allows the setup of signaling for outgoing communications without any specific requirement at the firewall. But for the media streams the firewall needs to be made aware of the incoming UDP streams, in order to forward them to the proper entity. Incoming calls need to be handled by a SIP signaling proxy of the firewall.

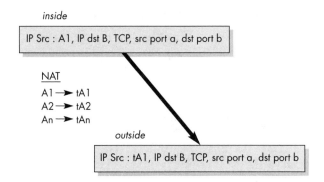

Fig. 2.21 : NAT

Note on NAT

Network Address Translation (NAT) is a technique used for security as well as to avoid readdressing issues.

SIP and H.323

What SIP does and H.323 does not

Speed

The first thing that strikes you when reading the SIP draft is its simplicity. SIP does in one transaction what H.323 version 1 did in four or five message exchanges, each of them specified in different ITU documents. In addition, SIP can use UDP, whereas H.323v1 and 2 must use TCP. The combination of these differences resulted in a much shorter setup time for SIP endpoints. This directly inspired some modifications introduced in H.323v2, namely the Fast Connect procedure and the ability to tunnel H.245 messages in Q.931 messages. Further improvements are on the way, such as the ability to use UDP signaling.

Multicast

The IETF has gained a lot of experience in multicast. There are thousands of regular users of the MBONE, and more and more multicast applications. SIP has been designed to work on a multicast enabled backbone, not only for the media streams, as H.323, but also for the signaling messages. For instance, an Invite message can be sent to a multicast group. This is useful for call centers, or when trying to find someone in a company. H.323 versions 1 and 2 need to use multi-unicast for the same purpose.

URL usage

The use of URLs as identifiers is powerful. At first sight there may seem to be no big difference between an H.323 email alias (*john@name.com*) and a SIP URL (sip: *john@name.com*). In fact, there is one: an H.323 email alias assumes the protocol used is H.323, whereas SIP specifies the protocol in the URL itself. Because of this, a SIP server can redirect a call to non-SIP servers in a flexible way. A SIP terminal, when called by another SIP terminal, may redirect the call to a web page, or to a mailto URL. This facilitates the integration of audio and video applications with other multimedia applications.

This feature is now available with the URL-ID type of AliasAddress in H.225v2, but the overall naming scheme of H.225 is starting to look a little cluttered (h323-ID, url-ID, transport-ID, email-ID, partynumber).

Call prioritization

The 'Priority' header field is a useful addition that was overlooked in H.323. Many countries have legal requirements to prioritize some phone lines.

Text encoding

The text encoding is a feature for some, and an issue for others. This is one of many endless religious wars between programmers. Text encoding has a lot of advantages – it is simple, can be debugged easily using simple network sniffers, and makes interoperability problems detectable 'visually'. Most programmers agree on these features.

The problem might be performance and size, as some argue that binary protocols are easier to code and decode. Obviously the size of text messages is much bigger than the size of binary encoded messages.

What H.323 does and SIP does not

Logical channels

H.323 makes a clear distinction between the media types that can be sent or received and the combinations that can be valid on one side (capabilities), and the media types that are active and actually sent over the network (logical channels) on the other side. SIP does not have such a distinction, as SIP endpoints advertise only the coders they can receive, and there is no procedure to open a media connection apart from actually sending the media. This simplifies the signaling and may seem an advantage at first sight.

However, in some cases, in particular when implementing resource-intensive servers, this can be a problem because each time a server advertises a capability, it needs to create a listening socket. In contrast, an H.323 client needs to open a socket only when it receives an OpenLogicalChannel message (if not in FastStart mode). This SIP behavior can result in a lot of idle sockets, and since most voice coders implement voice activity detection, and can be inactive even if the terminals are willing to send media data, the strategy to close these useless sockets is not completely trivial.

Conference control

H.323, alone or in combination with H.332, has powerful conference-control features. SIP has not been designed for conference control, and consequently many of the features required to do a controlled conference do not exist (yet).

Binary encoding

H.323 messages are encoded according to Q.931 for the subset of H.225 messages derived from Q.931. All other messages, as well as H.323 extensions to Q.931 messages, are encoded using abstract syntax notation 1 (ASN.1) packet encoding rules (PER). This is probably what has generated so much concern about H.323 'complexity'. The fact is that mixing two encoding methods with totally different rules is not the prettiest thing. It also implies a lot of programming efforts for companies who do not already have a Q.931 implementation and an ASN.1 compiler.

Finally, debugging the interoperability issues between H.323 terminals requires network monitors with both Q.931 and ASN.1 PER decoding capabilities. There are some around (one was distributed by Microsoft to ITU SG16 members as an extension to Microsoft's Network Monitor), but it is not yet a standard feature of most tools.

So there is indeed a steep learning curve, but once a company has an ASN.1 compiler and a Q.931 implementation, there are some advantages in using a binary encoding:

■ the PDU size is optimized
■ (maybe) the performance is better.

The size of the signaling PDUs is not, in general, a problem in modern networks. However, if H.323 was to be used on wireless networks (ETSI is considering H.323 for the third generation mobile system, UMTS), this would be an advantage.

Performance is arguable in the case of H.323. It is true that most binary protocols are extremely fast because programmers simply cast C structures to buffers
and vice versa. Both PER and Q.931 are much more complex than this, and the
performance depends on the implementation.

Gatekeeper discovery

In the present state of the SIP RFC, multicast GK discovery seems to be more solid
in H.323, allowing a terminal to know which gatekeeper is responding. But this is
a minor detail that could easily be fixed in later versions of the protocol.

H.323 to SIP gateways

Such gateways are feasible. The following information flow shown in Table 2.4
can be used.

If new logical channels are opened during the conversation by the H.323 endpoint, the proxy would send a new Invite message to the SIP endpoint, as shown
in Table 2.5.

Conclusion on the future of SIP and its relation to H.323

All IETF drafts start: It is inappropriate to use Internet-Drafts as reference material
or to cite them other than as 'work in progress'.

Mea maxima culpa – using a draft as reference material is exactly what I have
done throughout this chapter. I thought this would be useful to give an insight
into what could be a very serious challenger to H.323. Doing so before the protocol is mature and fully understood has probably led me into errors and
misunderstandings. The chapter was reviewed when SIP became an RFC, but the
reader is still encouraged to read the original RFC before ruling for or against SIP.

Saying that SIP is a work in progress of the IETF also explains its position compared to H.323. The ITU is an official body, and implementers are confident that
once a recommendation is published, it will not change. Therefore it was possible
to organize H.323v1 interoperability testing (the IMTC organizes such tests frequently) very early. Presently the industry is working on H.323v2 because
everybody is confident that now it has been approved it will remain stable. Some
operators have already invested a lot in IP telephony hardware, and in such an
immature market, the relative stability provided by H.323 came as a relief.

Now it seems that the market is focusing more on added-value services, and
their simplicity may be a real advantage. Someone probably has a SIP to H.323
gateway running, where SIP would be used in a private domain to allow more

Table 2.4 : Information flow between H.323 and SIP gateways

No	H323 side of proxy	SIP side of proxy	Comment
1	-> Setup with FastStart		Contains proposals for backwards logical channels
2	<- Call proceeding		The proxy acknowledges the receipt of the setup messages
3		Invite ->	Contains proposals for backwards logical channels in SDP format
4		180 Ringing <-	
5	<- Alerting		
6		200 OK <-	User picked up
7	<- Connect		
8		Ack ->	
N		Bye <-	On hook
N+1	<- Release		
N+2		200 OK ->	
N+3	-> Release complete		

flexible services, while H.323 would guarantee the interoperability with other solutions. But how simple is simple? Stimulus protocols, such as MGCP, which already has significant industry support, may be positioned as possible competitors to SIP, with more complex call controllers, but simpler terminals. The protocol war is far from over.

There is still no real industry support for SIP. However a SIP 'bake-off' meeting was held at Columbia University in April 1999 (*www.cs.columbia. edu/~hgs/sip/bakeoff.html*) and this may become the beginning of regular interoperability events, similar to those of IMTC for H.323.

Table 2.5 : Opening new media sessions

-> OpenLogicalChannel		
	Invite ->	Same call ID as the previous Invite (but Cseq is incremented).
		The SDP payload describes the new modified media channels list
	200 OK <-	Confirms the media channels list by including an SDP body.
<- OpenLogicalChannelAck		

Media gateway to media controller protocols (MGCP)

Introduction

It is interesting to note that once the technical credibility of carrying real-time data such as voice over IP was acknowledged by the carriers and service providers, the involvement of well known telecommunications equipment manufacturers in the definition of IP telephony protocols changed dramatically.

In the early days of IP telephony, 1995–1997, the VoIP market was created by the pioneers using the drivers of cheap, long-distance and international communications and the excitement of new technology. This trend was supported by endpoint-oriented – mostly PC vendors such as Intel and Microsoft. It is not surprising that the first incompatibility issues between IP telephony clients have been addressed by the ITU-T recommendation H.323 based on ISDN video-conferencing protocols, ITU-T recommendation H.320.

We have seen that the core of the signaling protocol uses a slightly modified version of digital subscriber signaling number 1 (DSS1) protocol, also known as ITU-T recommendation Q.931[1], a user to network interface (UNI) protocol. This protocol assumes that the endpoint has the capability of generating the rich set of signaling messages. The terminal must have the intelligence to assemble and disassemble ASN.1 PER structures and interpret the information and also maintain the state of the call. Those aware of the ISDN philosophy and protocols would immediately recognize the pattern that distributes the call-control functions between local exchanges (class 5 switches) and intelligent ISDN terminals.

The same basic assumption was used in drafting the H.323 recommendation: personal computers running the VoIP client software have all the intelligence and processing power necessary to use H.225 and H.245 for signaling and RTP for transferring real-time traffic. Using powerful PC endpoints was fully in line with the assumption that the market will be developed by corporate users eager to use video conferencing on their existing IP or IPX network.

But the market interest for real-time communications over IP came from another direction: new and incumbent carriers space.[2] Although the business model of various roles in carrier space may differ, they share at least one common denominator: they will make their revenue on services and the basic voice service is the necessary condition to be in this market. The early adopters of this market realized that their customers demand more and more bandwidth to carry their data traffic needs and IP is the right protocol for carrying both voice and data.

Now we can come back to the protocols. In mid-1998, when the important request for information (RFI) and request for proposals (RFP) for building large VoIP networks were sent to the vendors, those who did not have any product or any product plan based on H.323 were caught by surprise. They could not let such opportunities escape them knowing that time to market is the killer weapon in the high-tech market. On the other hand, some R&D departments realized that H.323v1 was not satisfactory in fulfilling some important requirements from carriers.

Lack of mature products, lack of some features in H.323v1, lack of marketing efforts in favor of H.323v2 and time to market issues (trying to stall the market until they were ready) pushed the incumbent vendors to react against H.323 and propose alternative protocols to address the needs of large-scale phone-to-phone deployments.

Which protocol?

The first proposal came from Bellcore (now Telcordia) and Cisco to address the needs of cable operators that want to become Competitive Local Exchange Carriers (CLEC) using IP on top of their HFC infrastructure. The simple gateway control protocol (SGCP) was introduced in early May 1998 by Cisco during a PacketCable™ meeting (later in other standards bodies, IETF, ITU-T SG 16 and ETSI TIPHON) as a cost-effective alternative and better suited protocol to implement and deploy than current H.323 implementations in the context of the cable operators' market.

The second proposal, the Internet protocol device control (IPDC) set of protocols, was presented to ITU-T SG 16, ETSI TIPHON and IETF a month later. IPDC addresses more or less the same requirements as SGCP but with a different transport approach. While SGCP depends solely on UDP, some reliability features and the application layer to fulfill transport requirements, IPDC proposes the use of Diameter (an extension and replacement for Radius) to carry PDUs between respective entities.

It was not long before the forces behind these two protocols realized that by unifying their efforts they could get bigger consensus and foster the adoption of their position.

Bellcore and Level3 played a key role in merging these two proposals into one: media gateway control protocol (MGCP). MGCP has been proposed to various standards groups, IETF (media gateway controller (MEGACO) working group), ETSI TIPHON and ITU-T SG 16. In addition, companies supporting this protocol created an industry forum, the multiservice switching forum (*www.msforum.org*), to develop complementary protocols and services necessary for providing different types of services on ATM (and, of course, IP) based networks.

The IP telephony industry, although very young, already has a legacy in the H.323-based VoIP products and solutions. Since the inception of H.323 there has been a lot of effort invested in the creation and improvement of the recommendation, in its marketing, its implementation and in interoperability testing. None of the companies behind these products is ready to throw away these efforts and lose the potential sales opportunities. The H.323 contenders are well aware of the limitations of the protocols composing this recommendation and they have chosen to adopt a different approach to address the new needs (*see* the requirements section) and any H.323 flaws – they will contribute to the improvement of H.323 rather than propose an alternative.

The first set of improvements came with release 2 of the recommendation (*see* the chapter on H.323) and at the time of writing this book more improvements were being made in release 3 of H.323 (*see* the chapter on H.323) to match the growing interest and the new requirements of service providers and corporate users and, of course, to fix some more bugs.

The third proposal comes from the H.323 supporters. It is based on the same set of requirements as MGCP (*see* the requirements section) and uses an object-oriented protocol to carry the information flow between the media gateway and media gateway controllers. As expected, this protocol fits in better with the H.323 architecture.

It is important to note that all the media gateway to media gateway controller protocols emphasize the interworking of network elements introduced in these new proposals with H.323 network elements. However, we would like to draw readers' attention to the fact that such considerations are over simplified – as we will see later, when considered together, MGCP and H.323 architecture present redundant network elements, especially the gatekeeper, the heart of an H.323-based network. It is obvious that the authors of these protocols had to comply with one of the unwritten rules governing technical wars: political correctness.

Having set the background we propose to review the general requirements being addressed with these device protocols, how they fit in a global voice over IP network architecture, what impact they have on the existing network models, and finally call flows for basic services.

All these questions are debated heavily in various standards bodies and industry consortiums, and none of the protocols is expected to be adopted as proposed by their authors. The selection process in standards groups follows more or less the natural selection process – it can only be hoped that the best technical solution among the various proposals will be adopted to serve the business needs of the IP telephony industry.

What about the requirements?

In 1998 there were a lot of contributions in standards groups concerning the requirements for IP telephony, focusing either on architecture issues and/or protocols questions. It is interesting to note that the number of contributions concerning requirements is much higher than it was in the early days of IP telephony standardization in ITU-T and ETSI. This is a good sign.

We are not going to focus on generic requirements for IP telephony or real-time data transport over IP networks but on those relating to architecture and protocol issues that were discussed on the different mailing lists related to IP tele-phony, especially the TIPHON and MEGACO standard groups.

The following documents specify most of the requirements expressed in various standards bodies with regard to media gateway to media gateway controller protocol. As IETF provides an easy access to its document through its web server, *www.ietf.org,* we have chosen to reference these documents through the IETF. These documents can also be found in TIPHON and ITU servers, with different names and format:

■ draft-taylor-ipdc-reqts-00.txt: Requirements for A Telephony Gateway Device Control Protocol

■ draft-taylor-megaco-reqs-00.txt:

■ draft-sijben-megaco-mdcp-00.txt:

The chairman of the MEGACO working group of IETF provided a list of require-ments divided into nine categories: accounting, applications, architecture, design efficiency, flexibility, scalability, performance, reliability and security. Obviously the list is not exhaustive and we expect some of these categories to be removed, or others added, as the standardization work proceeds.

Table 3.1 is based on the compilation of requirements provided on the MEGACO mailing list as the first summary. The term 'device control protocol' represents the media gateway controller to media gateway protocol.

A new architecture for IP telephony?

The requirements listed in Table 3.1 lead us to propose a reference network archi-tecture that will support the services to be provided by all the functional elements we will need to identify. Unfortunately, at the time of writing, there was no agreed reference architecture in standards bodies. We believe that it will be diffi-cult to reach a global consensus on the physical plane but there is a good chance of achieving a stable and lasting functional architecture for these requirements.

Whenever a network architecture is designed there are always some basic assumptions made. We will try to clarify the inevitable hidden words and suggest possible functional architectures that are likely to shape tomorrow's networks.

The first assumption is that these architectures and protocols are being designed to ease the interworking between an IP network carrying real-time data and a PSTN network. The corollary of this is that one day – hopefully within 5–10 years for incumbents and today for newcomers – the IP network will carry all types of data over high-speed backbone and access networks.

It is also assumed that in the carrier environment the direct routed call model of H.323 does not fit very well with the existing habits of service providers which are used to having the means to control the call from its beginning to its end.

Table 3.1 : Requirements compiled by MEGACO for MG to MGC protocol

Requirements	Category
Globally unique session ID	Accounting
Need to allow connections to modems (network access server function) This feature is very interesting: it allows an Internet access server to offer voice capabilities, especially if this feature can be offered through a single port (universal port)	Application
Neutrality of device control protocol with respect to signaling protocols used. The referred signaling protocol is the telephony signaling protocol. This can be SS7, TUP or any other protocol.	Application
An efficient way to set up and parameterize RTP associations, regardless of the way they are set up between MGCs, or between an MGC and an autonomous station	Application
Need to listen for tone signaling even on endpoints controlled by other types of signaling (e.g. Q.931), with consequent co-ordination issues	Application
Need for IVR-controlling extensions to scripting	Application
Need for support of detection and reporting of long tone (especially #) duration	Application
This is useful for calling card features. Need to consider how MGC and IVR interact in both directions	Application
MG able to provide event notification	Application
Need to support connections to complex network resources such as IVRs, wiretaps	Application
Need to support multimedia. This is definitely a new and important feature. The addition of this requirement clearly makes the MGCP-like protocols an alternative to H.323 or SIP	Application
Need to support use of network resources located in the MG or elsewhere	Application
Protocol should be able to refer to network resources such as announcements in the same way regardless of their physical location	Application

Table 3.1 : Continued

Requirements	Category
High-level protocol structure should be independent of bearer type. Here we can have, for example, an ATM layer instead of the IP layer	Application
Must provide for situation where requested connection or modified connection cannot be supported	Application
Specialized requirements for IVR application	Application
Permit synchronization of tone signaling and other media content at downstream points in the media path	Application
Requirement for reliable transport of event notifications to the MGC	Application
Requirement for ordered delivery of messages relating to a given session at the final point of consumption	Application
Potential need for pre-emption of outstanding requests	Application
Need to support provision of tones (particularly ringback) and announcements from different points in the call path	Application
Reliable detection of all valid supervision events (such as on/off hook transitions)	Application
Need to support different flavors and both ends of continuity tests	Application
Ability to request continuity test and report (transponder end)	Application
Ability to run continuity test over packet bearer connection	Application
Wireless IP support	Application
Potential need to leave DTMF in wave form for PSTN interaction	Application
Need to support DTMF as RTP payload type, as notifications to MGC, or both at once. This particular point was missing in original SGCP, IPDC and MGCP documents. Surprisingly, the protocol to carry real-time information, RTP, was not taken into account in these documents. A complete new protocol was used instead to carry DTMF tones	Application

Table 3.1 : *Continued*

Requirements	Category
Architectural requirement that integrated gateways have no need to implement MEGACO protocol. This leaves the option of having H.323 or SIP-based gateways and gatekeepers since if MGCP is not used the gateways will have to handle all the lower layer signaling issues anyhow	Architecture
The specification of the media gateway should be the minimum required to design the protocol, and beyond that should not constrain implementations	Architecture
Need for a clean syntactical separation between content which is of strictly local interest and content which the MGC must share with other network entities	Design efficiency
Reuse existing protocols where possible. It seems obvious that this decision was difficult to reach because it is sometimes easier to design a protocol from scratch. The use of RTP was long debated for DTMF signals	Design efficiency
Limit protocol scope to promote reusability	Design efficiency
Protocol syntax for requesting and receiving notification of signaling events should be independent of the application and the specific signaling system in use	Design efficiency
Need to distinguish static endpoint configuration from other functions and use appropriate protocol for purpose	Design efficiency
Need to specify structure of protocol formally at an early date	Design efficiency
Need to pass easily through firewalls	Design efficiency
Can upgrade different network entities independently	Flexibility
MG should be able to indicate a temporary resource unavailability	Flexibility
Need means for MGC to determine which optional capabilities a given MG supports	Flexibility
Need to allow for signaled flow characteristics on circuit as well as on packet bearer connections	Flexibility

Table 3.1 : Continued

Requirements	Category
Need to allow internal connections between any combination of bearer types	Flexibility
Potential need to specify which of multiple incoming streams on a bearer connection is to be monitored for tone signals	Flexibility
Should allow for possibility that protocol PDUs exceed UDP MTU size	Flexibility
Flexibility in distribution of call-processing control	Flexibility
Cannot assume proximity of MGC to MG	Flexibility
Need to allow multiple MGCs to have active access to the same MG	Flexibility
Need to consider various domain models for MGC-MGC, MG-MGC and MG-MG operation. But it is outside the scope of the MEGACO working group to specify protocols between these entities	Flexibility
Need for extensibility	Flexibility
Need to support distributed MGs	Flexibility
Ability for MGC to receive all notifications of DTMF detection on a single port, accompanied by associated call context information	Flexibility
Control of QOS for signaling path. There was a clear lack of QOS signaling in the early versions of SGCP	Performance
Take note of current PSTN performance standards when setting design performance targets	Performance
Need to consider critical resource consumption in design of protocol	Performance
Need to consider protocol PDU sizes vs transport MTU sizes in designing protocol	Performance
Need to support peak calling rates in order of 150 calls/s at MGC	Performance

Table 3.1 : *Continued*

Requirements	Category
Need to consider cost of encryption when designing wireline protocol	Performance
Reduce the number of unnecessary iterations between MGC and MG	Performance
Need to respect time constraints on processing of individual control messages	Performance
Allow for default/provisioned settings so that commands need only contain non-default parameters	Performance
Endpoint programmability	Performance
Need to minimize messaging required to perform continuity tests	Performance
Maximum 200 ms cross-MGC initial address message (SS7 message) propagation delay	Performance
Maximum 200 ms from end of dialing to IAM (initial address messsage) emission	Performance
Ability for MGC to delegate filtering to MG	Performance
MGC able to invoke scripts on MG	Performance, scalability
Avoid messaging avalanches on startup	Performance, startup
Need to minimize messaging required upon boot/reboot	Performance, startup
Need audits to return actual states in MG rather than requested states	Reliability
Should be possible to detect mismatches of perceived resource state between MG and MGC	Reliability
MGC and MG provide each other with booting and reboot indications	Reliability
MGC and MG able to detect loss of connectivity	Reliability
MG must offer its configuration to the MGC upon startup or association recovery	Reliability

Table 3.1 : *Continued*

Requirements	Category
Use names rather than physical addresses to locate network entities	Reliability
Allow for different control relationship profiles, then define a very few covering majority of industry needs	Reliability
Reporting of unexpected endpoint state (e.g. persistent off-hook after reboot)	Reliability
Explicit activation of endpoint programs by MGC on boot/reboot	Reliability
Appropriate handling of endpoint program activity status on failover	Reliability
MG detection and quarantine of endpoints generating 'showers' of supervision events	Reliability
Need to specify MG behavior for interactions between maintenance commands and resource (e.g. endpoint) states	Reliability
Need to correlate commands and responses	Reliability
Need to detect duplicate transmissions	Reliability
MGC able to activate/deactivate specific endpoint programs at any time	Reliability, application
Assure reliability, availability, security of services being provided	Reliability, security
Appropriate handling of endpoint supervision transients following boot/reboot	Reliability, startup
Need to inform MGCs on a per-endpoint basis that boot/reboot has occurred, if control associations are between MGCs and endpoints rather than between MGCs and MGs	Reliability, startup
Need to allow MGC control over order of reactivation of endpoints following boot/reboot	Reliability, startup
Large potential fanout from MGC to associated SGs and MGs	Scalability

Table 3.1 : *Continued*

Requirements	Category
MG/MGC can authenticate source of messages received	Security
Privacy of control messages maintained	Security
Protocol must operate across untrusted domains in secure fashion	Security
Need to ensure that commands come from sources authorized to use the resources affected	Security
Need for authentication and authorization of commands	Security
Non-repudiation in context of customer-located MG talking to operator MGC	Security
Minimize system cost by avoiding duplication of effort (DTMF detection)	System

Because SS7 is so essential for service providers as a network to network signaling protocol, the proposed architecture has to interface seamlessly with the existing SS7 network. This will allow carriers to control from either network circuit switched connections and supplementary services as specified in the intelligent network framework. This integration implies that the IP network with these network elements will be seen by the PSTN network as just another switch.

The original idea of interfacing PSTN and IP networks came in mid-1998 from carriers in the US facing congestion problems in their egress switch that terminates Internet telephony service numbers. The incredible success of the Internet and the price pattern of local calls in the US triggered a high usage by end users. Unfortunately, none of the incumbent network was designed and built to face such a call pattern. To overcome these problems most of the US carriers requested a solution from network access servers' vendors (*see* Fig. 3.1).

Another important point to mention is the actual physical separation of the SS7 signaling gateway from the call agent and the media gateway. One of the driving factors of such separation is the scarce number of SS7 point codes; other drivers are the need to improve the scalability and reliability, and allowing a pair of SS7 signaling gateways to be connected to a pair of signal transfer points.

From this architecture to an architecture integrating VoIP was just a small step, as shown in Fig. 3.2, and these views can be found in draft-greene-ss7-arch-frame-00.txt.

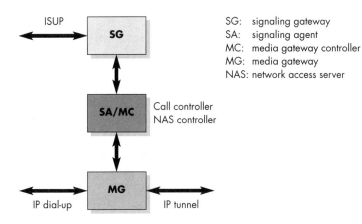

Fig. 3.1 : SS7 dialup access architecture

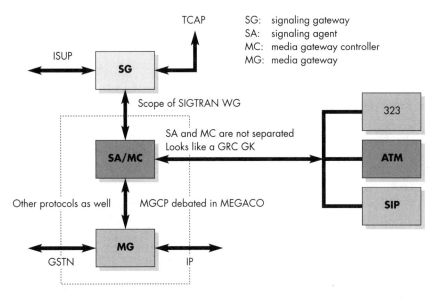

Fig. 3.2 : The media gateway to media gateway controller architecture with SS7 connectivity

It is important to note that SG and SA/MC can be combined, as well as all three boxes, of course. But the architecture is being designed to identify open interfaces and specify the protocols between these interfaces.

What is MGCP?

The media gateway controller protocol (MGCP) is specified in the informational RFC 2705.

MGCP is designed to interface a media gateway controller and media gateway. The protocol is text based[3] and supports a centralized call model. The media gateway controller is called call agent in MGCP terminology and the media gateways can be either different types of VoIP gateways (residential, trunking, corporate, etc.), network access servers or even voice over ATM gateways. The protocol is being built to serve gateways from 1 (a multimedia terminal adapter to connect an analogue phone to IP) to 100 000+ ports (class 4 or 5 switches). In the MGCP connection model the 'atoms' are endpoints (just like in H.323 and SIP) and connections (this is not the case in H.323 and SIP) that are 'virtually' connected (just like within a switch).

Only signaling and media planes are covered by the current MGCP draft. Both management and services planes have not been specified yet.

The protocol is based on SGCP version 1.1 (*sgcp.bellcore.com*) with CableLabs extensions and IPDC version 1.0. From the last protocol MGCP imports mainly the notion of event packages, a few new operations and some name changes. The end of the MGCP document describes in detail the changes made from SGCP v.1.1 and IPDC and incorporated in MGCP.

MGCP is a master/slave protocol. It uses other protocols to fulfill its requirements, such as the session description protocol which is used to describe the media aspects of the phone call. In its principle, MGCP is very close to the proprietary protocols of switch manufacturers that convey information back and forth between call control points (this terminology is not a 'standard' one used in intelligent network documents. IN does not define a standard interface between CCF and SSF) and service switching points.

This principle (in the context of MGCP) clearly places the intelligence on a physically separate element – the media gateway controller and not on the hardware endpoint, the media converter. But unlike the switch architecture as specified in IN documents where the call control remains close to the actual hardware endpoints, in the MGCP architecture the call control functionality is no longer attached to the media part.

Initially the protocol was designed to support only constant capabilities (for example, same codecs). But market needs and an ever-increasing number of requirements pushed the authors to consider adding dynamic capabilities, such as codec negotiation, a feature built in H.323. H.323 endpoints can negotiate their capabilities through H.245 messages and can even change one or more of their capabilities while the conversation is taking place. The origins of MGCP, known and published as SGCP, tried to avoid such dynamic features in order to keep SGCP as 'simple' as possible and be a competitive alternative to H.323. The addition of such functionalities and the expected addition of multimedia features will undoubtedly increase the complexity of MGCP.

In MGCP the session description protocol (*see* Chapter Two) is used to describe formally various parameters to enable establishment of connections between endpoints. MGCP does not use the multimedia features of SDP, such as the description of multiparty multimedia conferences. MGCP is not designed to support multimedia calls like H.323 or SIP does. It is nevertheless expected that this functionality will be added very soon (*see* requirements section). One of the other nice features of SDP is its flexibility and extensibility. New information elements can be added easily and registered to IANA. For a while, the use of Extensible Markup Language (XML) was considered as an alternative to describe telephony sessions (or multimedia) but due to lack of consensus at IETF the idea was abandoned. Also, as Christian Huitema, one of the head engineers of Bellcore, now Telcordia, describes: 'One advantage of a layered specification (such as using SDP in MGCP) is that it provides a clean partition between call signaling (as in MGCP) and media signaling (as in SDP).'

In its first release MGCP is composed of eight commands exchanged between the media gateway controller or call agent and the media gateway or simply gateway with the following features:

Notification Request	From call agent to gateway
Notification	From gateway to call agent
Create Connection	From call agent to gateway
Modify Connection	From call agent to gateway
Delete Connection	From call agent to gateway
Audit Endpoint	From call agent to gateway
Audit Connection	From call agent to gateway
Restart In Progress	From gateway to call agent

Readers may find all the details concerning MGCP in RFC 2705 (see above) and on the archive of the following mailing lists: *sgcp@bellcore.com* and *megaco@baynetworks.com.*

MGCP commands

Notification Request

This command requests the media gateway to watch for specific telephony events. These could be telephony signals, such as off-hook, on-hook, fax tones, modem tones, wink, flash hook, continue tone and detection, DTMF and pulse digits. One of the nice features of this command is the association of actions with each of the events. Using this facility, the communication and processing of information between the two entities can be optimized. For example, when the call agent requests the media gateway to watch for digits, it can request the media gateway to buffer the digits. By using this functionality the en bloc sending can be achieved easily.

One feature that is missing in this command is the ability for a media gateway controller to give other backup media gateway controllers' addresses. Should this functionality be included, MGCP could provide a built-in network reliability, just as H.323 version 2 does.

Notification Command

This command enables the media gateway to send back events that were requested by the media gateway controller. The media gateway can send one or several events in a notification command if it is asked to do so by the media gateway. Since the gateway is not supposed to have any 'intelligence', it sends the events in the order it detects them. It is up to the call agent to put events in the right order.

The collected information is sent by the media gateway to the call agent using the Notify command in the ObservedEvents field. From a protocol engineering point of view it would have been much more effective to use RTP (with compressed RTP headers) to send these events since RTP is designed to carry such information. Future releases of MGCP may adopt the use of RTP to send these messages back to the call agent.

Create Connection

This command is sent by the call agent to the media gateway to create a connection between two endpoints. In addition to the necessary parameters that enable a media gateway to create a connection, the LocalConnectionOptions parameter provides features for quality of service (echo cancellation, silence suppression), security, and network-related QOS fields (bandwidth, type of service, use of RSVP).

By sending a Notification Request command the call agent has the ability to request the gateway to execute simultaneous actions. In order to achieve this feature the call agent can use RequestedEvents, RequestIdentifier, DigitMap, SignalRequests, QuarantineHandling and DetectEvents parameters. The following example is given in MGCP:

■ 'ask the residential gateway to prepare a connection, in order to be sure that the user can start speaking as soon as the phone goes off-hook

■ ask the residential gateway to start ringing

■ ask the residential gateway to notify the call agent when the phone goes off-hook.

This can be accomplished in a single CreateConnection command, by also transmitting the RequestedEvent parameters for the off-hook event, and the SignalRequest parameter for the ringing signal.

This feature dramatically reduces the number of round trips necessary to establish a connection between two endpoints and improves the scalability of the call agent.

Modify Connection

This command enables a call agent to modify a connection that has already been set up by the gateway. The simultaneous feature mentioned below can also be used with the Modify Connection command. Modify connection can affect the following parameters of a connection: activation, deactivation, change codec, packetization period, etc.

Delete Connection

This command enables the call agent to terminate a call for a given connection. It should be noted that if there is more than one gateway involved, the call agent will send the Delete Connection command to each of the media gateways.

A nice functionality provided by MGCP (note that this is also provided by H.323) is that the media gateway, upon termination of a connection, has to send the call agent the following information:

- number of packets (RTP) sent
- number of octets (number of payloads) sent
- number of packets (RTP) received
- number of octets received
- number of packets lost
- interarrival jitter
- average transmission delay.

These parameters are fully described in RFC 1889.

MGCP allows also a media gateway to clear a connection on its own, such as when there is loss of a connection. In this context the media gateway issues a Delete Connection command to the call agent and sends all the parameters concerning call statistics back to the call agent as if it were a normal Delete Connection situation.

It is also possible for a call agent to delete multiple connections at the same time, using advanced hierchical naming structures and/or a wildcarding option (the wild card character is *). This command does not return any individual statistics or call parameters, making it unsuited for multiparty or conference calls. We believe that in the near future the media gateway will be required to send back this information.

Audit Endpoint
In order to check whether an endpoint is up and running the call agent can use this command. This feature is inherited from the switch environment.

Audit Connection
This command enables the call agent to retrieve all the parameters attached to a connection.

Restart in Progress
This command allows a gateway to make a call agent aware of an endpoint or a group of endpoints that have problems. The command allows three options: graceful (no connection lost), forced (connection(s) lost) and restart (the media gateway will restart soon). Further to these messages the call agent can decide if it wants to test these endpoints/connections before trying to make another call.

Fig. 3.3 shows MGCP protocol and architecture in use.

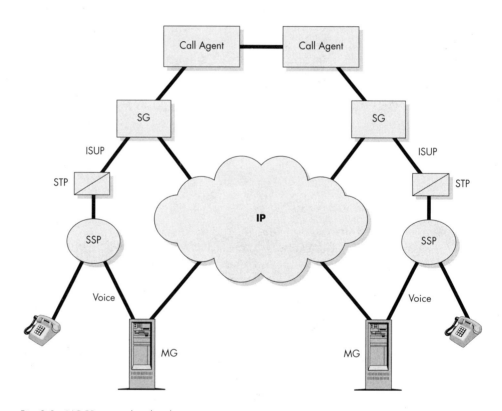

Fig. 3.3 : MGCP protocol and architecture in use

Protocols at work

Having seen the architecture where and media gateway to media gateway controllers protocols fit, we propose now to describe the call flows for some simple scenarios. We hope that, as we did for H.323, it will help readers to better understand the usage of the protocol. In addition to these call flows we have included an H.323 call flow for the same scenarios.

Scenario 1

User A calls user B through two residential gateways, A and B (*see* Fig. 3.4). There is no use of SS7 facilities. MGCP is used by the call agent to control the two residential gateways. We made the following assumptions for this scenario:

■ residential gateway (RGW) to RGW

■ no state hold in the GW

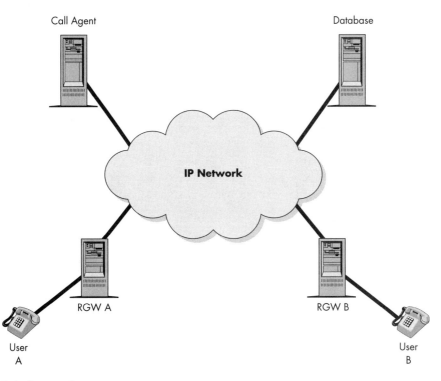

Fig. 3.4 : Scenario 1

- one centralized call agent that controls the two residential gateways
- no supplementary services, just basic call
- no data call (no network access server)
- no charging or accounting
- no QOS signaling
- no network or equipment failure.

Network configuration

The configuration analyzed here is a simple network topology. The call agent which provides the intelligence for the IP telephony service controls two gateways. These gateways serve two non-overlapping geographical areas. The call agent functions in this configuration can be compared to the functions of a gatekeeper using the gatekeeper routed call signaling model.

Call flows

Table 3.2 shows the call flows for Scenario 1.

Round trips	User A	RGW A	Call Agent	RGW B	User B	Steps
(initial)		←	RQNT			1
		ACK	→			2
0.5	Off-hook	NTFY	→			3
1		←	ACK			4
1	Dial-tone	←	RQNT			5
1.5		ACK	→			6
1.5+x	Digit	NTFY	→			7
2+x		←	ACK			8
2+x	(Progress)	←	RQNT+CRCX			9
2.5+x		ACK	→			10
5.5		←	CRCX			11
6		ACK	→			12
N			Database lookup			13
			(call processing)			
6.5			CRCX	→		14
7				← ACK		15
7.5		←	MDCX			16

Table 3.2 : Call flows for scenario 1

Round trips User A	RGW A	Call Agent	RGW B	User B	Steps
Table 3.2 : *Continued*					
8		ACK →			17
8.5		RQNT →		Ring	18
9		← ACK			19
9.5	(ringing)	← RQNT			20
10		ACK →			21
10.5		←	NTFY	Off-hook	22
11		ACK	→		23
11.5		← RQNT			24
12		ACK →			25
12.5		← MDCX			26
13		ACK →			27
		(call established)			
		(Talking)			
0.5	On-hook	NTFY →			28
1		← ACK			29
1.5		← DLCX			30
2		DLCX	→		31
2.5		← RQNT			32
3		ACK →			33
3.5		RQNT	→		34
4		← ACK			35

1 Call agent: instructs the RGW A to look for an off-hook event and report it. Sends a Notification Request to the RGW A.

2 RGW A: sends an acknowledgement message to the call agent.

3 RGW A: user A goes off-hook, the gateways detect the event and send a Notification to call agent.

4 Call agent: sends an acknowledgement message to the RGW A.

5 Call agent: the call agents look at the services associated to an off-hook action and send a Notification Request to the RGW A asking for more digits and request the GRW A to play the dial tone to user A.

6 RGW A: sends an acknowledgement message to the call agent.

7 RGW A: accumulates the dialed digits and sends a Notification to the call agent.

 8 Call agent: sends an acknowledgement message to the RGW A.

 9 Call agent: sends a Notification Request to stop collecting digits and watch for an on-hook transition. At this stage the call agent has got the necessary information to resolve the dialed number.

10 RGW A: sends an acknowledgement message to the call agent.

11 Call agent: seizes the incoming circuit. It sends a Create Connection message to the RGW A.

12 RGW A: sends an acknowledgement message to the call agent along with the session description used to receive audio data.

13 Call agent: the call agent queries a database to resolve the E.164 address and to find the remote gateway, RGW B, serving this number. This query may take a few other sets of messages. This request may also encapsulate authentication and authorization queries.

14 Call agent: the call agent knows the IP address of the RGW B and having seized the incoming trunk will now seize the outgoing trunk by sending a Create Connection command to the RGW B.

15 RGW B: sends an acknowledgement message to the call agent along with the session description used to receive audio data.

16 Call agent: can now relay the received information back to the RGW A by sending a Modify Connection to the RGW A. At this point two legs of the call are established in half duplex mode.

17 RGW A: sends an acknowledgement message to the call agent.

18 Call agent: instructs the RGW B to generate ringing tones by sending a Notification Request.

19 RGW B: sends an acknowledgement message to the call agent.

20 Call agent: notifies A that B is ringing.

21 RGW A: sends an acknowledgement message to the call agent.

22 RGW B: the user B answers the call and the RGW B sends a Notification to the call agent that the user B is answering the call.

23 Call agent: sends an acknowledgement message to the call agent.

24 Call agent: sends a Notification Request to the RGW A to stop ringing.

25 RGW A: sends an acknowledgement message to the call agent.

26 Call agent: sends a Modify Connection message to the RGW A to change the communication mode from half duplex to full duplex.

27 RGW A: sends an acknowledgement message to the call agent. The call is now taking place.

28 RGW A: the user A terminates the call and the RGW A sends the on-hook event to the call agent through the notification message.

29 Call agent: sends an acknowledgement message to the call agent.

30 Call agent: sends a Delete Connection message to the RGW A. No ACK is necessary from the GW.

31 Call agent: sends a Delete Connection message to the RGW B. No ACK is necessary from the GW.

32 Call agent: issues a new Notification Request to the RGW A asking it to be ready for the next off-hook event.

33 RGW A: sends an acknowledgement message to the call agent.

34 Call agent: issues a new Notification Request to the RGW B asking it to be ready for the next off-hook event.

35 RGW B: sends an acknowledgement message to the call agent.

Scenario 2

In this scenario we examine the call setup flows of a basic call. The user A calls user B. Basic assumptions are:

■ use of quasi associated mode
■ signaling is separated from voice.

Network configuration

The user A is attached to an analogue terminal (*see* Fig. 3.5). The CO (central office) that serves the user A is connected to the SS7 network through signaling transfer points. The service provider uses an IP backbone to carry its extra traffic. The interconnection between the circuit switched network and the IP backbone is done at two logical layers:

■ at the signaling layer, the STP is connected to the call agent through a signaling gateway that converts ISUP over MTP messages into a protocol over IP[4] (kind of ISUP over IP, and not Q.931 over IP) . The call agent acts as an intermediary between the signaling gateway and the trunking gateway;
■ at the voice layer, the switch is connected to a trunking gateway. The trunking gateway is controlled by the call agent as well as the residential gateway by using the MGCP.

The functional split of the call agent is shown in Fig. 3.6.

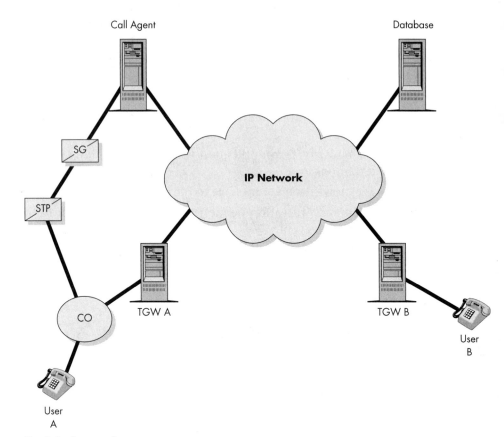

Fig. 3.5 : Scenario 2

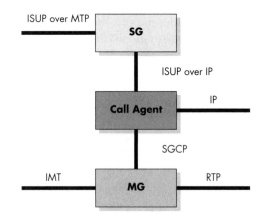

Fig. 3.6 : Call agent's functional design

Call flows

Table 3.3 shows the call flows for scenario 2.

Table 3.3 : Call flows for scenario 2							
Round trips	**CO**	**SS7**	**TGW**	**Call Agent**	**RGW**	**User**	**Steps**
0.5	IAM	→					1
1		IAM		→			2
1.5				Database lookup			3
2			←	CRCX			4
2.5			ACK	→			5
3				CRCX	→		6
3.5				←	ACK		7
4			←	MDCX			8
4.5			ACK	→			9
5				RQNT	→	Ring	10
5.5				←	ACK		11
6			←	ACM			12
6.5	←	ACM					13
						Off-hook	14
7				←	NTFY		15
7.5				ACK	→		16
8				RQNT	→		17
8.5				←	ACK		18
9			←	MDCX			19
9.5			ACK	→			20
10			←	ANM			21
10.5	←	ANM					22
				(Talking)			23
						On-hook	24
0.5				←	NTFY		25
1				ACK	→		26
1.5				DLCX	→		27
2			←	DLCX			28
2.5			←	REL			29

1 CO: issues an initial address message (IAM) to the call agent through its STP.

2 SS7: the Signaling Transfer Point (STP) routes the ISUP message to the signaling gateway attached to the call agent.

3 Call agent: queries a database to find out the IP address of the residential gateway serving the destination number.

4 Call agent: sends a Create Connection message to the trunking gateway to connect to the incoming trunk (uses the circuit identification code (CIC)).

5 TGW: sends an acknowledgement message to the call agent.

6 Call agent: seizes the incoming trunk and reserves the outgoing trunk circuit by sending a Create Connection message to the residential gateway.

7 RGW: sends an acknowledgement message to the call agent.

8 Call agent: will now indicate this information to the TGW by sending a Modify Connection to the TGW.

9 TGW: sends an acknowledgement message to the call agent.

10 Call agent: requests the residential gateway to ring the called line by sending a Notification Request message to the RGW.

11 RGW: sends an acknowledgement message to the call agent.

12 Call Agent: when the call agent receives the ACK from the RGW, it issues Address Complete message to the signaling gateway.

13 SS7: the STP conveys this information back to the CO.

14 User: terminal goes off-hook.

15 RGW: detects this event and notifies the call agent by sending a Notification message.

16 Call agent: sends an acknowledgement message to the call agent.

17 Call agent: in order to be able to detect the termination of a call, the call agent asks the RGW to report an on-hook event by sending a Notification Request message.

18 RGW: sends an acknowledgement message to the call agent.

19 Call agent: now the voice channel has to be turned into the full duplex mode; the call agent does this by sending a Modify Connection message to the TGW.

20 TGW: sends an acknowledgement message to the call agent.

21 Call agent: can now send an answer message to the signaling gateway.

22 SS7: the STP sends this information to the CO.

23 Both parties are talking.

24 RGW: the user B's terminal goes on-hook.

25 The RGW sends a Notification message to the call agent.

26 Call agent: sends an acknowledgement message to the call agent.

27 Call agent: sends a Delete Connection message to the RGW.

28 Call agent: sends a Delete Connection message to the TGW.

29 Call agent: issues a RELEASE message to the signaling gateway.

30 SS7: the STP conveys this information back to the CO.

Analysis

It should be noted that MGCP specification allows the combination of commands to be sent in one PDU, e.g. steps 24–27 in scenario 1 and steps 17–20 in scenario 2, and can be combined as MDCX+RQNT PDU. This combination allows a reduction in the number of messages necessary to set up a call.

On the other hand:

■ in order to establish a phone to phone call, MGCP requires at least 11 round trips;[5]

■ in the MGCP architecture, the call agent has to manage explicit interactions with the media gateway, as opposed to the current H.323 model where these interactions are performed by an H.323-compliant gateway;

■ MGCP gives the flexibility for per user or per call-based events to be created. A dialing plan per user, for example;

■ MGCP gives more control to the call agent or the media gateway controller, since it allows the call agent to act as a call-control element like an H.323 gatekeeper using the gatekeeper routed call model, while at the same time controlling tightly the media gateway functionality that is not available in H.323v2;

■ when MGCP is used in the trunking mode, its advantage with respect to the number of PDU exchanges between the call agent and the media gateway is obvious. This is due mainly to the fact that MGCP uses the UDP as the transport protocol as opposed to TCP in H.323;

■ MGCP architecture and its related functionalities enable the decrease of cost per port for a media gateway but increase the cost per port for a call agent or media gateway controller.

The H.323 case

This is the same as scenario 2 but using H.323 (*see* Fig. 3.7). Basic assumptions are:

- using gatekeeper routed call model
- the signaling gateway communicates with the gatekeeper and not with the gateway
- using Fast Connect procedure
- there is no GRQ; the GK addresses are statically configured
- no media can be sent by the called endpoint prior to the Connect message (calling endpoint sets the media WaitForConnect element to True in the Setup message)
- no call proceeding message will be sent by the gateway, since it is expected that the Connect message will arrive before four seconds elapse
- the RGW and TGW belong to the same zone – they are under the control of the GK
- there are no Admission Request messages per call. We use the pregranted mode with the following flags set to true by the gatekeeper in its RCF messages to the gateways:

  MakeCall

  UseGKCallSignalAddressToMakeCall

  AnswerCall

  UseGKCallSignalAddressToAnswer

- the RGW exchange admission messages prior to Setup message.

Network configuration

The user A is attached to an analogue terminal. The CO that serves the user A is connected to the SS7 network through signaling transfer points. The service provider uses an IP backbone to carry its extra traffic. The interconnection between the circuit switched network and the IP backbone is done at two logical layers:

- at the signaling layer, the STP is connected to the gatekeeper through a signaling gateway that converts ISUP over MTP messages into a proprietary protocol over IP. The gatekeeper acts as an intermediary between the signaling gateway and the trunking gateway;
- at the voice layer, the switch is connected to a trunking gateway. Both of the gateways are controlled by their own media gateway controllers and the gatekeeper.

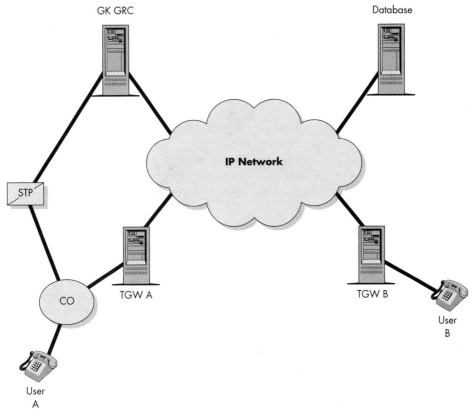

Fig. 3.7 : Scenario 3, the H.323 case

Functional decomposition of the gatekeeper is shown in Fig. 3.8.

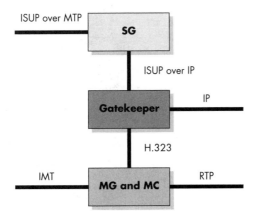

Fig.3.8 : Gatekeeper functional decomposition

Call flows

Table 3.4 shows the call flows for h.323.

Table 3.4 : Call flows for H.323

Round trips	CO	SS7 GW	TGW	Gatekeeper	RGW	User
0.5			RRQ	→		
1			←	RCF		
				TGW registered		
1.5				←	RRQ	
2				RCF	→	
				RGW registered		
3	IAM →					
3.5			IAM	→		
4				Database lookup		
4.5			←	TCP SYN		
5			SYN ACK	→		
5.5			←	SETUP (fastStart)		
6				TCP SYN	→	
6.5				←	SYN ACK	
7				SETUP (fastStart) →		
						Ring
7.5				←	ALERTING	
8		←		ACM		
8.5	←	ACM				
9						Off-hook
9.5				TCP SYN	→	
10				←	SYN ACK	
10.5				←	CONNECT	
11			←	TCP SYN		
11.5			SYN ACK	→		
12			←	CONNECT		
12.5		←		ANM		
13	←	ANM				
				(Talking)		
						On-hook
0.5				←	DRQ	
1				DCF	→	
1.5			←	DRQ		
2			DCF	→		
2.5		←		REL		
3	←	REL				

1 The trunking gateway registers with the GK.

2 The GK confirms the registration of the gateway and indicates it will use the GRC mode and exchanges any necessary tokens that can be used for the next coming protocols exchanges and indicates also the use of pregrantedARQs.

3 The same exchange occurs for the residential gateway.

4 Idem.

5 The initial address message is sent by the ingress CO to the GK through the SS7 signaling gateway.

6 On receipt of this message the GK looks up its database in order to decide where to route the incoming call.

7 Because H.323 version 2 mandates the use of TCP for call-control signaling messages, the GK must first establish the TCP channel with the trunking gateway.

8 Once the TCP connection is established, the GK issues the Setup message using the fastStart procedure as described in the specification.

9 The GK goes through the same exchange of messages with the residential gateway.

10 At this time logical channels are opened by the endpoints and they know where to send the RTP packets for the IP interface and where to send the PCM for the telephony interface.

11 The user's phone rings and the residential gateway sends the Alerting message to the GK.

12 The GK issues the ACM message to the CO through the SS7 signaling gateway and the switch gets ready to send the incoming PCM to the outgoing port of one of its voice trunks.

Analysis

The observation of these simplified call flows shows that the current H.323 protocol is not suited for trunking as well as MGCP is. One of the reasons is the use of TCP. Although more reliable, TCP does not fulfill the performance requirements imposed by the SS7 signaling network. There are at least two solutions to this problem:

■ use of long-live TCP connections between gateways and the respective gatekeepers. This solution assumes that the configuration of the network is more static than dynamic, therefore these connections can be kept alive for long periods (improves steps 9.5, 10, 11, 11.5);

■ use of UDP instead of TCP. The release 3 of H.323 will allow as an optional mode (*see* Annex E of H.323) the use of UDP for the fastStart procedure. It is possible to extend the proposed communication model of this annex to other signaling protocols (H.225 and H.245) of H.323.

Obviously, H.323 does not have the same features as the MGCP with regard to media control, but on the other hand MGCP as defined today does not have all the features of H.323, especially those being provided by H.245 that are very useful with intelligent endpoints.

Notes

1 In fact DSS1 is defined in ITU-T Recommendation Q.931.

2 The term carriers might have a different meaning – service providers, ITSP, cable operators, clearing houses. etc.

3 The authors claim that text-based protocols, by being easier to read and debug, improve application interoperability as opposed to binary protocols that require a specific decoder.

4 The IETF SIGTRAN working group is standardizing this protocol.

5 The current PSTN signaling network combines channel associated signaling (CAS) or digital subscriber signaling number 1 (DSS1) and SS7 signaling to establish a phone to phone call. The connection time in most of the advanced networks is below 1 s (this is a very large figure; in fully digitized networks this figure is around 200 ms).

VOICE TECHNOLOGY BACKGROUND

Voice quality

Introduction

A common joke among IP telephony engineers is to say that if they had proposed to carry voice over IP a couple of years ago, they would have been fired. This remains a private joke until you make your first IP phone call to someone who does not own a headset, and find out that the only person you hear is yourself.

Another way to find out why there really is a problem with IP telephony is to try a simple game: 'collaborative counting'. Collaborative counting has a simple rule: if you hear the person you talk to say 'n', you immediately say 'n+1'. In order to compare classic telephony with IP telephony, you first make a regular phone call to someone you know and say '1', he goes '2', etc. Keep an eye on your watch and see how long it takes to count to 25. Then you make an IP phone call and play the same game. In all cases, it will take much longer – if you ever reach 25.

The problems we have just emphasized – echo and delay – have been well known to telephone network planners since the early days of telephony, and today's telephone networks have been designed to keep those effects imperceptible for most customers. When carrying voice over IP, it becomes much more difficult to control echo and delay. As we will see, it will require state-of-the-art technology and optimization of all components to make the service acceptable to all customers.

Reference connection

The media path of IP telephony calls can be modeled as illustrated in Fig. 4.1 when there is no PSTN or ISDN terminal involved.

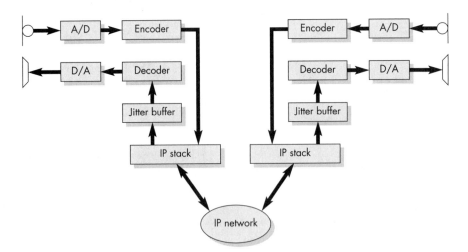

Fig. 4.1 : Media path with no PSTN or ISDN terminal

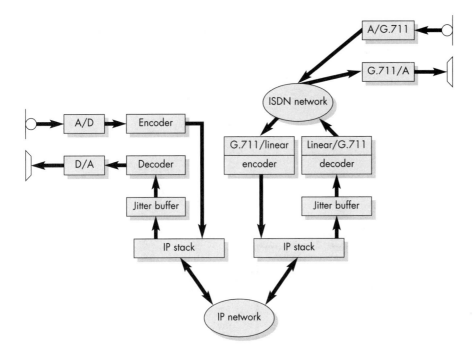

Fig. 4.2 : Interworking with an ISDN phone through a gateway

The situation becomes a little more complex when interworking with an ISDN phone through a gateway (*see* Fig. 4.2).

When the gateway interfaces with an analogue network, the user to network interface is in most cases using only two wires (incoming and outgoing signals share the same pair) and a four wire/two wire hybrid is required (*see* Fig. 4.3).

The model includes the most significant sources of voice quality degradation:

- the IP network introduces packet loss, delay and jitter;
- the jitter buffers (JB) influence end-to-end delay and frame loss;
- the acoustic interfaces introduce acoustic echo;
- the analogue interfaces introduce electric echo at hybrids.

This chapter is not a complete course on voice quality control in a telephone network. The subject is well covered by many ITU recommendations, and requires a lot of expertise. Here we try to describe the main factors influencing the end-user perception of voice quality. Most of these factors are common to switched circuit telephony and IP telephony. However, IP telephony has some unique characteristics, such as long delays, jitter and packet loss, and therefore requires a new framework for assessing voice quality. Work is ongoing at ETSI

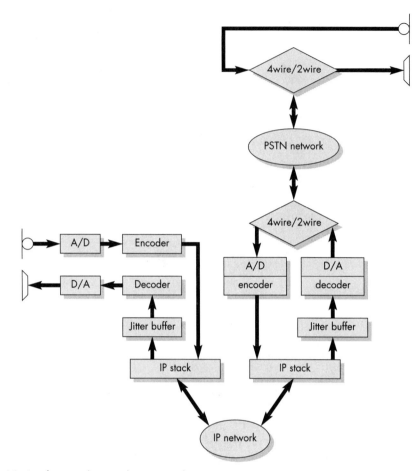

Fig. 4.3 : Interfacing with an analogue network

TIPHON (Working Group 5) on this subject, and we will follow their approach to the problem.

Echo in a telephone network

Talker echo, listener echo

The most important echo is the talker echo – it is the perception by the talker of his own voice but delayed. It can be caused by electric (hybrid) echo or acoustic echo picked up at the listener side. If the talker's echo is reflected twice it can

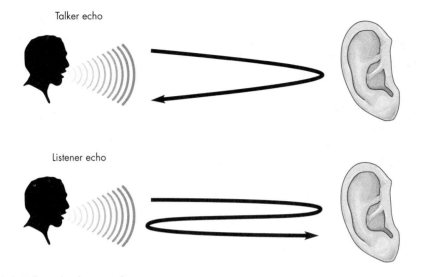

Fig. 4.4 : Talker echo, listener echo

also affect the listener. In this case the listener hears the talker's voice twice – a loud signal first, then attenuated and much delayed. This is the listener echo (*see* Fig. 4.4).

Hybrid echo

What is a hybrid?

The simplest telephone system would look like (a) (*see* Fig. 4.5). However, to use fewer wires, the phone system has been designed to use only two wires, and the first two wire phones looked like (b). Because of parasitic capacities on the line, most of the microphone signals were dissipated in the talker's loudspeaker (who then tended to speak more quietly), and almost nothing reached the listener. So the final design was (c), where Zref matches the characteristic impedance of the line. Now the microphone signal is split equally between Zref and the line, and the speaker hardly hears himself in his own loudspeaker (a small imbalance is kept for him not to have the impression that he is talking in the air). ETSI defined Zc (270Ω –750Ω//150 nF) as a 150 nF capacitor in parallel with a 750Ω resistor, wired to a 270Ω resistor. In France, Zref is a 150nF capacitor in parallel with a 880Ω resistor, wired to a 210Ω resistor. Depending on when a particular piece of equipment was installed, some older phones are also equipped with a real impedance of 600Ω. These values were found to be a good average value for a typical line. The actual impedance of a given line will vary according to its length (between 0 and 9 km, typically), so there is always some mismatch.

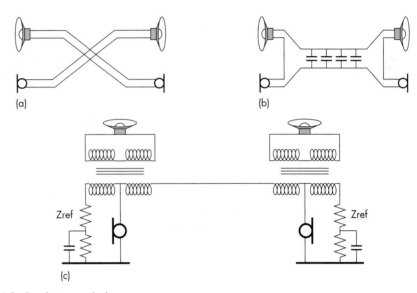

Fig. 4.5 : Developing a telephone system

The common way to symbolize this device is (d) (*see* Fig. 4.6), where each corner represents two wires. It is called a duplexer or a hybrid. Each half of (c) becomes (e). A hybrid can be integrated easily as in (f).

The hybrid is also commonly used in an analogue telephone network to allow line signals amplification using the configuration in Fig. 4.7.

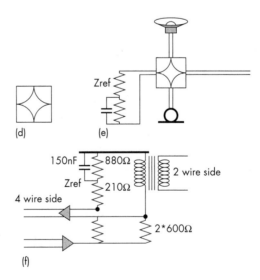

Fig. 4.6 : Integrating a hybrid

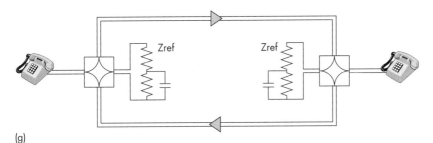

(g)

Fig. **4.7** : Using a hybrid in an analogue telephone network

In (c) or Fig. 4.7, Zref never matches exactly the characteristic impedance of the two-wire line, so a portion of the incoming signal is fed back in the outgoing signal. This parasitic signal is the hybrid echo and has all sorts of consequences:

■ in Fig. 4.7 the signals will loop between the two amplifiers and generate a 'cathedral effect' if the one-way delay is about 20 ms. To avoid instability in the network, a loss of 6 dB at least is introduced in the four-wire path;

■ a phone with a mismatched Zref will echo all incoming signals from the network, and the talker at the other side of the line will hear himself after a round trip delay.

In many countries, the transit network is entirely built using four wires (any digital link is a virtual four-wire link). The two to four-wire separation occurs at the local switch where the analogue phone is connected (Fig. 4.8). Because the echo

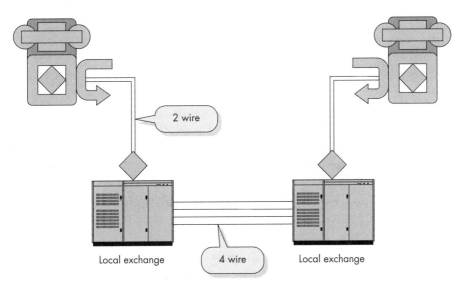

Fig. **4.8** : The two to four-wire separation

generated at the switch end coming back to the phone is not delayed, it has no effect. On the other hand the echo generated at the phone end travels back to the other phone through the network and is noticed as soon as the round trip time is above 50 ms (without echo cancellation in the four-wire path).

Acoustic echo

Here we call 'loudspeaker phone' an amplified phone without acoustic echo cancellation, and 'hands-free phone' an amplified phone with acoustic echo cancellation.

The acoustic echo is simply the part of the acoustic signal that is fed back from the loudspeaker of a device to the microphone of that same device. Typically the acoustic echo is a parasitic signal about 10–15 dB (case of a loudspeaker phone) below the acoustic signal of the person who actually talks into the microphone. Just like the hybrid echo, such a level of acoustic echo goes unnoticed if the round trip delay is below 20 ms. After 40 ms the person on the other end of the line gets the impression of talking in a well, and things are worse after 40 ms of round trip time.

An easy way to suppress the acoustic echo is to use a headset, but with appropriate devices it is possible to reduce the power of the parasitic echo to about 45 dB below the speaker's signal, even using a hands-free phone.

ITU recommendation G.167 gives some values for the typical echo path to use during testing:

■ 'for teleconference systems, the reverberation time (time after which the sound energy of an impulsion has decayed below 60 dB of the original power) averaged over the transmission bandwidth shall be typically 400 ms. The reverberation time in the highest octave shall be no more than twice this average; the reverberation time in the highest octave shall be no less than half this value. The volume of the typical test room shall be of the order of 90 m³;

■ for hands-free telephones and videophones, the reverberation time averaged over the transmission bandwidth shall be typically 500 ms; the reverberation time in the highest octave shall be no more than twice this average; the reverberation time in the highest octave shall be no less than half this value. The volume of the typical test room shall be of the order of 50 m³;

■ for mobile radio telephones an enclosure simulating the interior of a car can be used.(...) A typical average reverberation time is 60 ms. The volume of the test room shall be of 2.5 m³.'

The echo cancellers usually do not work with acoustic echo as well as with electric echo because the acoustic echo path varies much more, which makes it more difficult to dynamically adapt the synthesized echo to the real one. In particular echo cancellers compliant with ITU rec. G.165 performance might not be sufficient. A newer recommendation, G.168, is available and already implemented by some vendors. This recommendation contains useful additions, such as the ability to stop the echo cancellation when detecting the phase reversal tone of high-speed modems.

Typical values for acoustic echo attenuation in current devices are:

■ loudspeaker phones (80 per cent of the market in France): 10–15 dB;

■ hands-free phones: 35–40 dB;

■ phone with good quality handset: 35–40 dB.

How to limit echo

Two types of devices are commonly used to limit echo: echo cancellers and echo suppressors.

The electric echo and echo reduction are measured in the four-wire path with the reference points shown in Fig. 4.9.

Echo suppressors

Echo suppressors were developed in the 1970s. The idea is to introduce a large loss in the send path when the distant party is talking. This technique is widely used in low-end, hands-free phones, but tends to squelch the talker when the distant party talks at the same time.

Echo cancellers

The echo canceller functional model is shown in Fig. 4.10.

An echo canceller is much more complex than an echo suppressor because it actually builds an estimate of the echo to remove it from the incoming signal.

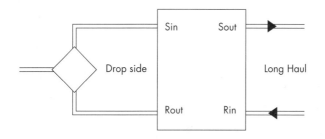

Fig. 4.9 : Measuring electric echo and echo reduction

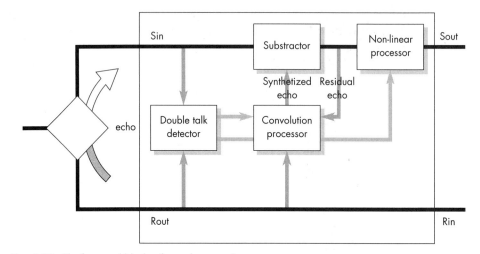

Fig. 4.10 : The functional blocks of an echo canceller

The echo is modelled as a sum of signals similar to the incoming signal but delayed and with a lower amplitude (a convolution of the incoming signal), therefore it works only with linear modifications of the signal between Rin and Sin. For example, clipping will ruin the performance of an echo canceller. The error signal is measured and minimized when only the distant party is talking, which is what the double talk detector is used for.

The echo canceller needs to store the amplitude of every returning delayed signal for each possible delay between 0 and the biggest delay on the drop side (this is the impulsive response of the hybrid). Therefore the echo cancellers that can handle large delays (e.g. 64 ms) on the drop side are more expensive than echo cancellers that handle only small delays – it is always best to place the echo canceller as close as possible to the source of echo.

Basically electric echo cancellers are adaptive digital filters (FIR: finite impulse response) placed in the network, for instance in an international switching center for a satellite link or in the mobile switching center (MSC) for digital cellular applications (*see* Fig. 4.11).

In the GSM cellular phone system, the one-way delay is around 100 ms due to:

■ the frame length of 20 ms
■ the processing delay of 20 ms (may be reduced by using powerful DSP.)
■ interleaving for channel protection
■ buffering and decoding.

So an electric echo canceller (EEC) must be included in the MSC as shown on (Fig. 4.12).

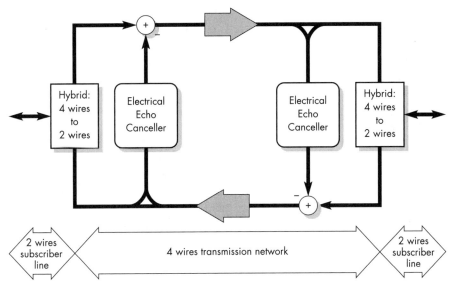

Fig. 4.11 : Electric echo canceller as adaptive digital filter

In the case of a real-time voice over packet switched network such as VoIP, the situation concerning the electrical echo is quite similar and it must be canceled if the IP gateway establishes a call between a PSTN two-wire terminal and a multi-media PC or workstation. The various functions of the IP telephony gateway will

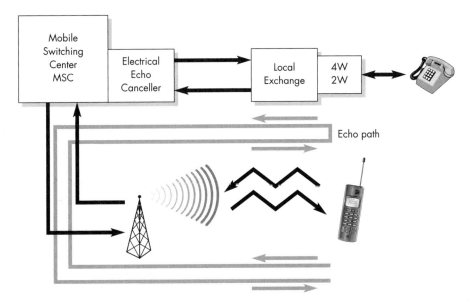

Fig. 4.12 : Need for an electrical echo canceller in a digital cellular system

be detailed later but one of them is the cancellation of the electrical echo generated by the four-wire to two-wire transformation. If the PC user has a handset and a microphone, there is no acoustic echo and there is no need for an acoustic echo canceller (AEC) in the PC sound card. As shown in Fig. 4.13, one EEC is needed in the gateway and one AEC is needed in the PC environment if the PC's user has a microphone and loudspeakers in a hands-free situation. If there is no EEC, the electrical echo will disturb the PC side, and if there is no AEC the acoustical echo will disturb the PSTN side.

On an IP network the delay is often large and unpredictable. For a switched network such as PSTN or ISDN, this is not generally the case, but for very large countries such as the US (from the East Coast to the West Coast, it's a long way for a phone call too) the transmission delay is so high that even for these terrestrial calls (using fiber optic links) an EEC is needed. It was one of the main drivers for the new ITU low-delay coding scheme at 16 kbit/s (the future G.728 aimed to replace the 32 kbit/s G.726). This avoids the need to update the installed base of EEC in the US.

Even when using low-delay coding schemes for digital cellular mobile systems, VoIP, voice over frame relay or even voice over ATM, the need for EEC is really mandatory and this impacts the overall cost of the system. Nevertheless, a speech coding with a low algorithmic and processing delay will relax the requirements for the performances of the EEC (echo rejection). To tackle the acoustical echo, one AEC must be installed in the hands-free terminal whatever network and transmission link are used.

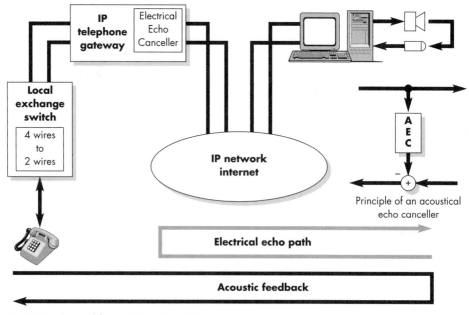

Fig. 4.13 : The need for an EEC and an AEC

The AEC works in a similar way to the EEC. It is an adaptive digital filter associated with some gain variations procedures. The larger the total round trip delay, the more difficult it is to tune all the parameters of the AEC systems (speed of convergence, range of gain variation, etc.) in order to reduce sufficiently the echo level and to keep a good interactivity.

Ideally, for any phone call or video conference, a low delay is highly desirable.

The performance of an echo canceller involves many parameters (*see* G.165 for more details). The most important ones are echo return loss enhancement (ERLE in dB) which is the amount of reduction of the echo level between the Sin and Sout port, and the size of the window modeling the impulse response (some echo cancellers are optimized to cancel all echoes coming with a delay of 0 to Tmax, some are optimized to model only echoes coming with a delay of Tmin to Tmax). Other parameters are the convergence time and quality of the double talk detection.

Delay in a VoIP telephone network

Influence of the operating system

Most IP phone applications are just regular programs running on top of an operating system such as Windows. They access the sound peripherals through an API (e.g. the WAVE API for Windows) and they access the network through the socket API. As you speak the sound card samples the microphone signals and accumulates the samples in a memory buffer (it may also perform some basic compression such as G.711 encoding). When a buffer is full the sound card tells the operating system, using an Interrupt, that it can retrieve the buffer, and stores the next samples in a new buffer.

Interrupts stop the regular activities of the operating system and trigger a very small program called an interrupt handler that in our case may simply store a pointer to the sound buffer for the program that has opened the microphone.

In the case of the WAVE API, the program registered a call-back function when it opened the microphone to receive the new sample buffers, and the operating system will simply call this function to pass the buffer to our IP phone application. When the call-back function is called, it will check that there are enough samples to form a full frame for a compression algorithm such as G.723.1, and if so put the resulting compressed frame (wrapped with the appropriate RTP information) on the network using the socket API.

The fact that the samples from the microphone are sent to the operating system in chunks using an Interrupt introduces a minimal accumulation delay because most operating systems cannot accommodate too many Interrupts per second. For Windows, many drivers try not to generate more than one Interrupt every 60 ms. This means that on such systems the samples come in chunks of more than 60 ms, independent of the codec used by the program. For instance, a program using G.729 could generate six G.729 frames, and a program using G.723.1 could generate two G.233.1 frames for each chunk, but in both cases the delay at this stage is 60 ms, due only to the operating system maximum interrupt rate.

The same situation occurs when playing back the samples, and there are further delays introduced by the socket implementation.

The conclusion is that the operating system is a major parameter that must be taken into account when trying to reduce end-to-end delays for IP telephony applications. To bypass this limitation, some IP telephony gateway and IP phone vendors use real-time operating systems such as VxWorks (by Wind River Systems) or pSOS (ISI) which are optimized to handle as many Interrupts as needed to reduce this accumulation delay.

Another way of bypassing the operating system limits is to do all the real-time functions (sample acquisition, compression and RTP) using dedicated hardware, and perform only the control functions from the non real-time operating system. IP telephony board vendors such as Natural Microsystems, Dialogic or Audiocodes use this type of approach to allow third parties to build low-latency gateways with Unix or Windows on top of their equipment.

Influence of the jitter buffer policy on delay

An IP packet needs some time to get from A to B through a packet network (*see* Fig. 4.14). This delay $t_{AB} = t_{arrival} - t_{departure}$ is composed of a fixed part L characteristic of the propagation delays and the average queuing delays, and a variable part characterizing jitter caused by variable queue length in routers and other factors.

Terminals use a jitter buffer to compensate for the jitter effects. This buffer will hold packets in memory until $t_{unbuffer} - t_{departure} = L+J$. The time of departure of each packet is determined by using the timestamp information provided by RTP. By increasing the value of J, the terminal is able to resynchronize more packets. Packets arriving too late ($t_{arrival} > t_{unbuffer}$) are dropped.

Terminals use heuristics to tune J to the best value: if J is too small, too many packets will be dropped; if J is too large, the additional delay will be unacceptable to the user. For some terminals the configuration of the size of the jitter buffer is static; this is not optimal when the network conditions are not stable. Other terminals can dynamically resize their jitter buffers using heuristics. These heuristics may take some time because the terminal needs to evaluate jitter in the network, e.g. the terminal can choose to start initially with a very small buffer, and pro-

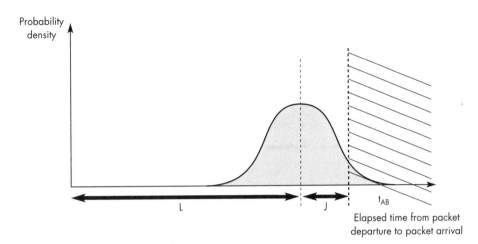

Fig. 4.14 : Delay through a packet network

gressively increase it until the average percentage of packets arriving too late drops below 1 per cent.

Influence of the codec, frame grouping and redundancy

Most voice coders are frame oriented. This means that they compress fixed-size chunks of linear samples, rather than sample per sample. Therefore the audio data stream needs to be accumulated until it reaches the chunk size, before being processed by the coder (*see* Fig. 4.15). This sample accumulation takes time, and therefore adds to the end-to-end delay. In addition some coders need to know more samples than those contained in the frame they will be coding (this is called lookahead).

A quick conclusion is that in order to reduce delays on an ideal network, the codec chosen should have a short frame length.

Unfortunately a good rule of thumb is the more you know about something, the easier it is to model it efficiently. Therefore coders with larger frame sizes tend to be more efficient, and have better compression rates. Another factor is that each frame is not transmitted as it is through the network – a lot of overhead is added by the transport protocols themselves for each packet transmitted through the network. If each compressed voice frame is transmitted in a packet of its own, this overhead is added for each frame, and for some coders the overhead will be comparable to if not greater than the useful data. To lower the overhead to an acceptable level, most implementations choose to transmit multiple frames in each packet (*see* Fig. 4.16).

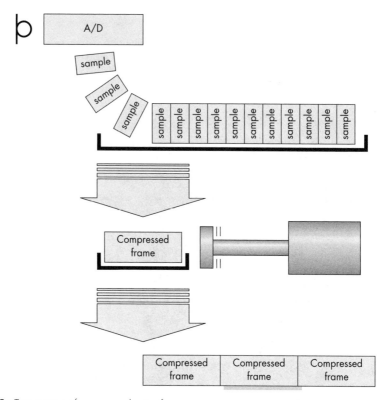

Fig. 4.15 : Transmission of compressed voice frames

If all the frames accumulated in the packet belong to the same audio stream, this will add more accumulation delay. In fact, using a coder with a frame size of f and three frames per packet is absolutely equivalent, in terms of overhead and accumulation delay, to using a coder with a frame size of 3f and one frame per packet. Since a coder with a longer frame size is usually more efficient, the latter solution is likely to be more efficient also.

Note that if the operating system gives access to the audio stream in chunks of size C ms rather than sample per sample, then samples have already been accumulated and it is best to use a coder with a frame size of F = C, or if C is too large to put floor(C/F) frames per packet.

A much more intelligent way of stacking multiple frames per packet without any impact on delay is to put frames from different audio streams but with the same network destination. This is often the case for VoIP trunks between corporate sites, or between gateways inside a VoIP network. Unfortunately, the way to do this RTP-multiplexing (or RTP-mux) has not yet been standardized in H.323, SIP or other VoIP protocols, and manufacturers need to use proprietary

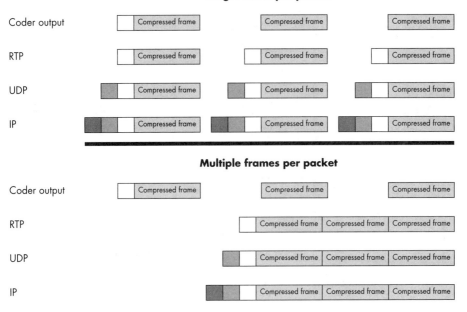

Fig, 4.16 : Comparison of frames per packet

implementations (such as using a logical channel with a 'coder' that actually encodes many channels and remains open permanently between the gateways, and for each new communication using a dummy coder type when opening the logical channel).

Another parameter that needs to be taken into account when assessing the end-to-end delay of an implementation is the redundancy policy. A real network introduces packet loss, and a terminal may use redundancy to be able to reconstruct lost frames. This can be as simple as copying a frame twice in consecutive packets, or more involved.

Redundancy will add to the packet size, but may not worsen the congestion if it is due to an insufficient switching capacity. The terminal may use a heuristic to determine the best redundancy strategy.

Redundancy influences the end-to-end delay because the receiver needs to adjust its jitter buffer in order to receive all redundant frames before if transfers the frame to the decoder. Otherwise if the first frame got lost, the jitter buffer would be unable to wait until it had received the redundant copies, and they would be useless. This can add significantly to the end-to-end delay, especially if the redundant frames are stored in non-contiguous packets to resist correlated packet loss (Fig. 4.17).

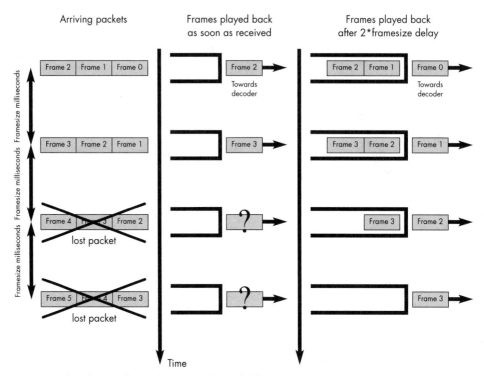

Fig. 4.17 : The influence of redundancy on end-to-end delay

Consequence for measuring end-to-end delay

In order to assess the delay performance of a particular IP telephony hardware or software, it is necessary to simulate various network conditions, characterized by parameters such as the average transit delay, jitter and packet loss. Because of the many heuristics used by IP telephony devices to adapt to the network, it is necessary to perform the end-to-end delay measurement after allowing a short convergence time.

A simple measurement can be done according to the following method:

1   The IP telephony devices IN and OUT are connected back to back through a network simulator.

2   The network simulator is set to the proper settings for the reference network condition considered for the measurement. This includes setting the average end-to-end delay L, the amount of jitter and the jitter profile, the amount of packet loss and the loss profile, and possibly other factors such as packet desequencing.

3   A speech file is fed to IN with active talk during the first 15 seconds (Talk1), then a silence period of five seconds, then an active talk again for 30 seconds (Talk2), then a silence period of ten seconds.

4   The speech file is recorded at OUT.

5   Only the Talk2 part of the initial file and the recorded file is kept. This is facilitated by the silence periods.

6   The average level of both files is equalized.

7   If the amplitude of the initial file is IN(t), and the amplitude of the recorded file is OUT(t), the value of D maximizing the correlation of IN(t) and OUT(t+D) is called Dmin. This can be done manually with an oscilloscope and a delay line, adjusting the delay until the input and output speech samples coincide, or with some basic computing on the recorded files (for ISDN gateways the files can be input and recorded directly in G.711 format). Please refer to ITU recommendation P.931 for details.

The delay introduced by both sending and receiving devices is Dmin-L. With this method it is impossible to split this delay between the sending terminal and the receiving terminal.

Note that a very crude, but efficient way of quickly evaluating the end-to-end delay is to use the Windows sound recorder.

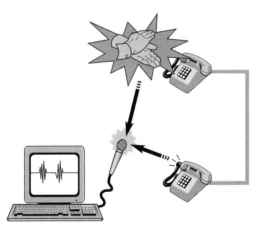

Fig. 4.18 : A (very) simple yet efficient method for measuring end-to-end delay

Acceptability of a phone call with echo and delay

The G.131 curve

The degree of annoyance of talker echo depends both on the amount of delay and on the level difference between the voice and the echo signals. This level difference is characterized by the 'talker echo loudness rating' (TELR) as described in G.122 and Annex A/G.111.

G.131 provides in figure 1/G.131 the minimum requirements on TELR as a function of the mean one-way transmission time T (*see* Fig. 4.19). According to G.131, in general, the acceptable curve is the 1 per cent curve (1 per cent means that on average 1 per cent of the users will complain about an echo problem) is the one to follow. The 10 per cent curve is an extreme limit that should be allowed only exceptionally.

This figure clearly shows that echo becomes more audible as delay increases. This is the reason why echo is such a problem in all telephony technologies that introduce high delays, which includes most compressed voice technologies, satellite transmissions – and of course IP telephony.

Note: What is TELR?

We use the reference circuit described in G.131 for the talker echo (Fig. 4.20).

For analogue phones: TELR=SLR+RLR+R+T+Lr, where R and T stand for additional loss introduced in the analogue circuit in order to have a 0 dBr point at the

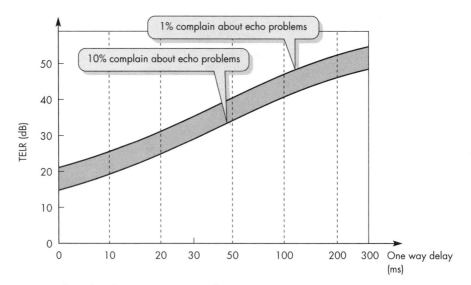

Fig. 4.19 : Talker echo tolerance curves (G.131 figure 1)

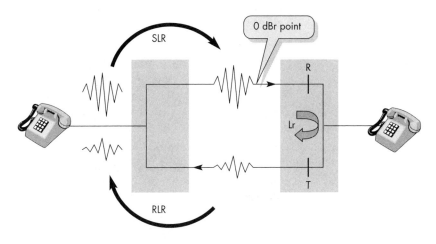

Fig. 4.20 : Talker echo

exchange. The send loudness rating (SLR) and receive loudness rating (RLR) model the acoustic to electric efficiency of the receiver and the emitter respectively (*see* ITU recommendation p. 79). For software IP phones these values can be affected by the sound card settings, and a good software should apply digital attenuation to make sure that the resulting SLR and RLR still have the recommended values.

For digital phones: TELR=SLR+RLR+TCL

Typical values:

- For typical phone sets G.121 states that SLRnom=7dB, SLRmin=2dB, RLRnom=3dB, RLRmin=1dB. The error margin is ±3 for digital phones, much greater for analogue phones.
- Most analogue phone connections have a Lr > 17 dB for an average length of subscriber cable; however, in some networks it can be 14 dB with a standard deviation of 3 dB.
- Most digital handsets have a TCL typically above 35 dB, and often in the 40–46 dB range.

In many networks R+T=6 dB (in France T=0 and R=7).

Examples:

For SLR=7dB, RLR=3dB, Lr=14dB, R+T=6 we get a TELR of 30 which leads to an acceptable limit for the one-way delay of 18 ms (33 ms in the limiting case). For a 'loud' telephone set with SLR=2dB, RLR=1dB and an Lr of 8 dB, we get a TELR of 17 and the limiting case is now 7 ms. When phoning to a digital handset (TCL=45dB) with the talker's phone having SLR=7dB, RLR=3dB, we get a TELR of 55 dB, and the one-way delay is 'acceptable' up to 400 ms.

Interactivity

In the previous examples 'acceptable' is regarding only echo. Interactivity must also be considered. Usually a delay below 100 ms one way provides a good interactivity. A one-way delay between 100 and 250 ms provides an acceptable interactivity (satellite hop). A 400 ms one-way delay should be exceptional (case of two satellite hops) and is the limit after which the conversation can be considered half duplex.

When there are large delays on the line, the talker tends to think that the listener has not heard or paid attention. He will repeat what he said and be interrupted by the delayed response of the called party. Both will stop talking – and restart simultaneously. With some training it is possible to communicate correctly, but the conversation is not natural.

A more complex model: the E-model

The E-model was originally developed in ETSI for the needs of network planning. It allows the subjective quality of a conversation to be evaluated as it would be perceived by a user. The E-model bases each degradation factor on the perceived voice quality by a value called an 'impairment factor'. Impairment factors are then processed by the E-model which outputs a rating R between 0 and 100. The R value can be mapped to a mean opinion score value, or to %Good or Better (%GoB) or % Poor or Worse (%PoW) values using tables. An R value of 50 is very bad, while an R value of 90 is very good.

The E-model takes into account parameters that are not considered in the G.131 curve, such as the quality of the voice coder. Most voice coders have been rated for their impairment factor without frame loss, and consequently the E-model (available as commercial software from various vendors) can readily be used to evaluate the perceived voice quality through an IP telephony network with no packet loss and low jitter. Such a work was published by the T1A1.7 committee in January 1999.

The impairment factor parameters are evaluated from real subjective tests to calibrate the model (*see* G.113). Therefore the usability of the E-model for a particular technology depends on how much calibration has been done on this technology.

IP telephony, in most cases, introduces perturbations that have not yet been thoroughly evaluated, such as the influence of the delay variation that may be introduced by endpoints trying to dynamically adjust the size of jitter buffers, voice clipping introduced by VAD algorithms, or correlated loss introduced by frame grouping. R&D labs specializing in voice quality and network planning are working on these issues, and new versions of E-model software packages with enhanced support for IP telephony should appear soon.

The E-model also takes into account psychological parameters that do not influence the absolute voice quality but the *perception* of the user. For instance, the 'expectation' impairment factor takes into account the fact that most users expect to have a degraded voice quality when using a cellular phone, and therefore will be more indulgent – and complain less – for the same level of quality than if they had been using a normal phone. IP phone manufacturers will have to find a recognizable design if they want to benefit from the 'expectation factor'.

The E-model is misleading if not used correctly. An impairment factor for a coder measured under specific loss profiles is not valid for other loss profiles (e.g. if there is correlated loss).

Consequences for an IP telephony network

In many ways the IP phone networks and mobile phone networks (such as GSM) face similar constraints regarding voice quality. On the IP phone side, as well as on the ISDN phone side, only acoustic echo is generated since there is no hybrid. With current technology, even 400 ms seems an optimistic end-to-end one-way delay over some wide area IP networks and any delay higher than 400 ms results in a real loss of interactivity between the talking parties, even with perfect echo cancellation.

The IP telephony connection is subject to the same echo/delay trade as any other telephony connection. Even with a toll quality coder, the kind of one-way delays encountered in IP telephony call for a TELR value of at least 55 dB. This is close to the highest achievable value for G.711 encoded voice signals, due to the quantization noise that is introduced by G.711. This echo cancellation level can be reduced to about 30 dB under double-talk conditions.

IP PC phone to IP PC phone: if we assume SLR+RLR = 10 dB, then the echo loss of the distant IP phone must be at least TCLw=45 dB. This might be implemented in the audio peripherals (sound board), or in the IP telephony software itself (although this will require a very high-end CPU).

IP phone to a regular phone: most ISDN phones have a TCLw value of 45 dB, so the IP telephony gateway does not need to perform echo cancellation on the ISDN phone side. This explains why so many demonstrations of IP telephony gateways propose to call a cellular phone from an IP phone. People will tell you this is a worst-case scenario because, after all, you are calling a cellular phone. In fact, this is very often done on purpose to hide the lack of echo cancelling devices in the IP telephony gateway. The cellular phone includes a powerful echo canceller, and the cellular phone network interface with the regular phone network is also via echo cancellers.

Obviously, the IP phone needs to have an echo canceller as well, or the ISDN user will hear echo.

IP phone to PSTN user and vice versa: the PSTN phone will generate hybrid echo and acoustic echo. Since the propagation time in the PSTN is usually low, many links may not implement sufficient echo cancellation (if at all). Therefore the gateway must implement echo cancellation. Again this will prove difficult because the gateway is not always close to the PSTN user and therefore the signal to echo delay may be delayed more than some echo cancellers can support. In fact, the echo cancellers are often characterized by the maximum skew between the signals that compose the echo. This signal is a superposition of signals s_i that are a copy of the original signal but attenuated by a factor A_i and delayed by a factor of $D+d_i$. Some echo cancellers work with $D=0$ and $0<d_i<\text{Maxskew}$ (18 ms for instance). Other echo cancellers work with D as large as 500 ms, and $0<d_i<\text{MaxSkew}$.

If a single gateway is implemented in a country the size of France, for instance, D is below 64 ms in 90 per cent of the cases, including call rerouting, but this would be too large for the first type of echo cancellers. These should be reserved only for IP/PBX-type applications with directly attached telephones.

The approach of ETSI TIPHON

ETSI TIPHON was one of the earliest standards bodies to work on QoS issues for IP telephony. TIPHON Working Group 5 has taken into account the following parameters of the quality perceived by the user:

- the setup time, which is influenced by directory lookups, round trips needed to establish the media channels, and the switched circuit network's own setup time for IP to SCN calls;
- the voice degradation caused by codecs and frame loss;
- the interactivity.

The goal of WG5 is:

- to allow some benchmarking of the quality of IP telephony networks. This is an end-to-end perspective;
- to allow network engineers to benchmark each component of the IP telephony network (gateways, terminals, software) in order to be able to do some planning. This also helps in choosing among various components the one that is best suited in each condition.

It was recognized in the first TIPHON meetings that the range of application of IP telephony was so broad that one type of QoS level would be insufficient. Imposing toll quality for all applications would in most cases rule out the public Internet as a voice transport backbone. Moreover the optimal tuning of an IP telephony terminal depends a lot on the network conditions – a terminal that has to work over a 28.8 modem connection will *have* to put multiple frames per IP packet, while an IP terminal designed to work over a 10 Mbps corporate LAN will probably be able to minimize delays by putting only one frame per IP packet, or even may use G.711 with no further compression.

Therefore TIPHON is working on defining four levels of end-to-end quality of service for IP telephony networks (from ETSI TR 101 329 V1.2.5).

Table 4.1 : End-to-end quality of service categories

	Best	High	Medium	Best Effort
Speech quality (one-way, non-interactive measurement)	Equivalent or better than G.711 for all types of signals	Equivalent or better than G.726 at 32 kbit/s for all types of signals	Equivalent or better than GSM FR for all types of signals	
End-to-end delay	<150 ms	<250 ms	<450 ms	
Setup delay (direct IP adressing)	<1.5s	<4s	<7s	
E.164 to IP address translation needed	<2s	<5s	<10s	
E.164 to IP address translation via clearing house	<3s	<8s	<15s	
Email alias to IP address	<4s	<13s	<25s	

The delay parameters are bounds for 90 per cent of the calls (including time and geographic variability). The measurements are taken with the actual network conditions found in the operational service. Using references to existing codecs facilitates direct comparison with recorded speech samples. The TIPHON members felt it was important to give delay bounds for the duration of the call setup. Table 4.1 was built after much debate, and it is indeed quite an achievement to have reached an agreement on such critical values for manufacturers and network providers. However, the exact numerical values are to be taken more as guidelines, representing a general understanding of what the limits were for each category.

The authors of this book also pushed TIPHON to define some characteristics of individual VoIP devices (terminals and gateways), in order to help network planners and to create a set of values that could be indicated in each technical manual.

Obviously the optimum characteristics expected from an endpoint differ according to the application: IP telephony over low bandwidth modem connections, IP telephony over bandwidth constrained corporate WAN connections, and high-quality IP telephony over high bandwidth networks. These situations were considered to be representative of the vast majority of current VoIP applications, and TIPHON created three 'device classes' – A, B and C – one for each type of application.

- class A devices (Fig. 4.21) are tuned for networks where bandwidth is not a concern, and quality is the main driver (low delays, high MOS);
- class B devices (Fig. 4.22) are tuned for operation within the constraints of an ISDN B channel bandwidth;
- class C devices (Fig. 4.23) are tuned for operation within the constraints of an analogue modem connection (< 30 kbit/s, typically).

It makes no sense to say that a class A terminal is better than a class C terminal – they are tuned differently. The class A terminal will perform much better on high bandwidth networks, but the class C terminal will perform better on a modem link. A terminal could even be configured by the user as a class A or B or C device. There may be higher quality requirements defined in the future over high bandwidth networks.

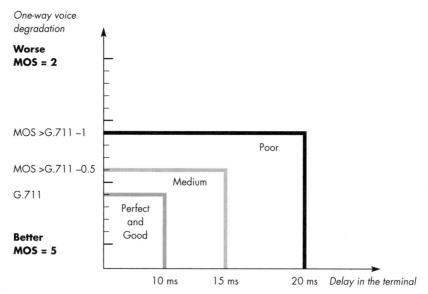

Fig. 4.21 : Class A devices. Boundaries of MOS and delay in the terminal depending on the reference network conditions (perfect, good, medium, poor)

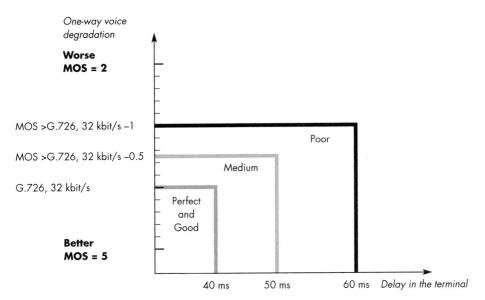

Fig. 4.22 : Class B devices

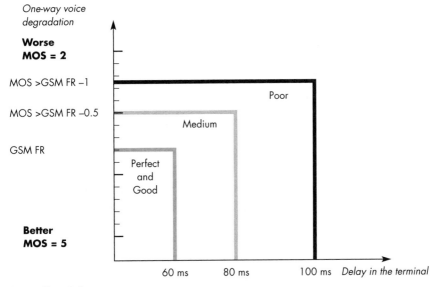

Fig. 4.23 : Class C devices

The characteristics expected from a device of each class depends on its environment. This is why reference network degradation conditions have been created (*see* Table 4.2):

Table 4.2 : Reference network degradation conditions

	Average (Gaussian) packet loss	Peak Gaussian jitter (standard deviation at half the peak)
	%	ms
Perfect	0	0
Good	3	75
Medium	15	125
Poor	25	225

The choice of Gaussian distribution models is debatable, but there is not enough common understanding today of IP loss and jitter to reach an agreement on anything else.

The 'delay in the terminal' is in fact an approximation of the delay budget per terminal (sender delay + receiver delay / 2). It can be measured easily using a network simulator (*see* 'Measurement of delays' below).

Other works

In February 1999 ANSI TIA (*www.tiaonline.org*) started a work on the same topic as ETSI WG5, which will be named 'Performance and interoperability requirements for voice-over-IP telephone terminals' (TR 41.3.4). This project will focus both on H.323 and protocols produced by the IETF MEGACO working group. The result is expected soon. Visit *http://www.tiaonline.org/standards/sfg/tr-41/*.

Measurement of delays

Figure 4.24 illustrates a 'delay indicator'. This is a convenience meant to represent the average one-way delay introduced by an IP telephony equipment, and facilitate the life of IP telephony network planners. This indicator is obtained as follows.

We call:

■ D the duration of the time sequence encoded in a single network packet (i.e. this may contain more than one frame of the underlying codec)

■ P_s the time needed to send the packet on the network link directly connected to the IP phone

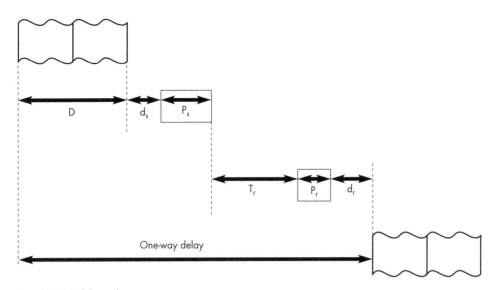

Fig. 4.24 : A delay indicator

- d_s the time elapsed between the end of the sound sequence and the time when the packet begins to be sent on the network (i.e. first bit is sent)
- d_r the time elapsed between the complete reception of the packet and the time when the sound sequence begins to be played on the loudspeaker
- T_r the transmission delay as seen in Fig. 4.24.
- P_r the time needed to receive the packet from the network link directly connected to the IP phone.

If party 1 is calling party 2, the one-way delay is $D+d_{s1}+P_{s1}+T_{r12}+P_{r2}+d_{r2}$ from 1 to 2, and $D+d_{s2}+P_{s2}+T_{r21}+P_{r1}+d_{r1}$ from 2 to 1. In most cases $P_s = P_r$ (but for users of satellite downstream connections this will not be true), but T_{r12} and T_{r21} can vary widely (e.g. in transatlantic connections). In order to separate the delay issue between the network side and the IP phone side, the composite indicator I called IP device delay is defined by $D/2+d_s/2+d_r/2$. Obviously this quantity will vary according to the number of frames stacked in a single packet, the jitter buffer resulting from the network condition, and the codec used. Therefore it has a meaning only within specific network conditions.

I can be measured easily by linking two IP telephony devices end to end over a high-speed network ($P_s = T_r = P_r = 0$), and evaluating the end-to-end speech delay. Therefore it does not require access to any internal reference point inside the IP telephony device. This gives us a good indication of the one-way end-to-end delay experienced by the user of IP phone 1 talking to the user of IP phone 2 by $I_1+I_2+T_r+P_s+P_r$. On a LAN I_1+I_2 is a good enough indication.

Other requirements for gateways and transcoding equipment

Average level, clipping

Even if the end terminals do not respect the average levels expected on a transmission line (microphone sensitivity can be adjusted in most implementations), the gateways and transcoding functions to the PSTN should implement automatic level control to respect ITU recommendation G.223: 'The long-term average level of an active circuit is expected to be –15 dBm0 including silences. The average level during active speaking periods is expected to be –11dBm0.' The methodology for measuring active speech levels can be found in ITU recommendation P.56.

PCM coding is capable of handling a maximum level of +3.14 dBm0 in A-Law (+3.17 dBm0 in μ-Law). The gateways should avoid clipping because it would heavily disturb echo cancellers in the network.

Note: About dB, dBr, dBm0, etc ...

A discussion of units can be found in G.100 Annex A. This is just a summary. Relative power is measured in dB. A signal of P1 mW is at level L dB compared to a signal of P2 mW if:

$$L = 10\log_{10}\left(\frac{P_1}{P_2}\right)$$

For relative voltages, currents or acoustic pressure, the formula uses 20 instead of 10 (power depends on the square of V). dBm refers to a power measurement in dB relative to 1 mW. dBr is used to measure the level of a reference 1020 Hz signal at a point compared to the level of that same reference signal at the reference point (0 dBr point). For instance, if the entrance of an X2 amplifier is the 0 dBr point, the output is a +3 dBr point (*see* Fig. 4.25). Digital parts of the network are at 0 dBr (unless digital gain or loss is introduced). To determine the dBr level at the analogue side of a coder or decoder, G.101 defines a digital reference sequence. When decoding the DRS, if the output of the decoder is an R dBm, then it is an R dBr point.

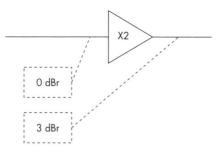

Fig. 4.25 : An X2 amplifier

dBm0 is used to measure the absolute level in dBm that a signal would have when passing through the reference point. For instance, if the power of a signal at the output of the amplifier is 10 dBm, then it is a 7 dBm0 signal.

Other requirements for gateways and transcoding equipment

VAD algorithms are responsible for switching the coder in active speech mode or background noise transmission mode (this can also be the transmit nothing mode). It they are not implemented properly these algorithms may clip parts of the active speech periods, such as the beginning of sentences, first syllables of words, etc. A general guideline for a good VAD algorithm is to keep the duration of clipped segments below 64 ms, and have no more than 0.2 per cent of the active speech clipped. These guidelines will be part of future ITU recommendation G.116. More detailed information is available in *'Subjective effects of variable delay and speech loss in dynamically managed systems'*, Gruber, J. and Strawczynski, L. (1982) IEEE Globecom, Vol 2: F.7.3.1-F.7.3.5.

Voice coding

Introduction

Transmitted bandwidth, sampling and quantization

The analogue to digital conversion is a process to represent an infinite precision signal originally in an analogue form, such as an electrical signal produced by a microphone, by a finite set of numbers at a fixed sample rate. This simple procedure, is mandatory to allow computer-based analysis, bitrate reduction, digital storage and transmission of any speech or sound signal. It has important factors that influence the quality of digitized speech:[2, 21, 22]

■ the rate of sampling

■ the total amount of different representatives (number of bits) used to encode the signal.

The sampling rate is directly related to the frequency bandwidth of the signal that needs to be transmitted or stored and the number of bits affects the correctness of the digital representation of the signal.

The sampling process can be viewed as multiplying an infinite and continuous pulse train of amplitude 1 spaced by the period of sampling and the analogue signal to be sampled. This leads to the well known PAM (pulse amplitude modulation) representation of the signal (Fig. 5.1).

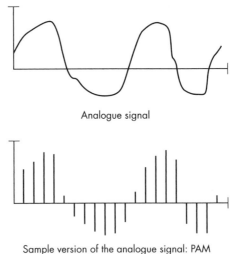

Analogue signal

Sample version of the analogue signal: PAM

Fig. 5.1 : Representing the signal as PAM

The basis of the 'sampling theorem' is that the frequency spectrum of this PAM signal is the copy (with a scaling factor) of the analogue and continuous spectrum repeated and shifted for any multiple of the sampling frequency Fs. This relies on the fact that the multiplication in the time domain extends to a convolution in the frequency domain. Although this new spectrum is 'infinite', it can be stated or, at least in a first step imagined, that the original spectrum can be recovered by low pass filtering this PAM signal – an ideal low-pass filter with a cutting frequency of Fs/2 is necessary. The unique condition to correctly recover the original analogue spectrum is that there is no frequency wrapping in the infinite PAM spectrum. The only way to achieve this is that the bandwidth of the original analogue signal is strictly limited to the band [0 to Fs/2].

Figure 5.2 shows an ideal situation and a frequency wrapping situation; in this latter, the recovered signal is spoiled by the frequency aliasing.

So the sampling frequency must be equal or greater than two times the bandwidth to be transmitted. This is known as the NYQUIST frequency or 'SHANON theorem'. If it is not the case (and, as far as speech and audio signals are concerned in telecommunication or multimedia applications, it is generally not the case), the signal must be frequency-limited by an 'anti-aliasing' analogue filter. Modern oversampled noise-shaping analogue to digital converters (also called sigma delta coders) use a very high sampling frequency but internally they do have digital decimation (sub sampling) filters which perform the same task. The reconstruction filter in the digital to analogue chain plays an important and quite symmetric role.

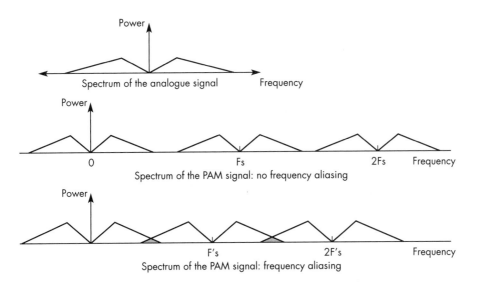

Fig. 5.2 : From ideal to frequency wrapping

The value of the sampling frequency determines the transmitted bandwidth but also impacts greatly the amount of information to be transmitted, especially for wide-band, high-quality, audio signals.

Although we have spoken of analogue to digital converters, we are not yet in the digital world. The PAM signal is essentially an analogue signal which can be displayed on an analogue traditional oscilloscope. Nevertheless, storage, analysis, computation for bitrate reduction and digital transmission need a digital representation of this PAM signal.

It can be figured out that a folding rule can be used to measure the amplitude of the PAM signal. Depending on the graduation or precision of the scale, the number which represents the PAM signal can be more or less precise. This is the basic rule of the quantization process: as the measuring scale gets less precise, the noise power increases.

At this point it must be emphasized that once this quantization noise is introduced in a speech or audio transmission chain, there is no chance to improve the quality; this can be correlated to the frequency band limitation prior to the sampling process. It would be meaningless to encode with 24 bits a speech signal which is intentionally band limited to 300 to 3400 Hz range; the limitation in frequency is much more perceptible (even annoying) than the 'gain' in precision brought by the 24 bits of the ADC chain.

If uniform quantization is applied (note that in Fig. 5.3, a non-linear quantizer is shown), the power of the noise can be easily derived. Uniform means that the

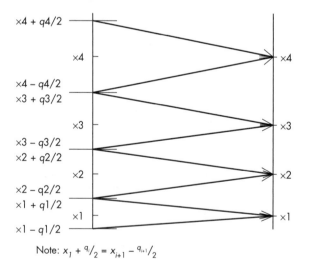

Note: $x_1 + {}^q/_2 = x_{i+1} - {}^{q_{i+1}}/_2$

Quantization process (here non-linear quantizer):

Any value belonging to: $[x_i - {}^q/_2, x_i + {}^q/_2]$

is quantized and converted in: x_i

The noise value spans in: $[- {}^q/_2, + {}^q/_2]$

Fig. 5.3 : A non-linear quantizer

scale of the previous folding rule is linear. All the step sizes of the quantizer have the same value: D. So the error spans between −D/2 and +D/2 and it can be shown that the power of this error is:

$$E^2 = \frac{D^2}{12}$$

More important, for a uniform quantizer using N bits (N is generally a power of 2), the maximum signal to noise ratio achievable (expressed in decibel) is given by:

$$SNR(dB) = 6.02N - 1.73$$

This golden formula should be remembered. For example, a CD player uses a 16-bit linear quantizer and the maximum SNR (signal to noise ratio) is 94.6 dB. This impressive figure should not hide some problems when using uniform quantizers. This maximum value is obtained for a signal having the maximum amplitude, e.g. a sinusoid going from −32768 to +32767. This signal will be tremendous for the loudspeakers, your headphones and your ears. In fact, the SNR is directly proportional to the power of the signal, and the curve representing the SNR against the input power of the signal is a straight line. If the power of the input signal is reduced by 10 dB, the SNR is reduced too. It might be one reason for the old black vinyl audio disk outperforming the CD. For very low power sequences of music, experts can be disturbed by the granularity of the sound reproduced by a CD player.

As previously stated, the sampling frequency and the number of bits impact greatly on the quality of the digitized signal and some compromises are made. Table 5.1 gives an overview of the most common set of parameters for transmitting speech and audio signals.

Table 5.1 : The most common parameters for transmitting speech and audio signals

Type	Transmitted bandwidth	Sampling frequency	Number of bits in AD and DA converters	Bit rate in kbit/s	Main applications
Telephone Speech	300–3400 Hz	8 kHz	12 or 13	96 or 104	PSTN, ISDN networks, digital cellular
Wide Band Speech (and audio)	50–7000 Hz	16 kHz	14 or 15	224 or 240	Video and audio conferencing, FM radio
High Quality Speech and Audio	30–15000 Hz	32 kHz	16	512	Digital sound for analogue TV (NICAM)
	20–20000 Hz	44.1 kHz	16	706	audio CD player
	10–22000 Hz	48 kHz	up to 24	1152	Professional audio

A bitrate around 100 kbit/s is necessary to encode and transmit a telephone conversation as a PAM signal with uniform quantization. So impressive research and works were carried out to reduce this bitrate for many telecommunications applications. Even the well known A- or μ-Law PCM G.711 coding scheme, used worldwide in all the digital switching machines and in many digital transmission systems, can be viewed as a speech coder.

Some basic tools for digital signal processing

We will introduce in a very simple manner some mathematical tools intensively used in digital signal processing and especially in speech and audio coding: the Z transform, digital filters and linear prediction.

The Z transform

In the analogue domain, a linear time invariant system is characterized by its impulse response h(t). If the input of the system is e(t), then the output is obtained by the well known convolution:

$$s(t) = e(t) * h(t) = \int_{-\infty}^{+\infty} e(t - \tau)h(\tau)d\tau$$

Very often, it is more interesting to write this relation in the frequency domain, using the Fourier or the LaPlace transforms. It becomes:

$S(\omega) = E(\omega)H(\omega)$, where S, E and H are the Fourier transform of s, e and h.

$S(p) = E(p)H(p)$, where S, E and H are the LaPlace transform of s, e and h.

The LaPlace transform is well known and used by electrical engineers and the frequency response of the system is obtained by evaluating H(p) for $p = j\omega$.

Modern signal processing and especially speech and audio bitrate reduction use sampled version of signals to be processed. The sampling frequency (see previous paragraph) is directly related to the bandwidth of the signal. In the discrete and sampled domain, we have only a set of e(n) as input of the system and a set of s(n) as output of the system (to be more precise e(nT) and s(nT) with T equal to the period of sampling). It can be shown that the input and output are linked by the following equation, which introduces a sampled version of the impulse response h(n) (h(nT)):

$$s(n) = \sum_{k=-\infty}^{k=+\infty} e(n - k)h(k)$$

This looks like the convolution equation in the analogue and continuous domain.

The previous equation introduces the concept of digital filters which can have a finite impulse response (FIR type, or non-recursive) or an infinite impulse response (IIR type, or recursive); note that if h(n) = 0 for n <= 0, then the system is causal or physically realizable. The equation for a FIR filter is:

$$s(n) = \sum_{k=0}^{k=N} e(n-k)h(k)$$

the h(k) for k=0 to N are constants (generally but they can be adapted) which characterize the system.

The equation for an IIR filter is:

$$s(n) = \sum_{k=0}^{k=N} e(n-k)a(k) - \sum_{k=l}^{k=L} s(n-k)b(k)$$

Here we have introduced the past values of the output (s(n–k)) in the computation and the a(k) and b(k) characterize the system. A powerful mathematical tool is used to manipulate discrete and sampled systems: the Z transform which plays a similar role as the LaPlace transform in the continuous domain. Given a sequence x(n), its Z transform is defined by:

$$X(z) = \sum_{k=-\infty}^{k=+\infty} x(n)z^{-n}$$

The Z transform has many interesting properties shared with the LaPlace transform (linearity, etc.) but shifts and convolution are the most important. If the Z transform of the set {x(n)} is X(Z), then the Z transform of the set (shifted by k) {x(n+k)} is: $z^k X(z)$ or shifted by –k ({x(n–k)}, $z^{-k}X(z)$).

Also, if {w(n)} is the convolution of {x(n)} and {y(n)}:

$$w(n) = \sum_{m=-\infty}^{m=+\infty} x(m)y(n-m) = \sum_{k=-\infty}^{k=+\infty} x(n-k)y(k)$$

then we have the following relation with the Z transform:

$$W(z) = X(Z)Y(Z)$$

Just as for the Fourier and LaPlace transform, a convolution in time is transformed in a simple product in the transformed domain (here the Z domain). As a simple application we compute the Z transform of:

$s(n) = \sum_{k=0}^{k=N} e(n-k)a(k) - \sum_{k=l}^{k=L} s(n-k)b(k)$ which is a time domain equation for an IIR

filter, we obtain: $S(z) = E(Z) \sum_{k=0}^{k=N} z^{-k} a(k) - S(z) \sum_{k=l}^{k=L} z^{-k} b(k)$ or $S(z)$

$(1 + \sum_{k=l}^{k=L} z^{-k} b(k)) = E(Z) \sum_{k=0}^{k=N} z^{-k} a(k).$

This gives the input to output relation:

$$S(z) = E(Z)H(z) \text{ with } H(z) = \frac{\sum\limits_{k=0}^{k=N} z^{-k} a(k)}{\sum\limits_{k=1}^{k=L} z^{-k} b(k)}$$

H(Z) is the Z transform of the IIR filter and its frequency response is obtained by evaluating H(Z) for $z = e^{j2\pi fT}$, with T the period of sampling (note that the frequency response as for all sampled systems is periodic with period equal to the sampling frequency).

In the following sections, some figures will show boxes with input, outputs, adders and multipliers, as shown below:

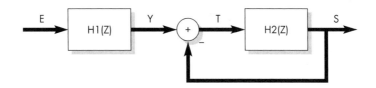

In this figure the sampled signal E is filtered by H1(z) giving signal Y. Then signal T is obtained by subtracting the previous output S (one sample delay) to signal Y. Finally signal S is obtained by filtering signal T by filter H2(z). Many figures of this type will be used to explain speech coding schemes.

Linear prediction for speech coding schemes

Linear prediction is used intensively in speech coding schemes – it uses a linear combination of previous samples to construct a predicted value that tries to approach the new input samples. So:

$s_p(n) = \sum\limits_{k=1}^{k=P} a_k s(n-k)$ gives the predicted value at time n. The coefficients a_k must be chosen to approach the s(n) value. If $s_p(n)$ is quite similar to s(n), then the error signal $e(n) = s(n) - s_p(n)$ can be viewed as a residual signal resembling a white noise. So the issue to transmit the speech information (the waveform) can be translated to the transmission of the set of coefficients a_k (or some coded representations) and some information related to the error signal e(n).

This is a very basic scheme to compress information for transmission purposes and if by chance e(n) is actually a white noise, only its power should be sent. In reality, e(n) is not a white noise and the challenge for speech coder experts is to model correctly this error signal and to transmit it with a minimal number of bits. The a_k coefficients are called linear prediction coefficients (LPC) and p is the order of the model. Methods for computing precisely and efficiently the a_k coefficients will be given later. They are generally computed on a frame basis of 10 to 30 ms during which the speech spectrum can be considered as stationary.

More important for understanding what follows is to highlight the LPC modeling filter which can be considered as a filter which produces a signal with a spectrum resembling the speech spectrum when a white noise is applied to its input. For that, we can use the previous equation, replacing $s_p(n)$ by its computation with the past values:

$$e(n) = s(n) - \sum_{k=1}^{k=P} a_k\, s(n-k) \text{ or in the Z domain: } E(z) = S(z)(1 - \sum_{k=1}^{k=P} a_k\, z(n^{-k})$$

So we have: $S(z) = \dfrac{E(z)}{(1 - \sum\limits_{k=1}^{k=P} a_k\, z^{-k})}$ which gives the 'speech' signal when filtering a

'white' noise signal. The digital filter $H(z) = \dfrac{1}{(1 - \sum\limits_{k=1}^{k=P} a_k\, z^{-k})} = \dfrac{1}{A(z)}$ is called the LPC modeling filter.

It is an all-pole filter (no zero) that models the source (speech) and if we want to obtain the residual signal we need only to filter the speech signal $(s(n))$ by the filter $A(z)$ because we have: $E(z) = S(z)A(z)$. $A(z)$ is often called the LPC analysis filter (giving the residual signal) and $H(z) = \dfrac{1}{A(z)}$ the LPC synthesis filter (giving the speech signal from the residual). These concepts are used intensively in low bitrate speech coder schemes discussed here.

The A or μ law ITU-T 64 kbit/s G.711

All the previous topics on quantizers were for linear ones. An important feature was that the quantization noise is independent of the energy of the signal. This is not always an optimal solution and it can be mathematically demonstrated that if the probability density function (PDF) of the input signal may be known, an optimal quantizer can be derived leading to an optimal SNR for this signal.[21, 22]

Of course, the main issue is to know this PDF for a given signal; for speech and audio signals, this is a very difficult task and the quantizer is generally not linear. Setting some other constraints on the final SNR, mathematics tools can also be used to derive the quantizer with the best characteristics.

Among these constraints, one is peculiarly interesting: could we find a quantizer giving an SNR which is level independent? The basic idea (issued by the digital telecommunications pioneers) was to say that the linear 12 or 13-bit quantizer (*see* Table 5.1) needed to encode correctly speech for telecommunications applications was useful only for very low input levels and that the SNR obtained for high-level input signals were somehow too high or irrelevant for such telecommunication applications. Some mathematics show that a logarithm type quantizer must be used to get a level independent SNR. The continuous logarithmic curve mathematically obtained is not very feasible in practice but an efficient approximation can be used. This can be figured out easily because if we double the step size of the quantizer each time the input level is doubled, we will obtain a constant SNR.

This is the basic idea behind of the international A (Europe and international links) and μ (North America and Japan) ITU-T G.711 PCM recommendation. There are subtle differences between A and μ law. The latter is intrinsically better than the A law but in practice, due to the least significant stolen bit used for signaling purposes, this advantage is somehow zeroed in many circumstances.

The two laws rely on the same approximation of the mathematics logarithmic curve: using straight lines with slope increasing by a factor of two. This will be demonstrated on the international A law.[1]

Starting with a digital linear quantized (generally the AD converters are linear) on 12 bits (sign + amplitude; very often AD outputs are 2's complements which need some bit manipulation before A or μ law encoding), the A law converter will output an 8-bit code (Table 5.2).

Table 5.2 : An 8-bit code

S	E2	E1	E0	M3	M2	M1	M0

With S as the sign bit, E2E1E0 as the exponent value and M3M2M1M0 as the mantissa value, A or μ law encoding can be viewed as a floating-point representation of the speech samples.

Table 5.3 gives the digital procedure to encode. It can be seen that the shaded area corresponds to the quantization noise which is clearly proportional to the input level. The X,Y,Z,T values are the ones coming from the input code that are transmitted directly as M3,M2,M1,M0 (the mantissa). This is a seven-segment A law characteristic (we have eight segments for the straight lines approximating the log curve, but segments 0 and 1 use the same slope). We can also see that this encoding process is easy to build using simple and off-the-shelf logical IC (priority encoder, etc.). The MIPS (millions of instructions per second) figure of A law encoding and decoding is very low and in the early days of digital telecommunications, this was mandatory.

On the receiving side, the 8-bit A law code is expanded into a 13-bit (sign + amplitude) code. In order to minimize the decoded quantization noise, an extra bit is used for the two first segments (see Table 5.4).

Table 5.3 : Digital procedure to encode

Segment number (sign bit omitted)			Amplitude coded with 11 bits (sign + amplitude, sign bit omitted)										
			B10	B9	B8	B7	B6	B5	B4	B3	B2	B1	B0
0	0	0	0	0	0	0	0	0	0	X	Y	Z	T
0	0	1	0	0	0	0	0	0	1	X	Y	Z	T
0	1	0	0	0	0	0	0	1	X	Y	Z	T	N
0	1	1	0	0	0	0	1	X	Y	Z	T	N	N
1	0	0	0	0	0	1	X	Y	Z	T	N	N	N
1	0	1	0	0	1	X	Y	Z	T	N	N	N	N
1	1	0	0	1	X	Y	Z	T	N	N	N	N	N
1	1	1	1	X	Y	Z	T	N	N	N	N	N	N

Table 5.4 : Minimizing decoded quantization noise

Expo-nent	Sign bit	Decoded amplitude using 1/2 quantization step (12 bits)											
		B10	B9	B8	B7	B6	B5	B4	B3	B2	B1	B0	B-1
0	S	0	0	0	0	0	0	0	M3	M2	M1	M0	1
1	S	0	0	0	0	0	0	1	M3	M2	M1	M0	1
2	S	0	0	0	0	0	1	M3	M2	M1	M0	1	0
3	S	0	0	0	0	1	M3	M2	M1	M0	1	0	0
4	S	0	0	0	1	M3	M2	M1	M0	1	0	0	0
5	S	0	0	1	M3	M2	M1	M0	1	0	0	0	0
6	S	0	1	M3	M2	M1	M0	1	0	0	0	0	0
7	S	1	M3	M2	M1	M0	1	0	0	0	0	0	0

Figure 5.4 shows the 'gain' obtained by using the A or µ law encoding process. Clearly, the gain is not in quality but in bitrate by using 8 bits at 8 kHz (8 times 8 equals the famous basic telecommunication bitrate of 64 kbit/s). The only drawback is to reduce the SNR for relatively high-powered input signal but the overall perceived (and subjective) quality is not dramatically impacted (some granular and signal independent noise is introduced). Starting from a clean and high-quality speech sample recorded with 16 bits at 44.1 kHz on a CD or at 48 kHz on a DAT recorder, the most impressive loss of subjective quality lies in the sub sampling process from 44.1 or 48 to 8 kHz on 16 bits; there is an obvious loss of clarity and introduction of extra loudness, especially for female voice. Then going from 16 to 12 bits of quantization introduces some granular noise and finally the A or µ law compression is not the worst in this 'degradation'

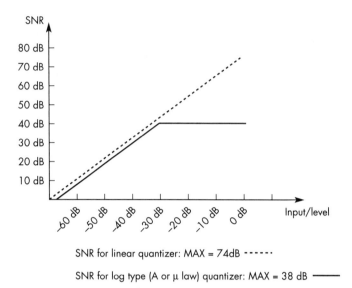

SNR for linear quantizer: MAX = 74dB ‑‑‑‑‑‑

SNR for log type (A or μ law) quantizer: MAX = 38 dB ————

Fig. 5.4 : SNR is reduced for loud signals

chain. Also, the PCM signal is low pass filtered (the conventional transmitted band is 300 Hz to 3400 Hz in Europe and 200 Hz to 3200 Hz in the US and Japan). This band limitation for the low frequencies of the speech signal throws out some essential spectral components of the speech and was initially set for compati-bility with analogue modulation schemes for telephone multiplex. Today, with the ISDN network going directly to the customer's premises, this limitation is not mandatory and somehow out of date (this also applies to the digital cellular mobile phone system).

By nature, the A or μ law compression scheme is a lossy compression. It means that some noise is introduced and the input signal (on 12 bits) cannot be recovered exactly. This is a feature of all the speech coders that will be addressed here and an important task of speech coder designers and telecommunications networks planners is to assess the quality of the coding schemes and to determine acceptable ranges. So, before reviewing the basic tools used to build modern speech coders, we will focus on subjective quality evaluation and specification of speech coders.

Specifications and subjective quality of speech coders

Generally, the aim of a speech coder is to reduce the bitrate while maintaining as much as possible the resulting subjective speech quality. Sometimes, though rarely, it is envisaged that the quality can be enhanced while keeping the original bitrate. This was the case for the speech and audio ITU-T G.722 64 kbit/s wide band [50–7000 Hz].[15] A speech coder must be defined and created by adhering to several settings and requirements. Among these, we can point out the following:

- field of application (PSTN, digital cellular mobile, voice storage system)
- original bandwidth and transmitted bandwidth
- bitrate (fixed, several, switched, embedded or scalability)
- encoding-decoding total delay (including algorithm delay, processing delay and system delay)
- level of speech quality to be achieved (tested in several circumstances)
- capabilities for correctly encoding various music signals
- input level dependencies
- impact of several types and level of background noise (bubble, hall noise, etc.)
- idle noise
- sensibility to errors (bit errors and frame erasure)
- tandems and cascading with other speech coders
- ability to transmit in band signaling tone (e.g. DTMF)
- maximum speed of voice band modems (V.32, V.34, etc.)
- complexity (MIPS, RAM and ROM figures).

Very often, this list is shortened by emphasizing four parameters: bitrate, complexity, delay and quality. Depending on the target application, this shortcut may or may not be relevant. The complexity factor is of course very much impacted by the three other requirements. As an example, Table 5.5 is a summary of the terms of reference set to specify the 8 kbit/s coder (G.729). This new coder was intended to replace the G.726 at 32 kbit/s or the G.728 at 16 kbit/s.

Speech quality assessment

In order to determine the level of quality of a speech coder, objective measurements are not relevant and subjective measurements of speech quality, which require a substantial effort and are time consuming, are indispensable. These tests are well defined and specified in ITU-T recommendations (ITU-T P.800 and P.830).[1, 3] The next part will give a rapid overview of these methods and their outputs. We will focus on listening-opinion tests although others, such as conversation-opinion tests, are possible.

In order to obtain reliable and reproducible results, a number of precise guidelines must be followed:

Table 5.5 : Terms of reference for the 8 kbit/s coder[19]

Items	Parameters	Requirements	Objectives
Quality for speech		Not worse than that of ITU-T G.726 at 32 kbit/s	
Performances in presence of transmission errors (bit error)	Random bit error: BER <= 0.1	Not worse than that of ITU-T G.726 at 32 kbit/s under similar conditions	Equivalent to ITU-T G.728
Performances in presence of frame erasure	Indication of frame erasure (random and burst)	Less than 0.5 MOS when 3% missing frame	As small as possible
Input level dependency	−36 dB, −16 dB	Not worse than that of ITU-T G.726 at 32 kbit/s	As small as possible
Algorithmic delay		<= 16 ms	<= 5 ms
Total codec delay		<= 32 ms	<= 10 ms
Cascading		2 asynchronous coding <= 4 asynchronous ITU-T G.726 at 32 kbit/s	3 asynchronous coding <= 4 asynchronous ITU-T G.726 at 32 kbit/s
Tandem with other ITU-T standard		<= 4 asynchronous ITU-T G.726 at 32 kbit/s	3 asynchronous coding <= 4 asynchronous ITU-T G.726 at 32 kbit/s
Sensibility to background noise	Car noise Bubble noise Multiple speakers	Not worse than that of ITU-T G.726 at 32 kbit/s	

- ensure that the total number of listeners is sufficient in order to have statistically reliable results;
- ensure that the ears of the listeners are 'good enough' (some medical tests may be necessary);
- enstruct the listeners of the methodology of the tests;
- ensure that the speech material is diversified – gender of talkers, pronunciation, age of the talkers (children);

- ensure that the test is performed in several languages by several experimental organizations (it may happen that a language other than English, Japanese, German, Italian, Spanish or French scratches a well standardized speech coder);

- ensure that all conditions of use of the candidate coder are tested (such as level dependencies, sensibility to ambient noise and type of noise, error conditions);

- choose the pertinent listening conditions – equipment (headphones, telephone handsets, loudspeakers), loudness of the samples.

We reiterate that these tests are time-consuming, expensive and need well-trained and experienced organizations, and more than just one if possible.

ACR subjective test or what is the MOS

For low bitrate telephone speech coders (between 4 and 32 kbit/s), the most used subjective measurement method to obtain reliable and reproducible test results is the absolute category rating (ACR) giving the famous but maybe unclear MOS (mean opinion scores) figure. For ACR subjective tests, listeners are asked to rate the 'absolute' quality of speech samples without comparison to a reference. The listening quality is generally assessed and the following scale is commonly used (Table 5.6):

Table 5.6 : Listening quality scale for absolute category rating

Excellent	5
Good	4
Fair	3
Poor	2
Bad	1

This is an absolute judgement without references, but in order to ensure coherency and calibration between successive tests, some anchor is needed. Very often, the modulated noise reference unit (MNRU) is used. This device simulates a noise equivalent to the one produced by the A or µ law PCM coding scheme.

Experiment results are reported by numerical means in the form of MOS. The relevance of MOS must be determined by statistical analysis requiring a lot of experiments – this leads to meaningful confidence intervals. Generally, an ACR subjective test requires an average of 24 listeners (three groups of eight). The simple test consists of a double sentence: 0.5 seconds of silence, 2 seconds for sentence #1, 0.5 seconds of silence, 2 seconds for sentence #2.

Although waveform coders, hybrid or analysis by synthesis coders, linear predictive coders or vocoders have not yet been described, Fig. 5.5 gives an overview of the MOS values for such speech coders against bitrate.[6]

More precisely, Table 5.7 gives the MOS figure and type for well known ITU-T standardized speech coders.

Table 5.7 : MOS figures for different types of coder

Standard	G.711	G.726 or G.721	G.728	G.729	G.723.1
Date of approbation	1972	1990 (1984)	1992	1995	1995
Bitrate in kbit/s	64	16/24/32/40	16	8	6,3–5,3
Type of coder	Waveform: PCM	Waveform: ADPCM	ABS: LD-CELP	ABS: CS-ACELP	ABS: MP-MLQ, CS-ACELP
Speech quality (MOS figure)	4.2	2/3.2/4/ 4.2	4.0	4.0	3.9/3.7

Table 5.8 gives MOS figures for the mobile standards.

Table 5.8 : Mobile standards

Standard	ETSI GSM 06.10	ETSI GSM 06.20	ETSI GSM-EFR	ETSI TETRA	U.S.A. IS54 TDMA	USA IS96 CDMA	JAPAN JDC 1	JAPAN JDC 2
Date of approbation	1988	1994	1995	1994	1989	1992	1990	1994
Bitrate in kbit/s	13	5,6	13	4,56	7,95	8/4/2/1	6,7	3,6
Type of coder	ABS: RPE-LTP	ABS: VSELP	ABS: ACELP	ABS: ACELP	ABS: VSELP	ABS: QUALCOM CELP	ABS: VSELP	ABS: PSI-CELP
Speech quality (MOS figure)	3,6–3,8	3,5–3,7	4	3,3–3,5	3,5–3,7	3,3–3,5	3,4–3,6	3,4–3,6

Table 5.9 gives MOS figures for the US Department of Defense (DOD) standards.

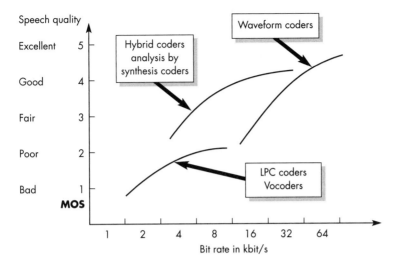

Fig. 5.5 : MOS values against bitrate

Table 5.9 : DOD standards

Standard	American DOD FS1015	American DOD FS1016	American DOD
Date of approbation	1984	1990	1995
Bitrate in kbit/s	2,4	4,8	2,4
Type of coder	Vocoder: LPC 10	ABS: CELP	ABS: MELP
Speech quality (MOS figure)	Synthetic quality	3	3,2

The improvement in speech quality is quite significant from the LPC speech coder[8] in 1984 to the MELP (Mixed Excited Linear Predictive) coder[7] in 1995 for the same bitrate.

Other methods to assess speech quality

ACR is not the only method for speech quality assessments. The degradation category rating (DCR giving DMOS) and the comparison category rating (CCR giving CMOS) are also possible. The DCR is preferred when good quality speech samples are to be compared. The range of degradation is shown in Table 5.10.

Table 5.10 : Degradation category rating

Degradation is inaudible	5
Degradation is audible but not annoying	4
Degradation is slightly annoying	3
Degradation is annoying	2
Degradation is very annoying	1

In DCR, pairs of samples (A–B) or repeated pairs (A–B, A–B) are presented, with A being the quality reference. CCR is similar to DCR, but the order for reference sample and processed sample is random. Thus the second sample may be assessed as better than the first one and it can be peculiarly interesting for speech enhancement systems.

Finally, and as far as VoIP is concerned, conversational tests may be instructive because they are intended to reproduce the real service conditions experienced by final users. Echoes, noises, hang-up and delays can be evaluated in that way. People are asked to speak using the system under test (e.g. DCME or VoIP) and then instructed to follow some scenario or to play some game and finally give their opinion on the communication quality and on other parameters such as clarity, level of noise, perception of echoes, delays, interactivity and so on. Once again, the two participants give a score (1 to 5 as described in ITU-T P.800 recommendation) and statistical methods are implemented to output results in communication MOS (MOS c).

It must be pointed out that these time-consuming tests are difficult to control and consistency and repeatability are hard to obtain. An example of international experiments conducted by ITU-T when selecting an 8 kbit/s candidate is given in Table 5.11.

Table 5.11 : International experiments conducted by ITU-T when selecting an 8 kbit/s candidate

Experiment number #	Description
Experiment 1	Clean speech quality and random bit error performances
Experiment 2	Tandem connection and input level dependency
Experiment 3	Frame erasure: random and burst
Experiment 4	Car noise, bubble noise, multiple speakers and music
Experiment 5	Signaling tones: DTMF, tones, etc.
Experiment 6	Speaker dependency: male, female, children

Final comments on MOS figures

As MOS figures represent a mean value, extreme care must be taken to select or promote a speech coder for a dedicated application. All the candidates' coders must be evaluated in the same conditions (clean speech, level dependency, background noise with several types and level of noise, sensibility to bit errors, frame erasure). International bodies such as ITU-T, TIA, ETSI, JDC are well aware of this. New organizations or companies wishing to market their speech coding schemes quickly are inclined to shorten this long and expensive process.

Speech and auditory properties

Speech production

Speech sounds are characterized by the excitation production and the shape of the vocal tract which consists in the vocal cords, the lips and the nose.[21, 23] The rough frequency spectrum of a speech sound is determined by the shape of the vocal tract and the lips which can modify this spectrum. The vocal tract introduces resonance called formants which carries information.

They are mainly three types of speech sounds: voiced, unvoiced and plosive. Closing and opening the vocal cords periodically produces a voiced speech. The period of this closing and opening procedure fixes the frequency at which the cords vibrate. This frequency is known as the pitch of this voiced speech. The pitch frequency is in the range of 50–400 Hz and is generally lower for male speakers than for female or child speakers. So the spectrum of a voiced speech sample presents periodic peaks on the resonance frequency and its odd harmonics, the formants.

During unvoiced speech such as s, f, sh, the air is forced through a constriction of the vocal cords. Unvoiced speech samples have a noise-like characteristic and consequently their spectrum is flat and almost unpredictable. By contrast, the voiced speech spectrum can be easily modeled by an all-pole filter with five poles or ten real coefficients computed on a frame length of 10–30 ms.

Speech is produced by the varying state of the vocal cords and by the movement of the tongue and the mouth, and all speech sounds cannot be classified as voiced or unvoiced type – there is also the plosive type such as the p in 'puff' and many speech sounds are complex and based on superimposing modes of production.

All this sums up the basic difficulties in correctly modeling the speech production process and encoding speech efficiently at low bitrate. Figures 5.6 to 5.11 illustrate voiced, unvoiced and mixed speech segments and their corresponding frequency spectrum associated with the 10 order LPC modeling filter frequency response.

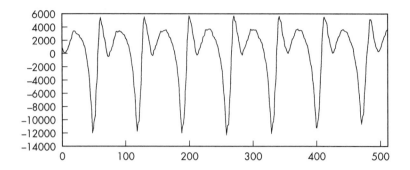

Fig. 5.6 : Time representation of a voiced speech sequence (in samples)

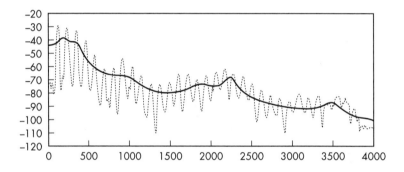

Fig. 5.7 : Frequency spectrum of the voiced speech segment (in dotted line) and the 10 order LPC modeling filter response

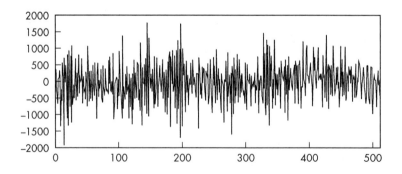

Fig. 5.8 : Time representation of an unvoiced speech sequence (in samples)

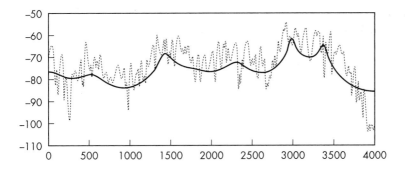

Fig. 5.9 : Frequency spectrum of the unvoiced speech segment (in dotted line) and the 10 order LPC modeling filter response

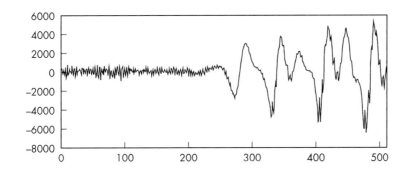

Fig. 5.10 : Time representation of a mixed speech sequence (in samples)

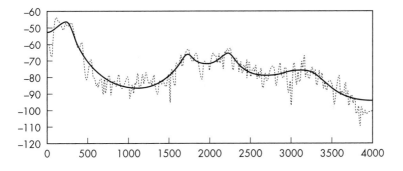

Fig. 5.11 : Frequency spectrum of the mixed speech segment (in dotted line) and the 10 order LPC modeling filter response

So a basic and simple source filter model of speech (Fig. 5.12) can be established and a corresponding source speech coder (also called vocoder, Fig. 5.13) can be built and used.

The DOD 2400 bit/s LPC10[8] speech coder (called LPC 10 because it has 10 LP coefficients) is a vocoder which has the parameters outlined in Table 5.12.

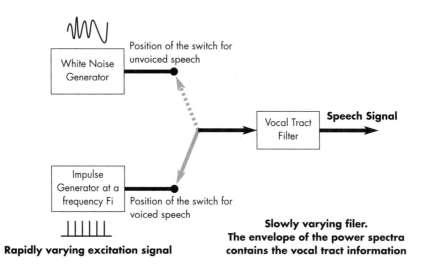

Fig. 5.12 : Source filter model of speech

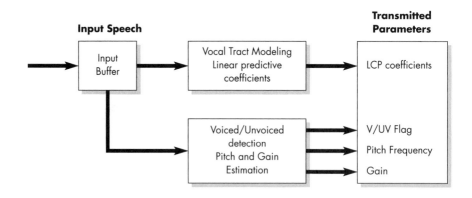

Fig. 5.13 : Basic principle of a source speech coder or Vocoder

Table 5.12 : Vocoder parameters

Sampling frequency	8 kHz
Frame length	180 samples = 22.5 ms
Linear predictive filter	10 coefficients = 42 bits
Pitch and voicing information	7 bits
Gain information	5 bits
Total information	54 bits per frame = 2400 bit/s

The main disadvantage of vocoders, based on this simple voiced/unvoiced speech production model, is that they generally give a near-synthetic speech quality. The reproduced speech is also very 'buzzed'. They are not tailored to toll quality for commercial telephone applications.

Auditory perception used for speech and audio bitrate reduction

The human ear is very complex and auditory perception is based on critical band analysis. There are 24–26 critical bands which are overlapping bandpass filters with increasing bandwidths from 100 Hz for signals below 500 Hz and 5000 Hz for signals at high frequency. All acoustical events are not audible and there is a curve giving the loudness threshold of audible signals depending on the sound pressure level and the frequency of the sound.[4, 9, 14] All signals 'under' this threshold cannot be perceived – the maximum of the human ear sensitivity is between 1000 and 5000 Hz. This means that if an incoming signal is inaudible, there is no sense in wasting bits to encode it. This is one of the basic principles of the perceptual coding scheme applied especially to audio coding (*see* Fig. 5.14). Also, a low-level signal can be inaudible or masked by a stronger signal – there is an area (predictable by mathematics tools) almost centered on the masker signal that makes all the signal inside this area inaudible. This is the simultaneous frequency domain masking phenomenon which is used intensively in perceptual audio coding schemes.

A temporal masking phenomenon including pre and post masking effects can be exploited in perception-based coding schemes. Although these methods are not commonly used in low (4 to 16 kbit/s) speech coders, they are included in all modern audio coders (ISO MPEG-1 Layer I, II, III – known also as MP3 for web uses – MPEG–2 AAC, AC3 or DOLBY-DIGITAL).

These coders rely on a temporal to frequency domain transformation (analysis filter bank) coupled to an auditory system modeling procedure giving a masking threshold that drives a dynamic bit allocation function. Bits are allocated in each band in order to fit the overall bitrate and masking threshold requirements.

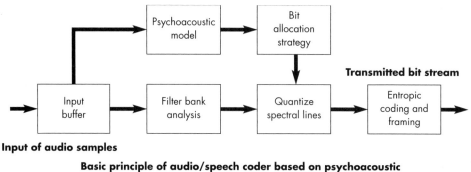

Input of audio samples

**Basic principle of audio/speech coder based on psychoacoustic
and high number of sub bands**

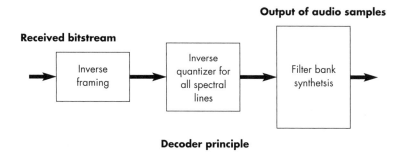

Decoder principle

Fig. 5.14 : Decoder principle

Today, audio signals can be efficiently encoded with the most advanced audio coding scheme (AAC) in 64 kbit/s for one monophonic channel, giving almost CD-like quality.[9, 10, 11, 12]. Wide-band (20 Hz to 7000 Hz) speech and audio coders can use the same scheme to encode in 24 or 32 kbit/s, although there are some issues related to the analysis filter bank (overlap and add procedure in the decoder) which give some annoying pre-echo phenomena. This is due mainly to the non-stationary characteristic of the speech signal and is very perceptible when it appears.

As far as low bitrate speech coders are concerned, auditory properties are found essentially in analysis by synthesis speech (ABS) coders in which some error signal used in the closed loop search procedure is pondered by a perceptual weighting filter derived from the global spectrum of the speech. The function of this perceptual weighting filter is to redistribute the quantizing noise into regions where it will be masked by the signal. This filter significantly improves the sub-jective coding quality, especially for analysis by synthesis coders, by properly shaping the spectrum of the error – the error noise is constrained to stay below the audible threshold when the correlated signal is present. In the ABS decoders, a post filter is often used to reduce noise between the maxima of the spectrum (formants) to improve significantly the perceived quality, especially on the MOS scale. Nevertheless, very efficient post filters can alter the naturalness (fidelity) of the decoded speech.

Quantization and coders

Adaptive quantizers

Linear or logarithmic quantizers are time unvarying systems – their step sizes are fixed. One basic idea related to the concept of adaptive quantizers is that if the probability density function of the input is known, one optimal quantizer can be computed, i.e. to adapt the quantizer (modify temporarily the characteristic) instantaneously or near instantaneously to the statistics of the signal. The rules and types of adaptation may or may not be transmitted. This is the basic principle of forward or backward adaptive quantizers (Fig. 5.15).

Also, the characteristics of the adaptive quantizer can be selected (or computed) by a sample-based procedure or by a block (often called in speech and audio processing a frame of samples) based procedure. Intuitively, it may be figured out that, in the forward adaptive quantizer types, some extra information needs to be transmitted to inform the decoder side of the selected characteristic used at this time. A block adaptation procedure is more efficient in terms of transmitted bitrate. Care must be taken to select the size of the block – if the size is too small, there may be a large overhead for transmitting the scaling information, but if the block size is too large, big disparities can appear on the samples (very low and very high values), leading to large errors in the quantization process. Figure 5.16 shows the principle for the inverse forward adaptive quantizer.

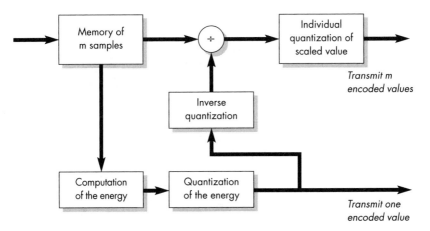

Fig. 5.15 : Principle of a forward adaptive quantizer

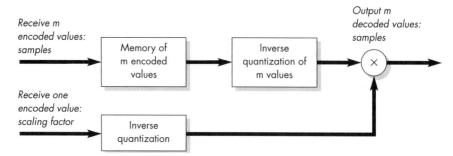

Fig. 5.16 : Principle of a forward adaptive inverse quantizer

To illustrate simply the forward adaptive quantizer concept, the NICAM (near instantaneous companding and multiplexing) system used to transmit the audio stereo signal in a digital way on analogue TV channels (at least on PAL and SECAM TV color systems in Europe) is selected. The NICAM system transmits one stereo audio channel sampled at 32 kHz at a bitrate of 728 kbit/s. The main idea is to memorize a buffer of samples for evaluating the mean power during this period and to normalize the input samples by the estimated mean power (the variance). A buffer of 32 samples is used and a scaling factor coupled with a fixed 10-bit logarithmic quantizer which converts each sample in the buffer. In the transmitted frame, some parity bits are added to the individual codes, scaling factor information and framing information, to protect the compressed audio signal against transmission errors.

It has been shown that, for the same subjective quality, the use of the quasi instantaneous (32 samples) system requires 10.1 bits per sample compared to 11 bits per sample for a classical sample by sample logarithmic quantizer. The use of the block analysis and forward 'adaptive' quantizer spares 1 bit per audio sample. That was the beginning of audio compression and NICAM is now used worldwide (*see* Fig. 5.17).

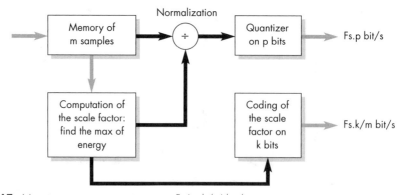

Fig. 5.17 : Near instantaneous quantizer using Fs.(p+k/m) bit/s

In a backward adaptive quantizer, there is no need to transmit any information related to the scaling procedure – the mean power is estimated in the quantizer and in the inverse quantizer in a symmetrical way, as shown in Fig. 5.18 and Fig. 5.19.

A very simple but efficient backward adaptive quantizer called one-word memory is largely used in the ADPCM G.726 and G.727 ITU-T speech coders.[13] A simple coefficient M_i depending only on the previous quantized sample determines the quantization step for the next sample. If the quantizer has 4 bits (one sign bit and eight ranges of quantization), there are 8 M_i fixed coefficients ensuring the compression or expansion of the quantizer. When large values are input to the quantizer, the multiplier value is greater than 1, and for small previous values the multiplier value is less than 1. This tends to force the adaptive quantizer to track the dynamics of the input signal. A fixed quantizer can be used and there is no need to transmit side information to the decoder side (*see* Fig. 5.20 and Fig. 5.21).

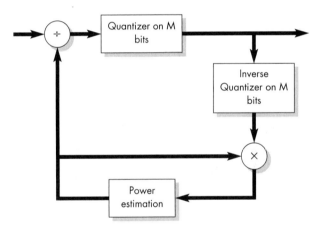

Fig. 5.18 : Principle of a backward adaptive quantizer

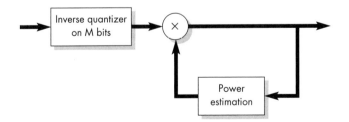

Fig. 5.19 : Principle of a backward adaptive inverse quantizer

Table 5.13 gives the M_i values for a 16-level quantizer optimized for an exponential distribution.

Table 5.13 : M_i values for a 16-level quantizer

MO	0.969
M1	0.974
M2	0.985
M3	1.006
M4	1.042
M5	1.101
M6	1.208
M7	1.449

Differential (and predictive) quantization

In speech and audio signals, some strong correlation exists between the present sample and the previous one and consequently it can be easily imagined that if we subtract the previous sample from the present one, the variance of the difference signal will be lower than the original and will require fewer bits to be

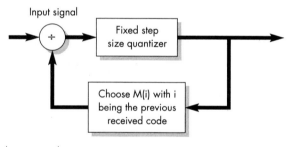

Fig. 5.20 : One-word memory adaptive quantizer

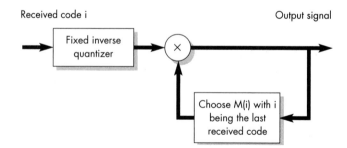

Fig. 5.21 : One-word memory adaptive inverse quantizer

quantized. Unfortunately, we cannot directly use the previous value because the decoder side will be unable to reconstruct correctly the decoded signal. In its place, the locally decoded value must be used. This, in fact, relies on a local decoder which is often used in speech and audio compression schemes.

So: $E(n) = X(n) - X_d(n-1)$, with $X_d(n-1)$ the decoded value at time n–1. We transmit the quantized version of $E(n)$, which is $Q[E(n)]$. At the decoder side, we can compute the decoded value at time n, by: $X_d(n) = X_d(n-1) + Q^{-1}[Q[E(n)]] = X(n) + (Q^{-1}[Q[E(n)]] - E(n))$. So $X_d(n)$ looks like $X(n)$ but with the small difference introduced by the quantization noise: $(Q^{-1}[Q[E(n)]] - E(n))$. If Q is ideal, then the noise is zeroed.

Differential quantization relies on some prediction of the signal to lower the dynamic of the signal to be encoded. Figure 5.22 illustrates the basic principle of a waveform speech or audio coder – all the concepts such as prediction and differential encoding are present.

Linear prediction of signal to be quantized

In the previous scheme, which is, in fact, a non-realistic one due to its overly high sensibility to transmission errors, a more efficient solution is to use the average value (fixed coefficient) of the first correlation coefficient of the input signal. There are two advantages. The first is that the predicted value will be generally a better estimation than when using a coefficient of one. The second addresses the sensitivity to transmission errors. If an error occurs on the transmitted and decoded codeword, the predictive loop in the distant decoder can 'explode' and

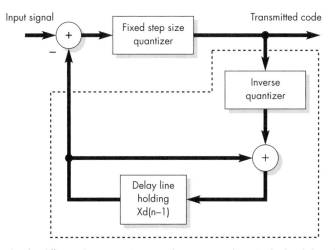

Fig. 5.22 : Principle of a differential quantizer (one-word memory prediction). The local decoder is in the dotted box (identical to the distant decoder)

will become unable to track the original input signal. So the previous equation leading to the difference signal to be encoded: $E(n) = X(n) - X_d(n-1)$ is replaced by: $E(n) = X(n) - C_1*X_d(n-1)$ with C_1 being the first correlation coefficient (C_0 is the variance or the root mean square of the sliding energy of the input signal).

Of course, what was just said about differential quantization and first order prediction cannot be applied if the input signal exhibits a flat frequency spectrum (white noise) because there is then no correlation between adjacent input samples. There is no chance to predict the future sample knowing the previous one. By contrast, speech and audio signals, due to their production mode, exhibit a non-flat spectrum and consequently a relative high correlation exists between samples. Moreover, to reach optimal performances, our average value (fixed coefficient) of the first correlation coefficient of the input signal should be replaced by the real (dynamically computed) value of C_1.

This is the very basic principle of linear prediction used intensively in many speech coding schemes, whatever the type:

- source coder or vocoder
- waveform or temporal coders
- frequency or analysis by synthesis coders.

In waveform or temporal coders working on a sample by sample basis, a temporal prediction of the signal is built around a linear combination of previous (and decoded) samples. The coefficients are not transmitted and computed by a symmetrical procedure in the decoder. For vocoder or ABS speech coders, the input signal is filtered by an inverse modeling (based on correlation coefficients) and this is the residual signal (output of the filter) which is encoded and transmitted with the modeling filter coefficients called linear predictive coefficients. The LPC analysis is performed on a frame of signals from 10–30 ms at a sampling frequency of 8 kHz. This is a period of time during which the speech signal can be considered as stationary.

An adaptive quantizer can be of the forward type (in that it needs to transmit side information) or the backward (looped) type. Linear prediction follows the same classification: backward linear prediction is generally used in ABS speech coders (transmission of the LTP parameters form a frame; though some exception exists, such as in the Low-Delay CELP 16 kbit/s ITU-T G.728).

The following equation gives the value of the predicted signal based on previous samples: $X_p(n) = \sum_{i=1}^{i=N} A_i X(n - i)$ and so in the previous scheme of differential (and predictive) quantizers, the term $X_d(n)$ is replaced by $X_p(n)$.

As indicated in Fig. 5.23, coefficients A_i can be fixed or adaptive, i.e. computed for each new sample. When fixed, they are non-optimal and derived from the average frequency spectrum (if it really exists) of the signal through the correlation coefficients. The computation of the set A_i requires the brut mathematical force[22] of an inversion matrix (solving a set of linear equations). Even for a frame

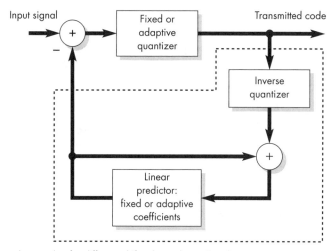

Fig. 5.23 : General principle of a differential (fixed or adaptive) coder

by frame analysis such as in a vocoder or ABS coder, this requires a very high computational task which is beyond the scope of many real-time implementations. For temporal or waveform coders, it is impossible and many theoretical works coupled with algorithmic optimizations have been carried out to simplify this procedure.

For waveform coders, the set A_i, which is generally not transmitted, is continuously adapted (on a sample by sample basis) by the 'stochastic gradient algorithm' (sometimes by the 'sign' algorithm). For frequency or analysis by synthesis speech coding schemes, the set A_i must be quantized and transmitted to the decoder side. In that case, the set of coefficients A_i or similar quantities modeling the short-term (10–30 ms) spectrum of the speech signal have to be computed. The direct inversion matrix relying on the autocorrelation method is not actually used and many powerful mathematical methods and algorithms have been studied and tuned to efficiently compute the LPC coefficients and to quantize them.

Among them, the Levinson-Durbin algorithm and the Schur recursion are the most used iterative methods to compute the A_i (Levinson-Durbin algorithm) or some partial coefficients called parcors (Schur recursion). The parcors coefficients are very interesting to control the stability of the LPC filter – for the time being it is an all-pole digital filter and if one pole is outside the unity circle, the filter can 'explode'. In order to ensure stability, the absolute value of the parcors coefficients must be less than 1. Digital lattice filters can be used to compute the parcors coefficients and the residual signal (output of the inverse LPC modeling filter when the input signal is applied) in one iterative procedure; on the decoder side, a symmetrical lattice filter using the transmitted and decoded parcors coefficients can be used to reconstruct the synthesized signal by feeding it the transmitted (and of course quantized) residual error.

Line spectrum pairs have also been used more recently to represent the coefficients of the LPC filters as they are more efficiently quantized.

Long-term prediction for speech signal

Once a linear predictor (LPC[21]) has been used to filter the speech, the correlation between adjacent samples is quite removed. The LPC filter $\frac{1}{A(z)}$ models the average (short-term) spectrum of the speech and the output of the inverse filter $A(z)$ looks like white noise. But all the fine structure of the speech spectrum is present in this residual signal. Especially for voiced speech, the pitch introduces a long-term correlation. Due to this quasi periodicity, the residual signal exhibits large variation.

One way to remove the correlation into an adjacent period of the residual signal is to use a pitch predictor. The simplest form of this pitch predictor, called LTP filter: (long-term predictor) is: $B(z) = 1 - \beta z^{-M}$, where M is the pitch period and beta a scalar gain. This means that this filter subtracts from the speech the past sample (at a distance equal to M samples) times the beta gain. This procedure reduces the quasi periodic behavior of the residual signal. A more generalized form of this LTP filter is: $B(z) = 1 - \sum_i \beta z^{-M-i}$, called a multi taps LTP filter.

In speech processing and coding, the main issue is to find the parameters of this LTP filter – gain and lag values (beta and M). The most efficient way (although it needs a high computational load) is to compute inter correlations between frames of speech with different lags and to find the maximum of these inter correlation values – this fixes the lag value. Then the gain can be obtained by a normalization procedure (division of the power of the frame by the maximum inter correlation found; LTP gain greater than unity can be found).

This procedure is known as an open loop search procedure as opposed to the closed loop search found in some advanced CELP coders (an adaptive codebook which deals with the long-term prediction). Also very often, since the frame length of speech coders is generally in the range of 160–240 samples and the number of samples between two pitch periods is 20–140, an LTP analysis is carried out on a subframe basis. This is also due to the fact that the pitch lag varies faster than the vocal tract (LPC filter).

Moreover, the pitch lag may not be equal to an entire number of samples leading to the concept of the fractional lags used in the LTP filter. The procedure to find this fractional lag must up-sample the signal to be analyzed. For example, up-sampling by a factor of 8 allows us to find the lag with a precision equal to $\frac{1}{8}$ of the sampling period (generally for speech, 125 µs). This fractional LAG LTP is much more time-consuming but it improves significantly the quality of the decoded speech.

Vector quantization

Vector quantization is one of the most powerful tools used in modern speech and audio coders. Some vectors of samples (or other quantities such as LPC or LSP coefficients) can be formed to be encoded jointly in a single operation. With sample by sample or scalar quantization, each sample is mapped or rounded off to one discrete element of the codebook. In vector quantization, a block of M samples (or other items such as the linear predictive coefficients) forms a vector which is mapped to predetermined points in the M-dimensional space portioned into cells. Figure 5.24 shows the case for a two-dimensional space.

For scalar quantization, a quantization noise is added to each sample to be encoded and decoded; for vector quantization, the noise is concentrated around the selected vector. So generally vector quantization is more efficient than scalar quantization. For example, in vocoders such as the LPC10 type, independent scalar quantization of the 10 LPC coefficients requires about 50 bits per frame (20–30 ms) and vector quantization needs only 25 bits per frame for the same subjective and perceived quality. This is a significant improvement, but the counterpart is that vector quantization is much more CPU time-consuming and the sensitivity to errors is more important than for scalar quantization – an error on one decoded vector impacts all the individual elements of the vector.

There are several types of vector quantization procedures such as binary, gain-shape and split. A detailed description is beyond the scope of this book, but as far

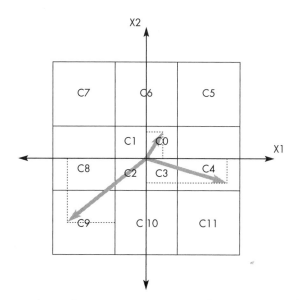

Fig. 5.24 : Two-dimensional space for a vector quantizer. Vectors of components X1 and X2 are localized in cells C0 to C11; the index of the cell is transmitted at the decoder

as speech and audio coding is concerned, the design and optimization of the codebook is of prime importance.

Partitioning the space or finding the best vector representatives needs a very large database on which the codebook is trained and optimized. Distortion measures correlated with human perception and some subjective tests are sometimes required to choose the best codebook.

Entropy coding

This tool is not generic to speech and audio coders. The basic idea is to use a short (minimum number of bits) codeword to represent the more frequently transmitted parameters and a long codeword for the less used. Hufmann codes and RLC (run-length code) are some representatives of such codes. This entropy coding scheme can be placed after a classical speech or audio coder on the bitstream to be transmitted.

Waveform coders: the ADPCM ITU–T G.726

Waveform coders, or temporal speech coders, rely on a time domain and sample by sample approach. They use the correlation between continuous samples of speech and are based on adaptive quantizers and adaptive (generally backward) predictors. They are very efficient in the range of 40–24 kbit/s but the quality becomes degraded around 16 kbit/s.

The most common standardized waveform coder (excepting the PCM A or µ ITU–T G.711[3] which is actually a waveform coder) is the well-known ADPCM ITU–T G.726 speech coder[13] which operates at 16, 24, 32 or 40 kbit/s: (Note: the old ITU–T. G.721 speech coder at 32 kbit/s, which is very heavily used in voice storage systems, is equivalent to G.726 at 32 kbit/s.) ADPCM stands for adaptive differential pulse code modulation, which explains the basic principle of the G.726 speech coder (see Fig. 5.25).

The adaptive quantizer is a one-word memory type (or Jayant type) as described in the basic tools part. The adaptive predictor is a mixed structure with six zeros and two poles. This means that it works on the reconstructed signal with a two-coefficient adaptive filter (the poles) and on the decoded difference signal with a six-coefficient adaptive filter (the zeros).

The basic scheme (Fig. 5.25) does not include some useful features such as a dynamic switch for selecting optimal strategies when a voice band modem signal is detected in order to allow the ADPCM coder to 'pass' the modem signal. This is one of the major drawbacks of coding schemes, reducing the bitrate and more or less relying on the speech characteristics (production model). Voice band modem signals are completely synthetic signals that do not fit the prediction

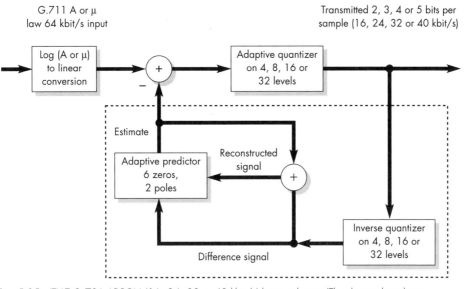

G.711 A or μ
law 64 kbit/s input

Transmitted 2, 3, 4 or 5 bits per
sample (16, 24, 32 or 40 kbit/s)

Fig. 5.25 : ITU-T G.726 ADPCM (16, 24, 32 or 40 kbit/s) basic scheme. (The distant decoder is equivalent to the local decoder inside the dotted box)

and adaptation procedures tailored for speech signal. The dynamic switch allows the speed of voice band modem transmitted by G.726 at 32 kbit/s to be boosted to 9600 bit/s. At 40 kbit/s, modem speeds up to 14 400 bit/s are possible.

The G.726 and its derivative was the first (G.721 was introduced in 1984) bit-rate reduction scheme for speech applications in GSTN or PSTN (as far as the civil telecommunications and standardization bodies are concerned, excluding the military area). Whatever improvements there are in modern speech coders, the G.726 is the most used for terrestrial and submarines cables. It is used in the DCME equipment (digital circuits multiplication equipment) which combines speech interpolation and ADPCM speech coders.

Speech interpolation relies on the statistical aspect found in the speech activity on a relatively large number of affluent speech links. In a conventional conversation, each speaker is active less than 50 per cent of the time on one side of the transmission link; then the freed bandwidth can be used to transmit another voice channel. Using DSI (digital subscriber signaling) and ADPCM (G.726 ADPCM at 32 kbit/s), DCME can achieve a compression gain of 4–5. G.726 speech quality is very good (not for 24 and 16 kbit/s), as indicated in Fig. 5.26.

One interesting feature of the ADPCM coder is its relative insensitivity to bit errors compared to that of the PCM. As shown in Fig. 5.27, there is a net difference for a BER (bit error rate) of 10E–3 in favor of the ADPCM coder. There are two main reasons for this. The first is that PCM 8 bit log A or μ code is very sensitive to an error on the sign bit. The second is that the ADPCM structure acts as a 'mixer' for the state variables of the algorithm and consequently it becomes more robust.

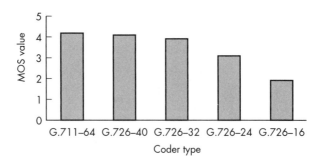

Fig. 5.26 : G.726 speech quality

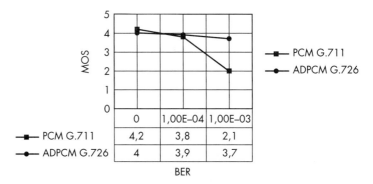

Fig. 5.27: Net difference for a BER in favor of the ADPCM coder

Although ADPCM coders are not based on a frame by frame analysis and speech coding procedure, in some circumstances (such as voice over IP), ADPCM codes may be transmitted in a packet form. One packet assembles several codes, each corresponding to one unique sample. In case of packet loss or frame error, the situation with PCM or ADPCM can be disastrous compared to hybrid or ABS speech coders, which can rely on the last valid received parameters (such as LPC and LTP coefficients) to rebuild an approximation of the complete form of the signal for the lost frame. For ADPCM, the distant decoder is constantly synchronized to the local decoder. If there is a significant loss of codewords, then the distant decoder loses it synchronization.

Detailed description and digital test sequences

The G.726 (in fact the G.721) was the first speech coder including a detailed description and an exhaustive set of digital test vectors. This is required to ensure interoperability between pieces of equipment built by different manufacturers. This constraint is necessary even for modern speech coder designs for cellular digital mobile systems or multimedia applications. Fixed-point implementation is also a strong request for economic design in DSP (digital signal processor) or dedicated VLSI (very large scale integration). So the ITU–T recommendation determines all the formats (fixed points) of the variables, constants, state variables and tables used in the algorithm. Also, it determines precisely all the arithmetical and logical operations such as addition, subtraction, fixed-point multiplication and control of possible saturation (that may happen frequently in fixed-point arithmetic).

This was not a C reference program but a huge documentation that designers had to follow to adhere to the recommendation. To help them and to ensure that the implementation did conform to the recommendation, a set of test vectors was designed and is included of part of the recommendation.

The designers have to understand the documentation and to translate it into assembly language for a DSP or gates, registers and flip flop for a VLSI. Then the verification test (trying to pass all the digital test sequences) finalizes the design, which can operate with another.

The well known and intensively used 'Basic Operations' were introduced for the first time by ETSI for the GSM RPE-LTP Full Rate13 kbit/s speech coder for the first European (and nowadays worldwide) standard for the digital cellular mobile system. When these were introduced, the ANSI C code was not provided as part of the standard, but a 'pseudo' C code was given. Today, an ANSI C reference code relying on the use of Basic Operations (fixed point) is the main part (and the basis) of the recommendation of many speech coders such as ITU-T G.723.1 or G.729.

Floating-point versions of some algorithms are often required for use in PCs and workstations (some sort of native signal processing may be useful for efficient implementation) for multimedia applications such as video conference, audio conference or voice over IP.

There are several big issues with floating-point implementation. The first is to ensure interoperability between a fixed-point implementation (if it exists) and a floating-point implementation – an example is a VoIP gateway using fixed-point DSPs and a client PC software using native floating-point arithmetic for efficiency. The second, more paradoxical, issue is to ensure interoperability between different floating-point implementations.

This is due to the internal representation of floating-point values in the floating-point processor used to realize the implementation of the speech coder. Generally, processors (Pentium, Power PC, Sparc) as well as some floating-point DSPs (AD SHARC, TI C67xx) conform to the IEEE floating-point standard (32 bits for single float or 64 bits for long double float) but other processors do not (AT&T 32C, TI C3x and C4x). Some processors use a floating-point format which does not use 32 bits (24 bits for example). To cope with these issues, some test vectors must be designed with companion software tools to assess the level of confidence for the tested implementation. Some segmental signal to noise ratio (or weighted SNR) can be used for this.

Due to the symmetrical form of the ADPCM encoder and decoder (they differ only in their quantizer procedures), there is no significant difference in CPU load and MIPS on either side – the G.726 encoder and decoder are around five (16-bit fixed point) DSP MIPS. This is not the case for hybrid or ABS coders, which exhibit a strong difference of complexity between the encoder (generally much more complex) and the decoder.

Embedded version of the G.726 ADPCM coder

Although many things should be said about scalability and hierarchical speech and audio coders, there is one interesting feature found in the ADPCM structure that confers the 'embedded' characteristic on this speech coder. The interpretation of 'embedded' here means that it will be possible to steal some bits from the transmitted codewords without breaking the distant decoder – the only consequence is to introduce a 'graceful' degradation in the decoded speech.

This feature is very useful in applications such as DCME or PCME (packet circuit multiplication equipment) when there is an overloaded situation (too many active channels present at the same time), or for 'in band' signaling or 'in band' data transmission.

The concept used in the embedded version of the G.726 (the ITU-T. G.727 recommendation[1]) is to have a core quantizer and an enhanced one with more bits which is a superset of the core quantizer. This means that the quantizer steps of the core quantizer are subdivided into more precise steps to form the enhanced ones. In order to ensure that the distant decoder tracks the local decoder correctly, and because this distant decoder may receive depleted codewords, the inner prediction loop relies on the inverse core version of the quantizer.

On the encoder side, the difference signal is encoded with the maximum number of steps of the enhanced quantizer, but the bits in excess in the enhanced version are masked before feeding an inverse core (adaptive) quantizer. On the decoder side, the received codeword is systematically masked to feed the core inverse adaptive quantizer used in the prediction and reconstruction inner loop. The entire received codeword enters the enhanced adaptive quantizer and then its output is used, along with the estimated signal coming from the inner loop, to build the enhanced reconstructed signal and final output.

If there is no robbed bit, the output is always enhanced but less precise than if the enhanced version of the quantizer was used in the inner loop of the encoder and decoder – that is the drawback or the price to be paid for the 'embedded' feature. Nevertheless, the system, without alerting the decoder, can rob some bits and even if it permanently robs all the enhanced minus core bits, the final quality will be that of the core ADPCM version. Fig. 5.28 and Fig. 5.29 illustrate this concept.

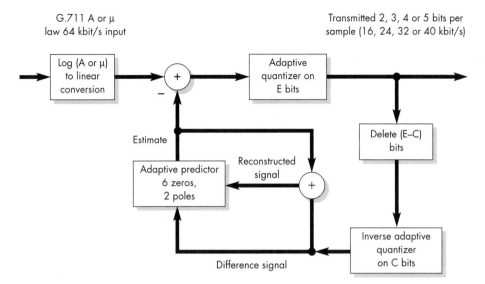

Fig. 5.28 : ITU-T G.727 embedded ADPCM (16, 24, 32 or 40 kbit/s) basic scheme. G.727 is characterized by the enhanced and core pairs (E, C) values for quantizers. C can have 2, 3 or 4 as its value and E2, 3, 4 or 5

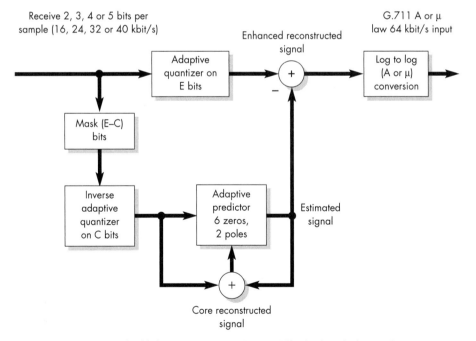

Fig. 5.29 : ITU-T G.727 embedded ADPCM (16, 24, 32 or 40 kbit/s) decoder basic scheme

Wideband speech coding using waveform-type coder

There were strong requirements to offer a better speech and audio quality for video-conference and audio-conference systems[4],[14] and when addressing speech and audio bitrate reduction technologies, two main objectives can be selected. The first is obviously to reduce the bitrate while maintaining the speech quality as much as possible. The second is to increase the quality while keeping the same bitrate. The latter was selected to design a coder with better quality for video-conference and audio-conference systems. As the scientists and engineers were well aware of the possibilities of waveform ADPCM speech coders to reduce the bitrate by a factor near 0.5, they naturally tried to use these techniques for the wide band speech coding issues – wide band means a transmitted frequency band equal to 50 Hz up to 7000 Hz compared to the telephone bandwidth (300–3400 Hz).

The basic idea is to split the band to be transmitted into two subbands: a lower subband spanning from 0 to 4000 Hz and a higher subband spanning from 4000 to 8000 Hz. Then, after a sub sampling procedure reducing the sampling frequency from the original 16 kHz down to 8 kHz, two 'classical' ADPCM encoders can be applied to reduce the bitrate.

The analysis synthesis procedure uses a pair of quadratic mirror filters; under certain constraints on the coefficients, the QMF filter can achieve a perfect analysis synthesis chain. QMF filters are the precursors of the filter bank theory – these filter banks (with a number of bands from 32 up to 1024) are used intensively in audio bitrate reduction (ISO-MPEG, AAC, Dolby Digital)[14]. The wide band ITU-T G.722 speech and audio coder can also be viewed as a precursor of the modern psychoacoustic audio coder because splitting the original band into two subbands and allocating more bits in the lower subband is directly related to efficiency of the prediction and to noise quantization masking. The energy of speech signals is more concentrated in the lower subband and allocating more bits in this subband provides the means to increase the quality of the decoded speech. The quantization noise will be masked in each subband. Moreover, using one separate predictor in each subband allows a better efficiency in prediction for each subband.

So G.722 allows the transmission of a wide band signal at 64 kit/s (the basic PCM bit rate) by using QMF filters and two ADPCM encoders with a structure borrowed from G.726. In the lower subband, 6 bits are used for the adaptive quantizer with an embedded characteristic; the core quantizer uses 4 bits and the enhanced one uses 6 bits.

This scheme is similar to the one found in the embedded version G.727. This allows the system to rob some bits for signaling purposes (framing with H.221) and to transmit some ancillary data. The decoder should be notified of the mode of operation (64, 56 or 48 kbit/s), although some realizations do not signal the mode of operation (64, 56 or 48 kbits) and use permanently the 6-bit enhanced inverse quantizer to build the reconstructed signal to be fed to the synthesis QMF filters.

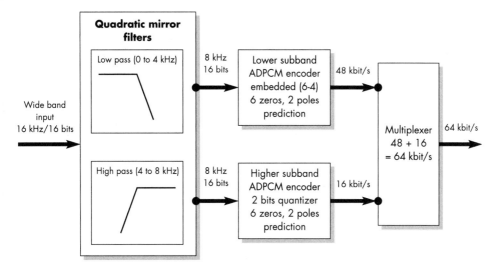

Fig. 5.30 : ITU-T G.722 wide band encoder, subband ADPCM with QMF filter. 48 kbit/s embedded ADPCM in lower subband, 16 kbit/s ADPCM in higher subband

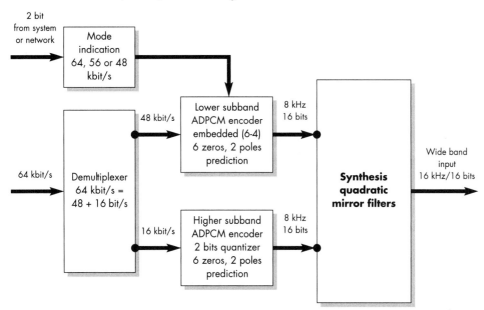

Fig. 5.31 : ITU-T G.722 wide band decoder subband ADPCNI with QMF filter. 48 kbit/s embedded ADPCM in lower subband, 16 kbit/s ADPCM in higher subband

In the higher subband, a 2-bit adaptive quantizer (non-embedded) is used, giving a 16 kbit/s bitrate for encoding compared to the 48 kbit/s for the lower (and more perceptually important) subband. The basic coding scheme of G.722 is shown in Fig. 5.30.

The decoding principle of G.722 is shown in Fig. 5.31.

The ITU-T G.722 wide band speech coder is used largely in teleconference systems adhering to the H.320 recommendation. The quality is quite good for speech and music at 64 and 56 kbit/s (MOS of 4.3 and 4 compared to an original with the same bandwidth rated at 4.3). As there is no specific production model (e.g. for speech) in that waveform coder, samples of music are quite well encoded, although another bit allocation in the two subbands such as 5 in the lower and 3 in the higher has shown better performance on many music samples.

As the main applications were for teleconference systems, preference was given to the fixed bit allocation strategy that favors speech quality. When used at 48 kbit/s, the reproduced speech becomes more noisy (due to the 4-bit quantizer in the lower subband).

The G.722, like other waveform ADPCM coder types, is relatively insensitive to bit errors, and is more robust than the direct PCM stream. One major advantage compared to new audio coding schemes is the low delay characteristic of the G.722. All the waveform coder types such as ADPCM and PCM have very low delay ranging from three to four samples (300 to 500 μs with a 8 kHz sampling frequency). In the case of the G.722, the QMF analysis and synthesis filters add a delay around 3 ms – a very good figure to ensure good interactivity in teleconference systems.

Studies and prototypes of new coding schemes have shown the possibility of encoding a wide band signal in a net bitrate of 24 kbit/s. This will be a future ITU-T recommendation to replace the old G.722. Two main competitive approaches are imminent. One is based on the 'psychoacoustical high number of subbands' audio coder type, while the second relies on a CELP approach. The first gives better performances for music and the second is advantaged for speech signals.

Speech coding techniques

Hybrids and analysis by synthesis speech coders

Waveform coders are essentially based on the inter-sample correlation between samples which is removed by linear prediction. A differential coding scheme is used with adaptive quantizers giving good performances between 32 and 24 kbit/s. A linear predictive coder or vocoder uses a simple model of the speech production (voiced or unvoiced) and a slowly variable filter (updated on a 20–30 ms frame basis) is used to shape the spectrum of the decoded speech. They are used for very low bitrate speech coders (1200–2400 bit/s) but the speech is synthetic.

Hybrids and analysis by synthesis coders try to pick the best of the two approaches for building efficient coding schemes in the range from 16 to 6 kbit/s. They will use a frame of samples to compute the LPC filter coefficients that model the vocal tract and a long-term predictive filter to remove the 'pitch' correlation. The LPC and LTP coefficients are encoded (vector quantization is often used) and transmitted. Hybrids and Analysis by synthesis (ABS) speech coders avoid the need as in LPC of coders or vocoders to classify the analyzed frame of samples as voiced or unvoiced type. In LPC coders, a flag indicating whether a voiced or unvoiced frame of signals is present is transmitted to the receiving side, but one of the big issues is to decide the type (voiced or unvoiced speech) of the current frame of speech.

With hybrids or ABS speech coders, there is (generally) no need to decide this type. Hybrid coders use several techniques to encode the residual signal (after passing the input signal through the inverse LPC filter and in some cases the LTP filter – *see* Fig. 5.32).

In residual excited linear predictive (RELP) speech coders, the residual signal is low pass filtered and the resulting signal is classically encoded in a PCM form. RELP coders give good results around 10 kbit/s by transmitting the LPC coefficients and the encoded residual signal. Nevertheless, they do not remove the pitch contribution because they do not apply a dedicated long-term predictive filter.

ABS speech coders cannot be strictly classified as waveform coders, but in reality the looped minimization procedure tends to produce output waveforms that try to follow the original waveforms. The ABS principle is shown in Fig. 5.33.

ABS speech coders try to select the best vector representative in the excitation generator. This best vector, searched by a looped error minimization procedure on the perceptual error between the original speech and the synthesized one, is the one which resembles the residual signal as much as possible. So ABS coders

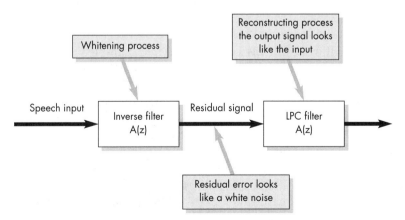

Fig. 5.32 : Encoding the residual signal with a hybrid coder

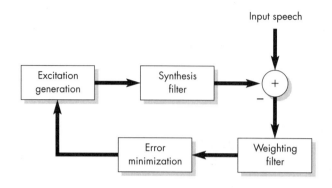

Fig. 5.33 : ABS encoder principle

can be considered as hybrid waveform speech coders. The synthesis filter is a cascade of the inverse LPC filter and inverse LTP filter. The ABS decoder is very simple, as shown in Fig. 5.34.

The GSM Full Rate RPE-LTP speech coder

The most well known and most used ABS speech coder is probably the GSM Full Rate RPE-LTP 13 kbit/s, standardized by ETSI in 1988 for the cellular digital mobile system.[6] This coding scheme uses a regular pulse excitation (RPE) with a long-term prediction (LTP). The choice of RPE for encoding the residual signal allows a low-complexity implementation compared to some multi pulse searches.

In the GSM FR, the signal is first buffered into a frame of 20 ms (160 samples). Then a classical LPC analysis finds the eight parcors coefficients that model the vocal tract. These coefficients are encoded and transmitted in the bitstream. The entire input buffer is inverse filtered by the inverse LPC filter and the next steps of the process will work on this 160 residual (LPC) sample. The process is subdivided into four subframes of 40 samples. In each, an LTP gain and delay will be searched (the pitch, which is between 75 Hz and 400 Hz depending on the age and gender of the speaker, varies more rapidly than the vocal tract).

The LTP lag and gain are encoded and transmitted for each subframe. The LTP contribution is subtracted from the residual signal for a subframe of 40 samples. This difference signal is encoded using the RPE procedure which in fact splits the original 40 samples of the difference signal into four subseries of values (the first one starts with index 0, then 3 up to 36; the second starts with index 1, then 4 up to 37; the third starts with index 2, then 5 up to 38; and the last starts with index 3, then 6 up to 39, the last index of the subframe).

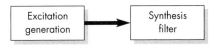

Fig. 5.34 : ABS decoder principle

This leads to a 'strange' subsampled process of one third (hard low pass filter with a frequency cutting around 1300 Hz) which in fact privileges male voice over female or child's voice. The subsequence that best approaches the original 40 residual samples is chosen – two bits per subframe are needed to signal it. Then the maximum energy of the samples in the selected subsequence is found and encoded with 6 bits. All the samples of the subsequence are normalized by this quantized and inverse quantized energy and all the normalized samples are scalar quantized with 3 bits. The bit allocation for one frame of the GSM RPE-LTP speech coder is given in Table 5.14.

Table 5.14 : Bit allocation for one frame of the GSM RPE-LTP speech coder

RPE-LTP frame length = 160 samples = 20 ms	
Vocal tract: LPC coefficients; 8 parcors = 36 bits	36
Subframe length = 40 samples = 5 ms (4 subframes)	
Grid selection = 2 bits	8
Maximum of energy of selected series = 6 bits	24
Scalar quantization of 13 samples = 13*3 = 39 bits	156
LTP lag = 7 bits	28
LTP gain = 2 bits	8
Total	260
Bit rate = 260/20 ms = 13 kbit/s	

Although the RPE-LTP yields a speech quality slightly lower than standard telephony, it is well suited for mobile communications systems because it is extremely resistant to transmission errors. The MOS figure of the RPE-LTP is around 3.8 compared to the 4.2 of the G.711 PCM A or μ law. The GSM RPE-LTP encoder principle is shown in Fig. 5.35 and the decoder in Fig. 5.36.

The ETSI 06–10 GSM RPE-LTP recommendation includes a detailed description in fixed point relying on the use of the Basic Operations. Digital test sequences are also given to check conformity to the standard. Although some floating versions of this standard exist and are used in some VoIP software, issues may arise in interoperability with the genuine fixed-point version.

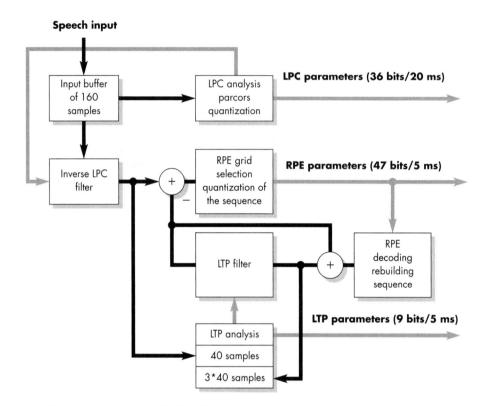

Fig. 5.35 : Basic principle of the RPE-LTP Full Rate (13 kbit/s) GSM speech coder

As the GSM RPE-LTP standard is aimed primarily at mobile applications a VAD (voice activity detection) DTX (discontinuous transmission) and CNG (comfort noise generation) was designed to save power in the terminal. The VAD detects if valid speech is present and if not, some parameters containing the noise information are transmitted less frequently. These parameters are based on the LPC parameters and on the energy of the noise. They are packed in a SID (silence description) frame which is sent every 80 ms (four frames compared to the 20 ms speech frame). The design of a good and efficient VAD is almost as complex as the design of good speech coders.

Code excited linear predictive (CELP) coders

CELP coders are in essence linear predictive coders equipped with an ABS search procedure. The main issue with linear predictive coders, after removing the short-term correlation with the LPC filter and the long-term correlation (or pitch

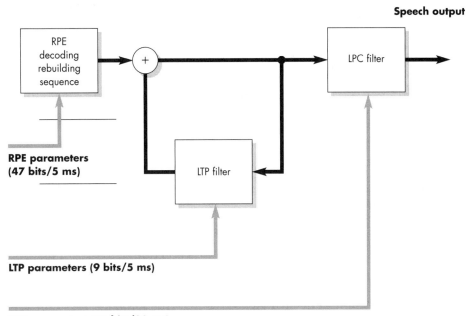

Speech output

Fig. 5.36 : Basic principle of the RPE-LTP Full Rate (13 kbit/s) GSM speech decoder

contribution), is to efficiently model the excitation signal. The RELP is the less complex but perhaps the more efficient one (as far as the bitrate is concerned).

The multi pulse solution tries to model the excitation with pulses – positions and amplitudes of these pulses are searched with an ABS algorithm. First the main pulse position is searched, then the second, and so on. The bitstream must encode the position and amplitude of each pulse modeling the excitation. The regular pulse solution used in the GSM FR is an elegant and efficient derivation.

In CELP coders, a codebook based on vector quantization is built (trained and optimized on a large 'speech' database) and its vectors are used as a generator for the LTP and LPC synthesis filters. The excitation signal (index in the codebook and gain) that best approximates the input signal is selected according to a perceptual error criterion. In that sense, CELP coders are somehow (as previously pointed out) waveform coders because they try to 'track' the temporal waveform of the input signal.

The role of the perceptual filter is to redistribute the quantization noise in a frequency range where it will be less audible due to the higher energy of the signal: the noise will be masked by the signal itself. Significant improvement of the subjective quality is observed when using this perceptual weighting filter.[3] The filter $W(z) = \frac{A(z)}{A(z/\gamma)}$ with a bandwidth expansion coefficient γ less than 1 forces

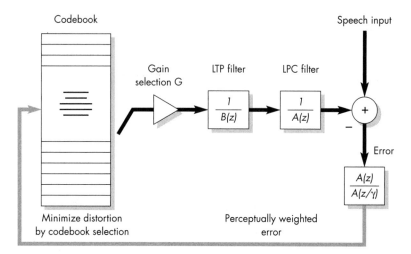

Fig. 5.37 : Basic concept of a CELP coding algorithm. The quantized LTP and LPC parameters are transmitted on a frame basis. The quantized gain G and the codebook index are transmitted (sometimes on a subframe basis)

the noise to be reinforced in the neighborhood of the formants and to be low-ered in the region where the signal is weak. Although the noise power is generally increased, listeners usually prefer this situation.

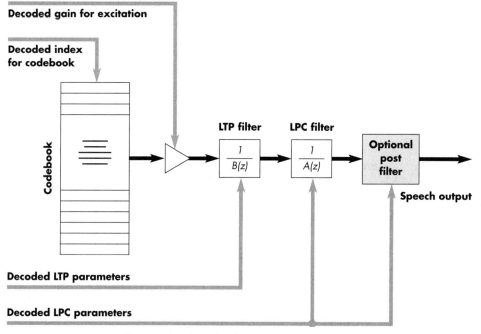

Fig. 5.38 : Basic concept of a CELP decoding algorithm

One big issue with the CELP coders type is the induced complexity to find the best index and associated gain in the codebook. For a long time, this has been a barrier to practical implementation in real time. Algorithmic simplification brought to the basic structure (efficient codebooks search or algebraic codebooks) and the growth of MIPS in modern DSP have simplified the situation. The basic scheme of the CELP coder is shown in Fig. 5.37.

The LPC coefficients are first computed and quantized for an entire frame of speech. Vector quantization and line spectrum pairs are used more and more due to their efficiencies. The LTP lags and gains are searched and quantized on a sub-frame basis as well as the codebook index and associated gain G_i.

The decoder is much less complex than the encoder (no ABS search procedure) and can include an optional post filter, as shown in Fig. 5.38.

In order to improve the perceived quality, the post filter is aimed at reducing noise between the maxima of the spectrum (located near the harmonics). This applies to the concept of the short-term (the most common) post filter which is derived from the LPC coefficients in a similar way as the perceptual weighting filter in the encoder. Modern post filters can include a long-term prediction post filter and a tilt compensation post filter. The introduction of the post filter can significantly increase the MOS rating of CELP decoders using it. Nevertheless, although the post filter removes some quantization and coding noise, it may affect the 'fidelity' of the decoded speech if its action is too important.

The previous explanation on the basic schemes for the CELP encoder relies on an open loop search for the long-term contribution. A more advanced implementation is based on the closed loop search in two codebooks:

- the adaptive codebook which is devoted to the long-term prediction
- the innovation which deals with the components in the residual signal that are not predictable; this is also called a stochastic codebook.

The closed loop search is now based on the joint selection of four parameters:

- an index in the stochastic codebook
- a gain for the index in the stochastic codebook
- a lag (integer or fractional) in the adaptive codebook
- a gain for the adaptive lag found.

To avoid a too CPU-time-expensive search, an open loop search for a raw LTP lag is first conducted. Then, in the closed loop search, the different LTP lags are tested and selected in the neighborhood of this initial and raw lag. So the contribution to the LPC synthesis filter is modified, as shown in Fig. 5.39.

Equipped with this advanced concept coding scheme (ABS with stochastic and adaptive codebooks and LSP vector quantization), CELP speech coders excel in the range from 4.8 to 16 kbit/s. Many of the international standards in that range

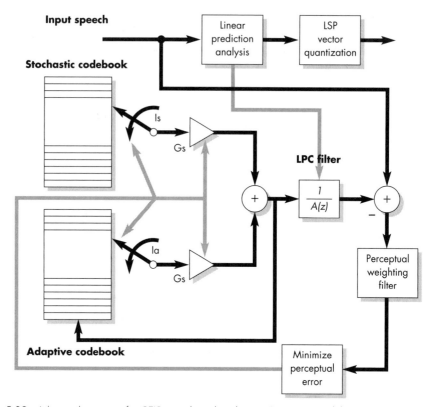

Fig. 5.39 : Advanced concept of a CELP encoding algorithm. Is, Gs, Ia, Ga and the LPC (LSP) parameters are transmitted

of bitrates are CELP or derivative CELP speech coders. This is the case for the Federal Standard 1016 4800 bit/s CELP voice coder,[17] the ITU-T 8 kbit/s G.729 CS-ACELP, the dual rate multimedia ITU-T G.723.1 (5.3 and 6.3 kbit/s, ACELP, MP-MLQ), the Enhanced Full Rate GSM ETSI speech coder, and the Half Rate GSM speech coder.

This is, of course, a non-exhaustive list and the Low Delay CELP ITU-T G.728 16 kbit/s plays a particular and important role in this class of CELP coders due to the fact that, in order to fulfill the stringent requirement of low delay, a long LPC backward adaptive filter is used in place of the LPC and LTP classical filters – no LPC coefficients are transmitted to the decoder side and only the index vector and associated gain is transmitted. We will look at this scheme later.

One of the most difficult tasks is to design the stochastic codebook which contains samples closely resembling noise. In the case of the adaptive codebook, the chosen values must be selected during the ABS-MSE (mean squared error) procedure. For the stochastic codebook, there are two main design concepts. The first is to build the codebook before the execution phase of the encoder by using training and optimization on a large speech database. The second, used for example in ACELP or MP-MLQ (multipulse maximum likelihood quantization), is to build the vector samples during the ABS-MSE procedure (selecting the pulse location and associated gain).

Each method, in this second class, has its advantages and drawbacks, but one important criterion is to reduce the complexity for finding the best combination of pulse location and associated gain. Overlapping codebooks, sparse codebooks, binary, ternary or algebraic codebooks can be used. Multiple codebooks allows faster algorithms but the bitrate may need to increase to obtain the same subjective quality.

VSELP (vector sum excited linear predictive) used in the Half Rate GSM speech coder belongs to this last multiple codebooks procedure.

Some details on the ITU-T G.729 8 kbit/s and G.723.1 6.3 and 5.3 kbit/s speech coders will be given before some explanations on the LD-CELP ITU-T G.728 16 kbit/s. It must be noted that the GSM EFR at 13 kbit/s is very similar to the high bitrate extension of G.729 at 11.8 kbit/s (an ACELP coder in both cases).

The ITU-T 8 kbit/s CS-ACELP G.729

The ITU-T G.729 has a frame length of 10 ms with two subframes of 5 ms.[18] The short-term analysis and synthesis are based on a tenth order linear prediction filter. Due to the short frame length of 10 ms, LSP (line spectral pairs) are quantized by using a fourth order moving average (MA) prediction. The residue of the linear prediction is quantized by an efficient two-stage vector quantization procedure (conjugate structure: CS in the name). An open loop search for the lag of the LTP analysis is made to select a candidate for refining closed loop search for each subframe.

In the ABS-MSE procedure, the lag of the LTP and the optimal algebraic codebook is found and the gains of the adaptive (LTP) and fixed (algebraic) excitations are jointly vector quantized using 7 bits. Pitch gain is around 1, but the fixed codebook gain varies much more.

To tackle this wider range, a fourth order MA gain predictor with fixed coefficient predicts the fixed codebook gain by considering the sequence of previous fixed codebook excitation vectors (this is the only main difference between the G.729 encoder scheme and the previous one described in Fig. 5.39; this gain predictor appears in the decoder in Fig. 5.40).

The innovation codebook is built by combining four pulses of amplitudes +1 or −1. The location of the four pulses is picked in a predetermined set, as shown in Table 5.15.

Table 5.15 : Location of pulses in the innovation codebook

Amplitude	Positions of pulses
+/–1	0,5,10,15,20,25,30,35
+/–1	1,6,11,21,26,31,36
+/–1	2,7,12,17,22,27,32,37
+/–1	3,8,13,18,23,28,33,38
	4,9,14,19,24,29,34,39

The pulse positions of the first three pulses are encoded with 3 bits (eight possibilities) and the fourth is encoded with 4 bits (two times eight possibilities). Each pulse needs 1 bit to encode the amplitude (+/– 1). This gives a total of 17 bits for this algebraic codebook in each subframe. Since only four non-zero pulses are in the innovation vector, very fast search procedures are possible. Four nested loops corresponding to each pulse are used. Finally, the bitstream of the 8 kbit/s is the one given in Table 5.16.

Table 5.16 : Bitstream of the 8 kbit/s

Parameter	Subframe of 40 samples		Frame of 80 samples
	1st	2nd	
LSP	–	–	18
Pitch delay	8	5	13
Pitch parity	1	–	1
Algebraic code	13+4	13+4	34
Gain codebook	4+3	4+3	14
Total	–	–	80

The decoder includes a post filter consisting of three filters: a long-term post filter, a short-term post filter and a tilt compensation post filter. The structure of the G.729 decoder is shown in Fig. 5.40.

The ITU-T G.729 includes a detailed description in fixed and floating point with associated digital test vectors. A VAD/DTX/CNG scheme similar to the G.723.1 (this was designed before the G.729 one) is used and will be discussed later. A lower complexity version (10 MIPS for the encoder compared to 18 MIPS), the G.729A was initially designed and recommended for DSVD (digital

Received bit stream: coded parameters into frames

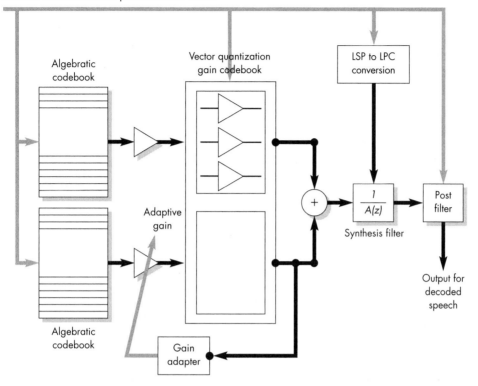

Fig. 5.40 : Basic principle of the ITU-T G.729 CS-ACELP 8 kbit/s speech decoder

simultaneous voice and data systems). There are also extensions at 6.4 and 11.8 kbit/s aimed to be used in DCME and PCME applications. G.729 is also recommended for use in a voice over frame relay system. The low-complexity version G.729A (8 kbit/s, 10 MIPS), designed primarily for DSVD applications, is sometimes used in VoIP systems.

The ITU-T G.723.1

In order to offer an efficient speech coding scheme at low bitrate for PSTN (public switch telecommunications network, now called GSTN – general instead of public due to deregulation) video-conference applications using a 28.8 or 33.4 kbit/s V.34 voice band modem, a dedicated speech coding expert group had been mandated by ITU-T for selecting the best candidate. After a short but hard competition, a compromise between the two best candidates was found.

So it was the birth of the G.723.1 proposed by Audiocodes and DSP Group on one side and University of Sherbrook and France Telecom on the other. This explains the two modes of innovation codebooks found in that standard – the MP-MLQ (Audiocodes) for the higher bitrate and the ACELP (USH) for the lower bitrate.

Some subtle differences lie between the general advanced CELP speech coding scheme presented previously and the G.723.1 general structure, but the basic principles and algorithmic tools are the same. The excitation signal for the high rate coder is MP-MLQ and for the low rate coder is ACELP, the same principle as in G.729 and GSM EFR. The frame size is 30 ms and there is an additional look-ahead of 7.5 ms, resulting in a total algorithmic delay of 37.5 ms. The subframe duration is 7.5 ms. The MP-MLQ block vector quantization resembles the algebraic vector quantization procedure: six pulses with sign +/–1 for even subframes and five pulses with sign +/–1 for odd subframes are searched with an ABS MSE procedure.

There is also a restriction on pulse positions. These can be either all odd or all even. This will be indicated by a grid bit. For the lower bit rate, the ACELP codebook was tuned to fit the bitrate of 5.3 kbit/s. Table 5.17 and Table 5.18 give the bit allocation for the two bitrates. The 189 bits of the higher bitrate are packed in 24 bytes and the 158 bits of the lower bitrate are packed in 20 bytes. So 24 or 20 bytes must be sent each 30 ms. Two bits in the first byte are used for signaling the bitrate and for VAD/DTX/CNG operations, which will be discussed later.

The ITU-T recommendation has a 16-bit fixed-point detailed description and a floating-point reference program. Both are furnished (as well as for the G.729 and its annexes) in the form of ANSI C programs. G.723.1 is specified in both fixed-point and floating-point C code. The complexity in fixed-point for the encoder and both bitrates (5.3 and 6.3 kbit/s) is around 16 MIPS. The floating-point C code, running on a Pentium 100, takes about 35–40 per cent of the processor. The conformance to the standard must be checked by passing all the digital test sequences. For the floating version, software tools were designed to allow the programmers to check their implementations.

An Annex C devoted to mobile application includes some mobile channel error coding schemes. Annex B deals with discontinuous transmission and the comfort noise generator. One important characteristic of the G.723.1 speech coder is that it has been selected to become the standard speech coder for voice over IP by IMTC. The ITU-T SG 16 does not have a default coder apart from G.711 and only vaguely recommends using G.729 or G.723.1 for low bitrate application.

Table 5.17 : Bit allocation table for the 6.3 kbit/s G723.1 encoder (MP-MLQ)

Parameters coded	Subframe 0	Subframe 1	Subframe 2	Subframe 3	Total
LPC indices					24
Adaptive codebook lags	7	2	7	2	18
All the gains combined	12	12	12	12	48
Pulse positions	20	18	20	18	73 (Note)
Pulse signs	6	5	6	5	22
Grid index	1	1	1	1	4
Total:					189

Note: by using the fact that the number of codewords in the fixed codebook is not a power of 2, 3 additional bits are saved by combining the 4 MSB of each pulse position index into a single 13-bit word

Table 5.18 : Bit allocation table for the 5.3 kbit/s G723.1 (ACELP)

Parameters coded	Subframe 0	Subframe 1	Subframe 2	Subframe 3	Total
LPC indices					24
Adaptive codebook lags	7	2	7	2	18
All the gains combined	12	12	12	12	48
Pulse positions	12	12	12	12	48
Pulse signs	4	4	4	4	16
Grid index	1	1	1	1	4
Total:					158

Discontinuous transmission and comfort noise generation

In order to reduce the transmitted bit rate during silent periods of speech, silence compression schemes have to be designed. Typically, they are based on VAD and CNG which reproduce an artificial noise at the decoder side. The VAD must precisely detect the presence of speech and send this information to the decoder side. The G.723.1 VAD operates on a speech frame of 30 ms and includes some spectral and energy computations.

One interesting feature of the VAD/DTX/CNG of the G.723.1 coding scheme is that, when the characteristics of the environmental noise do not change, nothing at all is transmitted. When needed, the spectral shape and the energy of the comfort noise to be reproduced at the decoder side are sent. The spectral shape of the noise is encoded by LSP coefficients quantized with 24 bits and its energy with 6 bits. With the two signaling bits, this fits in 4 bytes. The two signaling bits in each packet of 24, 20 or 4 bytes indicates either a 24-byte 6.3 kbit/s speech frame, a 20-byte 5.3 kbit/s speech frame or a 4-byte CNG frame. The G.723.1 can switch from one bitrate to the other on a frame by frame basis (each 30 ms). At the decoder side, four situations can appear:

■ receiving a 6.3 kbit/s frame (24 bytes)

■ receiving a 5.3 kbit/s frame (20 bytes)

■ receiving a CNG frame (4 bytes)

■ receiving nothing at all (not transmitted frame).

In the first three situations the decoder reproduces the speech frame or generates the comfort noise signal with parameters indicated in the CNG frame. In the final situation, the decoder incorporates some special procedures to reproduce a comfort noise based on the previously received CNG parameters. This characteristic may be interesting to tackle some asynchronous issues found in packet transmission such as VOIP systems. Similar VAD/DTX/CNG schemes have been included in G.729 and its annexes.

The low delay CELP coding scheme: ITU-T G.728

The previous chapter emphazises the requirement to lower the overall delay of a speech coding scheme is of prime importance. All the PCM and ADPCM (as well as the subband ADPCM wide band speech coder G.722) waveform speech coders introduce very low delay and they do not significantly impact on the network planning (introduction or not of electrical echo cancellers).

In large countries such as the US, long-distance calls must use EEC (electrical echo cancellers) and one of the ITU-T requirements when looking at updating the ADPCM G.721 or G.726 coding scheme by a more efficient one (say at 16 kbit/s) was to avoid the introduction of a new EEC or to avoid the need to increase the complexity of the existing ones.

ITU-T fixed a maximum encoding-decoding delay of 5 ms. This was the beginning of the G.728 low delay coding scheme designed by AT&T.[20]

CELP coding schemes are very efficient in this range of 16 kbit/s where ADPCM cannot work properly, but their drawback is that, due to the LPC modeling principle, a frame length of 10–30 ms is needed to compute the LPC coefficient (average stationary period of the speech signal). So AT&T researchers and speech coder designers have efficiently and brilliantly merged the two concepts of stochastic codebook excitation (CELP) and backward prediction. In that scheme, there is no need to transmit the LPC coefficient which is computed in the encoder and decoder in a backward loop.

This synthesis filter used in the ABS-MSE loop procedure does not include any LTP filter, but in order to cope with high pitch values (and to efficiently encode generic signals such as music), its length is extended to 50 backward coefficients. The coefficients are not transmitted but adapted (computed) in a backward manner by using the reconstructed signal in the encoder and decoder. This highlights the concept of a local decoder found in waveform ADPCM speech coders. The frame length for the innovative codebooks is equal to five samples (0.625 ms), but the 50 LPC backward coefficients are updated every 20 samples (there are actually four distinct phases of computation in the detailed description). For each set of five samples, an index found in a 128 stochastic codebook is transmitted with a sign bit and a gain coded in 2 bits. This leads to the following bit allocation table for the LD-CELP G.728 (*see* Table 5.19).

Table 5.19: Bit allocation for the LD-CELP G.728

	Bit allocation per frame		Bitrate (bit/s)
	Parameters	Numbers of bits	
Excitation	Index	7	11 200
	Gain	2	3 200
	Sign	1	1 600
Frame length: 0.625 ms (five samples)			16 000

In fact, the gain is not actually encoded in 2 bits but a linear predictor is used to predict the gain. This is the error prediction of this predicted gain which is encoded and transmitted. In order to obtain an optimized codebook structure (the vectors), a very long and time-consuming training sequence on a large speech signal database was necessary. The LD-CELP speech encoder principle is shown in Fig. 5.41.

To increase the resistance to transmission errors, the index of the codebooks are GRAY encoded. The introduction of the post filter in the decoder shown in Fig. 5.42 significantly improves the quality of the decoded speech (this has allowed the AT&T proposal to fulfill the ITU-T requirements). The G.728 has a very good score on the MOS scale (around 4) and it is used in the H.320 video-conference system (to replace the G.711 64 kbit/s and to allow one video

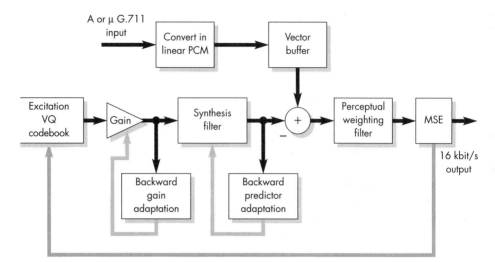

Fig. 5.41 : Low delay CELP ITU-T G.728 encoder principle

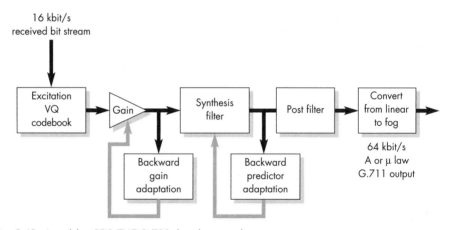

Fig. 5.42 : Low delay CELP ITU-T G.728 decoder principle

conference using only one 64 kbit/s ISDN B channel, leaving almost 48 kbit/s for the video). Also, some modern DCME are beginning to use the G.728 and its recent extensions to 9.6 and 12.8 kbit/s to replace the G.726 at 16, 24 and 32 kbit/s.

Nevertheless, in spite of all its intrinsic qualities, the LD-CELP coding scheme has two major drawbacks. The first is its difficulty in passing voice band modems and an extension to 40 kbit/s is being studied. The second is its overly high sensitivity to frame erasure due to the very long backward LPC filter and gain adaptation predictor. Recent works have significantly improved this robustness and led to a new annex in the ITU-T G.728 suite of recommendation.

Surprisingly (but it can be explained by the tightened backward LPC loop), the first detailed description introduced in 1992 was for floating-point DSP and two years (1994) of work were needed to finalize a fixed-point (16 bits) description. This detailed description, either in floating point or in fixed point, is not an ANSI C program but a huge document (pseudo code) which is very complex for DSP software code designers to interpret. The complexity in fixed point is around 20 MIPS for the encoder and 13 MIPS for the decoder.

Another issue that G.728 shares with the G.729 coder as opposed to G.723.1 is that there is no framing information in the transmitted bitrate. G.723.1 uses 2 bits in the first transmitted byte to indicate the contents of the packet. G.728 produces a 10-bit code for each five-sample frame (2 bits per sample gives 16 kbit/s at an 8 kHz sampling frequency) but actually the decoder must be precisely aware of the first, second, third and fourth packet of 10 bits to synchronize the backward LPC filter adaptation procedure. So strictly speaking, the G.728 has a delay not of 0.625 ms but in fact of 2.5 ms. In the H.320 suite of recommendations, the H.221 framing procedure specifies the way to correctly position the four packets of 10 bits of G.728 (2 bits per byte of a 64 kbit/s stream) or the 80 bits of the G.729 8 kbit/s (1 bit per byte of a 64 kbit/s stream). If we lose the start of the frame in G.729, the decoding process forces a mute after several ms. It is the same situation with G.728 when feeding the decoder an incorrectly positioned 10-bit word, but unfortunately in that decoder there is no muting procedure. More subtly with the G.728 decoder, if the sequence of the four 10-bit packets is misinterpreted (taking the second for the first, the third for the second and so on), the decoded speech is quite intelligible and seems of 'good' quality, but in fact is severely affected (at least for speech coder experts) by the desynchronization of the backward LPC filter.

Partial conclusion on speech coding techniques and their near future

Many coding schemes have not been addressed in this document, such as the mixed excitation LPC (MELP coder retained in the new 2400 bit/s US Federal Standard), the VSELP (Vector Sum Excited LP coder used in the half rate 5.6 kbit/s GSM system) and the multirate Q-CELP (QUALCOM CELP at 1, 2, 4 and 8 kbit/s used in the cellular US IS96 CDMA system). It is impossible to review all these coding schemes in detail and we have also not described the multiband excitation (MBE) or sinusoidal transform coders (STC).

Recent works carried out by ETSI have settled the basis of an adaptive multirate (AMR) speech coder for the new generation of mobile GSM systems. This relies on the fact that the speech coding scheme can be efficiently combined with the channel coding scheme in order to offer the best quality depending on the transmission quality (C/I carrier on interference value) of the air interface (radio link) at a precise time. A wide band version (WB-AMR) is being investigated by ETSI to transport a wide band signal (50 to 7000 Hz) at a 13 kbit/s bitrate.

ITU-T is planning to replace the SB-ADPCM wide band speech coder by a coding scheme giving an equivalent quality of the 'old' G.722 at 64 and 56 kbit/s but for an actual bitrate of 32 and 24 kbit/s. There are also plans to define a 4 kbit/s ITU-T speech coding standard.

Many competitors try to fulfill the severe requirements but despite all the advanced speech coding proposed, there is still no real solution. Today, speech is quite correctly encoded with one bit per sample (8 kbit/s) but all the solutions, including the recent ITU-T standards such as the G.729, at this bitrate have great difficulties in encoding speech with background noise or in situations where there are multiple speakers.

Moreover, except G.728 at 16 kbits, GSM EFR and the extension of G.729 around 12 kbit/s, these CELP-based coders have poor, or even catastrophic, results with encoding various music signals and they cannot compete with the higher bitrate 'old' encoded parameters.

And finally, as the level of compression is increased, the stream of encoded parameters becomes more and more sensitive to bit errors and frame erasure, so extra bits and procedures are necessary to protect this highly reduced bitrate. It seems that for the moment the situation corresponding to the bitrate for speech coders will be fixed.

Some other features, such as hierarchical coding and scalability, will be introduced in the coding scheme (the ISO-MPEG-4 speech and audio software tools box is tailored for that), but the net bitrate will not be reduced. In order to ensure the scalability and hierarchical possibilities, the bitrate will be increased for an equivalent level of quality – flexibility has a price.

Remarks applicable to VoIP telephone gateways

Placing a phone call over the IP network needs, in most cases, a speech coding algorithm to reduce the bit rate, but in spite of the huge processing load to perform this task it is not the most complicated one that a PC or an IP gateway must perform. The receiving side is much more complex than the sending side.

Electrical echo canceller

The EEC is required in a VoIP gateway (it is not needed when two PC users communicate over IP). This EEC must be well tailored (excellent performances are required) and the drawbacks are an increase in the total cost of the gateway and a negative impact on the speech quality.

Sending voice packet over IP is just a matter of signal processing and computer science. The only task to do on the sending site (from the microphone of the PC or from the handset's microphone for the IP gateway) is to collect frames of uncompressed speech, pass them to the software or DSP-based compressor, and pack the bitstreams of coded parameters into IP/UDP packets by adding proper headers and eventually some payloads for RTP protocol (Forward Error Control, etc). These are of course time-consuming tasks, but not difficult ones.

The IP gateway must extract the correct time slot in the received ISDN bitstream (E1 or T1) and manage the signaling information to translate it to an RTP stream to the correct IP address. The number of frames and the frame length of the speech coder can degrade the efficiency of the speech coding scheme (*see* below). Eventually, in most cases, some signaling tones such as the DTMF cannot be handled properly by the speech compressor and an alternative control message protocol must be used.

Best effort

On the sending side, the VoIP gateway task can be summarized as 'compress, send and forget' but on the receiving side the task is much harder. First there is a lack of synchronization. The IP network sends as best it can (best-effort network) the IP/UDP packet labeled with an address to the destination and timestamps included in the header packet. Whatever may be the sequencing of packets on the receiving side, the decoding procedure must send a continuous audio stream to the loudspeakers of the PC or a continuous 64 kbit/s A or µ law G.711 time slotted stream into the E1 or T1 connected to the local exchange of the PSTN user for the IP gateway.

Due to the unpredictable delay brought by the IP network, the receiver procedure must maintain a dynamic buffer to collect the received packet. If the size of this buffer is too small, the decoder will lack the packet for decoding, and if it is too large, this will introduce an unbearable delay (in the case of broadcasting, this is of course not an issue).

Moreover, a clock synchronization mechanism must correct the clock drift found between the timestamps of the received RTP packets and the local clock (either the digital to analogue clock of the PC sound card or the network clock of the E1 or T1 link connected to the gateway).

These two tasks are the main issues dealt with by the receiver. Associated with these, and not the easiest part of the job, procedures to cope with frame erasure concealment or error dissimulation have to be precisely and efficiently tailored in the receiver. Although the RTP payloads can be used to include some signal processing redundancies (such as the LPC parameters of the next frame inducing, again, an extra delay) or some forward error control procedure, it seems that voice over IP calls do not mix very well with this 'protection' scheme.

The fact is that either IP/UDP packets are correctly received in a 'time constrained' window, or they are lost (or declared as lost by the receiver).

So the work of the receiver is to build a continuous audio stream with holes in the decoded parameters. This needs accurate knowledge of the speech encoder and decoder algorithmic structure and experienced digital signal processing engineers to imagine the rebuilding of lost frames without impacting too much on the reproduced quality.

Non-standardization

The strategies used, which are of course proprietary, depend on the type of encoder, and some are less resistant to frame erasure than others. A CELP encoder such as the G.723.1 or the G.729 is less robust than a speech audio encoder based on a filter bank and psychoacoustical bit allocation. In the latter case, there is no prediction from frame to frame and it is easier to rebuild (repeat) the last frame for producing the continuous audio stream.

In the case of CELP encoders, there are many predictive loops which are highly disturbed by the loss of several consecutive frames. Some tests on a 24 kbit/s wide band coding scheme (filter bank) intended to be used in IP video conferences have emphasized the net superiority of this 'non-looped' coder type over CELP ones in the presence of a 10 per cent loss of IP packets.

So the overall speech quality of a voice over IP call is directly (and surely highly) correlated to the refined and tuned procedures in the decoder to tackle the synchronization clock and lost packet issues. This is not standardized, and all the IP phone software packages as well as the IP gateways' DSP software are not equivalent and do not have the same level of quality, even if they do use the same coding scheme.

Annex A

Main characteristics of ITU-T standardized speech coders

Standard	G.711	G.721	G.726	G.727	G.728	G.729	G.723.1	G.722
Date	1972	1984	1990	1990	1992	1995	1995	1988
Bitrate (in kbit/s)	64	32	16/24/32/40	16/24/32/40	16	8	6.3/5.3	48/56/64
Transmitted bandwidth	3.4 kHz	3.4 kHz	3.4 kHz	3.4 kHz	3.4 kHz	3.4 kHz	3.4 kHz	7 kHz
Complexity								
MIPS	0.1	10	12	12	33	22	16/18	10
RAM	2 w	256 w	256 w	256 w	3.4 kw	2.5 kw	2.1 kw	256 w
ROM	50 w	4 kw	5 kw	5 kw	8 kw	9.5 kw	7 kw	4 kw
Frame length (ms)	0.125	0.125	0.125	0.125	0.125	10	30	0.125
Overhead (ms)	0	0	0	0	0	5	7.5	1.5
Speech quality in MOS	4.2	4.0	4.0[1]	4.0[1]	4.0	4.0	3.9/3.7	+ 64, 56 kbit/s 0 à 48 kbit/s[2]
Noise quality	+	+	+[1]	+[1]	+	0	-	+2
Capability to encode music	0	0	0[1]	0[1]	0	-	-	+ 64 kbit/s[2] 0 56 kbit/s - 48 kbit/s
Robustness to errors	0/0	+/0	+/0[1]	+/0[1]	0/-	+/+	0/0	+/0
Maximum speed for modem (kbit/s)	28.8	4.8	14.4[3]	14.4[3]	2.4	-	-	-
Number of acceptable tandems	14	4	4[1]	4[1]	3	2	2/1	3
Coder type	Waveform PCM	Waveform ADPCM	Waveform ADPCM	Waveform ADPCM embedded	ABS LD-CELP	ABS CS-ACELP	ABS MP-MLQ ACELP	Waveform SB-ADPCM

Note 1: quality for 32 kbit/s (at 16 and 24 kbit/s, a continuous use is not recommended), at 40 kbit/s, MOS figure is 4.2.
Note 2: MOS figures do not have the same meaning for a wideband signal; the reference is a wideband (10–7 000 Hz) signal and the following scale will be used: + = near the original, good; 0 = medium quality; − = bad quality.
Note 3: possible with a bit rate of 40 kbit/s.
The total delay is around several samples (3–4) for the waveform-type coders (but for the G.722 QMF filters add 3 ms). For the analysis by synthesis speech coder type, the total delay is around four times the frame length (+ overhead if present).

Annex B

Main characteristics of cellular mobile standardized speech coders

Country	ETSI EUROPE				TIA USA			CRC JAPAN	
Standard	GSM 06.10	GSM 06.20	TETRA	GSM 06.60	IS54 TDMA	IS96 CDMA	IS136 TDMA	JDC 1	JDC 2
Date	1988	1994	1994	1996	1990	1992	1996	1990	1993
Bit rate (in kbit/s)	13	5.6	4.56	12.2	7.9	8/4/2/1	7.4	6.7	3.6
Bit rate for channel coding	9.8	5.8		10.6	5.1		5.6	4.5	2
Transmitted bandwidth	3.4 kHz	3.4 kHz	3.4 kHz	3.4 kHz	3.4 kHz	3.4 kHz	3.4 kHz	3.4 kHz	3.4 kHz
Complexity MIPS	2.5	17.5	15	15.4	14	10–12	16.1	14/18	30–40
RAM	0.8 kw	3.2 kw	4 kw	4.7 kw	?	?	2.4 kw	?	?
ROM	2 kw	18 kw	7 kw	5.9 kw	?	?	5.4 kw	?	?
Frame length (ms)	20	20	20	20	20	20	20	20	40
overhead (ms)	0	?	?	0	5	5	5	5	10
Speech quality	3.6–3.8	3.5–3.7	3.3–3.5	4.1	3.5–3.7	3.3–3.5	4.	3.4/3.6	3.4/3.6
Noise 'quality'	-	-	-	+	-	-	+	-	-
Capability to encode music	-	-	-	-	-	-	-	-	-
Robustness to errors	+/+	+/+	+/+	+/+	+/+	+/+	+/+	+/+	+/+
Maximum speed for modem (in kbit/s)	-	-	-	-	-	-	-	-	-
Acceptable number of tandems	2	2	2/1	2	2	2/1	2	2	2/1
Coder type	RPE-LTP	VSELP	ACELP	ACELP	VSELP	CELP	ACELP	VSELP	PSI-CELP

THE NETWORK

Quality of service

What is QoS?

Quality of service (QoS) was largely ignored in the initial design of IP. IP, like other packet network technologies, was built and optimized to transport data, not voice or video. The only 'quality of service' that was required was that the data should not be corrupted or get lost. Today, the improvement of networking technology makes it feasible to transport real-time data over an IP network. Therefore it becomes extremely important to be able to characterize and control jitter and transit delays in the network. Jitter is important mainly in real-time applications which need to maintain worst-case buffers to allow for timely delivery of the packets.

Packet loss is also an important parameter of the packet network QoS. It usually occurs when there is congestion on the packet's path, causing router buffers to overflow. On TCP connections, it will cause a significant drop in the connection's throughput due to the Van Jacobson algorithm. A loss of several packets will switch TCP in slow start mode and result in a slow connection long after the actual network congestion has stopped. On UDP connections, packet loss will also cause delay (if an acknowledgement and retransmission scheme, or a forward error correction method is used) or quality degradation in multimedia applications when loss cannot be recovered due to latency constraints.

Telephony is not the only application which poses severe constraints on the network QoS. Transaction applications (the round-trip delays will slow the setup time of all applications using TCP, and may, in extreme cases, slow the overall transmission speed), interactive applications (such as simulations and games) and some protocol encapsulations such as SNA in IP are also very sensitive to the network QoS. *See* Fig. 6.1.

The main parameters characterizing QoS in a packet network are therefore:

- latency
- bandwidth
- packet loss and desequencing.

Bandwidth seems an easy issue to tackle – just throw more leased line capacity at the problem. In fact, there is more than just providing overall bandwidth – a provider must also ensure that each user of the network gets a fair share of it. As we will see, this is especially tricky when dealing with TCP traffic, and it is only recently that efficient, fair sharing techniques have been deployed.

Packet loss and desequencing is closely linked with the bandwidth issue, but is also heavily influenced by the route stability of the network, efficient queue management in the routers, and proper use of congestion control (Internet Control Message Protocol – ICMP – source quench, etc.) at the edge of the network and within the backbone.

- **Packet loss**

- **Transmission end-to-end delay**: extremely important for conversational services, heavily influences echo perception

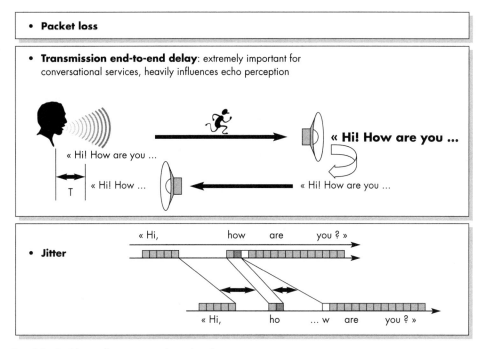

- **Jitter**

Fig. 6.1 : Problems affecting network quality of service

Latency is by far the most difficult issue. A common opinion is to say that IP is simply unsuitable for the transport of latency-controlled data. This is *not* true. Parekh and Gallager found a very useful approach in 1993, leading to a family of queuing algorithms called weighted fair queuing. These algorithms, although difficult to implement in practice, can guarantee an upper bound on latency for certain flows. RSVP is simply a reservation protocol that makes possible the use and implementation of this approach.

Describing a data stream

The simplest metaphor that can be used to model a data stream is called the fluid model (Fig. 6.2). In this model the data stream granularity (packets) is ignored, as if it was a continuous stream of bits, and even portions of bits. A popular model of such a stream is the token bucket regulated stream. The token bucket uses two parameters, the token bucket size (in bits) and the incoming traffic long-term average rate ρ in bits/s. The bits of the incoming traffic must remove a token from the bucket before being forwarded to the output. To regenerate the tokens, a new one is created each $1/\rho$ second until the number of

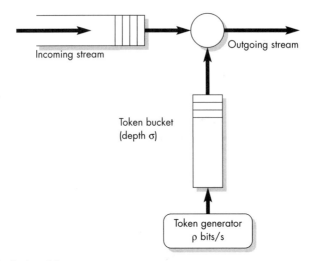

Fig. 6.2 : The fluid model

unused tokens stacked in the bucket reaches a depth of σ tokens. After this limit the bucket is full and the new tokens are rejected. Therefore σ represents the size of the traffic bursts. At any point in time the traffic getting out of the leaky bucket regulator is lower than σ+ρt, if it is the duration of the data stream.

The token bucket model is widely used to represent data traffic. It captures some of the burstiness characteristics of a stream, as well as the stream's average rate.

Queuing techniques for QoS

What causes so much trouble in a packet network is that, at each node, every packet must be received, processed and finally forwarded to the next hop as soon as some bandwidth is available over the appropriate link. The delay between the reception and the emission of a packet is highly variable: it can be extremely long if the network is congested or if a very long packet is already being emitted on the interface, or very short if the packet is the only one in the network. There has been a great deal of effort to design a scheduling policy that would minimize these delays and allow each stream a fair share of the available bandwidth.

The art of queuing is the art of managing congested queues in order to give specific bandwidth, latency and loss to some flows through each node. Several technologies exist, which can be grouped into two categories. The first takes care of packet ordering in the output queues:

■ FIFO (first in first out), also called first come first served (FCFS), simply outputs the packets in the order in which they have been received;

- class-based queuing (also called custom queuing by CISCO) assigns packets to prioritized logical queues;
- fair queuing and weighted fair queuing (WFQ) algorithms. Here we will present mainly an algorithm called PGPS, which is the reference fair scheduling algorithm.

Those techniques can be combined with any packet loss management technique of the second category:

- simple overflow
- random early detection and weighted random early detection.

Class-based queuing techniques

Class-based queuing techniques (CBQ) sort flows into several logical queues, each of which is usually assigned a priority. Arriving packets are sent to the appropriate logical queue, each working in FIFO mode. A scheduler then picks candidate packets from the logical queues according to their priority and forwards them to the interface physical FIFO queue.

Several scheduling algorithms are commonly used, including: weighted round robin – (see Fig. 6.3) if there are more than two packets waiting to be serviced the scheduler picks two packets in the high priority queue, then services one packet from the low priority queue, and this goes on until there are no packets left to be serviced.

Class-based queuing is extremely useful. A common configuration is to prioritize UDP (DNS, real-time applications) and interactive (TELNET) traffic. This is simple and efficient, but does not guarantee any delay to any flow, and someone could easily misuse the service by creating applications running on prioritized traffic.

The sorting algorithm can rely on the value of the Type Of Service (TOS) field, or sort the packet according to a combination of source address, destination address and port. It can also be controlled by RSVP, especially to support the controlled load mode of RSVP.

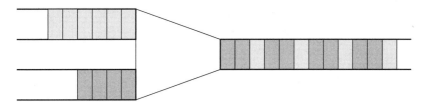

Fig. 6.3 : Class-based queuing

Fair queuing techniques

The notion of fairness can have many interpretations. The idea is that all flows should be given the same service, or a service proportional to their priority. Depending on the exact interpretation, several queue management techniques can be used.

Simple fair queuing: bitwise round-robin fair queuing algorithm

The model of fairness that bitwise round-robin fair queuing tries to emulate is a TDM (time division multiplex) link. If each flow is allocated a time slot on the TDM link, the service will be equal between all flows. If some priority is needed, one flow could be allocated two or more slots.

To emulate TDM on an interface, each queue keeps track of the total received byte count. Initially all queues start with a byte count of zero. Each arriving packet is assigned a tag with the value of the byte count of the queue just after it arrived. Then the scheduler serves packets in the order of their tags.

As described above, the TDM emulation will allocate the same bandwidth share to each flow. But it is simple to allocate different bandwidth shares: for instance, if queue 1 needs to be configured to use 50 per cent of the available bandwidth, queue 2 30 per cent and queue 3 20 per cent, then the tags will not be the byte count but the byte count divided by five for queue 1, by three for queue 2 and by two for queue 3.

This TDM model is quite good to allocate different shares of the bandwidth for each queue in an interface, but it has a major flaw – streams not using bandwidth accumulate the right to use this bandwidth later. A flow which has not sent data for a while could potentially send a huge burst and be serviced immediately. During this time, even if other flows have to send data, they will be blocked. In other words, the TDM model does not achieve stream isolation.

However, it is possible to limit this effect by controlling the maximum amount of data that can get in each queue in any given period, for instance through a leaky bucket regulator.

GPS policy in a node

Generalized processor sharing (GPS) is another view of fairness which is better than TDM. For GPS, the best node would ideally allocate a fair share of the available bandwidth to each stream. This share would be *immediately* available as soon as there was some data to be sent, even if other flows happened to be in a burst period at the time.

Unfortunately, this is possible only if we consider that the data of each stream can be arbitrarily fragmented, and that many data elements from different streams can be sent at the same time through the output link of a node. In the real world of packet data, a packet which is being sent takes all the bandwidth, even if another packet arrives simultaneously and would need its share of the bandwidth immediately.

If for a moment we accept that packets can be arbitrarily fragmented (this is called the fluid approximation), the best possible node looks like a toothpaste tube: the 'red' stream and the 'white' stream each get a fair share of the output. We can estimate the worst case delay that an element of data belonging to a stream (r,b) would face going through such a node – it would be b/R, where R is the bandwidth allocated to the stream through the node (R>r) and b is the token bucket depth of the stream's description.

More formally, under the fluid approximation, this bandwidth sharing policy between several streams is called GPS (Fig. 6.4). In this policy the processing power of the router and the output bandwidth on each interface are shared among the competing streams. Each of these streams receives at least a share ϕ_i of those resources ($\sum_{i=1}^{N} \phi_i = 1$). A good analogy is the sharing of CPU cycles between threads in a multitasking operating system. A GPS node is non-idling as long as at least one stream is still queued (which means that the scarce resource, output bandwidth, is never wasted transmitting nothing).

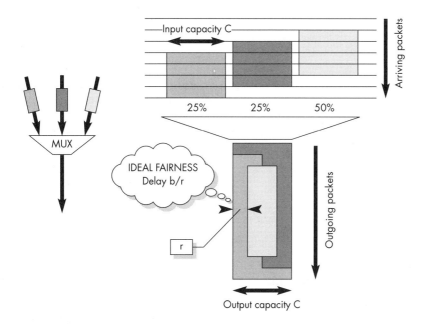

Fig. 6.4 : GPS and fluid approximation

More precisely, if $S_i(s,t)$ denotes the volume of a stream that has gone through the node between instants s and t, then

$$\frac{S_i(s,t)}{S_j(s,t)} \geq \frac{\phi_i}{\phi_j},$$

for each session i continuously backlogged between s and t. The backlogged active sessions share the resources of inactive sessions (not backlogged) proportionally to their ϕ_i.

In other words, each session i can use at least the capacity ϕ_i*C at any time, where C is the total capacity of the output interface considered. If *all* sessions are active, each session i uses exactly ϕ_i*C.

The service received by the token bucket regulated session i in a system where N token bucket regulated sessions share the scarce resource is always better than the service received by session i if all other sessions start with their token bucket full, then send the longest allowed traffic burst and finally keep sending data at the maximum long-term average rate allowed by the token bucket regulator. With this remark, the largest delay through the node (σ/ϕ_i*C) and the buffer size needed for the worst backlog (σ) can be calculated.

GPS policy has a very important property – the order of departure (i.e. last bit of the packet has been output) of two packets i and j is independent of packet arrivals. The reason for this is that if another packet arrives, the transmission speed of i and j is changed homogeneously (the factor of change is the same for i and j), which preserves the departure time. The exact time of departure of i and j, however, is obviously changed.

PGPS policy in a node

The fluid model behind GPS is not valid for real-world networks, where packets are received as whole entities (i.e. nothing is processed until the final packet

The router calculates in real time the way packets would be handled under fluid approximation, to find in which order they would finish

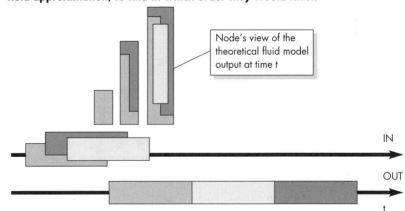

Node's view of the theoretical fluid model output at time t

IN

OUT

t

Fig. 6.5 : Weighted fair queuing

Cyclic Redundancy Check – CRC – is checked) and put in the output queue as blocks of contiguous bits. Taking into account these real-life facts leads to 'packet by packet GPS'.

The idea behind PGPS is to serve the packets in the order in which they would leave under a GPS policy. This order of departure is not changed by arrivals, so packets that have already been ordered keep the same order – only newly arrived packets may be inserted in this arrangement.

Figure 6.6 illustrates the case where the transmission capacity of each input and the output link is 1. The two leftmost streams are given a weight of 0.25, whereas the rightmost stream is given a weight of 0.5. A packet arrives for each stream each $\frac{1}{4}$ time unit in our case (we take as a time unit the transmission time of a packet of size 1); a_i is packet i arrival time. In case you wonder why packet 1 is sent first while it finishes second under GPS, this is because at the time the PGPS node had to choose a packet for output (remember it is non idling), packet 3 had not yet arrived, so its departure time was not known.

Under PGPS, packets are sent in the order of departure of GPS as known when the decision to select a new packet for the output queue is taken. Because we cannot guess what the future will be, this can lead to errors as in Figure 6.6: a new packet (dark grey) arrives just after the selection of the new output packet (grey) but its GPS finishing time is lower than the GPS finishing time of the

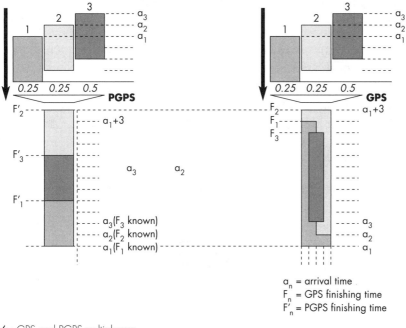

a_n = arrival time
F_n = GPS finishing time
F'_n = PGPS finishing time

Fig. 6.6 : GPS and PGPS multiplexers

packet being sent (on the right side, the dark grey packet finishes before the grey packet) but we must wait until this one is finished. So in some cases the rule 'sending in the same order as GPS finishing order' is not followed!

Therefore, under PGPS policy, some packets are finished after their finishing time under GPS policy. There is added delay attached to this:

$$F'_p - F_p \leq \frac{L_{MAX}}{C}$$

where L_{max} is the maximum size of a packet and C the throughput of the outgoing interface. This limit is approached in the example if we grow stream 3 weight to nearly 1 and we make packets 1, 2 and 3 arrive closer together.

The worst delay through the node for stream i becomes under PGPS (L_{MAX} is the maximum packet size on the inbound links):

$$D^*_i \leq \left. \sigma_i \middle/ r_i \right. + \left. L_{MAX} \middle/ C \right. + Tr$$

where $r_i = C*\phi_i$ is the capacity reserved for stream i and C is the total capacity of the output link. Tr is the duration of processing in the router.

Regarding the buffers we have:

$$Q^*_i \leq \sigma_i + L_{MAX}$$

under the stability condition $\rho_i \leq r_i$.

It is obvious from these that it is better not to have big packets, which was one of the design goals of ATM. However, if the link has a big capacity, then this is less important.

To prove the validity of the delay bounds, let us number the packets in the order they are processed by the PGPS server since the last busy session. For any packet p_k there are two cases:

■ all packets p_j leaving PGPS before p_k (j<k) also leave the GPS server before p_k. Therefore at the time f_k when packet p_k finishes under GPS, GPS has already served all other packets p_j (j<k). Because PGPS is work-conserving it will have served the same volume as the GPS server between the beginning of the busy

Latency evaluation

- with WFQ, the delay through the node can be guaranteed to be lower than:

$$\sigma/r + Lmax/C$$

- r is the bandwidth reserved for that stream
- C is the total bandwidth of the output link
- Lmax is the MTU of the input link
- σ is the token bucket depth characterizing the stream

Fig. 6.7 : Latency evaluation

session and f_k. All packets p_j ($j \leq k$) fit in this volume because GPS has served them, so PGPS has also served them before f_k, so $f'_k \leq f_k$

■ at least one packet p_m leaving PGPS before p_k ($m<k$) leaves after p_k under GPS. Among those packets, let us consider the one leaving PGPS last: p_M. If a_i denotes the arrival time of packet i, then we have:
$\forall i \in [M+1,k]$, $a_i > f'_{M-1}$, otherwise, if packet i had arrived before f'_{M-1} (this is when PGPS must choose which packet will go after p_{M-1}), because packet i finishes before packet M under GPS (otherwise M would not be the biggest integer lower than k having $f_M > f_k$), p_i would have been scheduled next, not p_M.

So it is now the case that no packet p_i, i between M and k, had arrived before f_{M-1}. But they have all been served before f_k (otherwise M would not be the biggest integer lower than k having $f_M > f_k$). So we can write:

$$f_k > f'_{M-1} + \sum_{i=M+1}^{k} \frac{L_i}{C}$$

where L is the size of the packet and C the bandwidth of the output.
Under PGPS we have exactly:

$$f'_k = f'_{M-1} + \sum_{i=M}^{k} \frac{L_i}{C}$$

which finally gives

$$f_k > f'_k - \frac{L_M}{C}$$

and because $L_M \leq L_{MAX}$ we have our result.

How to calculate the GPS departure time

A packet has arrived when its last bit has arrived. This moment is the arrival time for the kth packet arriving from flow i, which we call a_i^k. The length of the packet is L_i^k. Let s_i^k and f_i^k denote the moment at which packet k begins and finishes to be processed by the GPS server, then:

(a) $s_i^k = \max \{f_i^{k-1}, a_i^k\}$

(b) $f_i^k = s_i^k + t(L_i^k)$ where t is the time used by the GPS server to process L bits.

The difficult part is that the processing speed of the GPS server depends on its load and changes with each packet departure and arrival (called event). If t_i denotes the time of event i, the processing speed for session i is:

$$\frac{\phi_i}{\sum\limits_{j \in B(t)} \phi_j} * r$$

where r is the total throughput of the outgoing link and B is the group of buffered sessions at this time. This reflects the fact that a GPS server distributes unused reserved bandwidth to the active sessions according to their precedence.

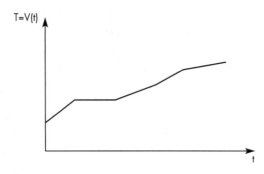

Fig. 6.8 : The 'virtual time function'

We call V(t) the piecewise linear function of t defined by its slope $\dfrac{r}{\sum_{j \in B(t)} \phi_j}$ then (b) can be rewritten:

(b) $\displaystyle\int_{s_i^k}^{f_i^k} \phi_i \, {}^*v'(t)dt = L_i^k$

writing S=v(s) and F=v(f) , (a) e and (b) become:

(a) $S_i^k = \max\left\{F_i^{k-1}, V(a_i^k)\right\}$

(b) $F_i^k = S_i^k + \dfrac{L_i^k}{\phi_i}$

with $F_i^0 = 0, \forall i$

This virtual time T (Fig. 6.8) respects the same order relations as t because v( ) is non-decreasing. So it is enough to calculate F, which is possible as soon as we receive a packet since a and L are known. The problem is solved and we can immediately classify a new packet among the queued packets.

However, this calculation requires that the PGPS server maintains the parameters necessary for the calculation of v(t): the co-ordinates of the last slope change, the current slope, and the number of backlogged sessions. Since each arrival and departure will change these values, and packets can arrive simultaneously, this is a real computation challenge.

PGPS multiplexers in a network

Along a path going through N PGPS multiplexers, the maximal delay is:

$$D_i^* \leq \frac{\sigma_i + (N-1)\, L_{MAX}}{r_i} + \sum_{n=1}^{N}\left(L_{MAX}\Big|_{C_n} + Tr_n\right)$$

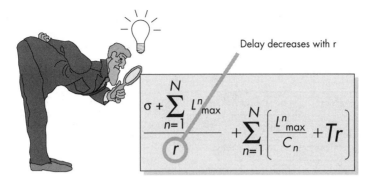

Delay decreases with r

$$\frac{\sigma + \sum_{n=1}^{N} L^n_{max}}{r} + \sum_{n=1}^{N} \left(\frac{L^n_{max}}{C_n} + Tr \right)$$

Fig. 6.9 : End-to-end delay

where r_i is the smallest bandwidth amount allocated to stream i along the path. (Caveat: Both the propagation time and the processing time should be included in Tr.)

There is a more accurate version of this if we consider the peak emission rate of stream i:

$$D_i^* \le \frac{\Sigma_i + C_{TOT}}{r_i} + D_{TOT}$$

with:

$$C_{TOT} = \sum_{n=1}^{N} L^n_{MAX}$$

$$D_{TOT} = \sum_{n=1}^{N} \left(\frac{L^n_{MAX}}{C_n} + Tr_n \right)$$

$$\Sigma_i = L + \frac{(\sigma_i - L)(p_i - r_i)}{(p_i - \rho_i)}$$

RSVP gives a receiver all the parameters in this formula. The receiver selects the rate r that he wants to reserve in order to have an acceptable end-to-end delay.

Signaling QoS requirements

The IP TOS octet

Ipv6 has a similar octet called a 'traffic class' octet (Fig. 6.10). The IPv4 TOS octet is structured as shown in Fig. 6.11.

The first three bits make up the IP precedence field which has values between 0 and 7. Packets with a higher IP precedence value should have a

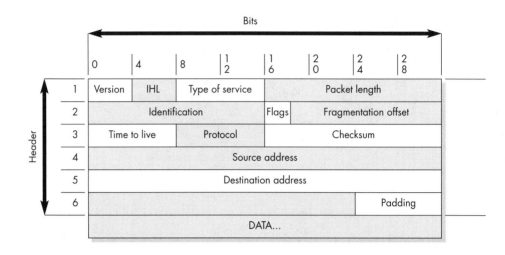

Fig. 6.10 : The IP TOS octet

higher priority in the network. The traditional meaning of the IP precedence (RFC 791) is described in Table 6.1. The vocabulary used reflects the military origin of IP; a 'flash' IP packet was supposed to be the electronic equivalent of a flash message. However, these values have never really been used in the context of the Internet, mainly because routers had FIFO queuing and were unable to process packets with various quality of service levels. As we will see, this is no longer true.

Fig. 6.11 : The IPv4 TOS octet structure

Table 6.1 : Traditional meaning of the IP procedence values

Value	Definition	
Network	packets with network control precedence	(7)
Internet	packets with internetwork control precedence	(6)
Critical	packets with critical precedence	(5)
Flash override	packets with flash override precedence	(4)
Flash	packets with flash precedence	(3)
Immediate	packets with immediate precedence	(2)
Priority	packets with priority precedence	(1)
Routine	packets with routine precedence	(0)

Levels 110 (6) and 111 (7) are reserved for routing and some ICMP messages (*see* RFC 1812 for details). Therefore only six levels (routine–critical) remain for user applications.

The following four bits form the TOS field and can be used to mark a desired trade-off between cost, delay, throughput and reliability, as described in RFC 1349. Originally RFC 791 used only the first three bits as the TOS field, and the two last bits were part of the MBZ field. RFC 1349 defines some values for the TOS field:

- 1000 – minimize delay
- 0100 – maximize throughput
- 0010 – maximize reliability
- 0001 – minimize monetary cost
- 0000 – normal service.

The idea is that TELNET, for instance, as an interactive service, should require TOS 1000. In the original RFC 791 it was legal to add those values to require combined properties. RFC 1349 no longer allows this, and value 1100, for instance, could mean anything. RFC 1122 and 1123 (host requirements) defined a few rules for setting TOS values for hosts, but they were based on a five-bit TOS field. RFC 1349 requires the last bit (MBZ) to be 0.

The MBZ (must be zero) field is for experimental use and is ignored by routers.

If you are beginning to think that things are not crystal clear, you are right. When sending traffic over the Internet with a specific IP precedence and TOS value, no one can be really sure of the behavior of routers along the path unless one provider controls the whole domain and has properly configured the forwarding policies of all routers. That is, of course, if the routers support forwarding policies according to the IP precedence value, because most UNIX forwarding implementations and many simple routers do not. The TOS value is simply ignored in most cases.

Using the IP precedence field

The IP precedence field can be used at the access level in conjunction with policy routing. Policy routing is the ability to bypass the regular routing mechanism to set custom next hops or custom IP precedence to packets getting through a router. For example, a router can be configured to set the IP precedence field of TCP traffic on to port 80 to critical (example for a CISCO router):

- interface Serial 0
- ip address 10.0.0.1 255.0.0.0
- ip local policy route-map test — *this activates policy routing on the interface*
- access-list 101 permit `tcp any any eq 80` — *defines an access list to match TCP port 80*
- route-map test permit 1 — *defines route map n°1*
- match ip address 101 — *sets TOS field to critical for all traffic matching access list 101*
- set ip precedence critical

Once this is configured in the customer's access router, the network provider has several options:

- prioritize the IP traffic in the backbone according to the value of the TOS field. This can be done using priority queuing, class-based queuing or weighted fair queuing.
- use a separate backbone (for instance based on ATM links) for IP traffic with critical priority. This can again be done using a route map.

(Re) defining the values of the IP TOS octet

There has been much theoretical work on the behavior of packet networks since the creation of the IP protocol, and people also have much more experience on the sophisticated queuing mechanisms used in QoS enabled equipment. The work done for ATM and frame-relay networks has also helped clarify the essential QoS related information that needs to be transported in each packet.

It was essential to review the original meaning(s) of the IP TOS octet and stop wasting four bits per IP packet. This is the charter of the IETF Diffserv group, with the intent to 'provide scalable service discrimination in the Internet without the need for per-flow state and signaling at every hop'. Work is ongoing, but there was enough consensus to redefine the semantics of the IPv4 TOS octet and IPv6 traffic class octet in RFC 2474 (December 1998) which makes RFC 1455 and 1349 obsolete. First of all, the name TOS (traffic class) is changed – this byte should now be called DS (differentiated services) byte.

The DS is subdivided into a six-bit DSCP (differentiated services codepoint) field, and CU (currently unused) field, as shown in Fig. 6.12.

The codepoint value should be used as an index to the appropriate packet handler, or per hop behavior (PHB). A PHB applies a particular forwarding treatment to all packets with a particular codepoint and direction (this class of packet is called a behavior aggregate). For instance, each behavior aggregate can be mapped to a particular queue in a weighted round robin, CBQ or WFQ scheduler (*see* Fig. 6.14).

The index is based on an exact match on the six bits of the DSCP (the two CU bits being ignored). Each specified PHB should be assigned a unique default codepoint among the 64 that could potentially be available with six bits. In fact, RFC 2474 has allocated three pools of codepoints:

- xxxxx0 for 'standard actions'. Eight codepoints (yyy000), called class selector codepoints, are already allocated for backward compatibility with the IP precedence field of RFC 791. RFC 2474 states that the set of PHBs mapped to those codepoints must satisfy the following requirements: offer at least two independent queues, expedite forwarding according to yyy values (the higher the yyy, the lower the average queuing delay), and prioritize yyy=110 and 111 (routing traffic) over yyy=000 (best-effort traffic). Note that this set of requirements does not imply the use of one particular scheduling algorithm (WFQ, CBQ or priority queuing could be used). This philosophy will be retained when defining other PHBs;

- xxxx11 for experimental or local use;

- xxxx01 for experimental or local use, or extension of the standard actions pool if it gets fully allocated.

Even if each PHB is allocated a default codepoint, Diffserv nodes are free to assign other codepoints to a particular PHB (except for xxx000 codepoints). In fact, codepoints may have a meaning that is only local to a domain. At the boundary of such Diffserv domains, it is important to control the forwarding of IP packets according to their codepoints, and if necessary to map some

Fig. 6.12 : The differentiated services byte

codepoints to other values. The configuration of the PHB to codepoint mapping is an administrative decision that may vary from domain to domain. Two service providers with service level agreements must either agree on codepoint values for each PHB, or properly configure codepoint translation at boundary nodes.

All packets with unknown codepoints (not part of the service level agreement of a service provider) are assumed to be part of the best-effort forwarding behavior. This PHB must always be present in a DS-compliant node. The default codepoint for the best-effort PHB is 000000, and this value must be recognized by all DS-compliant nodes.

So far only the class selector PHBs have been defined (in fact, this was mostly a mapping of the IP precedence semantics of RFC 791), but in the future there could be a strict priority queuing PHB with a different set of requirements.

In order to avoid mixing widely different traffic types into a single queue, providers of Diffserv networks are expected to perform some traffic shaping/regulation at the edge of the network, for instance with a token bucket. Occasionally there will be flows exceeding the regulator settings. It is not always a good idea to immediately mark such out-of-profile packets for best-effort for-

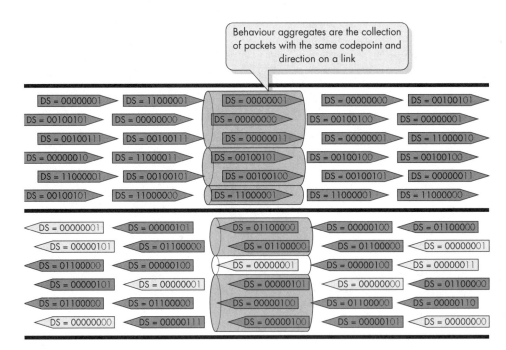

Fig. 6.13 : Behavior aggregates

warding, since this practice can introduce unnecessary desequencing. Maybe the network still has enough capacity to carry the excess packet in sequence; therefore the best solution is to mark this packet as being 'out of profile'. A node will forward this packet as if it was 'in profile' if there is enough capacity locally, and discard it otherwise (or mark it for best-effort forwarding). The solution recommended in RFC 2475 for marking in-profile and out-of-profile packets is to use two codepoints.

The CU field is not allocated yet, but could be used for forward/backward congestion notification. This has been very useful in frame-relay networks.

A more complete description of the differentiated services architecture has been published in RFC 2475 (December 1998). This RFC mainly introduces a specific Diffserv vocabulary (some of which appears in Fig. 6.14 and is reproduced in the glossary), and discusses the Diffserv paradigm and trade-off in comparison with other architectures supporting service level agreements.

Issues with IP TOS/DS octet

Sorting flows

Sorting flows based on the IP precedence value limits the number of queuing behaviors to eight (out of which six are available to end-user applications). It can be further refined by using filters based on the protocol number (for instance, to prioritize UDP over TCP) or destination/source addresses and ports. However, some applications are extremely difficult to prioritize using static filters, for instance all applications which use a dynamic port negotiation, such as H.323.

If the router has no proxy capability for the application, it has no way of knowing which port to prioritize. The only possibility is to prioritize an entire

Note: In a previous proposal, the first bit was allocated to mark an out-of-profile packet:

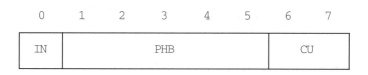

```
IN:  in (1) or out (0) of profile
PHB: per-hop behavior
CU:  currently unused (reserved)
```

range of ports, or all packets originated from the host. Obviously in many cases this is not enough. In a shared commercial backbone, this creates potential security issues because the prioritization will be static, and a witty user can decide to design an application which 'looks like' an authorized application but uses far more resources. For instance, if the provider prioritizes UDP in order to speed up small DNS queries, video-conferencing users will also benefit from it, while they obviously use far more resources.

Offering six classes of service to the end user may seem enough, and for most IP applications it will be. However, this will probably lead to merging different types of traffic to the same queues inside the backbone, and while in the short term it is not a real issue since many routers cannot maintain many queues, in the medium term six may be a bit short.

The recent Diffserv framework makes things potentially much better, since up to 32 packet-handling algorithms could be indexed. A service provider might choose to allocate specific codepoints for flows conditioned by an r,b token bucket. However, this will not help outside the intranet environment until providers have agreed on a set of standard codepoints, with *well defined meaning* (this was very long awaited in the ATM world, especially regarding profile control algorithms), and have put in place service level agreements that ensure

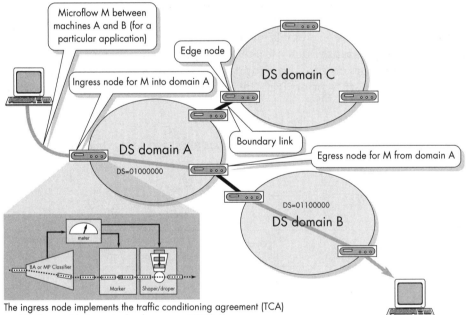

The ingress node implements the traffic conditioning agreement (TCA) used by the provider's service level agreement (SLA)

Fig. 6.14 : DS architecture

consistent quality of service levels across domains. Even then, some networks might choose to continue using the old definitions of the TOS octet because they might be unable to update the router software.

Pricing

For network dimensioning, it is useful to know the characteristics of the data streams that are being multiplexed. Let us compare the multiplexing of:

- flows having an average rate of 20 kbit/s, a maximum burst of 1 kbit at a constant rate of 100 kbit/s and a minimum constant bitrate of 10 kbit/s.
- flows having an average rate of 20 kbit/s, a maximum burst of 100 kbit at a constant rate of 100 kbit/s and a minimum constant bitrate of 10 kbit/s.

It is easy to calculate that in both cases the high bitrate occurs $\frac{1}{10}$ of the time, and the low bitrate occurs $\frac{9}{10}$ of the time. But for the first type of flow the bursts are very short ($\frac{1}{100}$s), while in the second case the bursts last one second. So in the first case the provider will be able to fit 1000 flows in just a little more than 1000*20 kbit/s – the excess traffic during bursts will accumulate in small router buffers, and the resulting delay will not be too large. But in the second case the bursts last much longer – the required buffers would be too large and the resulting delays unacceptable. So the provider needs to provide significantly more than 1000*20kbit/s in order to keep the buffer size low in routers.

In general, bursty traffic is much more expensive to carry than smooth traffic. In the next-generation IP networks, the provider will probably try to isolate these flows and apply a special pricing. In order to identify such flows, it would be useful to have a description of the characteristics of each data stream that a customer sends into the backbone. Based on this description, the provider could decide which streams could be grouped and how expensive it would be to carry these streams. The TOS value does not give any idea of the traffic characteristics, bursty and smooth traffic are mixed, and there is no easy way for the provider to sort similar streams together and have higher tariffs for the more bursty streams.

TOS value assignment

The internal backbone of a provider will have well defined TOS values/DS codepoints for each class of service. But different providers may use different values for each class, until Diffserv proposals are widely accepted and implemented. Even with the current Diffserv RFCs, only the relative behaviors of class selector PHBs are defined, but the quality of a particular codepoint could vary widely when changing providers. When designing a TOS-aware application, the programmer cannot know in advance which TOS value must be used, and will probably need some configuration. The average user will have no means of deciding which TOS is appropriate for each application. What are the implications on delay? Can this application recover from packet loss? Is it sensitive to jitter?

It is much easier for the programmer to be able to ask the network what it needs in terms of bandwidth and delay, and to let the network provide the required QoS.

For all these reasons, there is still a need for some more sophisticated signaling mechanism between the applications and the network, and this is where RSVP might fill the gap.

RSVP

RSVP is not about flowing packets on the Net, it's about flowing money on the Net . . . (John Wrocklowski, *Professor in computer science at MIT, one of the two heads of the MIT Internet Telephony Consortium and one of the two co-chairs of the RSVP working group*)

RSVP is a QOS protocol . . . and also a business enabling protocol. We have seen which difficulties were encountered when using only IP precedence as a way to signal a need for QoS. Commercial providers need to be able to:

■ promote native support of QoS by IP applications
■ arrange agreements to support QoS across networks managed by different entities
■ provide QoS guarantees when needed
■ bill for the service.

Therefore they need to:

■ give applications a uniform way to ask for a level of QoS
■ find a way to guarantee a level of QoS
■ provide authentication.

RSVP is an answer to all these issues.

Services provided by RSVP

RSVP offers two types of services:

■ the *controlled load* service – an application requesting controlled load service for a stream of given characteristics expects the network to behave as if it was lightly loaded for that stream. The exact meaning of this is not defined in

RSVP, but the general understanding is that packet loss should be very low or null. The absolute delay is not specified, but jitter should be kept as low as possible since in a lightly loaded network router buffers are empty;

■ the *guaranteed* service – this requests not only bandwidth, but also a maximum transit delay. RSVP guaranteed service is built on the PGPS paradigm. In the PGPS formulas, C and D parameters appear as sums along the path of the stream through the network; RSVP is used to calculate those sums and propagate the intermediary results between RSVP routers. The aim is to make C and D available to the recipient of the stream, together with the traffic characteristics of the flow such as σ, ρ and p. This information allows the recipient to calculate the bandwidth r he wants to reserve for that stream in order to achieve a particular delay bound. In the above formula the maximal delay D_i^* is a decreasing function of r_i , so by allocating a greater minimal rate r_i, the recipient can make the transit delay through the network as close as possible to D_{TOT}, which is the smallest value he can hope for.

In our description of PGPS, we emphasized that packets would not arrive later than the calculated PGPS delay bound, but they could also arrive *much* sooner. This means that RSVP cannot be used to specify a maximum jitter independently of the maximum delay. The jitter guaranteed by RSVP is just the difference between the minimum path latency (propagation delays) and the maximum guaranteed delay. The only way to request a very low jitter is to request a delay very close to the minimum path latency (we will see later that this is not very practical since the bandwidth reservation needed to request such a delay is extremely large).

Not having a fine control on jitter is in fact not very important for most applications – interactive applications need very low round-trip delays and can adapt to jitter using a jitter buffers and protocols such as RTP. But this could be a problem for applications using very large bitrate streams because they would need to allocate a lot of memory for the jitter buffers.

There are no clear guidelines in the IETF documents for the use of guaranteed service versus controlled-load service when writing RSVP-aware applications. The main difference is that controlled-load parameters do not include target end-to-end delay values. When several streams require controlled-load service, some may come from TCP applications needing an average bandwidth, and some may come from UDP real-time applications such as video conferencing. An RSVP-aware router that controls access to a low bandwidth or congested link will be unable to choose which packets need to go out first (or if a packet needs to pre-empt a packet already being transmitted) based on the parameters provided by the controlled-load RESV message (in the current RSVP specification).

Therefore real-time applications should preferably use the guaranteed service. Unfortunately this service is more complex to implement, and some expect that it will not be as readily available as controlled-load mode. So many programmers prefer to use controlled-load service even for interactive applications. We believe this is wrong. A real-time application should try to use guaranteed service first, and fall back to controlled load only if guaranteed service is unavailable.

RSVP messages

RSVP uses mainly two types of messages:

- *PATH*. Sent by the source of the stream, this message initially contains data describing the stream, in particular the bucket parameters σ and ρ. It follows exactly the same path as the stream itself (including multicast transmission), and each router updates the data elements CTOT and DTOT which are also part of that message. RSVP is useful only if the data follows the same path as the PATH messages. In order to enforce this for some complex routing algorithms, it is necessary to have a dialogue between the RSVP process and the routing process. This is the role of the RSRR (routing support for resource reservation) interface.

Figure 6.15 describes the propagation of PATH messages for a multicast stream. At each hop, an RSVP router modifies the PATH message to update the C and D parameters and includes its address. It also stores the last hop address that was originally in the PATH message. One of the routers is not capable of handling RSVP and simply forwards the PATH packet as it received it.

- RESV. This message (Fig. 6.16) is sent by the recipient(s) of the stream towards the source following the exact inverse path of the upstream packets and PATH messages. Each RSVP router, when receiving an RESV message for a flow, forwards it to the last hop address that was previously stored from the PATH message. The RESV message specifies the minimal bandwidth r_i required for stream i, calculated using the data from the PATH message in order to obtain a certain delay. Eventually it can also specify an error margin on that target delay, if it needs bandwidth but not low delays (e.g. a video-streaming application). The stream itself is characterized by a filter, so a single reservation can apply to several streams (e.g several sources in a conference). This is called a shared reservation.

Figure 6.16 shows how RSVP works even through non-RSVP routers – receiver A used the last hop address that it found in the PATH message as the destination address for the RESV message. This is in fact the address of the last RSVP router along the path – for RSVP, non-RSVP clouds between A and B appear as a direct link between A and B. If there is no congestion or significant delay in the non-RSVP cloud, end-to-end reservations made by RSVP will still be valid.

The example also shows how multiple reservations for a multicast stream can be merged. If receiver B requires a low delay (large reserved rate) and receiver C is prepared to cope with more delay for the same multicast stream, then only the largest reservation will be forwarded upstream.

During the reservation setup stage, it is important to avoid losing either the first PATH message or the RESV message, otherwise the reservation could be delayed by 30 seconds. For instance, over a Diffserv enabled backbone, the PATH and RESV messages could be transmitted over the net-ctrl (precedence level 7) class of service.

Using RSVP to set up a controlled-load reservation

The RSVP controlled-load service is simple, and can be implemented over custom queuing routers. If a stream requests a reservation of 200 kbit/s for a stream with bursts up to 10 kbit/s, each router can configure its scheduler to allocate an average 50 kbit/s to the stream – if the outgoing link is an E1 (2 mbit/s), the scheduler must service the queue allocated to the stream 10 per cent of the time at least.

This is not enough to guarantee a low packet loss if the traffic is bursty – each RSVP router must make sure that the queue buffer is large enough to accommodate bursts. In our example, if the scheduler services the stream 1 ms each 10 ms, the worst case is if the burst occurs just after the scheduler has finished servicing the stream. The stream traffic will accumulate for 9 ms – that is 10 kbit/s for the

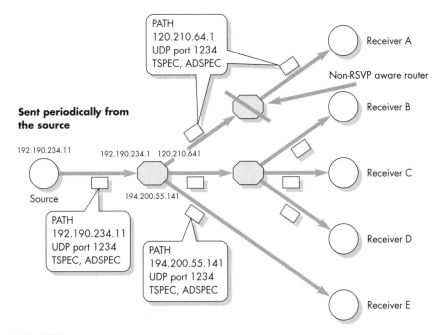

Fig. 6.15 : PATH messages

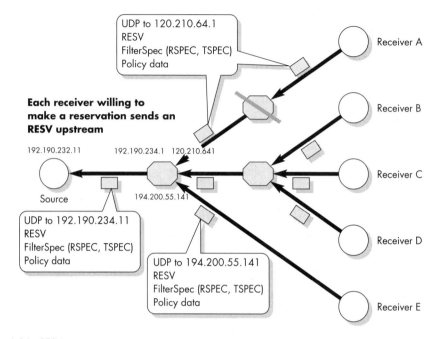

Fig. 6.16 : RESV messages

burst and 0.009*200 kbit/s for the regular flow after the burst. In this case the queue buffer needs to be large enough to accommodate 11.8 kbit of data.

And that is only for the first router. Each router can change the characteristics of the stream, and in general the traffic will become more and more bursty, so routers downstream will have to allocate even larger buffers and may choose to reshape the stream.

Some routers have low-capacity CPUs and may also become congested because of a lack of CPU power (this is especially true for flows generating small packets, such as IP telephony). The reservation algorithm should also make sure that enough CPU cycles will be saved for the processing of the flow.

There is a stricter interpretation of controlled load service saying that the bursts should be allowed to get through a node using the maximum available bandwidth (i.e. all the bandwidth except that used by guaranteed service streams, and some spare bandwidth saved for best-effort traffic to avoid BE starvation).

Using RSVP to set up a guaranteed service reservation

Let us look at an example. Source A sends a stream to B, and declares the following stream characteristics in the sender Tspec and AdSpec parts of the PATH message:

Tspec: (p = 10 mbit/s, L = 2 kbit/s, ρ = 1024 kbit/s, σ = 32 kbit/s)

AdSpec: (Ctot = 0, Dtot = 0)

The first RSVP router R1 keeps the Tspec part of the PATH message unchanged but modifies Adspec: (Ctot=11 kbit, Dtot = 0.05 sec). The second RSVP router R2 relays Tspec as it is and modifies AdSpec: (Ctot=55 kbit, 0.1 sec). The receiver B chooses the guaranteed QoS service to obtain a specific end-to-end delay. To find which reservation he needs as a function of the desired delay (which will always be greater than D_{tot} = 0.1s), he solves the equation derived from the above results:

$$r = \frac{(p - \rho)(L + C_{tot}) + (\sigma - L)p}{(D_{desired} - D_{tot})(p - \rho) + \sigma - L} \text{with the constraint r>}\rho.$$

For r=ρ the delay is simply $D = \dfrac{\sigma + C_{tot}}{\rho} + D_{tot}$ or 0.185s, so B can choose any delay between 0.1 and 0.184s. Table 6.2 shows the results obtained with some values: It is obvious that B must be reasonable (must pay!) because r 'explodes' when the desired delay approaches D_{tot}.

B chooses a delay of 0.15s and decides to request 1695.1 kbit/s. The reservation receiver Tspec = (p=10 mbit/s, M = 2 kbit/s, r = 1024 kbit/s, b = 32 kbit/s) and Rspec=1695.1 kbit/s is sent from the receiver B towards A along the path followed by the PATH messages.

The receiver can also specify the 'slack' Sn he can accept on top of D_{tot}. This is useful if B, for instance, needs a delay of 0.5s while asking simply for r=R already guarantees 0.185s. This slack value is then transmitted at the same time with Rn as the Rspec element. It can be used in a node if that node cannot allocate the requested r – in that case the node will 'eat' a part of Sn and pass on a decremented Sn.

Soft states

It would be a very bad idea to agree to do a reservation in a node if there was the slightest chance that this reservation was not properly terminated. In ATM or PSTN networks, this leads to a rather complex, but safe, signaling. RSVP works around this problem by committing only temporary reservations, which must be refreshed from time to time by the receiver of the stream – a reservation is a 'soft state' with a timeout.

Furthermore, the routes in an IP network can change at any time (when the network topology changes, for instance after a link failure). This is generally considered a feature which gives IP a lot of robustness in facing network failures. But when you consider a reservation along a given path, this becomes a serious issue. Again the soft state concept is the answer – since the PATH messages follow the

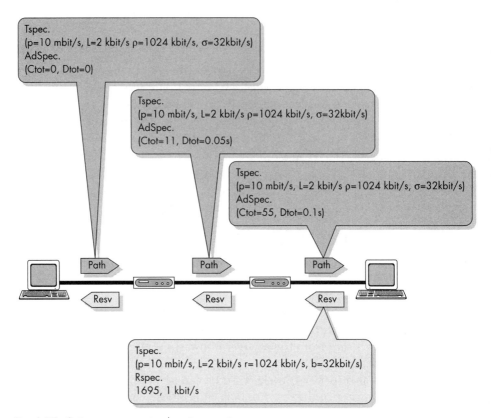

Fig. 6.17 : Setting up a guaranteed service rervation

Table 6.2 : Obtaining a spectic end-to-end delay

Desired delay (s)	r to ask (kbit/s)
0.15	1695.1
0.11	6777.1
0.101	20823.9

path of the stream, they will follow the new routes, and therefore the new RESV messages, which follow the inverse path, will attempt to do reservations along the new route. The old reservations will not be properly torn down, but they will time out.

In some cases it will not be possible to set up the reservation along the new path, for instance if the network is too congested or if the policy along this path is different, but this should not happen very often in a well designed network.

(The same situation could also occur in the PSTN if an important link broke down.) However, there could be a significant interaction between RSVP and dynamic routing algorithms assigning packets to the less loaded link. Those algorithms should ensure existing RSVP sessions remain intact, i.e. they should not change the route of PATH messages 'on the fly'.

Other features

In the case of multicast streams, the reservation requests are initiated by *any* receiver and merged in the network. This is a very powerful feature of RSVP, which so far has no equivalent on the ATM networks (although it could be included in UNI 4.0).

RSVP can 'work' over non-RSVP clouds, since those clouds will forward the PATH and RESV messages. But those clouds are seen as direct links by RSVP, and if they are congested it will not be reflected in the PATH parameters: therefore the RESV message will be wrong. So this is workable only when the non-RSVP cloud is a low-delay (compared to the delay in the RSVP region), uncongested area.

Note for Microsoft developers: Windows NT 5 beta2 (now Windows 2000) includes the following headers:

- winsock2.h
- qossp.h (included in winsock2.h)
- qos.h

which need to be included in the project in order to use the winsock2 RSVP implementation.

Scaling issues with RSVP

CPU limitations

RSVP is only a way to calculate and transmit the parameters that a node needs to perform a bandwidth reservation (including security and billing). It is not responsible for *actually reserving* bandwidth. So a router must implement a scheduling or resource-sharing mechanism such as PGPS. Usually the nodes are said to use weighted fair queuing, but this term might apply to PGPS or other simplified schemes such as SCFQ (self clocked fair queuing). The resulting performance and the actual delay bounds obtained vary widely according to what is actually used (RSVP expects PGPS).

The problem is that PGPS, while it leads in theory to the tightest bounds, is very difficult to implement and requires a lot of processing power. The first task is to be able to sort all incoming flows based on the source address and port, and destination address and port. This is commonly called a multi-field (MF) classi-fier. Most implementations are very sensitive to the number of flow filters to recognize, and have serious scalability limits when the number of filters exceeds a few dozen. The second task is to schedule the packets to be served in an opti-mal order, and a quick glance at the equations of WFQ gives an idea of the complexity of this.

In fact it is not the 'complexity' of RSVP that is an obstacle (actually RSVP is simpler than many other signaling protocols), but the complexity of PGPS and other WFQ mechanisms. For instance the most highly tuned kernel mode UNIX implementations of PGPS on a Pentium 166 (Ian Marsch, SICS) achieve a throughput on 90 mbit/s on ten flows.

It is quite obvious that PGPS cannot be applied stream by stream in a back-bone network. Most router vendors are using heuristics approaching the behavior of PGPS but requiring less CPU power. Still, it is impossible to scale per stream queuing techniques to the throughput required in modern backbones. Moreover, technologies such as MPLS explicitly group several streams, which shields the actual stream information from the nodes.

Over-provisioning

A more fundamental problem is the fact that the hard delay bounds derived above have nothing to do with what is observed statistically. For a given reser-vation r, the delay observed would be *much* lower than the delay guaranteed by PGPS for almost all packets. So what we do here leads to systematic over-reservations if the application can tolerate losing a delayed packet here and there. It is expected that most receivers, knowing that fact, will simply use the D parameter of RSVP PATH as an indication of what delay they are going to experience (for instance, to set retransmission parameters) and reserve the bandwidth announced by the source to prevent packet dropping. In other words, most applications will use the controlled-load mode of RSVP.

This over-provisioning is not as bad as it seems, however, in the case of a link that carries much more best-effort data than real-time data (which is con-troversial but reasonable, considering that software agents and other fancy applets on our desktops can eat as much bandwidth as the developers think they need, while we cannot speak more than 24 hours a day). Most scheduling algorithms, and of course PGPS, are able to reallocate the bandwidth not actu-ally used by a stream to the rest of the traffic – the extra bandwidth reserved but not actually used by RSVP will be used by best-effort traffic and *there is no waste* (*see* Fig. 6.18). However, if the real-time traffic is predominant, the net-work will refuse reservations that in reality it could have handled, and this is indeed a problem. This problem is not specific to RSVP, and also occurs on ATM-based networks.

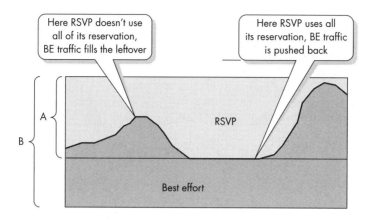

A: Reserved bandwidth for RSVP streams
B: Available bandwidth

Fig. 6.18 : *Extra bandwidth used by best-effort traffic*

State

RSVP is a connection-oriented technology. As such it requires the network nodes to store information (state) about each connection in the network. This is a fundamental move from the connectionless paradigm of IP, and probably the source of much of the debate around RSVP. Any other connection-oriented technology has the same problem: basically these techniques do not scale as the number of connections increases through the network. In the optimal case of multicast flows, the amount of state scales as the number of peripheral nodes. In the case of unicast traffic, the amount of state scales as the square of the number of peripheral nodes.

Compared with ATM for instance, RSVP has its advantages and drawbacks. The one major advantage is that RSVP requires state only for QoS connections, so if most of the traffic needs only best-effort transport, it is merely a small subset of the overall traffic. ATM will use a connection per stream, regardless of whether the stream has requested QoS or not. But ATM is based on hard states: there needs to be signaling activity only at call setup and call tear down. Since RSVP is based on soft states, each connection needs periodic signaling activity, so the work required for the same amount of streams is much higher for RSVP than it is for ATM.

So, in the current state of the specification, it is hard to decide whether RSVP is really better or worse than other connection-oriented QoS techniques, but there are some perspectives on the future of RSVP which could improve its scalability.

Some solutions

A layered architecture

The solution that seems to emerge is a layered architecture, which uses the fact that RSVP messaging can cross a non-RSVP cloud. This solution tries to focus on the business requirements for RSVP: in short, use RSVP where it is very useful, and avoid it as much as possible when it is not strictly necessary. The business requirements are:

1   To give applications a uniform way to ask for a level of QoS and describe data streams, in order to minimize the manual configuration and management tasks.

2   Find a way to guarantee a level of QoS, end to end, for each application and end user.

3   Provide authentication and facilitate billing.

4   Provide the necessary statistics in order to help the backbone provider to properly dimension its network.

Requirements 1, 3 and 4 are for the access nodes only. The only requirement which seems to require RSVP in the backbone is number 2. If we can find another way to guarantee QoS in the backbone, RSVP could be used only at the access network. Saying this, it is logical to divide the network into two separate concentric layers:

■   in the outer layer RSVP is used with flow by flow WFQ, which is possible because the bandwidth and the number of streams are still low for each router. The access routers also deal with security and billing;

■   in the core the streams facing similar constraints in terms of delay and required bandwidth are grouped using classes of service. The core routers do not perform any per flow accounting or policing, and are tuned to achieve a maximal throughput with minimal delay.

Classes of service in the backbone

Above are summarized some results related to the delay bounds achievable using a separate queue for each stream scheduled using WFQ. However, this scheme is not scalable due to the amount of processing power needed by WFQ. In this section we try to evaluate the impact of grouping several streams together in a single queue in the backbone.

Grouping of similar streams

We will call 'similar' streams those having similar characteristics in terms of average rate, maximum packet size, and burstiness. With this in mind, a 'class of streams' is composed of all streams whose characteristics fall within the following bounds:

- average rate equals $\rho \pm \Delta\rho$
- maximal burstiness $\sigma \pm \Delta\sigma$
- maximal packet size L_{MAX} is supposed to be common to all streams.

We now suppose that N streams fit in this definition (for instance, the rate and burstiness chosen are typical of the G.723.1 sound channel of an H.323 Internet phone). The resulting stream will have an average rate of $N\rho + N\Delta\rho$ and a burstiness lower than $N\sigma + N\Delta\sigma$. With these results we can calculate a delay bound at each backbone hop, where $_c$ means class:

(A) $$D_c^\star \le \left. \frac{N(\sigma + \Delta\sigma)}{N(\rho + \Delta\rho)} \right/ + \left. L_{MAX} \right/_C + Tr$$

assuming that the aggregate stream is assigned a portion of total bandwidth C equivalent to $N\rho + N\Delta\rho$ (stability condition).

If each individual flow had been assigned a separate queue under WFQ, the result would have been:

(B) $$D_i^\star \le \left. \sigma_i \right/_{r_i} + \left. L_{MAX} \right/_C + Tr$$

(A) and (B) are very similar, which shows that grouping similar streams in the backbone does not cause too much loss in the guaranteed end-to-end delay. Moreover, (A) is really a worst case bound since it assumes burstiness is an additive parameter; in reality, each individual stream is independent and the resulting burstiness would be much lower. How much lower is hard to say – it has to be measured – but for a sum of periodical streams with random phase it can be calculated exactly. In Fig. 6.19 sporadicity is defined as MaxThroughput(s)/averageThroughput(s), where $(P(\text{Throughput}(s,t))>\text{MaxThroughput}(s))<10^{-9}$:

If we now consider the end-to-end delay, grouping several identical flows might even be beneficial. In the end-to-end formula given for PGPS through H hops, one of the components of the delay was (H–1)L/r; when grouping several flows, this becomes (H–1)L/Nr, which is much less. If the grouped flows are similar in terms of sporadicity, less bandwidth is needed to achieve the same delay bound.

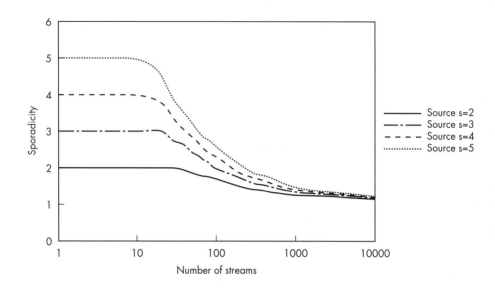

Fig. 6.19 : Sporadicity of aggregate streams

Bandwidth management

In the previous section it was assumed that N streams were grouped. In reality this number would vary with time, and it would be difficult to adjust dynamically the bandwidth reserved for that class of service each time N changed. A possible heuristic for bandwidth reservation could be some over-provisioning of bandwidth, which would be incremented if the class uses more than 90 per cent of the bandwidth or decremented if it uses less than 70 per cent (the threshold given here is arbitrary, and should be derived from effective dispersion of used bandwidth within the class). This hysteresis would reduce the number of bandwidth reservation changes in the backbone for that class.

Using class-by-class WFQ with some bandwidth over-provisioning does not waste bandwidth, since the unused reserved bandwidth is always available for best-effort traffic at any time. With this in mind, and given that best-effort traffic will probably be the bulk of the data carried over the backbone, this solution seems to be workable for real-world backbones.

Using DiffServ with RSVP tunneling

The easiest way to simplify the provision of QoS in the backbone and avoid per flow state is to ignore RSVP completely, relying on the simpler Diffserv architecture. Diffserv is an approach where all flows carried by the backbone are grouped in several classes of service, eliminating most of the scalability issues encountered by per flow QoS provisioning. There are many ways to implement classes of service in the core:

- using IP TOS – the internal routers can use class-by-class WFQ, where each class is determined according to the precedence bits of IP packets;
- using layer 2 capabilities:
  - providers with an ATM backbone can open several Virtual Channels (VC) between concentration routers with several levels of QoS, or use the ATM CLP bit (Cell Loss Priority)) to define two rough classes of service;
  - providers with a frame relay backbone can open several VCs between the border routers with various levels of QoS parameters, or use the DE (discard eligible) bit;
- in the future MPLS (multiprotocol label switching) backbones will also make it possible to have several levels of QoS for each path across the network. The level of QoS required will be marked in the label.

These techniques can be combined with congestion control mechanisms such as RED or WRED to smooth TCP traffic and improve fairness between flows within each class of service.

We have seen that RSVP is an end-to-end protocol, so RSVP messages need to be passed between hosts across the backbone. This is not as simple as it seems. First of all, RSVP messages must be ignored in the backbone, otherwise we would run into scalability issues. Each RSVP packet is marked with a 'router alert' option in order to help routers identify this packet as one needing special treatment. So in most cases it is enough to turn off the router alert option through the backbone. However, some implementations (e.g. ISI) do not rely on the router alert option but on an interception of protocol 46. In this case it is also possible to use a new IP protocol number that only access routers would recognize.

Work is ongoing at the IETF to clarify the expected behavior of a router regarding the router alert option. The last proposal is: 'The processing to be performed upon a message containing a router alert option should depend only upon the IP protocol Id field. In other words, a router does not have to look any deeper into the packet than the IP header' (Bob Braden on an IETF mailing list). This will probably lead to an update of the router alert RFC, and seems to indicate that the preferred method to hide RSVP messages from the backbone is to use a new protocol number. This number will have to be obtained from IANA.

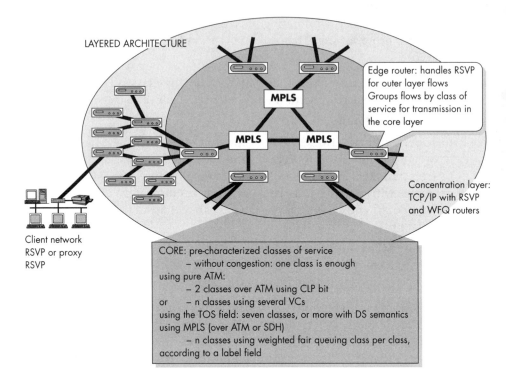

Fig. 6.20 : Scalable QoS

RSVP to Diffserv mapping

One technology that can be deployed in a backbone is Diffserv. The RSVP and the Diffserv paradigms are based on opposite models – RSVP gives precedence to a stream based on the receiver's wish, while Diffserv prioritization is controlled by the sender.

In the layered model, an edge router sits between the Diffserv domain and the Intserv (RSVP) domain (Fig. 6.21). This edge router can modify the TOS value of all packets injected into the backbone and therefore has complete control over the priority of these packets. In order to emulate the receiver-based RSVP behavior, this router must decide which class of service to use for a flow based on the QoS requirements contained in the RESV messages. Such a layered model is being studied at IETF (*see* Draft-bernet-diffedge-01.txt).

PATH messages

For the end-user application, the network must behave as if it was RSVP enabled, end to end. Therefore the PATH messages generated by the sender must cross the backbone and reach the receiver. When it receives a path message describing a flow, a receiver may choose to send back a RESV message in order to reserve resources for this flow in the backbone.

This is not enough. If an implementation transmits the PATH parameters transparently, the receiver will have a false view of the backbone because the parameters within the PATH messages will not have been updated to reflect the latency and other characteristics of the backbone. Therefore the receiver might be misled, thinking the backbone adds less delay than it actually does, and do a wrong reservation, especially in guaranteed service mode. In order to avoid this the egress router must update some of the PATH parameters, making the backbone appear as one node for RSVP.

So the PATH message parameters must be updated by the ingress or egress edge router. This is not straightforward. Each stream's PATH message must be updated with the C and D parameters found in: $Delay < \frac{\sigma + C}{\rho} + D$. But now the stream is included in a particular class of service grouping several flows, as there is no per-flow queuing in the backbone. Now the group average rate is $N\rho + N\Delta\rho$ and the average burstiness is $N\sigma + N\Delta\sigma$. We could try to calculate values for C and D, but

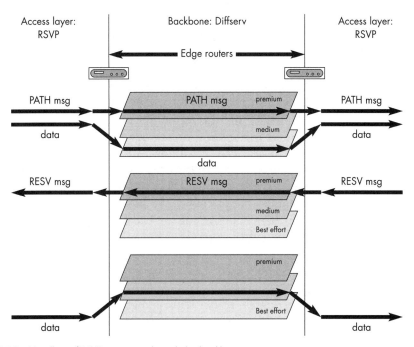

Fig. 6.21 : Handling of RSVP messages through the backbone

the result would depend on the values of N, $\Delta\rho$ and $\Delta\sigma$. N, $\Delta\rho$ and $\Delta\sigma$ depend on the class of service that has been chosen for the stream, and this class of service depends on the RESV parameters sent by the receiver. So we have a circular reference problem because the RESV parameters themselves depend on the calculated values of C and D.

To solve this chicken and egg problem, a practical approach is to propagate the value of C as is and update only the D parameter. In other words, we consider that the queuing delay added by the backbone is not very sensitive to the characteristics of the individual stream, and can be approximated by a value that does not depend on ρ. This approximation is generally valid if the number of aggregated streams is large, and one single stream has a negligible influence on the backbone transit delay. This delay is reflected in the update of parameter D. Therefore we update D with a value representing the propagation delays and the average queuing delay through the backbone.

If the backbone is built using powerful 'gigarouters', each PATH message can be updated at each hop. On the other hand, if the backbone is built using ATM or MPLS technology, the PATH message would have to be updated only once at the first ingress router with an evaluation of the overall transmission delay along the virtual circuit to the destination of that stream.

RESV messages

If the backbone uses routers that have enough processing power to handle RESV messages hop by hop, each RESV message can be propagated normally through the backbone, but instead of creating a separate queue for the stream as in regular RSVP operation, the router will direct that stream to the queue that is most appropriate for this class of service. Those routers will maintain the bandwidth usage information for each class of service, and eventually decide to add more bandwidth for a particular class.

If the backbone uses ATM or MPLS technology, the edge router receiving an RESV message can tunnel this message to the edge router used by that stream to enter the backbone. This router will then direct the stream to the appropriate PVC for that destination (or use special bits in the MPLS label to mark the class of each packet of that stream. The nodes inside the backbone could then only deal with this QoS information to put the packets in the appropriate queues).

Caveats

When all this is done, the ingress router will aggregate several flows over each class of service. This will not have a significant impact on the QoS level experienced by each individual flow except in some situations:

■ when one of the flows does not conform to its Tspec – if the provider has dimensioned each virtual link between the ingress and egress routers for an aggregate of flows with well defined characteristics, one non-conformant flow may be enough to ruin the quality of service experienced by all other flows on the same class;

■ when very sporadic flows are merged with smooth flows (e.g web with IP telephony).

Therefore the access router must have the ability to check the Tspec of each flow, and the service provider must avoid merging sporadic and smooth flows when defining the classes of service of the backbone. Each class will group streams having 'similar' burstiness and for which a 'similar' bandwidth has been requested. For instance, each class of service could be a square region in the σ, ρ space. *See* Fig. 6.22.

Improving QoS in the best-effort class

While it is easy to understand that a network provider will try to offer low loss rates and low latency to its premium customers, one might wonder what it can do for its best-effort customers. This amounts to only two things: improve fairness (each customer must have an equal opportunity to use the capacity of the best-effort class), and keep the backlog as low as possible in each router in order to minimize the transit delay.

Issues with UDP traffic

UDP traffic has no standard-rate limiting feature in case of congestion. Most properly written applications are able to detect network congestion and react by

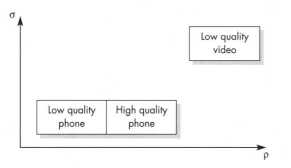

Fig. 6.22 : Classes of service

backing off the rate of UDP traffic – all applications using RTP/RTCP will detect congestion when RTCP reports increasing packet loss and higher latency. But on the best-effort class where everyone pays a flat fee it is tempting to create a UDP application with a high redundancy scheme and which reacts to congestion not by reducing its bitrate but by *increasing* it with more redundant and forward error correction packets.

And this will work because most best-effort queues are handled in FIFO mode, and packets are dropped when the queue overflows. Statistically, the packets which remain in the queue without being dropped represent a percentage of the total offered traffic – so the more you offer traffic to the node, the more packets you get through the node. Such behavior will cause 'honest' users to be gradually excluded from the network, while the greedy pirates will enjoy it all (*see* Fig. 6.23).

Issues with TCP traffic

All modern TCP stacks implement congestion control algorithms developed by Van Jacobson, as specified in RFC 1122 (and updated in RFC 2001). These algorithms interpret packet loss as a hint that the network is congested, and react by slowing down the rate at which TCP injects traffic into the backbone.

The Van Jacobson & Karels congestion control algorithm is one of the most popular. It works by defining, in addition to the usual receiver window size (the maximum number of bytes that the receiver is prepared to receive at once), a congestion window. The actual window size used during the transmission is the minimum of the receiver window size and the congestion window. The congestion window size begins with a size of one segment (512 or 536 bytes unless the other end requests a different size), and gets one segment larger for each acknowledgement received without loss. This exponential growth is characteristic of the slow-start mode.

If there is a timeout while waiting for an ACK, or if there are duplicate ACKs sent by the receiver, the sender deduces that there is some congestion and sets the congestion avoidance threshold to one half of the current window size. Then the sender sets the window size to one segment and increases it in slow-start mode. Once the window size gets larger than the congestion avoidance threshold, the sender increases the window size by (segment_size/window_size) segments for each ACK, and the window size increases linearly with time (*see* Fig. 6.24).

Modern TCP stacks (4.3 BSD 'Reno' stack) implement a specific fast retransmit/fast recovery procedure instead of going into slow start immediately when the receiver sends duplicate ACKs (duplicate ACKs are sent when the receiver receives out-of-sequence packets).

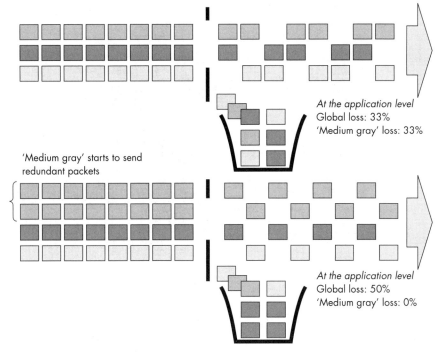

Fig. 6.23 : How 'pirates' can exploit the best-effort class

When a FIFO queue overflows, many active TCP sessions are likely to lose an IP packet *simultaneously*. These sessions will back off and hopefully the congestion will disappear. Then all these TCP sessions will see that they are not losing packets any more and will increase their window size little by little . . . after a while the congestion is back, packets are dropped, and all sessions back off again. This can lead to an oscillation of TCP traffic caused by a synchronization of VJ algorithms after a queue overflow.

RED and WRED

TCP implementations with congestion avoidance are friendly for the network, while UDP programs or hacked TCP stacks will continue to flood congested links. TCP stacks with congestion avoidance will rapidly back off and progressively let the aggressive traffic use the complete capacity of congested links.

It is possible to improve the behavior of the network by discarding packets 'intelligently'. Random early detection keeps the backlog in routers as low as possible, while avoiding TCP synchronization. A RED router starts dropping packets at random before the FIFO buffer actually overflows. Hopefully the session that

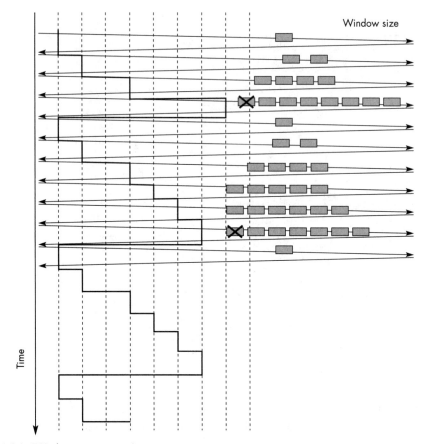

Fig. 6.24 : TCP slow start

experiences the packet loss will start reducing its bitrate. Little by little many sessions will experience some packet loss and reduce the aggregate bitrate smoothly before real congestion occurs. Without this policy, when the buffer overflows, all sessions experience some packet loss and reduce their bitrate simultaneously, which may cause undesired synchronization and possible oscillations.

With weighted RED, it is possible to go further and decide to increase the packet loss for a class of sessions. This can be useful for some basic prioritization, for instance traffic in 'premium' class would experience packet loss only after 'medium' class. Weighted RED can also be used to enforce fairness. In the above example, it is relatively easy to identify the greedy blue stream as one getting more bandwidth than it should, by analyzing the lost packets. The normal behavior of a router is to lose packets proportionally to the offered traffic which, as we have seen, actually encourages the use of redundancy schemes. WRED

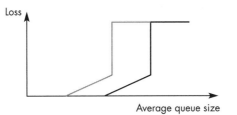

Fig. 6.25 : Selective loss (WRED)

introduces some non-linearity. In the above example, for instance, the router could decide to drop 80 per cent of the blue packets.

Issues with slow links

Slow links are especially challenging for delay-sensitive applications. For instance a 1500-octet packet (a common size since it is the MTU over Ethernet) needs about 400 ms (1500*8/28800) to be transmitted over a 28.8 kbit/s PPP link. This would not be an issue if there was only the delay-sensitive application on the link because this application could use smaller packets. Unfortunately, the line is often shared with other applications using larger packets, such as a web browser, and the urgent packets will be delayed if they are queued behind the large TCP packets. *See* Fig. 6.26.

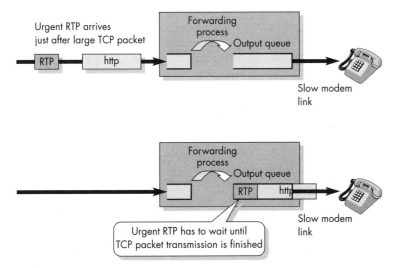

Fig. 6.26 : The implications of slow links

Another issue is that the overhead of the IP protocol suite is quite high. For example, in each packet of a telephony or video application, IP uses 20 bytes, UDP uses 8 bytes, and RTP uses 12 bytes. The link layer overhead is also significant: PPP+HDLC takes an additional 4 bytes per packet on a modem link.

To see how bad it is, this is what happens with a popular video-conferencing application such as Microsoft Netmeeting. The codec used is G.723.1, which has an audio frame length of 30 ms. In its 6.4 kbit/s mode (MP-MLQ), each frame is 24 octets long. When Netmeeting is putting only one frame per packet, each IP packet is 24+40 bytes long, and PPP+HDLC will make it 68 bytes long on the PPP link. A packet is sent every 30 ms, and the resulting bitrate is over 18 kbit/s. Only one-third of the bitrate is actual audio information from the G.732.1 codec. To leave some room for data and video over 28.8 bits/s modems, most audio applications (including NetMeeting) have to stack several frames per packet.

A popular trade-off is to put four G.723.1 frames in one packet. This reduces the bitrate to 7.7 kbit/s. The packetization delay becomes 4*30=120 ms (128 ms including lookahead). Then if we assume the best-case situation where this packet can be sent immediately, it will need 30 ms to get through the 28.8 modem link. Then we have the network delay, and again 30 ms at the egress modem. Unfortunately, this sets the conversational delay to a level that is unacceptable for most non-hobby users.

The PPPEXT/ISSLOW group of IETF is working on these issues. The overhead issue can be solved by using header compression. The queuing issue can be solved by allowing real-time packets to preempt non real-time packets.

Header compression is based on a simple idea. Since most of the overhead of an IP packet is constant for a given stream (for instance the source and destination IP addresses and ports are constant), it is possible to negotiate a shorter 'index' to those constant values when the stream is set up. Other variable values such as sequence numbers can be reconstructed at the receiving end if proper per-stream state is maintained. With this technique, the sending host replaces the large header by a small index, and the receiving host reverses the operation.

Such a technique is being developed by S. Casner and V. Jacobson for applications using RTP in 'Compressing IP/UDP/RTP headers for low-speed serial links' (work in progress draft-ietf-avt-crtp-04.txt, November 1997). Another technique is proposed by M. Engan, S. Casner and C. Bormann in 'IP header compression over PPP' (work in progress draft-engan-ip-compress-02.txt, December 1997) for IP flows over PPP.

Two techniques have been proposed for preempting:

■ using the PPP-MP protocol (RFC 1990). The original design of multilink PPP was to allow the bundling of several physical or logical links into one single virtual link. Compared to plain PPP, PPP-MP provides additional means to sequence and correlate fragments arriving from several links. Since multilink is able to fragment packets, it can be used to stop transmission of a long packet, send the urgent packet, and resume transmission of the long packet. Also the multilink short sequence number fragment format (only 12 bits instead of 24) can be used in order to reduce the overhead, and the address, control, and most significant PID bytes can be compressed.

This simple solution has the advantage of being compatible with existing PPP-MP implementations, but cannot be used for more than one preemption level. This is because the PPP-MP specification requires the sequence numbers of fragments of a packet to be monotonically increasing and contiguous.[1] Therefore the only way to send an urgent packet between fragments is to send it without the PPP-MP header, which is allowed by RFC 1990. (HDLC 0x7E flags at the beginning and end of each frame are not represented;)

■ work is in progress within IETF to further extend this fragmentation scheme to multiple classes ('The multi-class extension to multi-link PPP', Internet draft draft-ietf-issll-isslow-mcml-04.txt, valid until June 1999). Multiple classes could be used on slow modem links to allow video packets to suspend non real-time traffic, and audio packets to suspend all other types of traffic including video.

PPP header	Address 0×FF	Control 0×33
MP header	Pid (H) 0×00	Pid (L) 0×3d
	B E 0 0	seq. Number N
	Fragment data	
	PPP FCS	
PPP header	Address 0×FF	Control 0×03
	Pid (H) 0×00	Pid (L) 0×21
	Urgent packet	
	PPP FCS	
PPP header	Address 0×FF	Control 0×33
	Pid (H) 0×00	Pid (L) 0×3d
MP header	B E 0 0	seq. Number N+1
	Fragment data	
	PPP FCS	

- 003 is the protocol ID of multilink PPP

- 0021 is the protocol ID of IP (*see* RFC 1700, assigned numbers)

- the B and E bits indicate the beginning and the end of each frame

Fig. 6.27 : Insertion of an urgent packet in ML-PPP

Conclusion

Hopefully this chapter has demonstrated two things:

- quality of service over packet networks is not a trivial issue, regardless of the technology. There has been a lot of theoretical work and a consensus on the deployment strategy needed to build a large, QoS-aware IP backbone is slowly emerging;

- the main factor driving the latency aspect of the quality of service is the length of the data packet, divided by the transmission link speed. Large packets tend to introduce less overhead than small packets, but this is limited by the latency factor. This is the background behind the advantage of native ATM for small to medium links, typically below 2 Mbit/s. But as we enter the xDSL era, and WAN link bandwidth increases over the 2 Mbit/s threshold, the latency issue becomes irrelevant and IP will be the technology of choice.

Note

1 Extract from RFC 1990: 'On each member link in a bundle, the sender *must* transmit fragments with strictly increasing sequence numbers (modulo the size of the sequence space). This requirement supports a strategy for the receiver to detect lost fragments based on comparing sequence numbers. The sequence number is not reset upon each new PPP packet, and a sequence number is consumed even for those fragments which contain an entire PPP packet, i.e. one in which both the (B)eginning and (E)nding bits are set.

An implementation *must* set the sequence number of the first fragment transmitted on a newly-constructed bundle to zero. (Joining a secondary link to an existing bundle is invisible to the protocol, and an implementation *must not* reset the sequence number space in this situation.)

The receiver keeps track of the incoming sequence numbers on each link in a bundle and maintains the current minimum of the most recently received sequence number over all the member links in the bundle (call this M). The receiver detects the end of a packet when it receives a fragment bearing the (E)nding bit. Reassembly of the packet is complete if all sequence numbers up to that fragment have been received.'

Network dimensioning

Simple compressed voice flow model

Voice coders

Most recent vocoders implement a voice activity detection algorithm, which uses significantly less bandwidth in silence periods than in active speech periods. For most coders the activity bitrate is constant, and we call it M. In silence periods, very basic coders will have a null bitrate, but coders such as G.723.1 or G.729 actually send some information to describe the background noise level and other parameters. We will call the bitrate during silence periods m.

m and M values for popular coders are shown in Table 7.1.

Table 7.1 : m and M values for popular coders

Codec	Frames/IP packet	M (kbit/s)	m (kbit/s)
G.723.1 (5.3 kbit/s)	4	8	3.73
G.723.1 (6.4 kbit/s)	4	9.07	3.73
Lucent SX7003P	2	20.27	13.87

In the previous table, one may wonder why G.723.1 in its 5.3 kbit/s mode has an M value of 8 kbit/s. This is because 6.4 kbit/s per second is the bitrate at the output of the coder and does not include transport overheads such as RTP/UDP/IP headers. We want to properly dimension IP links and therefore we must take into account such overheads (*see* Table 7.2).

Table 7.2 : Transport overheads

IPv4 overhead (octets)	20
UDP overhead (octets)	8
RTP overhead (octets)	12
activity rate (%)	35

The template for calculating such values is straightforward (*see* Tables 7.3 and 7.4).

Additional input is needed to calculate the actual bitrate at the physical layer because IP packets themselves are encapsulated in Ethernet (+26 octets), HDLC (+7 octets), PPP frames (+7 octets), or ATM cells using AAL5 (*see* Fig. 7.1).

Table 7.3 : Sample spreadsheet for calculating coder bitrates with IP overheads

	G.723.1			SX7003P	
	G (5.3kbits/s)	(6.4kbit/s)	(silence)	(4.8kbit/s)	(silence)
Frame size (data octets)	20	24	4	18	6
Frame duration (ms)	30	30	30	15	15
Frames per IP packet	4	4	4	2	2
Bitrate without overhead (kbit/s)	5.33	6.40	1.07	9.60	3.20
Octets per IP packet	80	96	16	36	12
Overhead IPv4+UDP+RTP (octets)	40	40	40	40	40
Bitrate with overhead (kbit/s)	8	9.07	3.73	20.27	13.87
Average bitrate (with activity rate)	5.23	5.60		16.11	

Table 7.4 : Calculating m and M values

	Coder	
	activity	(silence)
Frame size (data octets)	FS_a	FS_s
Frame duration (ms)	FD_a	FD_s
Frames per IP packet	n_a	n_s
Bitrate without overhead (kbit/s)	$=FS\_a*8/FD\_a$	$=FS\_s*8/FD\_s$
Octets per IP packet	$=FS\_a*n=Payload\_a$	$=FS\_s*n=Payload\_s$
Overhead IPv4+UDP+RTP (octets)	$20+8+12=Ov$	$20+8+12=Ov$
Bitrate with overhead (kbit/s)	$=(Payload\_a+Ov)*8/(n*FD\_a)=M$	$=(Payload\_s+Ov)*8/(n*FD\_s)$
Average bitrate (with activity rate)	$=M*act\_rate+m*(1-act\_rate)$	

For instance, Fig. 7.2 illustrates an RTP packet captured using Microsoft's Network Monitor (the Ethernet preamble length and FCS fields do not appear), containing a single frame of G.723.1 encoded voice.

In order to reduce this enormous overhead, multiple compressed voice frames are frequently concatenated in each packet. Of course, the packetization delay increases accordingly (n*FD), so there is a limit to the number of frames per packet. The mouth-to-ear delay must preserve a good interactivity and must be

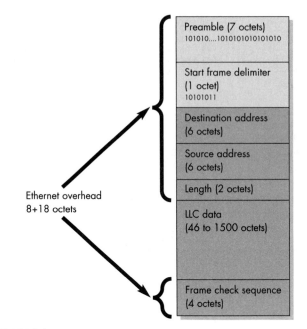

Preamble (7 octets)
101010....1010101010101010

Start frame delimiter
(1 octet)
10101011

Destination address
(6 octets)

Source address
(6 octets)

Length (2 octets)

LLC data
(46 to 1500 octets)

Frame check sequence
(4 octets)

Ethernet overhead
8+18 octets

Fig. 7.1 : The IEEE 802.3 frame

acceptable given the level of echo cancellation in terminal devices. For more details on acceptable mouth-to-ear delays, *see* Chapter Four.

Given the behavior of most voice coders, we model the one-way network bitrate during a voice conversation by a two-level function characterized by the suite of active speech intervals Tactive(i), and the suite of silence intervals Tidle(i) (Fig. 7.3). The activity rate a in Fig. 7.3 is defined as the limit when i gets infinite of sum(Tactive)/sum(Tidle+Tactive). A good average value is usually 0.35, but in order to be on the safe side we take a=0.5 in most of our calculations.

Model for N simultaneous conversations using the same coder

When there are N simultaneous uncorrelated conversations on the same link, they will not be active simultaneously, and therefore the required bandwidth will be less than N*M. When N gets very large it is intuitively obvious that the required bandwidth will be N times the average bitrate of a conversation: N*[aM+(1–a)m]. But for small values of N, some calculations are needed (*see* Fig. 7.4).

The probability for I conversations to be simultaneously active at any time can be expressed as:

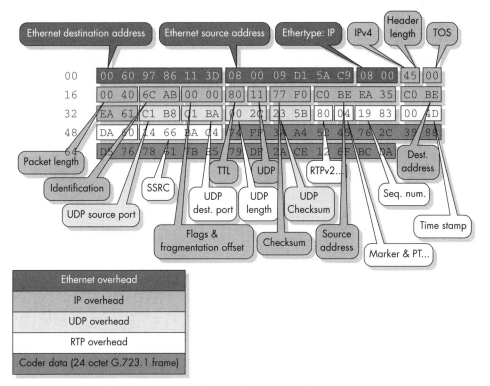

Fig. 7.2 : An RTP packet containing a single frame of G723.1 encoded voice

$$P(I) = C_N^I * (1 - a)^{N-1} = \frac{N!}{I!(N - I)!} * a^I * (1 - a)^{N-1}$$

(To check that the sum is 1, notice that it is the development of $[a+(1-a)]^N$.)

The average one-way bitrate on a link with N simultaneous conversations is therefore:

$$Average\_Bitrate = \sum_{I=0}^{N} P(I)*[IM + (N - I)m]$$

In fact, there is a much simpler expression noticing that:

$$\sum_{I=0}^{N} \frac{N!}{I!(N - I)!} * Ix^I * b^{N-I} = x \sum_{I=1}^{N} \frac{N!}{I!(N - I)!} * Ix^{I-1} * b^{N-1} = x\left(\frac{\partial(x + b)^N}{\partial x}\right) = xN(x + b)^{N-1}$$

and therefore

$$\sum_{I=0}^{N} I * P(I) = aN \qquad \text{(relation B)}$$

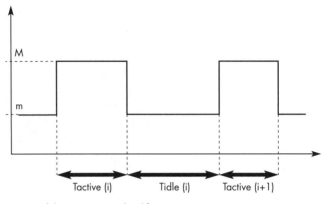

Fig. 7.3 : One-way network bitrate as a two-level function

which simplifies our average bitrate expression into:

$$\text{Average\_Bitrate} = MaN + Nm - maN = \mathbf{N(Ma + m(1-a))}$$

which is intuitively satisfying.

It can be shown, for such a probability law, that the standard deviation is:

$$\sigma = \sqrt{Na(1-a)}$$

This value measures the amount of dispersion around the average.

For large values of N, the probability P(I) can be approximated as a continuous function, and the Moivre and LaPlace theorem shows that:

$$P(I) \rightarrow \frac{1}{\sqrt{2\pi}\sigma} * e^{\frac{-(I-Na)^2}{\sigma^2}}$$

Compared to the exact calculation, it is much easier to use this function when N is larger than 30, and it can be found in most worksheets (in Excel this is the Normdist function).

Loss rate and dimensioning

From the previous results, we will try to evaluate which packet loss rate occurs when a bandwidth B is reserved on a link and there are N simultaneous conversations on that link. Once we know this, it will be possible to calculate the optimal value of B for a given acceptable loss rate. To facilitate the reading of the results, we will express B as a multiple of the elementary average bitrate of a single one-way voice channel during a conversation: aM+(1–a)m.

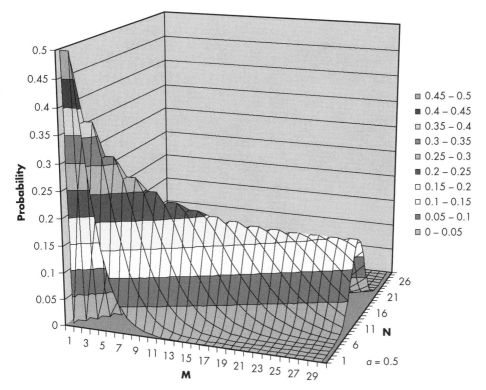

Fig. 7.4 : Probability of having N sessions simultaneously active among M

Loss rate (without queuing)

Each time I sessions are simultaneously active, the offered bitrate is:

$$Incoming\_Bitrate(I)=IM+(N–I)m$$

If we drop packets to reduce the bitrate to B, the loss rate when I sessions are simultaneously active is (with a fluid approximation):

$$Loss\_Rate(I,B)=MAX(Incoming\_Bitrate–B,0)/Incoming\_Bitrate$$

Over a time interval T, we group the packets lost for each subinterval during which I conversations are simultaneously active (the cumulated duration of each group is Ti=P(I) if T=1). We can calculate the average packet loss as follows:

$$Average\_Loss(N, B) = \left[\sum_{I=0}^{N}Loss(I,B)\right]/\left[\sum_{I=0}^{N}Ti(Nm + I(M–m))\right] = \frac{\sum\limits_{I=0}^{N}Ti^{*}\,MAX(Nm + I(n–m) – B,0)}{[Ma + (1–a)m]^{*}N}$$

where we used relations (A) and (B) to simplify the denominator.

To find what is the minimal bandwidth of a link that has to carry N calls, one must increase B until the calculated %loss equals the maximum tolerable average loss rate. As an example, this is what we get for the G.723.1 coder, in 6.4 kbit/s mode, with an activity rate of 0.5 and four frames per packet, where we considered that the average packet loss rate had to be kept below 1 per cent (*see* Table 7.5):

Table 7.5 : Calculating the minimal bandwidth of a link that has to carry N calls

Number of conversations	1	2	3	4	5	6	7	8
Average bitrate	6.4	12.8	19.2	25.6	32.0	38.4	44.8	51.2
Minimal link bitrate	8.9	17.6	25.7	32.2	39.2	46.3	52.5	59.8
Equivalent channels	1.4	2.8	4.0	5.0	6.1	7.2	8.2	9.3
Overhead bitrate	2.5	4.8	6.5	6.6	7.2	7.9	7.7	8.6
%overhead	40%	38%	34%	26%	22%	21%	17%	17%
%loss	1%	1%	1%	1%	1%	1%	1%	1%

We see that when a link is used to carry only a few conversations, it must be dimensioned almost as if all conversations were always active, which leads to a significant portion of the link bandwidth (as much as 40 per cent) being unused most of the time. As the number of conversations increases, the link size gets closer to the number of channels times the average bitrate of one channel, and the link utilization rate increases, as illustrated in Fig. 7.5.

One should keep in mind that what we call the 'loss rate' is an average value – during a single conversation it will be below this level most of the time, but can be significantly above it for short periods of time. Figure 7.6 illustrates this: for each rectangle i, the width represents the probability that i conversations are active (have a bitrate of M) simultaneously among T, and the height represents the loss rate when this occurs. The link itself is dimensioned to carry T conversations with an average loss of 1 per cent.

These are the calculated values for T=30. We have represented only the upper right corner of each rectangle for clarity.

Figure 7.7 can be interpreted as follows: for a conversation of 1000 seconds, there will be a 0 per cent loss rate during most of the conversation (820 seconds), a loss rate between 0 and 10 per cent for 175 seconds, and a loss rate of more than 10 per cent for five seconds or so. Of course, the good, bad and average quality periods will be interleaved in the conversation.

This calculation is relevant only for packet voice systems with silence compression. With traditional telephony systems, the only advantage of multiplexing several lines on a link is that not everybody phones at the same time, and hence

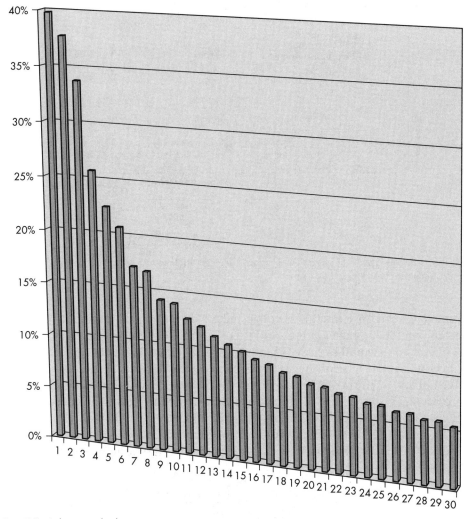

Fig. 7.5 : Link size and utilization rate

it is possible to put less capacity than the number of multiplexed lines (this is explained in the modeling call seizures section). This also applies to IP telephony, but IP telephony (and packet voice technologies in general) can also take advantage of the fact that not everybody *talks* at the same time.

Loss rate (with queuing)

The previous model only approximates what happens in an IP backbone because it considers that routers do not buffer packets (packets that cannot be forwarded

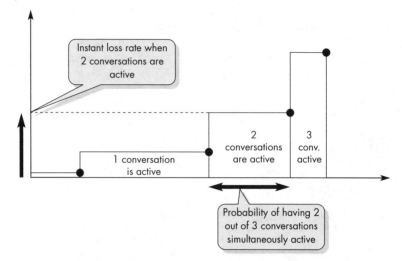

Fig. 7.6 : Loss profile on a link dimensioned to carry three conversations with an average loss of 1 per cent, when all three conversations are established

immediately because the link is congested are discarded). This is not true in fact because routers do have buffers, and therefore the real packet loss rates through an IP backbone would be lower than what we have calculated above (Fig. 7.8).

Eventually, packets will never be dropped by the network if routers have very large buffers. So in theory we should use a much more complex model that takes into account buffering. This model would also need to take into account the jitter buffer discard policy of the receiving terminals.

The following formula holds for a single conversation, where b is the average duration of the active periods, C the speed at which the buffer is emptied, and e the loss rate:

$$0 = \beta \times \exp\left(-\frac{buf\_size \times (C - m - a(M - m))}{b \times (1 - a)(M - C)(C - m)}\right) - \varepsilon = f(buf\_size, C)$$

$$\beta = \frac{(C - m - a(M - m)) + \varepsilon a(M - C)}{(1 - a)(C - m)}$$

This must be solved numerically to find the appropriate values of C for a target loss rate. Additional details and an approximation of C can be found in *Equivalent capacity and its application to bandwidth allocation*, by Roch Guerin *et al.*

Figure 7.9 (M=9.07 kbit/s, m=3.73 kbit/s, b=10s, ε=0.01, a=0.5) shows that C can be reduced significantly as the size of the buffer increases. But in our application, real-time telephony, we cannot take advantage of large buffers. The problem is that queued packets get delayed, reducing the interactivity of the conversation,

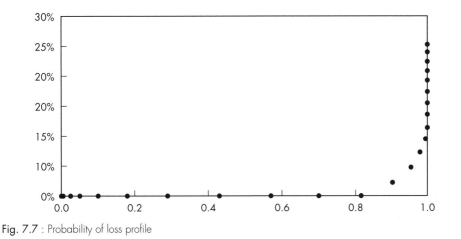

Fig. 7.7 : Probability of loss profile

and the increased jitter will cause some packets to be discarded by the jitter buffer of the receiving terminal if the extra delay exceeds a threshold.

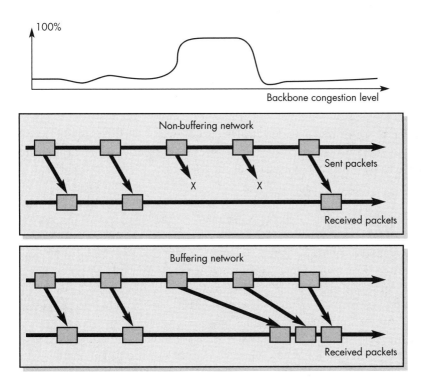

Fig. 7.8 : Packet loss through the buffer network

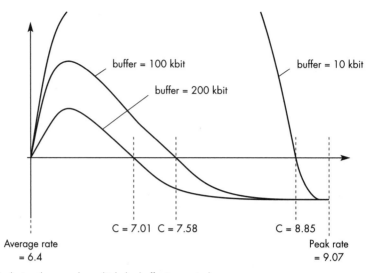

Fig. 7.9 : Reducing the speed at which the buffer is emptied

Do we really want to gain a few per cent of bandwidth at the expense of reduced interactivity? As we have seen in Chapter Four, the greatest constraint of IP telephony is the achievable end-to-end delay, which is in most cases at the extreme limit of what is considered acceptable for an average listener. By letting voice packets accumulate in the network, we would increase jitter and force terminals to adapt by building larger jitter buffers which would lead, inevitably, to additional delays.

Therefore we think it is good practice to dimension voice over IP links considering that there is no buffering. This leads, for small links, to some overprovision, but we will see that this overhead can be used by non real-time traffic.

Packet or frame loss?

What we have done so far is to calculate the characteristics of the offered bitrate and deduce how much of it could not get through a line of given bandwidth, using a 'fluid approximation'. In fact, routers will not throw away one bit here and there, but whole IP packets. However, this does not change our result which is also valid for the packet loss rate.

Is it the same as the frame loss rate? If, as we have assumed in our calculations, the frames generated by the coder are simply grouped in IP packets, then the answer is yes. But this is not always true, as some manufacturers use redundancy schemes to recover from packet loss. This is often the case for gateways optimized to work on the Internet, where the bandwidth is 'free'. The redundancy scheme used by such gateways leads to a greater bandwidth usage, but since it remains only a tiny fraction of the overall Internet traffic, it will in most cases not increase significantly the packet loss measured between two gateways.

A basic redundancy scheme is simply to copy one coder frame in two IP packets – if only one IP packet out of two is lost, the frame can be recovered and there will be no frame loss.

It is not as simple as that. The Internet will frequently drop entire sequences of packets in a row, so the basic redundancy scheme would not work that well under real conditions.

My advice is to be very careful when considering marketing material that proudly announces 'magic' redundancy schemes that beat the competition. Not only is it most unfriendly to jam the Internet with such a careless state of mind, but there is also frequently a delay trade-off when using redundancy, and that is often silenced.

If, however, you want to use redundancy, find out the performance of the redundancy scheme in the presence of grouped packet loss (or even better, test it). Then find out the packet loss characteristics of the network you will be using (isolated packets or many dropped packets in a row) and decide if the particular redundancy scheme in use will work as advertised. Finally, measure the end-to-end delay and check you are still in the 'acceptable' range.

Multiple coders

So far we have considered only one type of coder, with the same value of M and m for all voice flows. Different types of customers may require different qualities of service and therefore different coders may be used.

A possible approach to network dimensioning in this case is to rely on the Gaussian approximation of the traffic generated by one class of coders. Remember that in the case of N independent and identically distributed flows, the traffic distribution could be considered for large values of N to be a Gaussian distribution, with an average value of

$$N*average\_rate$$
and a standard deviation of
$$\sigma = average\_rate \times \sqrt{Na(1 - a)}$$

An interesting property of the sum of independent variables is that the standard deviation of the sum equals the sum of the standard deviations ($\sigma^2 = \sum \sigma_i^2$). In addition, if each variable follows a Gaussian law, the sum is also a Gaussian law.

So an approximation of the traffic distribution in the case of multiple coders is a Gaussian law, with an average value equal to the sum of the average values, and a standard deviation equal to the sum of the standard deviations obtained for each group of conversations with the same type of coder.

At this stage it is easy to calculate what proportion of the traffic is discarded for a given capacity C: this is the tail of the Gaussian distribution above C, which is well known. Finding C for a target loss rate ε amounts to calculating the inverse of this function. This can be done numerically, or using the following approximation (also given by Roch Guerin *et al.*):

$$C = mean + \alpha \times standard\_deviation$$

$$\alpha = \sqrt{-2 \ln(\varepsilon) - \ln(2\pi)}$$

Network dedicated to IP telephony

Is it necessary?

We will see in the following sections that it is feasible, and in fact desirable, to mix all types of IP traffic on one common backbone. But in order to keep a reasonable quality of service level for voice flows, it is necessary to have routers with sophisticated queuing capabilities. Even in this case, mixing large IP datagrams and small voice packets will have an impact on the end-to-end delay.

Therefore, in some cases, providers will want to build separate IP backbones dedicated to voice traffic, either because their routers cannot be configured properly or because they want to reduce the end-to-end delay as much as possible for high-quality applications.

Network dimensioning

Here we are, with six sites in three countries that need to communicate using IP telephony (Fig. 7.10). How do we dimension such a network?

Traffic matrix

The first step is the same as in switched telephone networks – we need to know who phones where, how often and how long. This information is usually derived from existing phone bills during a reference period. Then we need to choose an optimal route on the network for each of these calls. For this we need to know the cost of each link per unit of bandwidth. For instance, in the case of a leased line it is the monthly fee divided by the bandwidth (*see* Table 7.6).

Table 7.6 : Calculating the cost of each link per unit of bandwidth

From/to	1	2	3	4	5	6	A	B	C
1							2		
2							1		
3									1
4									1
5								1	
6								2	
A	2	1						10	10
B					1	2	10		
C			1	1			10	5	

The cost of carrying IP traffic from A to B or B to A is not always the same, since a provider could decide to use a satellite link one way. But satellite links add to the end-to-end delay, and we considered symmetric costs in our example. This cost matrix could also depend on time, as some providers have discount rates during off-peak hours.

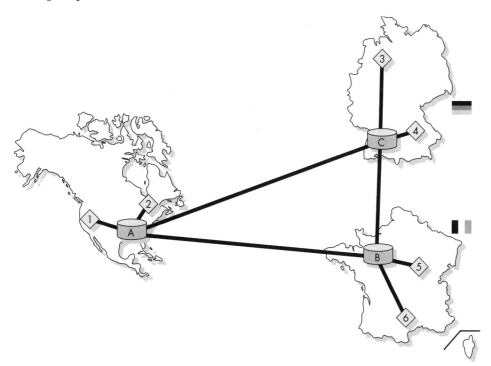

Fig. 7.10 : Network dimensioning across three countries

If there is only on-net traffic, the mapping of each phone call to a route in the network is straightforward – we simply take the least-cost route at the time of the call. For instance, a phone call from 1 to 6 will be routed through A and B (as opposed to A–C–B). When each call is mapped to a route, we need to calculate the maximum number of simultaneous calls over each link (the 'busy hour' traffic).

When there is also off-net traffic, the optimal route through the network is calculated by minimizing the on-net cost added to the cost of the hop from the last on-net node to the final destination over the switched telephone network. In most cases the route ends at the on-net node closest to the final destination, but things can get less rational when the last hop crosses national borders. Some calls (e.g. local calls) will not be routed through the corporate network at all.

Link sizing

Once each call has been mapped to an optimal route, we are able to calculate the number of simultaneous calls on each link at any given time. In general the link bitrate cannot be adjusted dynamically, so we must use the peak number of simultaneous calls (busy hour) as our input to dimension the link, and use the Erlang formula (*see* modeling call seizures section) to plan for variations during this busy hour. At this stage we know the maximum number of simultaneous calls that will be routed on each link.

The difficulty is that the link size also depends on the acceptable average packet loss rate. If we allow for more loss, the link can be adjusted to a smaller capacity, as in Table 7.7.

For a given coder in a given configuration, it is relatively easy to find what is the acceptable average packet loss using simple tests. This packet loss can be considered as our end-to-end budget that needs to be split among all the possible paths for a phone call through our network. There are many ways to split this budget, and they are not equivalent. If we consider two links, one of which is a transatlantic line (L2) with a cost of 10 000 monetary units for each supplemen-

Table 7.7 : Bandwidth overhead compared to the average bitrate for a given packet loss

Simultaneous calls	Loss rate 3.00%	1.00%	0.50%	0.10%	0.01%	0%
1	36%	40%	41%	42%	42%	42%
5	12%	23%	26%	39%	41%	42%
10	6%	14%	18%	25%	33%	42%
30	0%	6%	8%	14%	19%	42%
100	–2%	2%	3%	7%	10%	42%

tary unit of bandwidth, whereas the other is a local link (L1) with a cost of 10 units for each supplementary unit of bandwidth, and we have a loss budget of loss L1 + loss L2=1%, we can calculate the values shown in Table 7.8.

Table 7.8 : Calculating the end-to-end budget

L1 =	0.9%	0.7%	0.3%	0.1%
L2 =	0.1%	0.3%	0.7%	0.9%
channels on link 1	10			
channels on link 2	100			
ov(L1)	15%	16%	21%	25%
ov(L2)	7%	4%	3%	2%
distance on L1	1			
distance on L2	100			
cost on link1	10			
cost on link 2	10000			
Total overhead cost	661.23	451.39	252.43	187.95

In this example we see that the best way to split the loss rate is to give most of the loss budget to the transatlantic line.

This issue is very complex in general. The same transatlantic link could serve hundreds of smaller local access links, and in this case the cumulated overhead cost of all the local lines could become larger than the cost of the transatlantic link. This is a non-linear optimization problem and its resolution is outside the scope of this book.

Fault tolerance

The phone network is a mission-critical system, and the failure of one IP link should not jeopardize corporate communications. This is why a careful network planner will plan ahead for such failures and assess their consequences. This is done by considering the network without this link and rerouting all phone calls according to the new topology (this is done automatically by IP routers). The network must be dimensioned to handle this configuration.

Planning for link outages therefore lies in simulating all possible topologies with one link failure ($T(link_i)$), and dimensioning the remaining links to handle the rerouted flows. The final capacity of a link should be the maximum of its capacity calculated under all possible $T(link_i)$. Some critical backbones may even be dimensioned to handle the simultaneous failure of two links.

Note that this step is not necessary if the layer 2 protocol already has such fault protection (e.g. SDH rings, etc.).

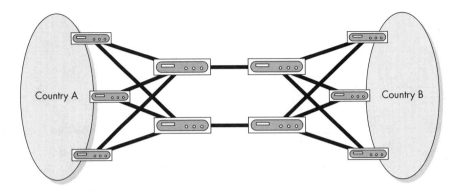

Fig. 7.11 : A redundant configuration

A potentially more significant problem is the loss of a router. If the router connects N links, then the situation is the same as if all these links were down. And
this is a layer 3 failure, which will not be recovered by layer 2 security mechanisms (SDH rings, etc.).

Some failures cannot be recovered by rerouting. This forces the network
providers to use redundant configurations such as that in Fig. 7.11.

Merging data communications and voice communications on a common IP backbone

We have seen that it is necessary to plan for some overhead capacity when
designing an IP network dedicated to IP telephony. It is very tempting to use this
spare capacity for best-effort data when it is unused by voice flows, but what are
the consequences?

Prioritization of voice flows

The first condition, in order to carry voice flows over a general purpose IP backbone, is to guarantee that packet loss and network delays and jitter will be kept
to a minimum. There are several ways to achieve this:

■ *do nothing*. TCP traffic backs off when facing a network congestion. Therefore
UDP traffic will tend to occupy whatever bandwidth it needs at the expense of
TCP traffic. However, this adaptation of TCP traffic is rather slow and works
by trial and error: send traffic first, and interpret packet loss as congestion.

Therefore TCP traffic will always grow until it congests the network, and then back off again. It will maintain the network in near congestion state and cause some marginal packet loss on UDP traffic in order to 'get a feel' of the state of network congestion. Moreover, there are some TCP stacks that do not respect this back-off strategy. All things considered, relying on TCP congestion control algorithms in order to prioritize UDP seems to be asking too much;

■ *prioritize all UDP traffic*. This is the easiest way to prioritize voice flows, since IP telephony RTP packets are carried over UDP. The side effect is to prioritize also all other UDP flows (such as DNS (domain name system) queries). This is fine in general because most applications written on top of UDP need minimal delays. In public networks, however, this is a dangerous practice. Soon someone will figure out that it is actually quite simple to simulate a TCP connection over UDP, and chances are that after a while more and more customers will begin to use all sorts of tricks to send most of their traffic, not just voice, over UDP. Our advice is to use this method only on corporate backbones, when the backbone traffic is well understood and connected networks are well behaved;

■ *use IP precedence levels*. Many routers can be configured to use the IP precedence, or DS, information in IP packets to prioritize classes of traffic. The routers can be configured in several ways:
 – assign a minimal bandwith to each class
 – assign a weight to each class, and share the available bandwidth between classes that have a backlog proportionally to those weights
 – give head of line priority to a class.

Each of these methods is discussed in detail in the QoS chapter, and many of them can be used depending on the other flows that are being carried on the network. It is important, when evaluating one method or the other, to verify the behavior of the scheduling algorithm being used regarding delays. We found that it was sometimes impossible to obtain such data from manufacturers, and it is not enough to have just the name of the algorithm (e.g. WFQ is now used as a marketing term by many manufacturers for all scheduling algorithms that more or less exhibit selective prioritization properties).

It is also necessary not to ignore the behavior of level 2 multiplexing algorithms: if your IP network is built on top of plain frame-relay links (without priority extensions), you may prioritize some IP packets at the IP level, but the frame-relay switches will gladly ignore this information. Connectivity providers using ATM or plain IP/TDM backbones are likely to offer a better support for differentiated classes of service, but it is always useful to check delays and jitter over a shared backbone before trying to use it for IP voice.

In an example configuration, we build a backbone supporting three classes of service:

- real-time class
- committed bandwidth class
- best effort

Each link between our backbone routers is bought from an ATM connectivity provider, and we asked for an ABR (available bitrate) capacity on the virtual channels. The minimal cell rate is calculated by adding the bitrate needed for IP telephony traffic (calculated as above) and the bitrate that we want to have available for the committed bandwidth class. The maximal cell rate depends on how much bandwidth we want to offer for the best-effort class.

If our provider does not have ABR, we can use CBR (constant bitrate) mode for the aggregate capacity of the real-time and committed bandwidth classes, plus the spare capacity that we always want to have for best-effort traffic. Then we configure our ingress routers to assign TOS=2 for all flows generated by IP telephony gateways (through a route-map for instance), TOS=1 for all flows that need a committed bandwidth (the ingress router for such flows must also be configured to check that the bandwidth of such flows does not exceed what was reserved). Best-effort traffic has TOS=0.

If class-based queuing (CBQ) is available on our routers, we configure the queue for TOS=2 to always get priority treatment over TOS=1 and TOS=0. Similarly, we configure the queue for TOS=1 to get priority over TOS=0. With

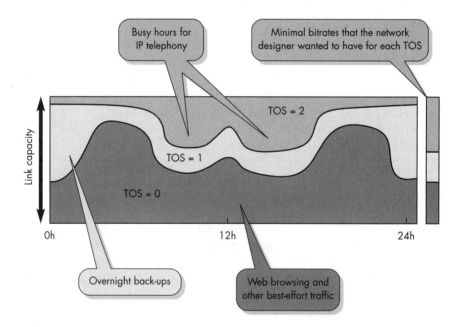

Fig. 7.12 : Network profile supporting three classes of service

this configuration, IP voice packets between our gateways will never have to wait for non real-time traffic, and committed bandwidth traffic pushes back best-effort traffic.

Figure 7.12 shows how the profile of the network load on our link will look.

On public backbones, this traffic mixing happens to be very favorable – business users will use a lot of bandwidth between 8am and 6pm, but this bandwidth will be freed for the 'web rush' of 8pm–11pm. During the empty hours (12pm–6am), the provider will be able to offer special pricing for bulk data transfers.

Impact on end-to-end delay

Mixing traffic of different types does have an impact on the end-to-end delay. This is because a router needs to wait until it has finished sending a packet before it can service the next one. Even if the next packet is a high priority one, it will need to wait. On backbones dedicated to IP telephony, all packets will be small (unless techniques such as RTP-mux are used) and therefore this waiting delay will be less than on a backbone on which most packets are 1500 octets long. This is worth considering only on low bandwidth links: the waiting time quickly becomes negligible as the link bandwidth increases (1500 octets are sent in 1.2 ms on 10 Mbps links).

On backbones carrying far more data flows than voice flows, the links used will have a much higher bandwidth than on a backbone dimensioned only for voice. If voice is prioritized, the delays offered on such a backbone may well be lower than those observed on a dedicated voice backbone.

Clearly the trend is an ever increasing data traffic, with voice traffic being limited to 24 hours per day per person. Letting voice take advantage of the high-capacity links of the data backbone is the way to go for future networks.

Multipoint communications

Audio multipoint conferences

Star topology with centralized flow mixing

This is the typical topology of a conference in multi-unicast mode with a central MCU. For a conference the activity rate a needs to be calculated by considering that the conference is active when at least one person speaks – the activity rate a will typically be in the 0.7–0.9 range, depending on whether people are bored or over-excited during the conference. *See* Fig. 7.13.

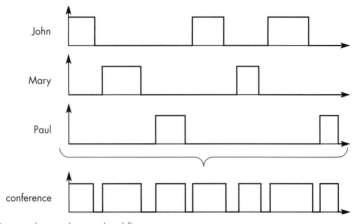

Fig. 7.13 : Star topology with centralized flow mixing

In this topology each link between the mixing server and a terminal carries asymmetric flows. If there are P participants in the conference, each speaking in turn and for the same amount of time:

■ from the server to each terminal the average traffic will be aM+(1–a)m, with a peak value of M;

■ from each terminal to the server, the average traffic will be (a/P)M+(1–a/P)m, with a peak value of M.

The problem with multi-unicast conferences is obvious: if many participants (say N) are behind the same link, then the average downstream traffic from the server is N*(aM+(1–a)m). Moreover, each flow from the server to a terminal is strongly correlated and therefore the peak bitrate N*M will be reached most of the time.

Another major issue, even if there is plenty of bandwidth, is delay (Fig. 7.14). The central server must decode the audio signal it receives from each terminal, calculate for each the sum of all signals except the signal from the participant himself, then recode these signals and return them. Before it can calculate the signals, the central server must receive enough voice frames from each partici-pant and synchronize them. This requires a jitter and synchronization buffer that will add at least the duration of the longest voice frame to the reception delay. All other delays depend on the CPU power available, but can generally be assumed to have a duration of two voice frames.

Another source of delay is the non-optimal route of the voice flows, which must get through the central server instead of reaching the receiving terminal through the shortest route. Finally, the receiving terminal still has a jitter buffer.

As a conclusion, multi-unicast conferences will work best when installed on non-bandwidth constrained networks, and the multipoint processor is inserted in the optimal path between the participants. The codecs should be used in low delay mode (i.e. minimal number of frames per packet as allowed by the band-

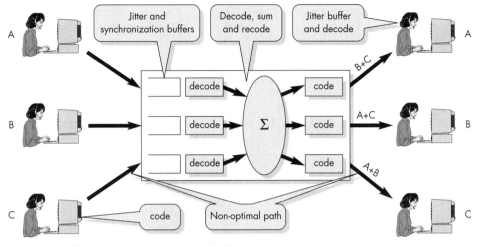

Fig. 7.14 : Multi-unicast conference – sources of delay

Note: For clarity all terminals are represented twice: once in their sending role, once in their receiving role

width constraints). Some conference bridges avoid the decoding stage by being able to sum encoded signals. However, this is possible only on some proprietary coders (i.e. Elemedia).

Star topology with flow switching

In this configuration the central server does not sum signals, but rather transmits to all participants the signal that has last been measured 'most active' . The traffic evaluation is the same as before, but the delays will be lower since the coding stage needed to compress the sum signal is not needed (the decoding stage is generally still needed to evaluate signal energy, unless silence detection is used by senders). This technique allows very simple and scalable multipoint processors to be built.

However this comes at a price: the conference becomes very sensitive to parasitic noise sent by senders, and the conference participants need a strong discipline as it is generally impossible to interrupt an active speaker.

It is possible to improve things by building multipoint servers that mix only the last two or three most active signals – they remain scalable and yet it becomes possible to interrupt the active speaker.

Using multicast with source-based trees

This is the technique used for conferences on the MBONE, the multicast backbone of the Internet. With multicast, traffic measurements depend a lot on the network topology between conference participants, and we will examine a few typical situations below. In all cases the end-to-end delay is improved because all flows now follow the shortest path and the decode/recode stage is avoided.

Conferences over an Ethernet LAN

Now, with the same assumptions and definitions as before, each participant generates an average traffic of $(a/P)M+(1-a/P)m$ with a peak bitrate of M. The traffic generated by the P participants is added on the network, and the average aggregate bitrate is therefore $aM+(P-a)m$, which is not much higher than the value obtained for a *single conversation*. If the value of a for the conference was the same as for a two-party conversation, and the coder was sending no data during silences – m=0, then it would be equal. Note that many coders have a discontinuous transmission feature (DTX), and we can actually have m=0 during long silences.

However, the possible peak value of the aggregate traffic is P*M, and is obtained if all voice flows are correlated, or if everybody talks simultaneously. Put another way, it is a bad idea to start a chorist club on the Internet with multicast technology based on source-rooted trees! For normal voice conversations, however, the probability of having such a situation is very low. It is possible to limit the peak rate to K*M deterministically by using terminals that refuse to send data if more than K different SSRCs are detected in the incoming RTP flows (or K different source IP addresses).

The previous calculation is valid for coax or thin-coax Ethernet and also when using a hub or a switch. However, when using a switch, there is a very important caveat: always check the behavior of your switch when receiving multicast traffic. People usually buy switches to prevent traffic generated by two hosts that communicate from affecting other hosts. However, some older or cheap switches will turn multicast traffic into broadcast. The technology does work and your multicast conference will be fine, but all other connected hosts will also receive the aggregate traffic of the conference. I have heard of networks with thousands of machines suddenly becoming desperately slow because just three people were having a chat.

Switches should have a way of taking into account multicast group membership information – protocols such as CGMP (Cisco) or GARP can be used, while another solution is to use switch/routers such as 3COM Corebuilder 3500 or Bay Networks accelerar 1200.

LANs connected to a central router

Now multicast packets are duplicated by the central router towards all terminals on other LANs. As before, the average traffic of each terminal to the central router is $(a/P)M+(1-a/P)m$ with a peak bitrate of M. If there are K participants on a LAN, then the average traffic from the central router to this LAN will be $(P-K)[(a/P)M+(1-a/P)m]$. It will be added to the traffic that is generated locally on the LAN, so the aggregate traffic is still $aM+(P-a)m$.

The same remarks as before apply for the peak bitrate.

Larger networks

On larger networks each source sends (a/P)M+(1–a/P)m to a tree that reaches each participant except the source. The tree duplicates traffic according to the topology (for DVMRP, if there are several possibilities the duplication is done where it leads to the shortest source-to-destination delays).

Comparing with the multi-unicast situation depends on the topology of the multicast tree built by the multicast protocol. If multicast packets are duplicated very close to the final users, the network load is minimized. The issue is that many multicast protocols are optimized to minimize delays, and packets are duplicated at the node which minimizes the number of hops to the destination. This may not be the optimal solution to minimize traffic. However, in some cases the shortest delay solution coincides with the lowest network load solution, and that is where there is only one possible distribution tree: in hierarchical networks (*see* Fig. 7.15).

If we call a 'level i' conference a conference in which all participants can be reached by using only nodes of level i and higher, and N(link) is the number of participants located on the part of the distribution tree rooted at 'link', then we will have for each link between a node of level j and level j+1 (j>=i) an average downstream traffic of

$$(P–N(link)–1)*[(a/P)M+(1–a/P)m]$$

and an upstream traffic of

$$N(link)*[(a/P)M+(1–a/P)m]$$

on each link of the distribution tree.

If we had been using a multi-unicast server at level i, the average value of the downstream traffic would have been

$$N(link)[(aM+(1–a)m]$$

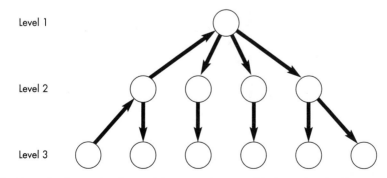

Fig. 7.15 : Hierarchical network – shortest delay tree is also optimal for lowest bandwidth usage
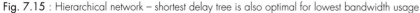

And the average value of the upstream traffic

$$N(link)*[(a/P)M+(1-a/P)m]$$

From those evaluations it is clear that the multicast solution scales much better as the number of participants increases for downstream traffic. For upstream traffic the scalability of both solutions is identical.

Using a shared-tree multicast technology

In this technique all traffic is sent to a node (this node can be different for each conference), and multicast diffusion starts at this node (Fig. 7.16).

In this case, when the node is located at level I the average downstream traffic is

$$P*[(a/P)M+(1-a/P)m],$$

and the average upstream traffic is

$$N(link)*[(a/P)M+(1-a/P)m]$$

We see that, due to the fact that local sources are heard through the central node, the result is not as good as before in terms of bandwidth. The delays are not optimal either. However, it remains much better than multi-unicast.

Using a hybrid unicast/multicast technique

This technique allows each source to send their flows in unicast to a central server, but the central server is allowed to use multicast. The central server can do voice switching and redistribute the most active flow in multicast mode. This is the most scalable design but the speaker cannot be interrupted.

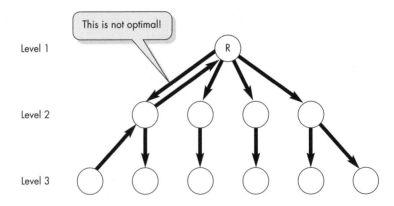

Fig. 7.16 : Shared tree – all sources send their flows to node R, which initiates multicast traffic

Another solution is to redistribute each source in multicast mode, without any mixing. This design has the same scaling properties as the shared tree multicast technique.

Note that it is impossible to perform mixing at the central node and redistribute the mixed flow in multicast to all conference participants because the active speaker would hear his voice echoed by the server. However, when there are a lot of passive participants (panel type of conference where there are a few speakers and a large audience), this mixing option is very attractive for the audience, while speakers can still use multi-unicast conferencing. This hybrid mode is used, for instance, in H.332 conferences.

Conclusion

Using multi-unicast servers for multipoint conferences is possible only for small-scale conferences. This model can be extended to the panel service by sending the mixed audio signal to all passive members using multicast. For larger scale conferences, the cheapest solution is to use audio switching with multicast, but it provides limited interactivity.

High-quality conferences with many speakers can be provided efficiently only using multicast technology. There is a small difference in the bandwidth scaling properties of shared tree and source-rooted trees, but not significant enough to be a good reason to choose one or another. If delay is a concern, source-rooted trees are a better option, but overall the major decision factor will be the scaling properties of such networks regarding the number of simultaneous groups that can be supported by routers.

Multipoint video conferencing

There is one major difference between audio and video conferences – video data grows linearly with the number of participants, whereas the audio data is auto-limiting (not everybody talks at the same time).

In order to limit the amount of video data, most conferencing systems use video switching, broadcasting the image of the last active speaker only. Another option is to build a composite image (mosaic) from all the incoming video streams. In this case we reach the same conclusions as for audio traffic:

- if multi-unicast is used, traffic on each link grows linearly with the number of participants connected via this link, which rapidly leads to scalability problems;
- if the central switching server broadcasts the selected image using multicast, the conference can grow to a larger number of active participants (sending video data), and is not limited in the number of passive participants (receivers only).

For high-quality 'continuous presence' conferences, the best solution is to have each participant sending their video data to all others using multicast. Network usage is proportional to the number of simultaneous active senders.

Conclusion
For video conferences with more than just a few participants, using multicast is unavoidable.

Modeling call seizures

Introduction to the Erlang model

We now model the traffic generated by a single phone line with an average pick-up frequency f and an average duration d, as illustrated in Fig. 7.17. This is more data than just the activity rate a (and of course, we have a=fd).

A line is served as soon as it is picked up if possible, but if there are already Mmax lines busy, the user needs to wait to be served, or the call is immediately rejected (d=0,w=0). This is the same as if f customers per hour were entering a ticket office with Mmax counters. It takes d hours to serve a customer. Customers can immediately proceed to a counter if one is available, or they have to wait in a single line if Mmax customers are already being served.

To experiment with this new model, let us assume first that Mmax is infinite and let us calculate the probability to have x lines simultaneously active in a system with N phone lines. We consider many (S) similar environments with N phone lines. If we take a picture at any time, some of those systems will have only one line busy, some of them will have two lines busy, etc. up to N lines busy. We call g(M) the number of systems with M busy lines ('M' systems). We consider the evolution of those S systems over a very short time interval t. So

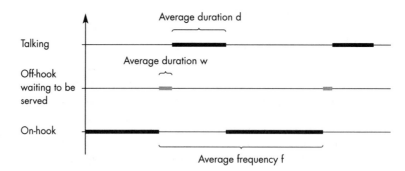

Fig. 7.17 : Traffic generated by a single phone line

short that there is a negligible probability to have more than one event like a new call, or completion of an active call for each system: the probability to transition from state 'M' to state 'M+2' is negligible.

Let us calculate the number of new calls received during t by an 'M' system. It may seem logical to say that this is Nft. In fact, it is more complex. f is the average pick-up (seizure) frequency over time, but a line can be picked up only if the line is on-hook. In a given M state, the instantaneous frequency will be higher if there are more on-hook lines. To take this into account we notice that the on-hook time during a unit of time is 1–fd on average and therefore the seizure frequency for on-hook machines is f/(1–fd). In a given state 'M' with N–M on-hook lines, the seizure frequency is therefore (N–M)f/(1–fd).

This flow of new calls will tend to turn a system with M busy lines into a system with M+1 busy lines. For our S systems during t, we will have g(M)*(N–M)ft/(1–fd) 'M' systems becoming 'M+1' systems. But in the meantime there will be t(M+1)/d*g(M+1) calls that will complete in systems with M+1 busy lines, tending to turn M+1 systems into M systems.

If we want the distribution g(M) to be steady, the number of M systems becoming M+1 systems must equal the number of M+1 systems becoming M systems during t, therefore we must have for each M:

$$0 = t(M+1)/d*g(M+1) - g(M)*(N-M)ft/(1-fd)$$

We have introduced a lot of unnecessary parameters to make the calculation less theoretic. In fact, g(M)/S is the probability P(M) to have M lines simultaneously busy, and the exact value of t has no importance. Our equations become:

$$P(M+1) = P(M)*(N-M)*fd/(1-fd)(M+1) \qquad \text{eq. M+1}$$

$$\mathbf{P(M) = P(M-1)*(N-M+1)*a/(1-a)(M)} \qquad \textbf{eq. M}$$

...

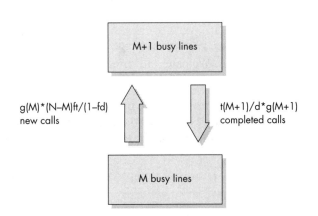

Fig. 7.18 : Statistical equilibrium of states M and M+1

which easily leads to:

$$P(M) = C_N^M \times \left(\frac{a}{1-a} \right)^M P(0)$$

since the sum over all M of P(M) equals 1, and we have

$$\sum_{M=0}^{N} P(M) = \left(\frac{a}{1-a} + 1 \right)^N$$

we can find P(0)=(1–a)N, and finally:

$$P(M) = C_N^M \times a^M \times (1-a)^{N-M}$$

Yes, this the same binomial distribution as the one we found in the first section when trying to calculate the probability of having M simultaneous active voice channels, with a more complex method. This was just to get familiar with it, before deriving more interesting results.

Before getting into more lines of algebra, there are a couple of additional notes:

■ the standard deviation of this distribution is $\sigma = \sqrt{Na(1-a)}$

■ if N gets very large while a gets smaller and smaller: N*a=A remains finite and represents the traffic in Erlangs of the whole system, then we can simplify P(M) into a Poisson Law: $P(M) = \frac{A^M}{M!} e^{-A}$ and we approximate $\sigma = \sqrt{A}$ which is slightly larger than the exact value.

Model for a limited set of servers and calls are rejected if no server is available

This is the most common behavior of PBXs controlling access to external lines, for instance. This will also be the behavior of gatekeepers controlling the usage of WAN resources.

We use the same definitions as above for t, N, a, A and d. We call B the probability that a call gets rejected. We calculate the new distribution P(M) with the same method:

■ the seizure frequency of an on-hook line now is f/(1–fd(1–B)), where the (1–B) factor appears because some of the offered calls now complete immediately (are rejected) instead of lasting d. Therefore there are (N–M)ft/(1–fd(1–B)) new calls offered during t;

■ as before there are Mt/d previously accepted calls that complete during the same period.

The equilibrium equation becomes:

$$P(M)=(N-M+1)/M*P(M-1)*fd/(1-fd(1-B))$$

from which we derive

$$P(M) = C_N^M \times \alpha^M \, P(0), \text{ where } \alpha = \frac{a}{1 - a(1 - B)}$$

and finally $P(M) = \dfrac{C_N^M \times \alpha^M}{1 + C_N^1 \times \alpha + C_N^2 \times \alpha^2 + \ldots + C_N^{Nmax} \times \alpha^{Nmax}}$ because

$P(M>Nmax)=0$. This is called the Engset distribution.

It is easy to show that $B = \dfrac{N - N\max}{N - aN(1 - B)} P(N\max)$ by considering that all calls arriving when Nmax servers are busy get rejected. This solves our problem by eliminating a, but there is no easy analytical expression of B. A way to approximate the result is to consider that B is very low and to write

$$\alpha = \frac{a}{1 - a}$$

Another useful approximation is to consider that each line is not very active and that there are many lines, and we know the total traffic (Na–> A); the equilibrium equation converges to:

$$P(M)=Na/M * P(M-1)$$

And we have $P(M) = \dfrac{\dfrac{A^M}{M!}}{\displaystyle\sum_{i=0}^{N\max} \dfrac{A^i}{i!}}$ and B=P(Nmax)

This result is the first Erlang law. It allows us to calculate the number Nmax of servers (e.g. external lines) that must be installed to ensure a given rejection rate B. It is always possible to compute P(Nmax) with increasing values of Nmax until we reach the desired B, but there is also a simple approximation (known as the Rigault rule): if the desired B is 10^{-k}, then $N\max \approx A + k\sqrt{A}$.

Calls per second

Another critical parameter to take into consideration when dimensioning a telephony system is the number of calls per second that can be processed. This involves a lot of signaling (especially in the case of IP telephony), and potentially each call can trigger many back-end services (accounting, IN, identity verification via DTMF). Therefore we must evaluate the distribution of incoming calls. This will be useful mainly to dimension gatekeepers.

A simple model is to say that if each line is characterized by an average call frequency f and a mean call duration d, then the traffic offered by N lines is A=Nfd, and the average call setup frequency for all lines is Nf. Therefore if we know only A (a gatekeeper serves ten gateways with 30 ports each: A=300), we can find the average call setup frequency by calculating A/d.

However, there is a probability that the instantaneous frequency will get larger than the average value, potentially increasing call setup delays if the systems cannot handle this peak. We go into more detail in the next section.

Poisson process

Let us number each new call setup as 'event number i', and its timestamp T_i. The time interval between event i–1 and event i is t_i.

If the probability of having a new call between t and t+dt does not depend on the previous events, and is proportional to dt (first order approximation) with a negligible probability that more than one call arrives, then it is a Poisson arrival process (Fig. 7.19).

If we call $P_k(D)$ the probability to have exactly k calls during a time interval D, then our assumptions can be written:

$$P_1(d) = \lambda \times d + o(d)$$

$$1 - P_0(d) - P_1(d) = o(d)$$

$$P_{k+1}(D + d) = P_{k+1}(D)(1 - \lambda d) + P_k(D) \times \lambda d + o(d)$$

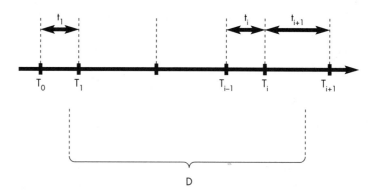

Fig. 7.19 : The Poisson arrival process

where the last line is obtained by considering that we can have k+1 events at D+d if we have (a) k+1 events at D and no event between D and D+d, or (b) k events at D and one event during d. This leads to a differential equation whose solution is

$$P_k(D) = \frac{(\lambda D)^k}{k!} e^{-\lambda D}$$

And if we call A(t) the probability that t_i<t, we have

$$A(t) = 1 - P(t_1 > t) = 1 - P_0(t) = 1 - e^{-\lambda t}$$

In fact λ is the average frequency of the event because

$$\bar{t} = \int t A'(t)dt = 1/\lambda$$

Incoming phone calls are often modeled as a Poisson process, even if one could argue that our hypothesis that an event does not depend on past events is not always true. This is because the superposition of N independent processes P_i with an average event frequency λ_i, even if they are not individually Poisson processes, converges to a Poisson process when N increases (Palm Kintchine theorem). The average frequency of this Poisson process is the sum of all λ_i. This is exactly what happens for a set of many telephone lines – call setup events can be considered as a Poisson process where $\lambda = Nf = A/d$. Fig. 7.20 is obtained for 100 lines and one call/hour per line.

   Now we suppose that a server can serve a maximum of Nmax calls simultaneously, the other calls being queued in FIFO mode. Each call requires on average d seconds to be serviced (database lookup, etc.). The server is servicing N lines with an average call frequency f. For instance, this could model a complex gatekeeper that needs d seconds to process a call setup, and processes no more than Nmax setups at a time. But the result can also be used for an IVR server which can accept only Nmax calls and interacts with the user for d seconds, or a call center with Nmax operators.

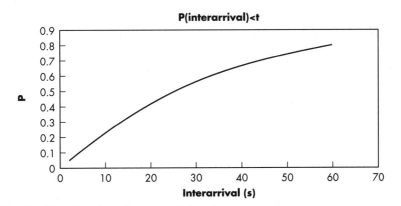

Fig. 7.20 : Model for a limited set of servers and phone lines can wait for a server

If we call A=Nfd, then the probability of waiting more than t is:

$$P(w>t) = \frac{\left(\dfrac{N\max}{N\max-A}\right) \times \dfrac{A^N\max}{N\max!}}{\left(1 + A + \dfrac{A^2}{2!} + \dfrac{A^3}{3!} + .. + \dfrac{A^{N\max}}{N\max!}\right) + \dfrac{A^{N\max}}{N\max!} \times \left(\dfrac{A}{N\max - A}\right)} * e^{-(N\max-A)\frac{t}{d}}$$

Conclusion

Systems with few users need to be dimensioned for peak values; systems with many users need to be dimensioned for average values. This allows a network to be used more efficiently as the number of users increases.

In a large 64 kbit/s telephony system, the network can be dimensioned for slightly more than the average number of simultaneous calls. This is also true for IP telephony systems, but in addition the usage of coders with voice activity detection allows us to perform some statistical multiplexing between active channels and idle channels – when there are many channels, the link needs to be dimensioned for slightly more than the average bitrate of the coder taking into account the activity rate of the conversation.

Finally many coders have a peak rate of less than 10 kbit/s, which is much more efficient than the 64 kbit/s used in the PSTN.

Therefore it would seem that IP telephony is far more efficient than the PSTN, and this is claimed by many manufacturers. In fact, this view must be taken with care. The tremendous overheads of RTP+UDP+IP+physical layer eat up much of what was gained with compression and VAD, and many systems do not even have VAD. Still, with well designed systems it is possible to reach a 1–5 efficiency ratio, and in extreme cases a 1–10 ratio. But in order to achieve such gains it is necessary to stack many frames per RTP packet and this degrades the delay performance.

Overall, it seems that claiming that *the* advantage of IP telephony is its bandwidth efficiency is misleading. Many other techniques can achieve the same, or even a better, efficiency (voice over frame relay or ATM, DCME equipment, etc.). But none of them can achieve such a large-scale connectivity. Voice over frame will work well inside a single company, but it will never work on the scale of a country (too many PVCs would be needed).

Other savings might be more significant than the bandwidth gain:

■ companies will be able to use fewer wires since all communications will be merged on the LAN;

■ carriers will merge all communications on a single backbone, reducing maintenance and operation costs;

■ the voice switching equipment (gatekeepers) will be cheaper than traditional switches because they have to care only about the signaling flows, not the media itself.

Last but not least, IP telephony will unleash all services that were previously less attractive because of geographic and wiring constraints, such as Centrex. IP Centrex services will allow corporations to outsource all their communication needs to the provider, buying no equipment except IP phones.

IP telephony is cheaper telephony, but it is richer telephony.

IP Multicast Routing

Introduction

Multicast is a real-time, network-level information distribution technology. It does not need any central server that would distribute the information at the application level. This chapter focuses on IP multicast routing technology and its applications.

Like many other IP technologies, multicast was designed in a university. It grew with an overlay network called the MBONE that is built on top of regular Internet links. Today multicast seems to have reached a critical level of maturity that makes it more suitable as a commercial service as the first professional-grade applications are being released – video-streaming servers, reliable data distribution servers, video-conferencing applications. These applications will soon trigger a need for IP multicast enabled intranets.

This chapter explains the advantages of network-level data distribution, describes the protocols used, and their limits. There is also a description of some widely used applications. As multicast is an evolving technology, we also cover the work at IETF regarding group address allocation and multicast inter-domain routing.

When to use multicast routing

A real-time technology

There are already many techniques that are used to distribute information to many recipients on the Internet. They were developed to solve specific problems encountered during the development of the Internet:

■ the domain name system (DNS) is used to distribute the mapping of domain names to IP addresses. DNS defines efficient caching and replication mechanisms among DNS servers;

■ NNTP, the network news transfer protocol, is used to replicate newsgroup messages among news servers worldwide;

■ IRC, the Internet relay chat, is a text chat protocol optimized to immediately send any sentence typed by any participant of a forum to all other relevant chat servers, that in turn send this sentence to all members of the forum that they host;

■ even HTTP, the protocol used to transfer web documents, was designed to let cache servers know how long they can keep a page in memory, in order to minimize unnecessary network traffic;

■ many small companies have emerged with content-pushing technologies.

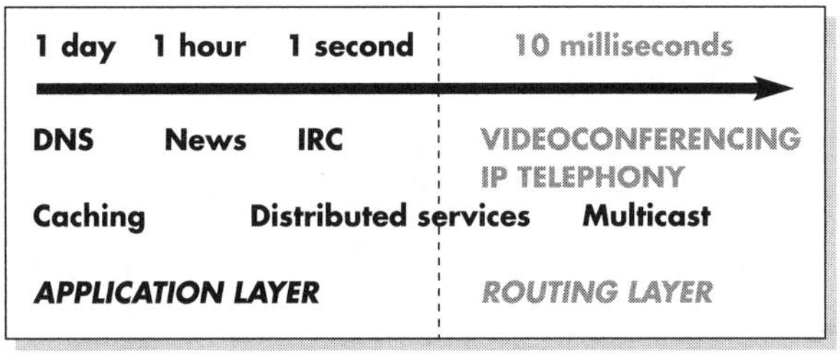

1 day	1 hour	1 second	10 milliseconds

DNS	News	IRC	VIDEOCONFERENCING IP TELEPHONY
Caching		Distributed services	Multicast
APPLICATION LAYER			*ROUTING LAYER*

Fig. 8.1 : Information distribution delay

All these techniques are very efficient at what they do, but they share a common characteristic: they are not real time. Because they duplicate and distribute information at the application layer, the classic information distribution techniques are unable to handle real-time information, i.e. information that must be distributed in less than 100 milliseconds or so. *See* Fig. 8.1.

Video-conferencing is the primary application of IP multicast, but there are many other situations in which several computers need to share the same information with a very low latency – interactive gaming or financial applications are also very likely to use IP multicast once it is widely available.

Network efficiency

The network efficiency of IP multicast is best demonstrated with an example. We can take the example of an IRC forum, with just one server. For this application each client opens a socket on a central server (or a set of replicated servers), which takes care of duplicating and sending all incoming messages back to the forum members.

The simplified IP network in Fig. 8.2 shows the 'packet storm' caused by a single packet sent from client a to the reflector. Several copies of the same packet (except the destination) are sent simultaneously over several links; moreover, the reflector has to be a powerful machine, since it has to handle a separate connection for every client.

A more scalable solution would ideally be to send only one copy of each packet over each link, and would not need a special machine to handle all the work. This is exactly what IP multicast is doing. Figure 8.3 illustrates that IP multicast can be supported by the underlying physical medium capabilities, here the multicast capabilities of an Ethernet LAN.

Many applications rely on broadcasts to find network resources. The Windows operating system is one of them. Broadcast is fine when only several workstations share a small LAN, but in bigger networks where hundreds of workstations are connected using hubs and switches it becomes a real problem. Because network managers want to avoid broadcast storms as much as possible, they usually

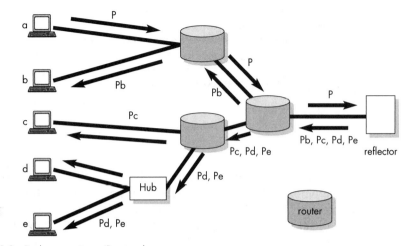

Fig. 8.2 : Packet storm in an IP network

configure their routers to not forward broadcasts across subnets. This limits the practical usefulness of broadcast discovery to just the subnet of the broadcasting host.

Multicast is one possible solution for those limitations of broadcast. (There are other useful approaches, for instance, the IEEE 802.1 WG defined the notion of VLANs for distributed working groups.) Multicast is a way to distribute information to a group which can easily span several subnets and still reach only the hosts that have requested to be members of the group. Moreover, multicast can be configured to do expanding ring searches, so a host can look to its immediate neighborhood for a resource without flooding the universe in the first instance.

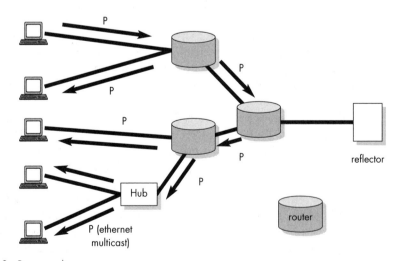

Fig. 8.3 : Resource discovery

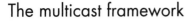

The multicast framework

Multicast address, multicast group

A multicast IP address format has been introduced in IPv4 and IPv6 to support multicast applications, in addition to the existing unicast and broadcast addresses. Another type of address, called anycast address, has been added in IPv6 – v6 Anycast addresses and v6 multicast addresses are used for different purposes and should not be mixed up.

In IPv4, a multicast address is a Class D address, which ranges from 224.0.0.0 to 239.255.255.255 (all addresses starting with 1110). Addresses 224.0.0.0 to 224.0.0.255 are reserved for multicast routing protocols. Combined with the port number (1024 to 65535) this leads to more than 16 000 billion possibilities.

In IPv6, multicast addresses will have a high order octet equal to FF.

The difference between a unicast address and a multicast address is the same as that between a regular email address and a mailing-list address. Clients who subscribe to a particular multicast address will receive all datagrams sent with this multicast address in the destination address field (*see* Fig. 8.4.)

A multicast group is a set of hosts that subscribe to the same multicast address. The subscription is done using a protocol called IGMP. The hosts are called the group members. A group is completely dynamic: at any time a machine can leave or join a group. There is no restriction on the number or location of members in the group.

A client is not required to be a member of a group to send a message to its members. However, there is a big difference between a mailing list and a multicast group. In the first case, the complete list of members is known to a central server. For multicast, the routers in the network know only if they have at least one member on each interface, without knowing who the members are.

Since groups are completely dynamic, the multicast addresses need to be obtained dynamically. The main issue is to choose an address that is not already

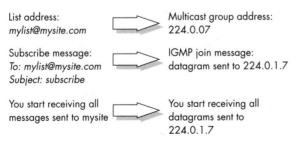

Fig. 8.4 : Destination address field in multicast

« all systems on this subnet »	224.0.0.1
« all routers on this subnet »	224.0.0.2
All DVMRP routers	224.0.0.4
All MOSPF routers	224.0.0.5
Routing Information Protocol (RIP)---Version 2	224.0.0.9
Network Time Protocol (NTP)	224.0.1.1
Audio news	224.0.1.7
IETF audio	224.0.1.11
IETF video	224.0.1.12

Fig. 8.5 : Well known multicast groups

in use. Usually the addresses already in use can be obtained via the SDR application (*see* p. 415), but some applications simply choose a random address. The second issue is to make this address known to the potential listeners. Here again it is possible to use SDR (this has the advantage of letting everyone know that you are using this address), but a simple web page also serves the purpose.

A permanent group is just a group with a well known address (registered by the Internet Assigned Numbers Authority) that is used for a particular application. It does not imply that there is some permanent member in that group. Some well known groups are shown in Fig. 8.5.

TCP cannot be used for multicast communications – multicast datagrams have to be standard UDP or RAW datagrams and are delivered to the group members with no guarantee. Reliable transmissions can be implemented on top of UDP.

Multicast on Ethernet

In addition to the reserved Class D addresses, the IANA owns a block of Ethernet addresses reserved for multicast, which in hexadecimal is 01:00:5E (the first byte of any Ethernet address must be 01 to specify a multicast address). This block is the high-order 24 bits of the Ethernet address, meaning that this block includes addresses in the range 01:00:5E:00:00:00 through to 01:00:5E:ff:ff:ff. The IANA allocates half of this block for mapping class D IP multicast addresses to IEEE-802 multicast addresses. So the Ethernet addresses corresponding to IP multicasting are in the range 01:00:5E:00:00:00 through to 01:00:5E:7f:ff:ff.

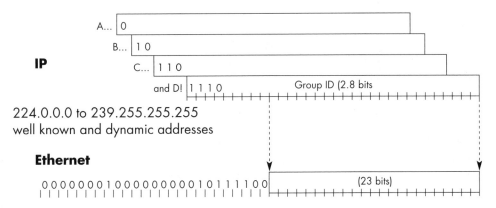

Fig. 8.6 : The 23 bits in the Ethernet address correspond to the IP multicast group ID

(A bit of history here: when Steve Deering designed IP multicast, he figured out that he would need to buy 16 blocks of 24 bits from IEEE, which were worth £2000 each. So he was allowed to use only half of a 24-bit block, which accounts for the 23 bits we have today.)

This allocation allows for 23 bits in the Ethernet address to correspond to the IP multicast group ID (*see* Fig. 8.6). The mapping places the low-order 23 bits of the multicast group ID into these 23 bits of the Ethernet address. Since the upper 5 bits of the multicast address are ignored in this mapping, it is not a one-to-one relationship: 32 different multicast group IDs map to each Ethernet address.

Because there is not a one-to-one mapping between Ethernet and IP multicast addresses, an Ethernet card can receive and forward wrong packets to the device driver. The device driver or the IP stack of the host must filter out these datagrams by checking the IP destination address.

IP multicasting on a single physical network is simple. The sending process specifies a destination IP address that is a multicast address, then the device driver converts this address to the corresponding Ethernet address and sends it. The receiving processes must notify their IP layers that they want to receive datagrams destined for a given multicast address, and the device driver must enable reception of these multicast frames. This process is triggered by joining a multicast group.

Group membership protocol

IGMPv1

IGMPv1 is specified in RFC 1112. In the same way that a special form of email is sent to the list server to subscribe to the list, a host sends a group membership protocol message to be included in a multicast group. IGMP has been assigned protocol number 2 (RFC 1700). *See* Fig. 8.7

When a host first subscribes to a multicast group, a couple of IGMP reports are sent to the group address to which the host subscribes with a TTL (time to live) of 1. Multicast routers promiscuously receive all multicast traffic (the network interface forwards all packets to the device driver) and are therefore informed of the new member. Because of the TTL, an IGMP message is never forwarded out of the subnet.

On each link, a multicast router is elected to be the querier and periodically (every minute, typically) sends an IGMP query message to the all-hosts group (224.0.0.1) with a TTL of 1. Each host on the directly connected subnets is supposed to issue an answer with an IGMP report sent to each group address to which it belongs. To avoid a synchronized storm of messages, the reports are sent after a random delay. When a host hears a report for a group and is also a member of that group, it resets the timer and keeps silent to avoid duplicate messages. The router will consider that there is no member left for group G on a link if it does not hear reports for group G after several queries on this link. *See* Fig. 8.8.

IGMP operates only over broadcast LANs or point-to-point links, but there are some ways to extend the subscription mechanism over NBMA (non broadcast, multiple access) networks. MARS is an example of such a solution over ATM.

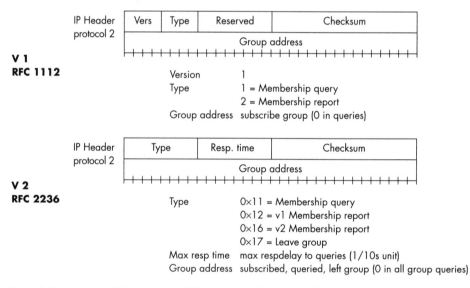

Type 1 for queries, 2 for reports. The group address is either the group concerned, or 0 in queries.

Fig. 8.7 : IGMPv1 format

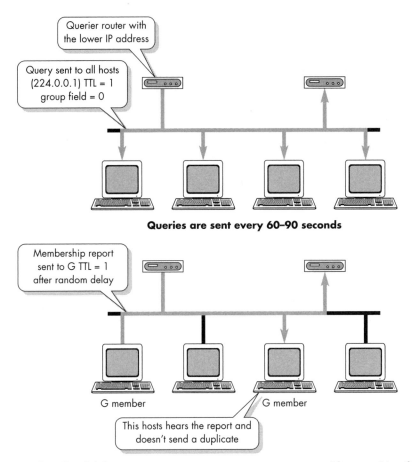

Queries are sent every 60–90 seconds

When first joining a group, two reports or more are sent without waiting for a query

Fig. 8.8 : Sending an IGMP query message

IGMPv2

In IGMPv1, a router considers a group has no members left if it does not receive IGMP reports addressed to the group after a number of queries. In the meantime it will keep forwarding useless and bandwidth-consuming datagrams. In IGMPv2, an additional 'leave group' message has been defined to reduce the latency of hosts leaving a group. IGMPv2 is specified by RFC 2236 and is backward compatible with v1.

The fields type and version have been merged into a new 8-bit type field (0x11 membership query, 0x12 v1 membership report, 0x16 v2 membership report, 0x17 leave group).

The group address now indicates the group being either queried, or reported, or left. It is left to 0 to query all groups. The reserved space has been allocated to indicate a maximal response time in one-tenth of a second.

The leave message for a group is sent only by a leaving host if it is the last one to have effectively sent a report membership for that group (otherwise it knows there are other members on the LAN). The querying router then sends a couple of group-specific queries with a small max response time to check no one else is still a member. If no report is heard for the group, the router considers there are no more members on the LAN.

The querier election for IGMPv2 is very simple. In the beginning all routers send queries, then only the one with the smallest IP address keeps sending queries. If the other routers do not hear queries for some time, they restart the election process.

IGMPv3

IGMPv3 will add source selection possibilities, such as listening to some sources only, or to all but a set of unwanted sources. This could be used, for instance, to exclude from large conferences some users who send background noise (e.g. they do not know how to switch off their microphones). This will also help prevent 'denial of service' attacks where the hacker sends a stream conflicting with the original session on the same multicast group and port.

Controlling scope in multicast applications

Scope versus initial TTL

Like any other IP packet, any multicast datagram has a TTL field. The TTL is decremented at each hop. When the TTL reaches 0, the packet is discarded by routers. For a unicast packet, this TTL is always set to a rather high value (127 typically) and is just used to prevent routing loops. The TTL field of a multicast datagram is also decremented at each multicast router. But in addition to preventing routing loops, it is an indication of the size of the datagram's scope. Consider the IP multicast sender as a radio station (*see* Fig. 8.9). The initial value of the TTL defines the power of the emitter. The larger the TTL, the larger the range that can be reached. Therefore multicast datagrams are usually sent with a small initial TTL.

The TTL can therefore be used as some basic form of 'power control' for a multicast broadcast. A multicast session sent using a TTL of two can only span a disk centered on the sender with a diameter of four routers. Increasing the TTL to six would expand this diameter to 12.

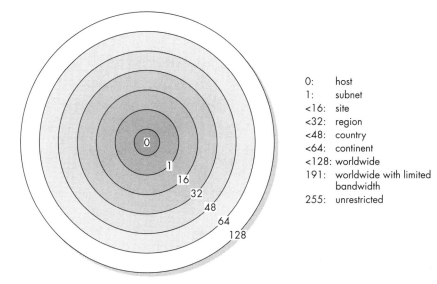

0:       host
1:       subnet
<16:   site
<32:   region
<48:   country
<64:   continent
<128:   worldwide
191:    worldwide with limited
         bandwidth
255:    unrestricted

Fig. 8.9 : Scope versus initial TTL

TTL threshold

The TTL can also be used to set a virtual administrative boundary to a domain. All multicast interfaces can be configured to forward only those packets having a TTL greater than a preset value. If an administrative domain can be approximately defined by a disk of diameter D, then setting the minimal forwarding threshold of all edge routers higher than D will prevent all sessions originating in the domain with a TTL of D to propagate to the outside world. Such sessions with an initial TTL of D will cover the whole domain but stay within the boundary of the edge routers.

This scheme applies to nested domains; for instance an internal subdomain could be configured with a threshold of 16, and the parent domain would have a TTL of 32. *See* Fig. 8.10.

Administrative scoping

The traditional way of limiting the scope of a multicast broadcast using TTL has a serious flaw: it does not allow administrative domains to overlap. Let us take the case of a company that has an engineering department A and an accounting department B. Two book-keepers are in charge of the engineering department and belong to both domains. We want to be able to do engineering-only conferences, accounting-only conferences, and company-wide conferences from any desktop in the relevant domains.

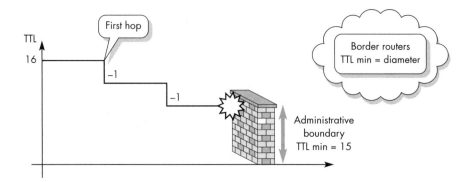

Fig. 8.10 : Using a combination of TTL and administrative TTL bounderies

In the setup shown in Fig. 8.11, a conference sent from domain A with a TTL of 16 will stay in domain A. A conference with a TTL of 32 will be company wide. But how do you do a conference for domain B only? If we set the outgoing threshold of the remaining common interfaces (left) to X>16, it will be impossible to initiate an 'A-only' conference from the book-keepers' desktops (an initial TTL<16 would stay in the intersection domain, an initial TTL>16 would leak into domain B). A threshold X below 16 creates the same impossibility for B-only conferences.

To allow administrators to have better control over the scope of a session, the multicast address range 239.0.0.0 to 239.255.255.255 (administratively scoped addresses) has been reserved for this use. Administrators can configure all edge routers to not forward some addresses in this range. All sessions sent using those multicast addresses will stay within the domain, regardless of the initial TTL. Overlapping multicast domains can be configured simply by using different administratively scoped addresses in each of the domains.

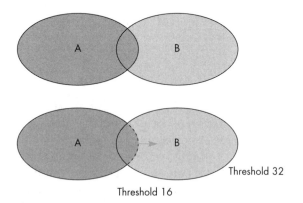

Fig. 8.11 : TTL scoping issues

An administrative scope is bi-directional: it prevents all 239.x.x.x traffic from getting out and getting in. This is useful since many site administrators on the Mbone forget to set the administrative scope and still use software that is set to send 239.x.x.x datagrams.

Building the multicast delivery tree

With IP multicast, the routers are responsible for duplicating the packets and sending them to the appropriate interfaces – but which interfaces? In fact, the construction of the multicast delivery tree is the most complex issue of the multicast technology.

We will call a 'source router' any router directly connected to a subnetwork with a source station. Several techniques can be used.

Flooding and spanning tree

The simplest way to send a packet to every member of a group is flooding. In this technique each router of the IP internetwork replicates every inbound multicast packet to all interfaces except the inbound interface. If the same packet arrives more than once, it is discarded. This is simple and robust (it is used for some military networks), but clearly not scalable.

An improvement of the flooding algorithm is to select a subset of the Internet routers. This subset should form a spanning tree of interconnected routers, in which two distinct routers are interconnected by one, and only one, active path (*see* Fig. 8.12).

This topology ensures that there will be no routing loop, so it becomes unnecessary to detect duplicate packets and flooding is much more efficient. Unfortunately it is computationally difficult to build a spanning tree for large networks, and spanning trees tend to concentrate a lot of traffic near the root of the tree.

Shared trees

Shared tree techniques use only one spanning tree for the group. A simple way to build a common spanning tree is to choose a 'rendezvous' point. Then all sources send a message towards the rendezvous point, and each multicast router seeing this message on its way marks the interface from which it arrived and the outgoing interface. Now any multicast datagram received on the outgoing interface will be copied to all other marked interfaces.

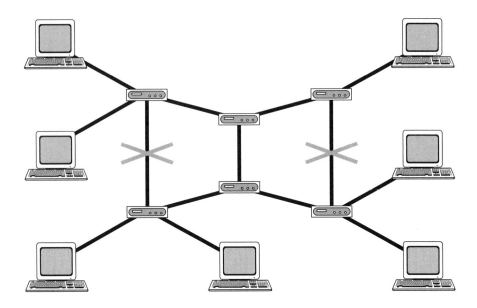

Fig. 8.12 : A spanning tree – there is one path between any pair of nodes

For a source router, sending a datagram to the group is just a matter of sending an encapsulated datagram to the rendezvous point, which decapsulates it and forwards a copy on all of its marked interfaces.

Source-based trees

A spanning tree can be shared between all source routers, but some algorithms build a different tree for each source router. When a host sends a datagram to the group, the datagram will be duplicated according to the spanning tree rooted at the host's router. This leads to more efficient paths and smaller delivery delays.

Dense and sparse mode protocols

Multicast routing techniques fall in two broad categories: sparse mode protocols, and dense mode protocols. Sparse mode protocols are optimized for large networks where only a small portion of all connected hosts are members of each group. Dense mode protocols are optimized for networks where most hosts are members of active multicast groups. These are not necessarily small networks. For instance, at an exchange between large ISPs, it is very likely that there will be at least one member in each ISP domain for all active groups.

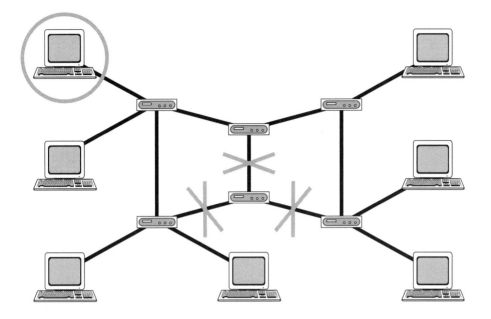

Fig. 8.13 : A source-rooted treee

Technically, sparse mode protocols tend to use a shared tree, and a router needs to subscribe to a group to become a member. Dense mode protocols tend to use source-rooted trees (*see* Fig. 8.13), and include by default all multicast routers in the distribution tree. Routers need to send 'prune' messages if they are not interested.

Reverse path broadcasting and truncated reverse path broadcasting

Reverse path broadcasting (RPB) is a technique to build source-based spanning trees. For each source, if the packet arrives on the link that the router believes to be the shortest way back towards the source (this information is derived from the protocol's own routing table in the case of DVMRP, or from the unicast routing table in the case of PIM), the router duplicates the packet and forwards it to every interface except the originating one. Otherwise, if the packet comes from a link that is not the shortest one back to the source, the packet is dropped. *See* Fig. 8.14.

This algorithm has one main limitation: it includes all routers and subnets in the tree, even if some of them are not part of the destination multicast group.

A possible enhancement of RPB is truncated reverse path broadcasting (TRPB), where the routers use the information obtained with IGMP to avoid sending

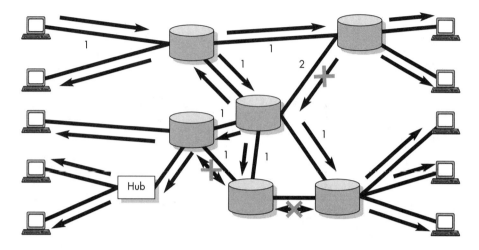

Fig. 8.14 : Reverse path broadcasting

multicast datagrams to leaf subnets in which no host is a member of the destination multicast group. However, the delivery tree between routers still makes no use of IGMP information, even though some parts might be useless.

DVMRP v1 (distance vector multicast routing protocol), the original Mbone routing protocol, used the TRPB forwarding algorithm. DVMRP is similar to RIP, except that it tracks distances to the source, not the destination.

Reverse path multicasting

Reverse path multicasting (RPM) builds source-based trees that span only subnets with group members and routers along the shortest path to subnets with group members. The first packet is forwarded using the TRPB algorithm, but if the edge routers see that none of their leaf subnets are members of the destination group, they send a 'prune' message to the parent router. The parent router stores this information and disables this child interface for this source and this group. If all child interfaces are disabled for a given source and group, this router itself sends a prune message upstream.

To allow dynamic group expansion, the prune information has a limited life, and so the network is periodically flooded again with TRPB. It is a big improvement, but it requires the routers to store a lot of prune information (for each active [source, group] pair), and the periodic flooding wastes bandwidth. RPM, being a dense mode algorithm, is especially suitable for networks with plenty of bandwidth and many receivers.

Multicast routing protocols

DVMRPv3

DVMRPv3 is a routing protocol which uses an RPM algorithm to forward multicast packets. It is the dominant protocol of the Mbone.

As we have seen, when a router R running an RPM algorithm receives a multicast datagram, it needs to know:

■ if the packet was received on the interface closest to the source (RPF check) from the multicast topology perspective. If it is not, the packet should have been received first by the interface closer to the source, so this packet is probably a duplicate and must be dropped. Note that in most cases all links on the network are not multicast enabled, so the interface closest to the source from the unicast topology perspective and the interface closest to the source for the multicast topology will often differ. For this reason, DVMRP maintains its own routing protocol to take into account the multicast topology;

■ if the source of this datagram is closer to R or closer to R's neighbor routers. If neighbor routers are closer, they will receive the datagram first, so there is no need to forward the current packet to those routers.

In unicast routing protocols, such as RIP, each router advertises its best route *from* the router *to* each destination for the unicast topology. The result is that each router knows the length of the unicast way *from* it *to* each destination.

Here what we really want to know is how long it is *from* the source *to* the router in the *multicast* topology. This is very often the same, but not always, as in the case of asymmetric links or when using tunnels. All multicast routing protocols assume that links are symmetric (the DVMRP draft encourages the configuration of tunnels with symmetric administrative distances), so the first issue tends to be ignored rather than solved. DVMRP solves the second issue by using its own routing protocol to discover the topology of the multicast network.

For each directly attached subnet S, a DVMRP router R advertises the distance from S to R to each neighbor router N (in this case just one hop). When N receives such an advertisement from a neighbor saying that S can reach R in h hops, it first checks that no other router R has sent a message saying that S is closer to it (if this is the case, the advertisement is not forwarded). Otherwise N will send a message to each of its neighbors saying that S can reach N in h+d hops, where d is the administrative distance associated with the interface connected to R. The interface can be a physical interface or a virtual tunnel interface. *See* Fig. 8.15.

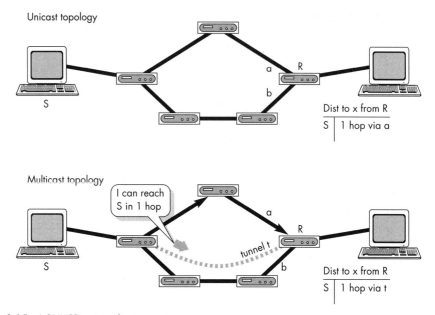

Fig. 8.15 : A DVMRP router advertisement

Table 8.1 is an example of how a DVMRP routing table might look.

Table 8.1 : A DVMRP routing table

Source Prefix	Subnet Mask	From-Gateway	Metric	Status	Entry Lifetime(s)
128.1.0.0	255.255.0.0	128.7.5.2	3	UP	200
128.2.0.0	255.255.0.0	128.7.5.2	5	UP	150
128.3.0.0	255.255.0.0	128.6.3.1	2	UP	150
128.3.0.0	255.255.0.0	128.6.3.1	4	UP	200

DVMRP also builds a forwarding table since the routing table does not include group membership information. This table includes by default all interfaces connected to neighboring DVMRP routers (including virtual tunnel interfaces). After prune messages have been received, those interfaces are pruned for certain groups. On interfaces with directly attached hosts, the forwarding information is based upon IGMP queries and reports.

Table 8.2 : A DVMRP forwarding table

Source subnet prefix	Multicast group	TTL	In interface	Out interface(s)
128.1.0.0	224.1.1.1	200	1p (prune sent)	2p (prune received), 3p
	224.2.2.2	100	1	2p 3
	224.3.3.3	250	1	2
128.2.0.0	224.1.1.1	150	2	2p 3

The prune states have a timer of about two hours on the Mbone. The number of prunes that the routers need to maintain (per source, group and interface) is the main limitation of the scalability of DVMRP. This is an interesting property: as the number of listeners increases for a source, the state required in the router decreases. DVMRP is really a dense mode protocol. *See* Fig. 8.16.

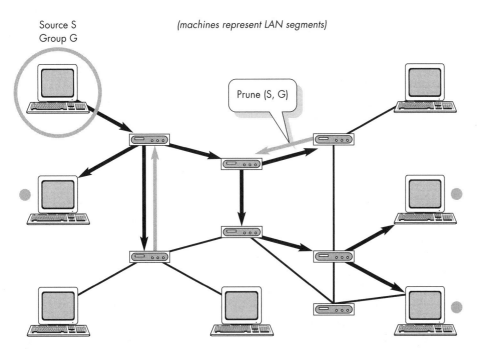

Fig. 8.16 : A prune message

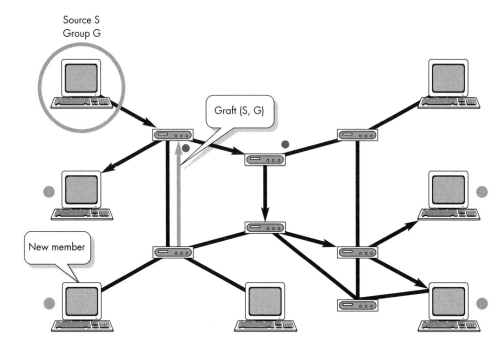

Fig. 8.17 : A graft message

DVMRPv3 also has a notion of 'graft' messages (*see* Fig. 8.17). Those graft messages g(source,group) are sent by a router to indicate that it is willing to reattach to a multicast tree for which it had previously sent a prune message.

All messages exchanged by DVMRP routers are encapsulated in IP datagrams with protocol number 2 (IGMP), and IGMP packet type 0x13.

Some further improvements of DVMRP are under way, such as CIDR-like aggregation.

The main issue with the scalability of DVMRP is the periodic flooding which occurs when prune states expire. All DVMRP routers will receive unwanted multicast traffic until they have sent a prune back. However, the measurements made on the Mbone show that this is not yet a real problem. Figure 8.18 is a graph of flooding activity for two pruned sessions (one audio and one video) which can be found on *http://ganef.cs.ucla.edu/~mbone/tunnel.html*. The graph shows that most of the time the session is pruned back immediately after the first packet of the session reaches the router, so the flooding activity is really minimal. The aggregate flood/prune rate for all sessions typically never exceeded 40 packets/s.

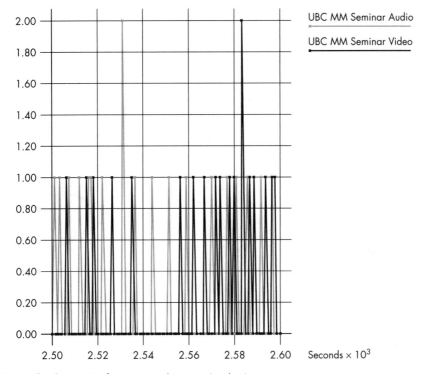

Fig. 8.18 : Flooding activity for two pruned sessions (packets)

Other protocols

MOSPF

Description of operation in a single OSPF area

The multicast extension to OSPF is described in RFC 1584. MOSPF uses the link state information built by OSPF to calculate a shortest path tree on the fly for each source, group pair. The router knows the multicast topology because the link state advertisements (LSAs) comprise a multicast capable bit, so the tree spans only MOSPF routers and subnets that are members of the group. *See* Fig. 8.19.

In addition to the regular OSPF routing table, each MOSPF router maintains a group membership table. On each subnet, one or two MOSPF routers maintain multicast group memberships in a local group database using IGMP. The designated router DR performs the IGMP queries on each subnet and both the DR and the backup designated router (BDR) listen to the IGMP host membership reports. The DR then floods the entire OSPF area with group membership link state advertisements.

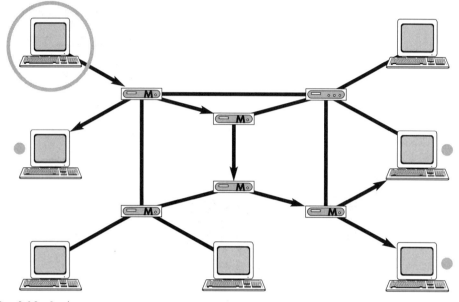

Fig. 8.19 : Single area operation

Since each MOSPF router has all the necessary information locally, the multi-cast tree built using Dijkstra's algorithm spans only subnetworks that have members of the group, so it does not have to be pruned. This is a major difference with DVMRP (DVMRP floods the networks for each new multicast flow and then periodically when prune state expires).

Inter-area routing

In OSPF, area border routers (ABR) are used to forward datagrams outside the OSPF area. In MOSPF, some of them are also configured to act as inter-area multicast forwarders. An inter-area multicast forwarder sends new group membership LSAs to the backbone area for each group which has at least one member within the local OSPF area. The inter-area multicast forwarder is a 'wild card multicast receiver' for the local OSPF area, i.e. it receives all multicast traffic generated within that OSPF area, and decides whether to forward it to the backbone based on the LSAs received from the backbone. *See* Fig. 8.20.

PIM

The Inter-Domain Multicast Routing working group of the IETF develops a set of standards describing multicast routing protocols. For the moment the working group has defined PIM (protocol independent multicast), which comes in two flavors: PIM dense mode and PIM sparse mode (now an experimental RFC).

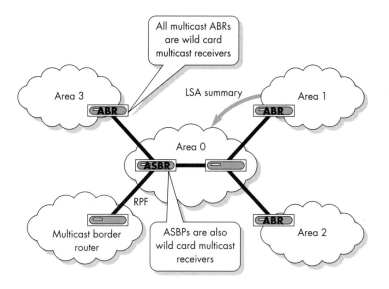

Fig. 8.20 : Area multicast border router and AS boundary routers handle inter-area and inter-AS multicasting

PIM-DM

PIM-DM relies on the routing tables established by any unicast routing protocol. This topology information is used to find the route back to the source and build a spanning tree using the reverse path multicasting algorithm. PIM-DM forwards the multicast packets to all downstream interfaces (flooding) until a prune message is received. (In comparison, DVMRP determines child interfaces, i.e. interfaces which are known to be on the shortest path back to the source for the downstream router.)

PIM-DM also uses graft messages to reattach a pruned part of the delivery tree if a new member joins the group (*see* Fig. 8.21).

PIM-SM

PIM-SM is specified in RFC 2362. By design, PIM-SM is suited for WAN nets, with limited bandwidth and scarce group members. With this constraint, it is impossible to use flooding, so DVMRP would not scale well.

PIM-DM and PIM-SM must be used in separate multicast domains; however, the packet forwarding and control messages operate seamlessly between the two.

In PIM-SM, designated routers must explicitly join a group by sending a message to a 'Rendezvous' point for that group. There is only one rendezvous point per group, which is determined by a deterministic hash function of the group address. Each multicast router in the path of the join message to RP point creates a forwarding entry for that group.

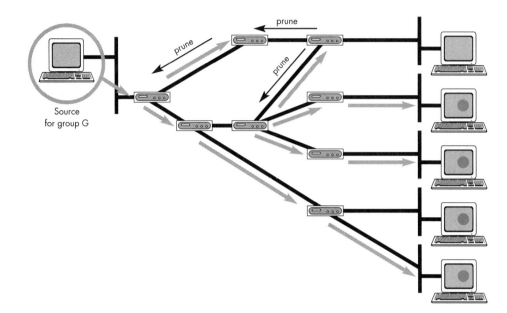

Fig. 8.21 : PIM – Dense Mode

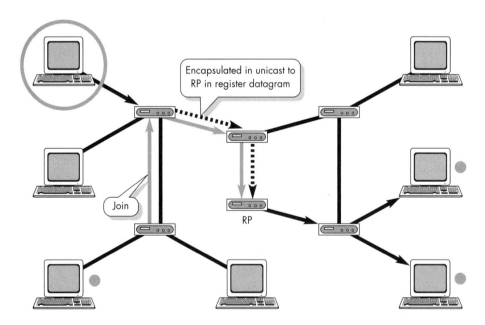

Fig. 8.22 : PIM – Sparse Mode

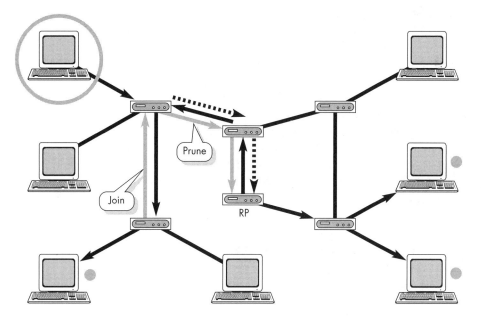

Fig. 8.23 : Sending a join message

Also, the first packet of a multicast stream is sent encapsulated in a unicast reg-ister packet sent to the RP (*see* Fig. 8.22). Each router in the path of this register packet creates a forwarding entry so that future multicast datagrams for this group can be sent unencapsulated.

If the traffic from a source exceeds a certain threshold, the last hop router has the option (it is in no way mandatory) to stop using the RP for that source and build a source-based shortest path tree by sending a join message towards the source of the stream (*see* Fig. 8.23). Once the tree is built, the last hop router sends a prune message for that source to the rendezvous point.

Core-based trees

CBT (RFC 2201) has been designed to be used in the context of very large networks, where scalability issues can prevent the use of other multicast techniques. CBT uses a bi-directional shared tree. Many features are identical to PIM-SM, including the notion of rendezvous point (called a core router) and the election mechanism. However, CBT design does not allow shortcuts to be established, and this is presented by CBT designers as a feature to preserve the scalability features of CBT. Because the tree to the rendezvous point is bi-directional, routers that are attached to a group do not need to encapsulate their multicast messages sent to the same group.

Security issues in IP multicast

Unauthorized listening

IGMP has no security features. Any host which knows the appropriate group and UDP port can attempt to become a member of any conference.

Any application using IP multicast must be designed having this limitation in mind and use strong encryption for any data sent to the group. Most of the popular applications can at least use 56-bit DES encryption.

In addition to this, all routers allow access lists for IGMP messages to be configured: this can be useful to restrict the number of directly attached hosts which can be members of a group. However, if multicast datagrams have to be forwarded to another router operated by a different administration, nothing prevents that administration from having a less restrictive policy.

Unauthorized sending and denial of service attacks

We emphasized in the IGMP chapter that it was not necessary to be a member of a group to send datagrams to the group. This potentially allows any host connected to the multicast backbone to send datagrams to any conference.

If the conference is encrypted, or if the media streams are authenticated, this is not a security breach since members will be able to sort valid packets and spoofed packets – if valid packets make it to the listener. By sending large numbers of spoofed datagrams, a sender can easily congest the leased lines to the listener. Usually access routers are configured to accept only a limited number of multicast packets to save some bandwidth for unicast applications, so these routers will start to drop multicast packets. They have no means of distinguishing spoofed packets from valid packets, so each stream – valid and spoofed alike – will experience a proportional packet loss.

This is a major threat to any commercial multicast service, since the customer will expect a good quality of service, and cannot easily distinguish those denial of service attacks from the effects of a poor congested backbone. For this reason, existing commercial multicast services are deployed on managed networks, with access lists dropping all multicast traffic at the access level by default. Customers are allocated a group and a set of ports, and only their access routers are allowed to inject multicast traffic for that group in the backbone (*see* Fig. 8.24).

This is not very efficient for address allocation, and does not work with applications using dynamic UDP ports because access lists cannot easily be reconfigured on the fly.

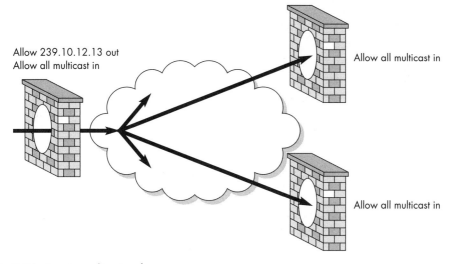

Allow 239.10.12.13 out
Allow all multicast in

Allow all multicast in

Allow all multicast in

Fig. 8.24 : Securing multicast conferences

Firewalls

Firewalls are configured using a set of rules which are usually based on the source and destination unicast addresses and port. IP multicast breaks this model because group membership is completely dynamic, and group members are unknown to the firewall – any router behind the firewall will duplicate and relay multicast packets to any attached host sending the appropriate IGMP message.

Therefore firewalling cannot be as precise with multicast traffic as it is with unicast traffic; the rules can be based only on sender and group (destination UDP port and destination address). There are some ways to improve this:

■ in the future firewalls could listen to domain-wide multicast reports in order to track group members;

■ another possibility is to poll hosts with ICMP ECHO packets for a group, but this obviously does not scale and works only with Unix hosts (W95 does not respond to multicast ICMP ECHO);

■ a third possibility is to track group membership at the application level; this is possible, for instance, with H.323 MCUs since they allocate the multicast addresses to be used.

Address translation can be used to hide internal addresses: the initial sender address can be replaced by the firewall address. This can break some applications.

The Mbone

The Mbone has grown from 40 subnets in four countries in 1992 to 3400 subnets over 25 countries in March 1997, and should reach nearly 6000 subnets in January 1998 (this can be seen easily by listing the DVMRP routing table of a router connected to the Mbone). The Mbone is composed of islands of multicast routers interconnected by tunnels over the regular Internet links. Multicast datagrams are conveyed on the tunnels as IP over IP datagrams (protocol 4).

Routing protocols

Most routers run DVMRP (MOSPFv2 does not handle tunnels), but the islands themselves may run MOSPF, PIM or CBT.

Topology

A quick look at the cover of this memo is enough to understand that the Mbone is not completely managed. However, the people in charge are trying hard to keep it hierarchical. Figure 8.25 shows the picture in France (made by *Christian.Donot@inria.fr*).

How to get connected

From the end-user perspective, multicast is available on most operating systems, including all flavors of Unix, Windows NT and MacOS. The issue is to get connected to one of the multicast routers of the Mbone, via a tunnel or directly. The best way is first to contact your network provider, and if he is not willing to establish a tunnel himself, to issue a message to a regional mailing list (Europe: mbone-eu-request@sics.se; North America: mbone-na-request@isi.edu; other: mbone-request@isi.edu). Hopefully you will find someone near you ('near' for the MBone topology) who will let you establish a tunnel.

You can expect a traffic in the 100–300 kbit/s range, but it depends on which sessions you plan to attend. It must be kept in mind at all times that if there are multiple tunnels on one physical line, the traffic will be several times the traffic of each individual tunnel. On slow links, you can adjust the amount of traffic you will be receiving by adjusting the TTL threshold of your router. IETF sets the TTL of high bandwidth video sessions lower than for audio sessions (*see* Table 8.3).

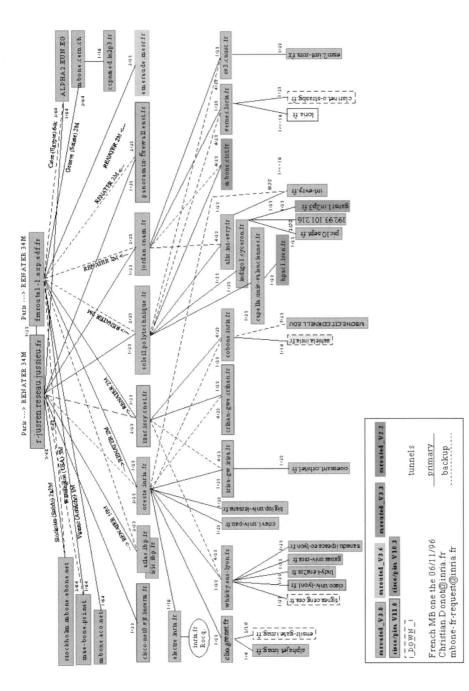

Fig. 8.25 : The Mbone in France

Table 8.3 : TTL for video and audio sessions

	TTL	Threshold
IETF chan 1 low-rate GSM audio	255	224
IETF chan 2 low-rate GSM audio	223	192
IETF chan 1 PCM audio	191	160
IETF chan 2 PCM audio	159	128
IETF chan 1 video	127	96
IETF chan 2 video	95	64
local event audio	63	32
local event video	31	1

A threshold of 128 may be used initially, and then raised to 160 or 192 if the 64 kbit/s voice is excessive (GSM voice is about 18 kbit/s), or lowered to 64 kbit/s to allow video to be transmitted to the tunnel.

Inter-domain multicast routing

Inter-operation between domains running different protocols

There are IETF drafts on the inter-operation between multicast domains running different protocols. Interoperability Rules for Multicast Routing Protocols (<draft-thaler-multicast-interop-02.txt>, <draft-ietf-idmr-gum-02.txt>) considers first a tree domain topology, as in Fig. 8.26.

The routers between domains are called multicast border routers (MBRs). They have an interface in each domain and run at least an instance of a multicast routing component for each domain they are attached to. All routing components can run the same routing protocol, or different ones (for instance DVMRP and PIM-SM). For each domain at level n, the parent domain at level n+1 is the default route. The domain at level n injects only the routes of its domain to level n+1.

All components share a common forwarding cache of (S,G) entries, each entry having one IIF (incoming interface) and a list of several interfaces (oiflist). The routing tables maintained by each component can be different (*see* Fig. 8.27). The information about each interface in the forwarding cache is maintained by the component which owns the interface (the determination of the owner according to the routing tables is made by an inter-domain component).

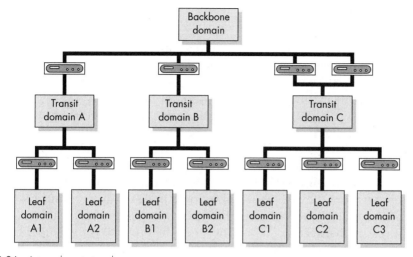

Fig. 8.26 : A tree domain topology

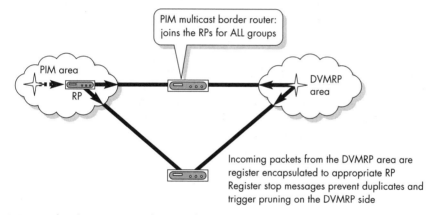

Fig. 8.27 : Interface between PIM and DVMRP domains

The component owning the interface performs the RPF check for packets coming from this interface. Once it is accepted it is forwarded according to the forwarding rules of all components.

When a new (S,G) entry is created, all components are advised so that they can set the forwarding state on their own outgoing interfaces in the forwarding table. When a component removes the last oif from a forwarding table entry, the iif owner must be alerted so it can send a prune. When the first oif is added to the forwarding table concerning an (S,G) entry, the owner of the iif must be alerted (so it can send a join or graft).

In most cases each component must be a wild card receiver for its domain.

BGMP

Some of the multicast routing protocols described above can be used in a wide area environment. DVMRP, and to a lesser extent PIM-SM, are used on the Mbone. However, the Mbone is still a small network compared to the Internet, and lives in the relatively friendly environment of inter-university and experimental networks. DVMRP creates state per source and per group in every router and would not scale to the size of the Internet. PIM-SM could potentially scale much better, but leads to another issue: third party dependency. If you decide to use a multicast address, it could very well happen that the RP for this address is in fact a router belonging to another service provider – not an easy situation.

For these reasons, work is continuing to define a multicast routing protocol which is both scalable, minimizing third-party dependency, and convenient, to establish policies between domains. The emerging protocol is the border gateway multicast routing protocol (BGMP), described in <draft-ietf-idmr-gum-02.txt>.

BGMP supposes that portions of the class D address space are allocated to domains. The mechanism to carry out this allocation is not yet very well defined, but the IETF is walking on a 'multicast-address-set advertisement and claim mechanism'.

BGMP is similar to both PIM-SM and CBT. BGMP uses a shared tree for each group like PIM-SM, and these trees are bi-directional like CBT (a bi-directional tree means that the forwarding state in each router is group specific and does not consider the source – a packet arriving from any interface is forwarded with no RPF check). The main difference with CBT is that now the root of the shared tree for a group is an entire domain. The advantage of using bi-directional trees is that packets in transit for a domain A to a domain B do not have to transit via the core domain if they are on the same branch of the tree. *See* Fig. 8.28.

Each domain advertises the groups for which it is a root domain using the EGP. Therefore the EGP (exterior gateway protocol) must be able to carry multicast prefixes. The multicast extension of BGP4, defined in RFC 2283, can be used for this purpose.

BGMP routers establish peer relations with TCP connections. When a domain wants to become a member of a group G, it sends a join message to its peer in the direction of the core for G, and the peer itself will forward this join if it is not already a member of the group. Join states are hard states, which is also a difference with PIM-SM. BGMP routers must send a prune message to leave a group.

Operation with DVMRP and PIM-DM

BGMP needs special arrangements to work with DVMRP and PIM-DM. The first issue is that DVMRP and PIM-DM perform an RPF check on incoming multicast datagrams. For this reason it must be possible to inject multicast packets from

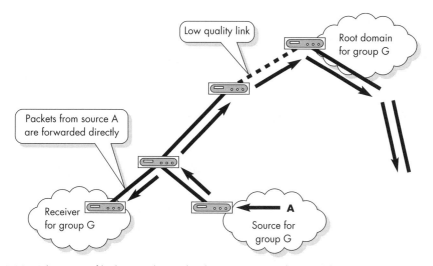

Fig. 8.28 : Advantages of bi-directional tree – local communications do not go through the net

different sources via different border routers, otherwise the RPF check may fail (*see* Fig. 8.29). This control will fail if the BGMP distribution tree is common to the group, for instance in Fig. 8.29.

In these situations any BGMP border router which receives a multicast datagram for the domain will first forward it – encapsulated – to the right border router (the one that will perform the RPF check). Then the right border router will – if not already receiving the packets from the shared tree – send a *source specific* join message towards the source, and create a source specific entry in the forwarding table. When this is done, it will receive datagrams directly and can send a prune message to the border router that was sending encapsulated datagrams.

It should be noted that this situation will never occur for domains connected through only one border router (stub domains).

The second issue with DVMRP and PIM-DM is that there is no explicit joining mechanism – DVMRP and PIM-DM routers join everything they do not prune. Therefore the border BGMP router has no easy way to know which groups have been joined inside the domain – unless it first joins all groups and forwards the packets inside the domain. This would ruin the scalability of BGMP. Another way to do it is to assume that all receivers are also senders, and to join a group as soon as there is a sender for it inside the DVMRP domain. This of course is far from being a perfect solution either.

Inter-operation with PIM-SM

PIM-SM routers also do an RPF check on incoming multicast datagrams. But in this case it is easier to deal with this problem: if the BGMP border router receiving

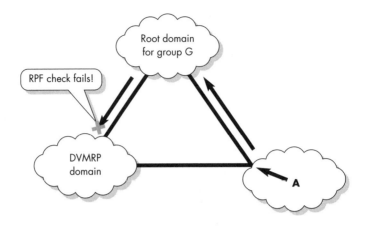

Fig. 8.29 : A failed RPF check

packets from the shared tree for a multicast group also becomes the RP for that group, RPF checks will succeed. In order to achieve this, the BGMP router should send candidate-RP advertisements in the PIM-SM domain.

Other multicast border routers may also receive packets for that group (the tree is bi-directional). In this case they must send them encapsulated in register messages to the RP.

In PIM-SM domains, the routers are allowed to switch a shortest path tree instead of the shared tree if a source exceeds a certain threshold. If the shortest path to that source is via the multicast border router which is also the RP, there is no issue. But it can also be via any other multicast border router. If this is the case, the MBR will send source specific join messages toward the source, as in the DVMRP case.

Inter-operation with CBT and MOSPF

The most significant interoperability issue with these protocols is that they are unable to process source specific joins or prunes. Although in most cases BGMP uses only group specific join and prune messages, we have seen above that in order to interoperate with multicast routing protocols that perform an RPF check, it was necessary in some cases to send source specific joins and prunes. The exact description of how this is done is quite complex (*see* draft-ietf-idmr-gum-02.txt), but in short the source specific messages are, under certain conditions, extended to the whole group.

Conclusion on multicast inter-domain routing

Multicast is quite hard to scale to very large networks. All efforts to reduce the necessary state to group specific data leads to interoperability problems, which can be solved, but make the protocol considerably more complex. BGP is already difficult to configure but still manageable – one wonders how long it will take to configure a large BGMP network dealing with not only the usual peering configuration headaches of BGP, but also all sorts of tricky RPF issues.

However, in the particular case of a domain with a tree topology (for the multicast links), the situation is much simpler. A network provider could implement either hierarchical-DVMRP or BGMP without major trouble. For the end customer, the situation is also easier since only a default route needs to be configured.

Multicast caveats

Multicasting on non-broadcast media

Bridged LANs

Modern LANs use bridges to reduce the number of collisions. A bridge forwards a packet only to the segment on which the machine with the destination MAC address has been detected. Packets with multicast MAC addresses are traditionally forwarded on all interfaces, which is wasteful.

There are several proposals to improve the situation.

IGMP snooping

This solution requires the bridge to inspect all multicast frames to decode IGMP reports. This allows the bridge to learn where the receivers are. In addition it decodes router messages like IGMP queries, DVMRP probes, MOSPF and PIM hellos to learn the position of multicast routers.

Because hosts never send duplicate IGMP reports, the bridge does not forward a report heard on one segment to another segment in order to have a view of which hosts are receivers on each segment.

This solution has some potential drawbacks. Because it relies on the content of IP multicast messages, it does not work for non-IP multicasts and even for IP it may stop working for new IP multicast algorithms. In addition, the inspection of all multicast frames possibly has an impact on performance.

Another issue is that connected multicast routers need to receive all multicast traffic. Since there is no such thing as a wild card IGMP membership report, switches need to be configured to know which ports are attached to multicast routers.

Cisco group management protocol (CGMP)

There is no public spec of this proprietary protocol (CGMP). The idea is to let the router add forwarding entries to the bridge's tables. The router sends CGMP control messages to the bridges. The bridge mechanism is left untouched; simply multicast MAC addresses are added to the forwarding tables for the segments on which the router has detected a member of the multicast group.

IEEE 802.1p group address resolution protocol

GARP is analogous to IGMP at the MAC layer. The hosts which want to receive frames with a particular multicast MAC address send a GARP message to the bridge. The bridge propagates this information to the other bridges.

The specification of GARP is still uncompleted. An obvious problem with GARP is that it requires a change in the hosts.

Windows operating systems

A protocol without users is useless, and obviously most users have either a Windows 95 or a Windows NT machine. Microsoft did take into account multicast and there are decent freeware ports of major Mbone applications on both W95 and NT. Microsoft research has even released a multicast add-on for Powerpoint.

Regarding IGMP, Windows 98 supports IGMPv2. Also, there is a winsock 2.0 update for Windows 95 on the web that carries with it a stack that supports IGMPv2. The IGMPv2 support for NT is in NT 4.0 Service Pack 4 (Q4 98).

Of course, there are some issues:

■ NT machines with several NIC cards will automatically add the 224.0.0.0 route to each interface. A multicast application has to bind to the particular interface on which they want to send the multicast datagram, or the operating system will send the packets on all of them. Most UNIX ports do not do that and will have difficulties running in such a configuration;

■ the WINS service uses 224.0.1.24 (knowledge base Q151761);

■ several issues with remote access service include adding default multicast routes on the RAS device, not responding to general IGMP queries on dynamic RAS connections, etc.

NICs

The performance of network cards is also very important for multicast applications. For instance, Ethernet NICs, as we have seen above, can filter multicast groups based on the multicast Ethernet address. Cheap cards will simply forward all multicast traffic to the operating system, and let the IP stack perform the filtering. This will keep the CPU busy even if there is no relevant traffic for this host and can be problematic on the smaller CPUs. On the most recent Pentium class CPUs, the impact will be typically below 20 per cent.

The more appropriate network cards have a hardware filter based on a hash table with N flags. They hash the destination MAC address to a number between 1 and N and forward the multicast traffic to the host's OS if the flag number N is set. The size of the hash table varies from 64 bits (Intel, Compaq) to 512 bits (DEC DE-500) (more information can be found at *www.stl.nps.navy.mil/~mcgredo/projectNotebook/mcast/EthernetMain.html*).

Flooding

As we said, the security aspects on the Mbone are still to be defined and supported. Expect surprises from time to time. Here are some examples:

- clever people know that 224.2.127.254 is used for SDR and most hosts receive it. They will use just that to flood the Internet;
- less clever people will play with multicast on routers having the full BGP routing tables – and inject the full BGP routing table on the Mbone. This happens frequently, and most routers have warning procedures when they see such a surge. For instance, CISCOs will say:

    %DVMRP-1-ROUTEHOG: Receiving 9993 routes from 204.70.74.61
    (Tunnel8) in the last 00:01:05

Common issues

We have discussed the issue of asymmetric links, and the reader may think that he is safe if there is no satellite hop or similar exotic thing in his network. In fact, some common situations can generate a lot of trouble with multicast protocols. *See* Fig. 8.30.

This is a common setup for companies willing to secure their IP access via two ISPs. Here the work around is to use special routes for multicast traffic (mroutes), or to change the topology.

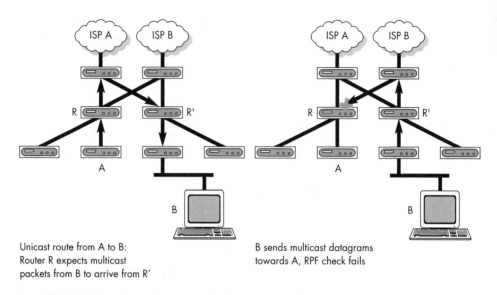

Unicast route from A to B:
Router R expects multicast
packets from B to arrive from R'

B sends multicast datagrams
towards A, RPF check fails

Fig. 8.30 : Failsafe topology with two egress links

Address allocation

There are several proposals being discussed at the IETF:

■ for inter-domain allocation, there is the multicast address set claim (MASC) protocol. In June 1998, the MASC draft was not a full specification, it was more a framework describing how a domain (a BGP autonomous system) could claim and advertise a set of multicast addresses. The domain may need this set of multicast addresses to populate the address pools of the internal MDHCP servers, for instance.

A domain D using MASC first signals that it is willing to use a set of addresses to other domains: this is called a claim. The domain must wait some time in order to allow other domains to warn that there is a collision with a set of addresses already allocated to them. If there is a collision, domain D may claim a different set of addresses until it finds an unallocated range. Once it has obtained such a free range, D can advertise that it is using it by injecting this set of addresses as a multicast route in the inter-domain routing protocol. For instance, if it runs BGMP, it can be included in the network layer reachabilty Information (NLRI) of BGP4+. This will ensure that the multicast distribution trees for the addresses allocated to a domain are rooted in this domain (*see* the section on BGMP).

In order to achieve good scalability and to allow address sets to be aggregatable, MASC proposes to organize the domains running MASC in a hierarchy. Initially, a specialized domain would advertise the entire class D (224/4). The child domains make their choice and claim a set of addresses (a subset of the range advertised by the parent domain). The claim is sent to the parent domain, which advertises it to the other child domains. At this stage the other child domains may generate collision announcements. Little by little, this procedure should settle and allow each child domain to use and advertise a subset of their parent domain.

The advantage of this approach is that allocation of addresses is driven by usage (you are not supposed to claim an address unless you actually plan to use it), and the address sets allocated are aggregatable;

■ for intra-domain address allocation, there are two proposals: AAP and MDHCP. The advantage of AAP is the well defined interface with MASC; the advantage of MDHCP is its integration with the already widely used DHCP. Here is a brief summary of the two proposals, as of June 1998:

– *the multicast address allocation protocol (AAP)*. A domain running AAP has one or more MAAS servers. The role of these servers is to manage the allocation of multicast addresses (the address set allocated to the domain by MASC and learned by listening to the MASC ADDRESS-SET-ANNOUNCE messages, or administratively scoped addresses) to individual clients. These addresses can be grouped in several scopes, and a client must first ask a MAAS server S about the available scopes.

Once this is done, the client chooses a scope and requests the right to use one or more multicast addresses in this scope for a certain amount of time. Since there might be several MAAS servers in the domain, S must first signal to all other MAAS servers in the domain the addresses that it is willing to use. If there is no collision, S can allocate these addresses to the client, and will periodically remind all other MAAS servers that it has allocated these addresses.

This allows a new MAAS server to learn, little by little, all the addresses in use in the domain. After a while, it can be fully synchronized with other MAAS servers and can become client server requests;

– *the multicast address allocation extensions to the dynamic host configuration protocol (MDHCP)*. This proposal extends DHCP to allow a host to request a multicast address from an MDHCP server. DHCP servers and MDHCP servers can be co-located or separate. MDHCP servers have a group address that a client can learn via DHCP or by configuration.

An MDHCP server manages a pool of multicast addresses available for each scope. In this context, a scope is an arbitrary group with a four-byte scope ID described by a string. A client can request the list of scopes managed by an MDHCP server using a new DHCP option defined in multicast address allocation extensions options (<draft-ietf-dhc-multopt-02.txt>) and the DHCP server will return a list like the one in Table 8.4.

Table 8.4 : List of spaces managed by an MDHCP server using a new DHCP option

Scope ID	TTL	Description
1	5	'Workgroup'
2	10	'Department'
3	15	'Company'
4	64	'World'
1001	15	'Engineering group'

This list can contain scopes characterized by a TTL (0xxx) or scopes using administrative addresses (1xxx).

Once the client knows the list of available scopes, it can request one or more addresses in an available scope by using MDHCP messages, which are similar to DHCP messages with an additional 'M' flag. The request can be multicast to all MDHCP servers (DHCPDISCOVER) or directed to one specific server using its unicast address. If the request is multicast, each MDHCP server will reply with the address(es) it offers (DHCPOFFER).

The client then selects the address it wants and makes a request for it to the appropriate server (DHCPREQUEST). There are some options that allow a client to specify the start time of the lease period, and the desired duration of the lease, and the number of addresses requested. The address server confirms the lease with a DHCPACK, and specifies the start time and duration of the lease, as well as the TTL to be used with the multicast addresses.

When the client has finished using one or more multicast addresses, it should send a DHCPPRELEASE message to the MDHCP server.

Mbone applications

Video conferencing with RTP on multicast networks

On unicast networks, RTP can be used for point-to-point communications, but requires a mixer or multi-unicast for multipoint communications. On a multicast network, such as the Mbone, RTC and RTCP can be used to establish multiparty video conferences.

For each media, two UDP ports are allocated, one for RTP and one for RTCP, but a single multicast address can be used for the whole conference. This multicast address and port are usually learned on the Mbone by receiving SDP encoded session descriptions transmitted using the session announcement protocol, but any other protocol or even a web page can be used.

A receiver knows who originated an RTP packet from the SSRC identifier of the RTP packet. This SSRC can be mapped to a CNAME as soon as an SR is received. A receiver should also try to synchronize audio and video streams for SSRCs corresponding to a common CNAME.

Using separate multicast addresses for audio and video allows receivers to choose to receive only audio if they do not have sufficient bandwidth. If a common multicast address is used, multiplexing can still be achieved using the port or payload type, but since the protocol used to subscribe to a multicast group, IGMP, cannot distinguish between payload types or UDP ports, a potential member of the conference could receive only all media streams.

In case of congestion during the conference, participants will become aware of it with incoming receiver reports, and can decide to reduce the number of frames per second of their video streams. They can also change the audio codec used dynamically, since the codec used can be learned from the value of the RTP packet payload type.

SDR: session directory

SDR uses 239.255.255.255 port 9875 for local scope groups and 224.2.127.254 port 9875 for global scope groups. For administratively scoped groups, the highest address in the scoped range should be used. Any port is suitable, but it seems that the tradition is to use 9875.

Table 8.5 shows an example announcement using the SAP protocol and SDP encoding.

For more details about SDP, *see* the SIP chapter.

VIC and VAT *(see* Fig. 8.31)

Reliable multicast

Why isn't there a multicast TCP?

We have stated that multicast could transport only UDP or RAW datagrams, but we did not explain why.

The explanation is rather easy. IP packets, multicast or not, are never guaranteed to reach their destination. There can be a route change, a congestion or an overloaded router along the path, and the poor IP packet gets killed. The only way to send information reliably is to get the receiving host to send back confirmation that it has received the IP packet; the sender uses timeouts to detect losses and eventually resends a copy of the lost IP packets. This traditional approach is called positive acknowledgments with retransmission (PAR). The receiver generates positive acknowledgments for every data packet that it receives.

Table 8.5 : An announcement using the SAP protocol and SDP encoding

SAP: 596 bytes		
version: 0		
message type: 0		
encrypt: 0		
compress: 0		
auth length: 0		
msgid: 8192		
address: 130.240.64.20		
v	=	0
o	=	demo 3066564173 3066564269 IN IP4 130.240.64.67
s	=	places all over the world
i	=	low bandwidth video (10 kb/s) with views from all over the world. It is probably wise to limit the overall bandwidth to 100 kb/s (that is, a maximum of ten 10 kb/s streams). Audio is primarily for feedback for the senders of video
e	=	Hakan Lennestal <hakanl@cdt.luth.se>
c	=	IN IP4 224.2.172.238/127
t	=	0 0
a	=	tool:mStar 1.0beta1
a	=	type:broadcast
m	=	video 51482 RTP/AVP 31
c	=	IN IP4 224.2.172.238/127
m	=	audio 20154 RTP/AVP 0
c	=	IN IP4 224.2.213.113/127
a	=	rtpred1:5
a	=	ptime:40
a	=	rtpred2:5
a	=	rtpmap:121 red/8000

For this purpose, TCP numbers the packets and sends acknowledgments based on this serial number.

Let us extend this concept to multicast. Send a data packet with serial number xyz, wait until you receive an acknowledgement from all group members for serial number xyz, and go on. This seems OK, but it will not work for the following reasons:

1 the sender has no idea of the number and identities of group members;

2 even if it had those identities through the use of a specific protocol (similar to RTCP, for instance) this scheme would not scale to thousands of users because each new IP packet would generate a storm of acknowledgments.

- VIC video tool
- VAT audio tool
- WB shared with eboard
- Network Text Editor

Fig. 8.31 : VIC and VAT

Reliability on a multicast network is not at all a trivial issue, and many approaches exist.

Reliable multicast techniques

All reliable multicast protocols need to detect transmission errors. There can be two approaches: either the receiver sends ACKs for received data and the sender must check those ACKs to determine whether all senders have received the data, or the receiver can try to find data losses locally, for instance by checking gaps in sequence numbers. Therefore there are two broad categories of reliable multicast protocols: those with sender-based error detection, and those with receiver-based error detection.

The first approach is based on ACKs, the second is based on NACKs. In each case there are scalability issues, which are usually addressed by aggregating those messages or multicasting them in order to let other endpoints know that it is useless to send the same information again.

When an error is detected, the concerned receivers must receive a copy of the packets they are missing. In hierarchical approaches this is done by intermediary servers which multi-unicast or multicast those backup copies. If multicast is used, the receivers must be prepared to revive duplicate packets and discard them.

In order to minimize the amount of retransmissions, RM protocols can use data interleaving and redundancy, i.e. they will repeat the same information in two or more packets separated by several other packets. This will reduce the effect of correlated loss in the multicast network.

One of the most complex issues with RM is flow control: the sender needs to adapt the sending rate to the receiving rate of the slowest receiver. In hierarchical approaches, there can be a level of buffering in the RM nodes which prevents a single receiver from slowing down the entire receiving group.

Reliable multicast protocols

There are about 15 implementations of reliable multicast protocols, some of which are described below. RM protocols can get very complex, and are in fact applications running on top of a multicast backbone.

SRM

The scalable reliable multicast (SRM) protocol is a layer above raw IP multicast that provides reliability and scalability. It was originally developed for the 'wb' collaborative whiteboard used on the Mbone.

To avoid the ACK explosion problem, SRM is based on NACKs. Those NACKs are multicast, which allows hosts to know if another endpoint has already requested information or replied to a retransmission request, and prevents duplicate queries and answers. This scheme works because hosts delay their requests and answers proportionally to their distance from the source.

SRM rate control is based on a token bucket, with a fixed rate or a variable rate depending on the particular implementation.

RMP

Reliable multicast protocol (RMP) was initially a university project, but has evolved into a commercial product sold by Globalcast Communications. RMP is real-time oriented.

RMP is a NACK-based protocol. The NACKs are multicast so that other receivers can have a chance of receiving them and avoid duplicate NACK sending as much as possible. The flow control uses TCP concepts (slow start, etc).

Lucent RMTP

Lucent's reliable multicast transport protocol focuses on file distribution in a multi-level hierarchical environment. The final receivers send periodic status messages to upper level designated receivers, and those receivers also report to their upper level designated receivers. Each status message indicates which packets have been lost relatively to the flow control window sequence number. The DR is responsible for retransmitting lost packets to lower levels.

Appendix: well known multicast addresses

The range of addresses between 224.0.0.0 and 224.0.0.255, inclusive, is reserved for the use of routing protocols and other low-level topology discovery or maintenance protocols, such as gateway discovery and group membership reporting. Multicast routers should not forward any multicast datagram with destination addresses in this range, regardless of its TTL.

224.0.0.0	Base Address (Reserved)	[RFC1112,JBP]
224.0.0.1	All Systems on this Subnet	[RFC1112,JBP]
224.0.0.2	All Routers on this Subnet	[JBP]
224.0.0.3	Unassigned	[JBP]
224.0.0.4	DVMRP Routers	[RFC1075,JBP]
224.0.0.5	OSPFIGP OSPFIGP All Routers	[RFC1583,JXM1]
224.0.0.6	OSPFIGP OSPFIGP Designated Routers	[RFC1583,JXM1]
224.0.0.7	ST Routers	[RFC1190,KS14]
224.0.0.8	ST Hosts	[RFC1190,KS14]
224.0.0.9	RIP2 Routers	[RFC1723,GSM11]
224.0.0.10	IGRP Routers	[Farinacci]
224.0.0.11	Mobile-Agents	[Bill Simpson]
224.0.0.12	DHCP Server / Relay Agent	[RFC1884]
224.0.0.13	All PIM Routers	[Farinacci]
224.0.0.14	RSVP-ENCAPSULATION	[Braden]
224.0.0.15	all-cbt-routers	[Ballardie]
224.0.0.16	designated-sbm	[Baker]
224.0.0.17	all-sbms	[Baker]
224.0.0.18	VRRP	[Hinden]
224.0.0.19–224.0.0.255	Unassigned	[JBP]
224.0.1.0	VMTP Managers Group	[RFC1045,DRC3]
224.0.1.1	NTP Network Time Protocol	[RFC1119,DLM1]
224.0.1.2	SGI-Dogfight	[AXC]
224.0.1.3	Rwhod	[SXD]
224.0.1.4	VNP	[DRC3]
224.0.1.5	Artificial Horizons – Aviator	[BXF]
224.0.1.6	NSS – Name Service Server	[BXS2]
224.0.1.7	AUDIONEWS – Audio News Multicast	[MXF2]
224.0.1.8	SUN NIS+ Information Service	[CXM3]

224.0.1.9	MTP Multicast Transport Protocol	[SXA]
224.0.1.10	IETF-1-LOW-AUDIO	[SC3]
224.0.1.11	IETF-1-AUDIO	[SC3]
224.0.1.12	IETF-1-VIDEO	[SC3]
224.0.1.13	IETF-2-LOW-AUDIO	[SC3]
224.0.1.14	IETF-2-AUDIO	[SC3]
224.0.1.15	IETF-2-VIDEO	[SC3]
224.0.1.16	MUSIC-SERVICE	[Guido van Rossum]
224.0.1.17	SEANET-TELEMETRY	[Andrew Maffei]
224.0.1.18	SEANET-IMAGE	[Andrew Maffei]
224.0.1.19	MLOADD	[Braden]
224.0.1.20	any private experiment	[JBP]
224.0.1.21	DVMRP on MOSPF	[John Moy]
224.0.1.22	SVRLOC	[Veizades]
224.0.1.23	XINGTV	[Gordon]
224.0.1.24	microsoft-ds	<arnoldm@microsoft.com>
224.0.1.25	nbc-pro	<bloomer@birch.crd.ge.com>
224.0.1.26	nbc-pfn	<bloomer@birch.crd.ge.com>
224.0.1.27	lmsc-calren-1	[Uang]
224.0.1.28	lmsc-calren-2	[Uang]
224.0.1.29	lmsc-calren-3	[Uang]
224.0.1.30	lmsc-calren-4	[Uang]
224.0.1.31	ampr-info	[Janssen]
224.0.1.32	Mtrace	[Casner]
224.0.1.33	RSVP-encap-1	[Braden]
224.0.1.34	RSVP-encap-2	[Braden]
224.0.1.35	SVRLOC-DA	[Veizades]
224.0.1.36	rln-server	[Kean]
224.0.1.37	proshare-mc	[Lewis]
224.0.1.38	Dantz	[Yackle]
224.0.1.39	cisco-rp-announce	[Farinacci]
224.0.1.40	cisco-rp-discovery	[Farinacci]
224.0.1.41	Gatekeeper	[Toga]
224.0.1.42	Iberiagames	[Marocho]
224.0.1.43	nwn-discovery	[Zwemmer]
224.0.1.44	nwn-adaptor	[Zwemmer]
224.0.1.45	isma-1	[Dunne]
224.0.1.46	isma-2	[Dunne]
224.0.1.47	telerate	[Peng]
224.0.1.48	Ciena	[Rodbell]
224.0.1.49	dcap-servers	[RFC2114]
224.0.1.50	dcap-clients	[RFC2114]
224.0.1.51	mcntp-directory	[Rupp]

224.0.1.52	mbone-vcr-directory	[Holfelder]
224.0.1.53	Heartbeat	[Mamakos]
224.0.1.54	sun-mc-grp	[DeMoney]
224.0.1.55	extended-sys	[Poole]
224.0.1.56	Pdrncs	[Wissenbach]
224.0.1.57	tns-adv-multi	[Albin]
224.0.1.58	vcals-dmu	[Shindoh]
224.0.1.59	Zuba	[Jackson]
224.0.1.60	hp-device-disc	[Albright]
224.0.1.61	tms-production	[Gilani]
224.0.1.62	Sunscalar	[Gibson]
224.0.1.63	mmtp-poll	[Costales]
224.0.1.64	compaq-peer	[Volpe]
224.0.1.65	iapp	[Meier]
224.0.1.66	multihasc-com	[Brockbank]
224.0.1.67	serv-discovery	[Honton]
224.0.1.68	Mdhcpdisover	[Patel]
224.0.1.69	MMP-bundle-discovery1	[Malkin]
224.0.1.70	MMP-bundle-discovery2	[Malkin]
224.0.1.71	XYPOINT DGPS Data Feed	[Green]
224.0.1.72	GilatSkySurfer	[Gal]
224.0.1.73	SharesLive	[Rowatt]
224.0.1.74	NorthernData	[Sheers]
224.0.1.75	SIP	[Schulzrinne]
224.0.1.76	IAPP	[Moelard]
224.0.1.77	AGENTVIEW	[Iyer]
224.0.1.78	Tibco Multicast1	[Shum]
224.0.1.79	Tibco Multicast2	[Shum]
224.0.1.80–		
224.0.1.255	Unassigned	[JBP]
224.0.2.1	'rwho' Group (BSD) (unofficial)	[JBP]
224.0.2.2	SUN RPC PMAPPROC_CALLIT	[BXE1]
224.0.2.064–		
224.0.2.095	SIAC MDD Service	[Tse]
224.0.2.096–		
224.0.2.127	CoolCast	[Ballister]
224.0.2.128–		
224.0.2.191	WOZ-Garage	[Marquardt]
224.0.2.192–		
224.0.2.255	SIAC MDD Market Service	[Lamberg]
224.0.3.000–		
224.0.3.255	RFE Generic Service	[DXS3]

224.0.4.000– 224.0.4.255	RFE Individual Conferences	[DXS3]
224.0.5.000– 224.0.5.127	CDPD Groups	[Bob Brenner]
224.0.5.128– 224.0.5.255	Unassigned	[IANA]
224.0.6.000– 224.0.6.127	Cornell ISIS Project	[Tim Clark]
224.0.6.128– 224.0.6.255	Unassigned	[IANA]
224.0.7.000– 224.0.7.255	Where-Are-You	[Simpson]
224.0.8.000– 224.0.8.255	INTV	[Tynan]
224.0.9.000– 224.0.9.255	Internet Railroad	[Malamud]
224.0.10.000– 224.0.10.255	DLSw Groups	[Lee]
224.0.11.000– 224.0.11.255	NCC.NET Audio	[Rubin]
224.0.12.000– 224.0.12.063	Microsoft and MSNBC	[Blank]
224.0.13.000– 224.0.13.255	UUNET PIPEX Net News	[Barber]
224.0.14.000– 224.0.14.255	NLANR	[Wessels]
224.0.15.000– 224.0.15.255	Hewlett Packard	[van der Meulen]
224.0.16.000– 224.0.16.255	XingNet	[Uusitalo]
224.0.17.000– 224.0.17.031	Mercantile & Commodity Exchange	[Gilani]
224.0.18.000– 224.0.18.255	Dow Jones	[Peng]
224.0.19.000– 224.0.19.063	Walt Disney Company	[Watson]
224.0.19.064– 224.0.19.095	Cal Multicast	[Moran]
224.0.19.096– 224.0.19.127	SIAC Market Service	[Roy]
224.0.19.128– 224.0.19.191	IIG Multicast	[Carr]

224.0.19.192– 224.0.19.207	Metropol	[Crawford]
224.0.252.000– 224.0.252.255	Domain Scoped Group	[Fenner]
224.0.253.000– 224.0.253.255	Report Group	[Fenner]
224.0.254.000– 224.0.254.255	Query Group	[Fenner]
224.0.255.000– 224.0.255.255	Border Routers	[Fenner]
224.1.0.0– 224.1.255.255	ST Multicast Groups	[RFC1190,KS14]
224.2.0.0– 224.2.127.253	Multimedia Conference Calls	[SC3]
224.2.127.254	SAPv1 Announcements	[SC3]
224.2.127.255	SAPv0 Announcements (deprecated)	[SC3]
224.2.128.0– 224.2.255.255	SAP Dynamic Assignments	[SC3]
224.252.0.0– 224.255.255.255	DIS transient groups	[Joel Snyder]
232.0.0.0– 232.255.255.255	VMTP transient groups	[RFC1045,DRC3]
239.000.000.000– 239.255.255.255	Administratively Scoped	[IANA]
239.000.000.000– 239.063.255.255	Reserved	[IANA]
239.064.000.000– 239.127.255.255	Reserved	[IANA]
239.128.000.000– 239.191.255.255	Reserved	[IANA]
239.192.000.000– 239.251.255.255	Organization-Local Scope	[Meyer]
239.252.000.000– 239.252.255.255	Site-Local Scope (reserved)	[Meyer]
239.253.000.000– 239.253.255.255	Site-Local Scope (reserved)	[Meyer]
239.254.000.000– 239.254.255.255	Site-Local Scope (reserved)	[Meyer]
239.255.000.000– 239.255.255.255	Site-Local Scope	[Meyer]

These addresses are listed in the Domain Name Service under MCAST.NET and 224.IN-ADDR.ARPA.

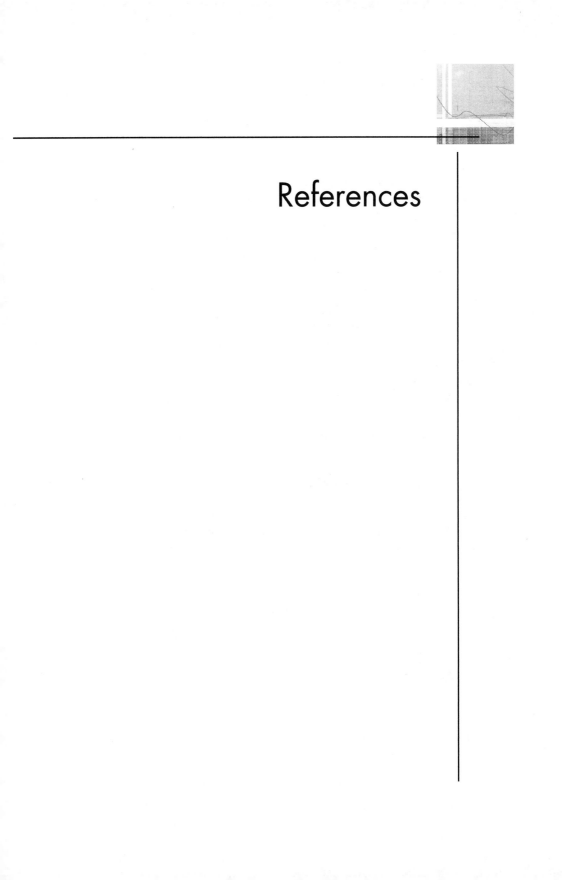

References

References

Chapter 1

ITU

The ITU, headquartered in Geneva, Switzerland, is an international organization within which governments and the private sector coordinate global telecom networks and services. ITU recommendations and draft documents:

ITU-T Recommendation H.323 (1998) *Packet-based multimedia communications systems*

ITU-T Recommendation H.225.0 (1998) *Call signaling protocols and media stream packetization for packet-based multimedia communications systems*

ITU-T Recommendation H.245 (1998) *Control protocol for multimedia communication*

ITU-T Recommendation H.235 (1998) *Security and encryption for H Series (H.323 and other H.245 based) multimedia terminals*

ITU Rec. H.261 (03/93) *Video codec for audiovisual services at p × 64 kbit/s*

ETSI standards

Use the publications download application located on *http://webapp.etsi.org/ publications-search*

Publications can be download freely in Adobe Acrobat Reader format (.pdf).

RFCs

RFC 1035: Mills, D. April 1992, *Network Time Protocol v3*
RFC 2190: H.263 RTP payload format
RFC 2032: Turletti, T. and Huitema, C. 1996, *RTP payload format for H.261 video stream*
RFC 1889: Schulzrinne, H., Castner, S., Frederick, R. and Jacobson, V. 1996, *RTP: A transport protocol for real-time applications*
RFC 1006: TPKT definition for transport over TCP

Draft IETF documents

Dieks, T. and Allen, C. (1997) *Internet engineering task force*, 'The TLS protocol version 1.0' draft-ietf-tls-protocol-03.txt.

About codecs

Cox, R.V. (1997) 'Current methods of speech coding' *International Journal of High Speed Electronics and Systems*, Vol. 8, 1, 13–68.

Cryptography

Gamel, T.E. 'A public key crypto system and a signature scheme based on discrete logarithms' *IEEE Trans. on Inf. Theory*, IT-31 (1985), pp. 469–72.

Chapter 2

RFCs

RFC 2327: SDP (Session Description Protocol)

Draft-ietf-mmusic-sip-09.txt

draft-ietf-mmusic-sip-cc-00.txt SIP call control services

DNS

RFC 2052: SRV record:

RFC 974: MX record

RFC 1035: CNAME or A record

RFC 2068: HTTP/1.1

RFC 2234: BNF (Backus-Naur form)

RFC 2279: ISO 10646/UTF-8 encoding

RFC 822: generic-message format

RFC 2396: SIP URL

RFC 1890: Schulzrinne, H. January 1996 *RTP profile for audio and video conferences with minimal control* January.

RFC 2326: Schulzrinne, H., Rao, A. and Lanphier, R. April 1998 *Real-time streaming protocol (RTSP)*

RFC 1305: Mills, D. March 1992 *Network time protocol (version 3) specification and implementation*

RFC 2396: Berners-Lee, T., Fielding, R. and Masinter, L. August 1998 *Uniform resource identifiers (URI): generic syntax*

RFC 2543: Handley, M., Schulzrinne, H., Schooler, E. Rosenberg, J. March 1991 *SIP: Session Initiation Protocol*

RFC 1890: IETF Codecs

RFC 1288: Zimmerman, D. December 1991 *The finger user information protocol*

RFC 2076: Palme, J. February 1997 *Common Internet message headers*

RFC 1423: Balenson, D. (1993) *Privacy enhancement for Internet electronic mail: Part III: Algorithms, modes, and identifiers*

ISO

ISO/IEC 10646-1: 1993. International standard – information technology – universal multiple-octet coded character set (UCS) – Part 1: Architecture and basic multilingual plane. Five amendments and a technical corrigendum have been published. UTF-8 is described in Annex R, published as Amendment 2 and also in RFC 2044

Chapter 3

ITU
ITU-T Recommendation Q.762 *General functions of messages and signals of the ISDN user part of signaling system No. 7*

RFCs
RFC 2327: Handley, M. and Jacobson, V. April 1998 *SDP: session description protocol*

Draft documents
draft-taylor-ipdc-reqts-00.txt: Requirments for a telephony gateway device control protocol

draft-taylor-megaco-reqs-00.txt:

draft-sijben-megaco-mdcp-00.txt:

Huitema, Christian *et al.* (October, 1998) 'MGCP: media gateway control protocol' draft-huitema-MGCP-v0r1-00.txt

Tom Taylor, draft-taylor-ipdc-00.txt: 'Internet protocol device control base protocol'

Cuervo *et al.* (July 1998) 'SS7-Internet interworking – architectural framework', draft-greene-ss7-archframe-00.txt

Calhoun, Zorn, Pan (May, 1998) 'Diameter framework', Internet-draft, draft-calhoun-DIAMETER-framework-00.txt

Chapter 4

ITU
ITU Recommendation G.100 *Definitions used in recommendations on general characteristics of international telephone connections and circuits*

ITU Recommendation G.107 *The E model, a computational model for use in transmission planning*

ITU Recommendation G.113 *Transmission impairments*

ITU Recommendation F.114 *One-way transmission time*

ITU Recommendation G.116 *Transmission performance objectives applicable to end-to-end international transmissions*

ITU Recommdnation G.122 *Influence of national systems on stability and talker echo in international connections*

ITU Recommendation G.131 *Control of talker echo*

ITU Recommendation G.122 *Influence of national systems on stability and talker echo in international connections*

ITU Recommendation G.111 *Loudness ratings in an international connection*

ITU Recommendation G.168 *Digital network echo cancellers*

ITU Recommendation G.167 *Acoustic echo controllers*

ITU Recommendation G.165 *Echo cancellers*

ITU Recommendation G.174 *Transmission performance objectives for terrestrial digital wireless systems using portable terminals to access the PSTN*

ITU Recommendation P.310 *Transmission characteristics for telephone band (300–3400 Hz) digital telephones*

ITU Recommendation P.79 *Calculation of loudness ratings for telephone sets*

ITU Recommendation P.56 *Objective measurement of active speech levels*

ITU Recommendation P.11 *Effect of transmission impairment*

ITU Recommendation G.175 *Transmission planning for private/public network interconnection of voice traffic*

ITU Recommendation G.173 *Transmission planning aspects of the speech service in digital public land mobile networks*

ITU Recommendation G.111 *Loudness ratings in an international connection*

IEEE
IEEE Gruber, J. and Strawczynski, L. (1982) *Subjective effects of variable delay and speech loss in dynamically managed systems* IEEE Globecom Vol. 2: F.7.3.1–F.7.3.5.

ETSI
ETSI TR 101329 V 1.2.5 *Telecommunications and Internet protocol harmonization over networks (TIPHON): general aspects of quality of service (QoS)*

Technical Report 56 T1A1.7 *Performance guidelines for voiceband services over hybrid IP/PSTN connections*

Chapter 5

ITUs
Bosi, M., Brandenburg, K.H., QuackenbushU, S., Fielder, L., Akagiri, K., Fuchs, H., Dietz, M., Herre, J., Davidson, G. and Oikawa, Y. (1997) 'ISO/IEC MPEG-2 advanced audio coding', *Journal of Audio Engineering Society*, Vol. 45–10, October, 789–814.

Other References
Brandenburg, K.H., Stoll, G., Dehéry, Y.F., Johnston, J.D., Kerkof, L.D. and Schröder, E.F. (1994) 'ISO-MPEG-1 audio: a generic standard for coding of high quality digital audio', *Journal of the Audio Engineering Society*, Vol 42, October, 780–792.

Campbell, J.P., Tremain, T.E. and Welsh, V.C. (1991) 'The federal standard 1016 4800 bps CELP voice coder', *Digital Signal Processeing*, Vol. 1, 145–155.

Chen, J.H., Cox, R.V., Lin, Y.C., Jayant, N. and Melchner, M.J. (1992) 'A low delay CELP coder for the CCITT 16 kb/s speech coding standard', *IEEE Journal on Selected Areas on Communications*, Vol. 10–5, 803–849.

Combescure, P., Le Guyader, A., Jouvet, D. and SORIN, C. (1995) 'Le traitement du signal vocal', *Annales des Télécommunications*, Vol. 50–1, 142–164.

Cox, R.V. (1995) 'Speech coders: from idea to product', *AT&T Technical Journal*, March/April, 14–21.

Daumer, W.R., Mermelstein, P., Maitre, X. and Tokizawa, I. (1984) 'Overview of the ADPCM coding algorithm', Proc. of Globecom, 23.1.1–23.1.4.

Dimolitsas, S. (1993) 'Standardizing speech coding technology for network application', *IEEE Communications Magazine*, November, 26–33.

Fielder, L.D., Bossi, M., Davidson, G., Davis, M., Todd, C. and Vernon, S. 'AC-2 and AC-3: low-complexity transformed-based audio coding', Collected papers on digital audio bit-rate reduction, 54–72. Editors Gilchurist, N. and Grewin, C. Audio Engineering society.

Gersho, A. (1994) 'Advances in speech and audio compression', Proceeding of the IEEE, June, 900–918.Combescure, P. and Mathieu, M. (1985) 'Codage des signaux sonores', *L'Echo des recherches*, 121, third trimester, 13–22.

Hellwig, K., Vary, P., Massaloux, D., Petit, J-.P., Galand, C. and Rosso, M. (1989) 'Speech codec for the European mobile radio system', Globecom conference, 1065–1069.

Kowdoz, A.M. (1994) *Digital Speech; Coding for low bit rate communications systems*, Chichester: Wiley.

Mahieux, Y., Petit, J-P. and Charbonnier, A. (1991) 'Codage pour le transport du son de haute qualité sur le réseau de télécommunications', *L'Écho des recherches*, 146, fourth trimester, 25–35.

Maitre, X. (1988) '7 kHz audio coding within 64 kHbit/s', *IEEE Journal on Selected Areas on Communications*, Vol. 6–2, February, 283–298.

Moreau, N. (1995) *Technical de compression des signaux*, Masson, CNET-ENST.

Noll, P. (1993) 'Wideband speech and audio coding', *IEEE Communications Magazine*, November.

Pascal, D. (1987) 'Méthodologie d'évaluation subjective de la qualité des systémes de communication', *Bulletin de l'IDATE*, third trimester.

Salami, R., Laflamme, C., Adoul, J.P., Kataoka, A., Hayashi, S., Moriya, T., Lamblin, C., Massaloux, D., Proust, S., Kroon, P. and Shoham, Y. (1998) 'Design and description of CS-ACELP: a toll quality 8 kbit/s speech coder', IEEE transcript on speech and audio processing, Vol. 6–2, March, 116–130.

Special features on ITU-T standard algorithm for 8 kbit/s speech coding, (1996) *NTT Review*, Vol. 8, 4, July.

'Speech technologies for telecommunications', (1996) *BT Telecommunications journal*, January.

Supplee, L.M., Cohn, R.P. and Collura, J.S. (1997) 'MELP: the new federal standard at 2400 BPS', Proc. of ICASSP conference, 1591–1594.

Tremain, T.E. (1982) 'The government standard linear predictive coding algorithm: LPC 10', *Speech Technology*, April, 40–49

Chapter 6

Abhay, K.P. and Gallager, R.G., (June 1993) *A generalized Processor Sharing approach to flow control in Integrated Services Networks, Part I*, IEEE/ACM Transactions on Networking, Vol. 1, No 3, pp 344–357

Abhay, K.P. and Gallager, R.G., (April 1994) *A generalized Processor Sharing approach to flow control in Integrated Services Networks, the multiple node case*, IEEE/ACM Transaction on Networking, Vol. 2, No 2, pp 137–150

Floyd, S. and Jacobson, V., (August 1993) *Random Early Detection Gateways for Congestion Avoidance*, IEEE/ACM Trans. on Networking, Vol. 1 No. 4, pp. 397–413

Golestani, S.J. *A Self-Clocked fair queuing scheme for broadband applications*, Bellcore, ATT Research Labs

Jacobson, V., (August 1988) *Congestion Avoidance and Control, Proc. ACM.SIGCOMM'88*, pp 314–329

Norival R.F. and Pasquale, J. (August 1995) An upper bound on Delay for the virtualClock Service Discipline, University of California, San Diego. IEEE/ACM transactions on Networking, Vol. 3, No 4

RFCs
RFC 1990: Slower, K., Lloyd, B., McGregor, G., Carr, D., Coradetti, T., (August 1996) *The PPP Multilink Protocol (MP)*

RFC 1661: Simpson, W., (Ed), (July 1994) *The Point-to-Point Protocol (PPP)*

RFC 1662: Simpson, W., (Ed), (July 1994) *PPP in HDLC-like Framing*

RFC 1812: Requirements for IPv4 routers F. Baker

RFC 2205: (Version 1 Functional Specification of RSVP)

RFC 2211: Specification of the controlled-Load Network Element Service

RFC 2212: Specification of the Guaranteed Quality of Service

RFC 2474: Definition of the Differentiated Services Field in the IPv4 and IPv6 headers

RFC 2475: An Architecture for Differentiated Services

RFC 1812: Requirements ofr IPv4 routers

RFC 2309: Braden, B., D. Clark, J. Growcroft, B. Davie, S. Deering, D. Estrin, S. Floyd, V. Jacobson, G. Minshall, C. Partridge, L. Peterson, K. Ramakrishnan, S. Shenker, J. Wroclawski, L. Zhang, (April 1998) *Recommendatiosn on Queue Management and Congestion Avoidance in the Internet*

RCF 791: Information Sciences Institute, (September 1981) *Internet Protocol*

Draft IETFT documents
draft-stevens-tcpca-specp01.txt

Nichols, K. and Blake, S. *Definition of the Differentiated Services Field (DS Byte) in the IPv4 and IPv6 Headers* draft-ietf-diffserv-header-00.txt

Deering, S. and Hinden, R. (November 1997) *Internet Protocol, Version 6 (IPv6) Specification, Internet Draft* draft-ietf-ipngwg-ipv6-spec-v2-01.txt

Carsten, Bormann (March 1998) *Providing integated services over low-bitrate links* draft-ietf-issll-isslow-03.txt

Casner, S. and Jacobson, V. (November 1997) *Compressing IP/UDP/RTP Headers for Low-Speed Serial Links* draft-ietf-avt-crtp-04.txt

Engan, M. Casner, S., Bormann, C. (December 1997) *IP Header Compression over PPP* draft-engan-ip-compress-02.txt

Bormann, C. (March 1998) *The Multi-Class Extension to Multi-Link PPP* draft-ietf-issll-isslow-mcml-03.txt

Bormann, C. (March 1998) *PPP in a real-time oriented HDLC-like framing* draft-ietf-isll-isslow-rtf-02.txt

Andrades, R., Burg, F. (September 1996) *QOSPPP framing Extensions to PPP* draft-andrades-framing-ext-00,txt

Bormann, C., (March 1998) *The Multi-Class Extension to Multi-Link PPP* draft-ietf-issll-isslow-mcml-03.txt

Barnet, Y., Yavatkar, R., Ford, P., Baker, F. Zhang, L. A Framework for End-to-End QoS Combining RSVP/Intserv and Differentiated Services, draft-bernet-intdiff-00.txt

draft-ietf-diffserve-rsvp-01.txt

draft-ietfrsvp-tunnel-01.txt

Baker, F., (August 1997) *RSVP Cryptographic Authentication* draft-ief-rsvp-md5-05.txt

Herzog., S. (April 1997) *RSVP Extensions for Policy Control*, Internet Draft, draft-ietf-rsvp-policy-ext-02.[ps,txt]

RSVP simulator

RSVP simulator written in PARSEC (see *http://pcl.cs.ucla.edu/projects/parsec* for more about PARSEC) available for download from *http://irl.cs.ucla/software.f.html#rsvp-simulator*. The simulator comes with a Java GUI that can be used to create test topologies and view the flow of RSVP messages.

A new RSVP Diagnostics client with a GUI front-end is now available from *http://irl.cs.ucla.edu*, The client is based on the 'rsvptrace' utility included in the ISI release RSVP. Also contained in the code are parts of 'mtrace' and 'traceroute' that are used for finding the path from the last hop to the sender in the process of finding 'black holes'. More on that, in the I-D or my presentation from the Chicago IETF.

The client was originally written by David Bibighaus, Tom O'Neil, Boris Shimanovshy. Modifications/changes by Andreas Terzis.

RSVP simulator for NS too: http://titan.cs.uni-bonn.de/~greis/rsvpns

Chapter 7

Guerin, R., Hamadi, H. and Naghshineh, M. (September 1991) 'Equivalent capacity and its application to bandwidth allocation' *IEEE* journal on selected areas of communicator, Vol. 9, 7.

Kleinrock, L. (1975) *Queuing Systems: Vol. 1: Theory*, Chichester, John Wiley and Sons.

Chapter 8

URLS

General web site: *www.mbone.com*
    www.best.com/~prince/techinfo/mbone.html

Cisco web site: *www.cisco.com*

Mbone topology: *www.cs.berkeley.edu/~elan/mbone.html*
    www.nlanr.net/viz/Mbone/

follow-up tool to Planet Multicast: *www.caida.org/Tools/Manta/*

IANA: *www.isi.edu/div7/iana/assignments.html*

Tools: *www.it.kth.se/~e93_mda/mbone/ripewg/resources.html*

Statistics: *www.dante.net/mbone*

Tools for windows NT: *www.uoregon.edu/~joelja/project/mbone.html ftp://cs.ucl.ac.uk/mice/sdr/2.5a5.*

Meccano project web: *www-ice.cs.ucl.ac.uk/multimedia/projects/meccano/*

'Well known' multicast addresses: *ftp://ftp.isi.edu/in-notes/iana/assignments/multicast-addresses*

Addresses used by SAP: *www.cs.columbia.edu/~hgs/internet*

Reliable multicast protocols comparison: *www.tascnets.com/mist/doc/mcpCompare.html*

RMP: *http://research.ivv.nasa.gov/RMP/*

SRM: Floyd, S., Jacobson, V., McCanne, S., Liu C.-G. and Zhang, L. (1995) *A reliable multicast framework for lightweight sessions and Application Level Framing*. In *Proceedings of SIGCOMM '95, Boston, MA, September ACM.*

Network card performance:
www.stl.nps.navy.mil/~mcgredo/projectNotebook/mcast/EthernetMain.html

RFCs and internet drafts
IGMP version 1: RFC-1112

IGMP version 2: Fenner, W. (1997) *Internet group management protocol, version 2*. RFC 2236, November.

DVMRP: original RFC-1065, 1075, DVMRP v3 *Distance vector multicast routing protocol*, draft-ietf-idmr-dvmrp-v3-06.txt

MOSPF: RFC 1584, 1585

CBT: Ballardie, A. (1997) *Core-based trees (CBT version 2) multicast routing*: Protocol specification. RFC 2189, September.

RFC 2117: PIM-SM: Estrin, Farinacci, Helmy, Thaler, Deering, Handley, Jacobson, Liu, Sharma and Wei (June 1997) *Protocol independent multicast-sparse mode (PIM-SM)*: protocol specification

Domain interoperability: *Interoperability rules for multicast routing protocols* draft-thaler-multicast-interop-02.txt (Exp Sept 98)

Border Multicast Protocol: *Border gateway multicast protocol*, draft-ietf-idmr-gum-01.txt

HDVMRP: Thyagarajan, Ajit S. and Deering, Stephen E. (1995) *Hierarchical distance-vector multicast routing for the MBone* in 'Proceedings of the ACM SIGCOMM', 60–66, October.

MBGP: Thaler, Estrin, Meyer *Border gateway multicast protocol*, draft-ietf-idmr-gum-02.txt

MASC: Estrin, Handley and Thaler, D. *Multicast-address-set advertisement and claim mechanism*, draft-ietf-idmr-masc-00.txt

Patel, S. Multicast address allocation extensions to the dynamic host configuration protocol, draft-ietf-dhc-mdhcp-03.txt

Patel, S. Multicast address allocation extensions options, draft-ietf-dhc-multopt-02.txt

AAP: Handley Multicast address allocation protocol, draft-handley-aap-00.txt

IPv6: Hinden, R. and Deering, S. (July 1997) *IPv6 multicast address assignments*, draft-ietf-ipngwg-multicast-assgn-04.txt

RFC 2283: BGP4+: Bates, T., Chandra, R., Katz, D. and Rekhter, Y. (1998) *Multiprotocol extensions for BGP-4*, February.

RFC 1771: Rekhter, Y. and Li, T. (March 1995) *A border gateway protocol 4 (BGP-4)*

Multicast and firewalls, *IP multicast and firewalls*, draft-finlayson-mcast-firewall-00.txt

RFC 1112: Multicast: Deering, S. (August 1989) *Host extensions for IP multicasting*

Firewall: Freed, N. and Carosso, K. (December 1997) *An Internet firewall transparency requirement*, work-in-progress, Internet-draft 'draft-freed-firewall-req-02.txt'

Administrative scoping: Meyer, D. (November 1997) *Administratively scoped IP multicast*, draft-ietf-mboned-admin-ip-space-04.txt

Domain-wide reports: Fenner, B. (November 1997) *Domain-wide multicast group membership reports*, draft-ietf-idmr-membership- reports-00.txt

UMTP: Finlayson, R. (February 1998) *The UDP multicast tunneling protocol*, draft-finlayson-umtp-02.txt

RFC 1928: SOCKS: Leech, M., Ganis, M., Lee, Y., Kuris, R., Koblas, D. and Jones, L. (April 1996) *SOCKS Protocol Version 5*

SOCKS: Chouinard, D. (July 1997) *SOCKS V5 UDP and multicast extensions*, draft-chouinard-aft-socksv5-mult-00.txt

Mailing lists

MBONE events: *Rem-conf-request@es.net*

MBONE engineering: *mbone-request@isi.edu*

MBONE deployement working group: *mboned@ns.oregon.edu*

Glossary

AAP Multicast address allocation protocol (draft-handley-aap-00.txt)

ACELP Algebraic-code-excited linear prediction

ACF Admission confirm, a RAS message defined in H.225.0

ACR Absolute category rating; subjective test (MOS)

ADM Adaptive delta modulation (modulation delta)

ADPCM Adaptive differential pulse code modulation (MICDA)

aggregate *See* 'Behavior Aggregate'

AMPS analogue mobile phone standard

ANSI American National Standard Institute

APDU Application protocol data units, *see* H.450.1

ARJ Admission reject, a RAS message defined in H.225.0

ARQ Admission request, a RAS message defined in H.225.0

ASN-1 Abstract syntax notation-1

Associate session A related session. Two related sessions must be synchronized. For instance, an audio session can specify a video session as being related: the receiving terminal must perform lip synchronization for those sessions

ASVD analogue simultaneous voice and data

ATC adaptive transform coding

ATM Asynchronous transfer mode

BA *See* Behavior Aggregate

BA Classifier A traffic classifier based on the DS field

BCF Bandwidth confirm, a RAS message defined in H.225.0

Behavior aggregate DiffServ Term defined in RFC 2474 as 'a collection of packets with the same codepoint crossing a link in a particular direction'

BER bit error rate

BFI bad frame indicator

BGMP Border gateway multicast routing protocol

BNF Backus-Naur Form, *see* RFC 2234

Boundary Link (RFC 2475) A link connecting the edge nodes of two domains

Boundary Node (RFC 2475) A DS node that connects one DS domain to a node either in another DS domain or in a domain that is not DS capable

BRJ Bandwidth reject, a RAS message defined in H.225.0

BRQ Bandwidth request, a RAS message defined in H.225.0

Call According to the SIP draft, all participants invited by a common source are in the same SIP call, identified by a globally unique CallID

CallID A globally unique call identifier

CBQ Class Based Queuing

CCF Call control function

CCR comparison category rating (subjective tests)

CDMA code division multiplex access

CELP code excited linear prediction (vector quantization of excitation)

CID Conference identifier. This is not the same as the Q.931 call reference value (CRV) or the call identifier (CID). The CID refers to a conference which is the actual communication existing between the participants. In the case of a multiparty conference, if a participant joins the conference, leaves and enters again, the CRV will change, while the CID will remain the same

CIF The Common Intermediary Format is a video format which has been chosen because it can be sampled relatively easily from both the 525 and 625 lines video formats

Class Selector Codepoint DiffServ Term defined in RFC 2474 as 'any of the 8 codepoints in the range xxx000' (x=0 or 1). *See* also 'Class Selector Compliant Codepoint'

Class Selector Compliant Codepoint DiffServ Term defined in RFC 2474 as a per hop behavior satisfying the class selector specifications as defined in RFC 2474. In short those requirements aim at ensuring a minimal level of backward compatibility with IP precedence semantics of RFC 791. *See* the QOS chapter for more details

CLR Circuit loudness rating: the loudness loss between two electrical interfaces in a connection or circuit, each interface terminated by its nominal impedance which may be complex. This is 0 for a digital circuit, 0.5 for a mixed analogue/digital circuit

CNG Comfort noise generator

CO Central office

Codec COder DECoder

codepoint Proposed name for the value of the PHB field of the DS octet, in the DIFFSERV framework. *See* RFC 2474, and also Class Selector Codepoint

Controlled load service An application requesting controlled load service for a stream of given characteristics expects the network to behave as if it was lightly loaded for that stream

CoS Class Of Service

CRC cyclic redundancy check

CRLF Carriage return, line feed (0x0d0a)

CRV Call reference value: a 2-octet locally unique identifier copied in all Q.931 messages concerning a particular call. *See* also CID

CS-ACELP conjugate- structure ACELP

CSRC Contributing source: when an RTP stream is the result of a combination by an RTP mixer of several contributing streams, the list of the SSRCs of each contributing stream is added in the RTP header of the resulting stream as CSRCs. The resulting stream has its own SSRC

CT cordless telecommunications

CT2 CT system two

CU Currently Unused: the last 2 bits of the DS octet

dBm Power level with reference to 1 mW

dBm0 At the reference frequency (1020 Hz), L dBm0 represents an absolute power level of L dBm measured at the transmission reference point (0 dBr point), and a level of L+ x dBm measured at a point having a relative level of x dBr. *See* G.100, annex A.4

DCF Disengage confirm, a RAS message defined in H.225.0

DCME digital circuit multiplication equipment

DCR degradation category rating test (subjective test: DMOS)

DCT Discrete cosine transform

DECT Digital European cordless telephone

DMOS Degradation mean opinion score

DNS Domain name system

Domain For MBGP: a set of one or more contiguous links and zero or more routers surrounded by one or more multicast border routers. This loose definition of domain also applies to an external link between two domains, as well as an exchange

DRJ Disengage reject, a RAS message defined in H.225.0

DRQ Disengage request, a RAS message defined in H.225.0

DS Differentiated service(s). The new name assigned by the IETF DIFFSERV group to the Ipv4 TOS field and the IPv6 Traffic Class field. *See* RFC 2474

DS-compliant Behaving according to the general rules of RFC 2474. *See* DS

DSCP Differentiated Services Codepoint: the name of the first six bits of the DS octet (in drafts before RFC 2474, those bits were called PHB)

DSL Digital Subscriber Loop

DSP digital signal processor (fix or floating point)

DSSI Digital subscriber signaling number 1

DSVD digital simultaneous voice and data

DTMF Dual tone multi-frequency

DTX Discontinuous transmission

DVMRP Distance vector multicast routing protocol

echo Unwanted signal delayed to such a degree that it is perceived as distinct from the wanted signal. A good source of definitions relating to echo is G.100.

Talker echo Echo produced by reflection near the listener's end of a connection, and disturbing the talker

Listener echo Echo produced by double reflected signals and disturbing the listener

EGP Exterior gateway protocol used for unicast interdomain routing, for instance BGP

Energy For an image in a particular color, the sum of the squared color values of the pixels is called the energy

EOL The end of line sequence for Group 3 fax (001H)

ETSI European Telecommunications Standardization Institute

FCC Federal Communication Commission

FCFS First Come First Served: another name for FIFO

FEC Forward error correction

FER frame error rate

FIB Forwarding information base = forwarding table

FIFO First In First Out, same as FCFS

Forwarding table For unicast routers, this is the list of the appropriate egress interface for each destination prefix. For a multicast router, this also includes the expected incoming interface (iif) and a list of outgoing interfaces (oiflist) for each destination group address (there can be one such entry for each source for some multicast routing protocols like DVMRP)

FPLMTS future public land mobile telecommunication system

FS1015 Federal Standard 1016: 2.4 kbit/s LPC speech coder (NATO)

FS1016 Federal Standard1016: 4.8 kbit/s CELP speech coder (NATO)

GCF Gatekeeper confirm, a RAS message defined in H.225.0

GPS Generalized processor sharing

GRJ Gatekeeper reject, a RAS message defined in H.225.0

GRQ Gatekeeper request, a RAS message defined in H.225.0

GSM Global system for mobile communications

GSM-EFR GSM enhanced full rate speech coder 13 kbit/s NPAG

GSM-FR GSM full rate RPE-LTP 13 kbit/s

GSM-HR GSM half rate VSELP 5.6 kbit/s

GSTN general switch telephone network (deregulated PSTN)

HDVMRP Hierachical DVMRP. *See* Ajit S. Thyagarajan and Stephen E. Deering. *Hierarchical distance-vector multicast routing for the MBone.* In 'Proceedings of the ACM SIGCOMM', pages 60–66, October 1995

IAM Initial address message (SS7 message)

ICMP Internet Control Message Protocol

IFT Internet fax transmission protocol, *see* ITU recommendation T.38

IGMP Internet group membership protocol

iif Incoming interface

IMT Inter machine trunk

IN Intelligent network

In profile Packets that are not Out of Profile

Inter mode Refers to a video coding mode where compression is achieved by reference to the previous, or sometimes the next, frame

Intra mode Refers to a video coding mode where compression is achieved locally, i.e. not relatively to the previous frame

IPDC Internet protocol device control

IRC Internet relay chat: the famous 'chat' service of the Internet, based on a set of servers mirroring text-based conversations in real time

IRQ Information request, a RAS message defined in H.225.0

IRR Information request response, a RAS message defined in H.225.0

ISDN Integrated services digital network

ISO international standardization organization

IS-xx intermediate standard xx (c.f. IS-54 VSELP)

ITU International Telecommunications Union

IVR Interactive voice response

Jitter Statistical variance of packet interarrival time: it is the smoothed absolute value of the mean deviation of the packet spacing change between the sender and the receiver. The smoothing is usually done by averaging on a sliding window of 16 instantaneous measures

jitter Varying delay

JND Just noticeable distortion

LARs Logarithmic area ratios

LCF Location confirm, a RAS message defined in H.225.0

LDAP Lightweight directory access protocol

LD-CELP Low-delay, code-excited linear prediction

log-PCM logarithmic pulse code modulation (G.711 A or µ)

LPC linear predictive coding

LR (loudness rating) As used in the G-Series Recommendations for planning; loudness rating is an objective measure of the loudness loss, i.e. a weighted, electro-acoustic loss between certain interfaces in the telephone network. If the circuit between the interfaces is subdivided into sections, the sum of the individual section LRs is equal to the total LR. In loudness rating contexts, the subscribers are represented from a measuring point of view by an artificial mouth and an artificial ear respectively, both being accurately specified

LRJ Location reject, a RAS message defined in H.225.0

LRQ Location request, a RAS message defined in H.225.0

LSP Line spectral, pair

LTP long-term predictor

MAAS Multicast address allocation server, running the AAP protocol

macroblock For the H.261 algorithm, a group of 4 8*8 blocks

MASC Multicast address set claim protocol (draft-ietf-idmr-masc-00.txt)

MBR Multicast border router: a router between two multicast routing domains

MC Multipoint controller: the H.323 which provides the control function for multiparty conferences

MCU Multipoint control unit

MCU Multipoint control unit: An H.323 callable endpoint which consists of an MC and optional MPs

MDHCP Multicast address allocation extensions to the dynamic host configuration protocol

Meter (RFC 2475) A device that performs metering

Metering (RFC 2475) The process of measuring the temporal properties (e.g. rate) of a traffic stream selected by a classifier. The instantaneous state of this process may be used to affect the operation of a marker, shaper, dropper and/or may be used for accounting and measurement purposes

MF Classifier A traffic classifier based on one or more IP header fields such as protocol number, source and destination IP addresses, port numbers, DS field value, etc ... *See* also BA classifier

MG Media gateway

MGC Media gateway controller

Microflow (RFC 2475) A single instance of an application-to-application flow of packets which is identified by source address, source port, destination address, destination port and/or protocol ID. *See* also MF classifier

MIPS millions of instructions per second

MNRU modulated noise reference unit

MOS Mean opinion score

MOSPF Multicast Extension to OSPF

MP Multipoint processor: the H.323 entity which processes the media streams of the conference and does all the necessary switching, mixing, etc.

MPEG moving picture expert group

MP-MLQ Multipulse maximum likelihood quantization

MTP Message transfer part

MTU Maximum transmission unit: The largest datagram that can be sent over the network without segmentation

Multicast RIB The routing information base, or routing table, used to calculate the 'next hop' towards a particular address for multicast traffic

MWI Message waiting indication

NFE Network facility extension, defined in H.450.1

NICAM near instantaneous companding and multiplexing

NLRI Network layer reachability information conveyed by BGP4+. This information is used by BGMP to inject multicast routes in the interdomain routing protocol

NMR noise to mask ratio

NNI Network to network interface

NNTP Network news transfer protocol

NPAG North American PCS 1900 Action GROUP

NTP A standard way to format a timestamp, by writing the number of seconds since 1/1/1900 with 32 bits for the integer part and 32 bits for the decimal part (expressed as number of $1/2^{32}$ seconds, for instance 0x80000000 is 0.5 seconds). A compact format also exists with only 16 bits for the integer part and 16 bits for the decimal part. The first 16 digits of the integer part can usually be derived from the current day, the fractional part is simply truncated to the most significant 16 digits

NTSC National Television System Committee

oiflist A list of outgoing interfaces which are part of each forwarding table entry

OLR (overall loudness rating) The loudness loss between the speaking subscriber's mouth and the listening subscriber's ear via a connection

Out of Profile Property of data packets within a flow that momentarily exceeds some envelope parameters of its profile (such as maximum burst size). For instance if the flow is regulated by a token bucket, packets arriving when there are no tokens and the backlog buffer is full are Out of Profile. *See* profile

PAL phase-alternation-line video format

PBX Private branch exchange

PCM Pulse code modulation

PCME packet circuit multiplication equipment

PCN personal communication network

PCS personal communication system

PDC personal digital communication

PDU Protocol data unit

P-frame Prediction frame obtained by motion estimation or otherwise, and representing only the difference between this image and the previous one

PGPS Packet by Packet General Processor Sharing

PHB group (RFC 2475) A set of one or more PHBs that can only be meaningfully specified and implemented simultaneously, due to a common constraint applying to all PHBs in the set such as queue servicing or queue management policy

Policing (RFC 2475) The process of discarding packets (by a dropper) within a traffic stream in accordance with the state of a corresponding meter enforcing a traffic profile

port An abstraction which has the ability to distinguish various destinations of the packets on the same machine. For instance, it can be transport selectors TSEL in the OSI model, or IP ports. On the Internet, many applications have been assigned 'well know ports', for instance a machine receiving an IP packet on port 80 using TCP protocol will route it to the web server

Profile Properties of a data flow, usually defined as envelope parameters (such as maximum burst size) and mean values (such as average bitrate)

Promiscuous An interface set in promiscuous mode receives and forwards to upper layers (the device driver) all the packets it has access to, even if the physical destination address of such packets shows it is destined to another interface

Proxy server An intermediary program that acts as both a server and a client for the purpose of making requests on behalf of other clients. Requests are serviced internally or by passing them on, possibly after translation, to other servers. A proxy interprets and, if necessary, rewrites a request message before forwarding it

Prune A message sent by a downstream multicast router to an upstream router meaning he is not interested in receiving multicast packets for a specific group and source. This marks a soft state in the upstream router, which usually expires after an hour or two

PSTN Public switched telephone network

PT Payload type as defined by RTP

QCIF Quarter CIF

QDU quantization distortion unit

QoS Quality of service

RAM random access memory

RAS Registration, admission and status. The name of the protocol used between the gatekeeper and a terminal, and between gatekeepers for those purposes

RAS protocol Registration, admission, status protocol, defined in H.225.0

RBP Reverse path broadcasting

RCF Registration confirm, a RAS message defined in H.225.0

RED Random Early Detection

RFI Request for information

RFP Request for proposal

RGW Residential gateway

RIB Routing information base. The list of all routes (next hop and distance to each destination prefix) from the router

RLE Run Length Detection

RLR (from G.111) receive loudness rating: the loudness loss between an electric interface in the network and the listening subscriber's ear. The loudness loss is here defined as the weighted (dB) average of driving e.m.f to measured sound pressure. The weighted mean value for G.111 and G.121 is 1–6 in the short term, 1–3 in the long term

ROM read-only memory

RPE-LTP Regular pulse excited LPC with long term prediction

RR RTCP receiver report

RRJ Registration reject, a RAS message defined in H.225.0

RRQ Registration request, a RAS message defined in H.225.0

RSP CISCO: Route Switch Processor

RSRR Routing Support for Resource Reservation interface

RTC Return to command: six consecutive EOLs which mean for a G3 fax that it has to return to command mode

RTCP Real-time control protocol, see RFC 1889

RTP Real-time transport protocol, as specified by RFC 1889 (*www.internic.net/rfc/rfc1889.txt*)

RTP/AVT Real-time protocol under the audio/video profile

S13-ADPCM sub band ADPCM (ITU-T G.722)

SAP Session announcement protocol

SBC sub band coding

SCN Switched circuit network: a generic term for the 'classic' phone network, including PSTN, ISDN and GSM

SECAM Sequentiel couleur à mémoire

Session ID A unique RTP session identifier assigned by the master. The convention is that the value of the session ID is 1 for the primary audio session, 2 for the primary video session and 3 for the primary data session. *See* Associate session

SG Signaling gateway

SGCP Simple gateway control protocol

SIP Session initiation protocol

SIP final response A SIP response that terminates a SIP transaction, e.g. 2xx, 3xx, 4xx, 5xx, 6xx responses. *See* provisional response

SIP provisional response A SIP response that does not terminate a SIP transaction, as opposed to a SIP final response. 1xx responses are provisional

SIP redirect server A redirect server is a server that accepts a SIP request, maps the address into zero or more new addresses, and returns these addresses to the client. Unlike a proxy server, it does not initiate its own SIP request. Unlike a user agent server, it does not accept calls

SIP registrar A registrar is a server that accepts Register requests. A registrar is typically co-located with a proxy or redirect server and *may* offer location services

SIP server A server is an application program that accepts requests in order to service requests and sends back responses to those requests. Servers are either proxy, redirect or user agent servers or registrars

SIP transaction A SIP transaction occurs between a client and a server and comprises all messages from the first request sent from the client to the server up to a final (non-1xx) response sent from the server to the client. A transaction is identified by the CSeq sequence number within a single call leg. The ACK request has the same CSeq number as the corresponding Invite request, but comprises a transaction of its own

SLA Service Level Agreement

SLR (from G.111) send loudness rating: the loudness loss between the speaking subscriber's mouth and an electric interface in the network. The loudness loss is here defined as the weighted (dB) average of driving sound pressure to measured voltage. The weighted mean value for G.111 and G.121 is 7–15 in the short term, 7–9 in the long term

SMR signal to mask ratio

Soft state Any state which times out after a certain delay if not refreshed

Source-router In this document only: any router directly connected to a subnetwork with a source station

SP Single space

SPL sound pressure level

SR RTCP sender report, *see* also RTP

SS Supplementary service, *see* SS-CFU

SS7 Signaling system number 7

SS-CD Supplementary service: Call deflection

SS-CFB Supplementary service: Call forwarding on busy

SS-CFNR Supplementary service: Call forwarding on no reply

SS-CFU Supplementary service: Call forwarding unconditional

SS-DIV All diversion supplementary services, including SS-CFU, SS-CFB, SS-CFNR, SS-CD

SSF Service switching function

SSL Secure sockets layer

SSRC Synchronization source: source of an RTP stream, identified by 32 bits in the RTP header. All the RTP packets with a common SSRC have a common time and sequencing reference

Stub domain A domain which has no transit traffic between its border routers, i.e. which is not used by other domains as a transit domain to destinations external to the domain

SUD Single use device, *see* H.323 Annex F

talker echo loudness rating (TELR) The loudness loss of the speaker's voice sound reaching his ear as a delayed echo.

Talkspurt A period during which a participant actually speaks, as opposed to silence periods

TCA Traffic Conditioning Agreement. The specification of all traffic shaping parameters, discard policies, in/out of profile handling rules used for a particular service level agreement (SLA)

TCL Terminal coupling loss: coupling loss between the receiving port and the sending port of a terminal due to acoustical coupling at the user interface, electrical coupling due to crosstalk in the handset cord or within the electrical circuits, seismic coupling through the mechanical parts of the terminal. For a digital handset it is commonly in the order of 40 to 46 dB

TCLwdt Weighted terminal coupling loss – double talk: the weighted loss between Rin and Sout network interfaces when echo control is in normal operation, and when the local user and the far-end user talk simultaneously

TCLwst Weighted terminal coupling loss – single talk: the weighted loss between Rin and Sout network interfaces when echo control is in normal operation, and when there is no signal coming from the user

TDM Time division multiplexing

TDMA time division multiplex access

TGW Trunk gateway

TIA Telecommunications Industry Association (USA)

TIPHON Telecommunication and IP harmonization over networks

TLS Transport Layer security: Internet Engineering Task Force, 1997 'The TLS Protocol Version 1.0' draft-ietf-tls-protocol-03.txt, T. Dieks, C. Allen

TLV Type, length, value format

TOS Type Of Service

TPKT A TCP connection establishes a reliable data stream between two hosts, but there is no delimitation of individual messages within this stream. RFC 1006 defines a simple TPKT packet format to delimit such messages. It consists of a version octet (« 3 »), two reserved octets (« 00 »), and the total length of the message including the previous headers (2 octets)

Transit domain A domain which has transit traffic between its border routers, i.e. which is used by other domains to reach destinations external to the domain

Transport address Combination of a network address (ex: IP address 10.0.1.2) and port (ex: IP port 1720) which identifies a transport termination point

TRPB Truncated reverse path broadcasting

TTL Time to live

TUP Telephony user part

UCF Unregistration confirm, a RAS message defined in H.225.0

UMTS universal mobile telecommunication system

UNI User to network interface

URI Universal resource identifier

URJ Unregistration reject, a RAS message defined in H.225.0

URL Uniform resource locator: an address used by SIP to indicate the originator, current destination and final recipient of a SIP request, and to specify redirection addresses

URQ Unregistration request, a RAS message defined in H.225.0

User agent client (UAC) Calling user agent: a user agent client is a client application that initiates the SIP request

User agent server (UAS) Called user agent: A user agent server is a server application that contacts the user when a SIP request is received and that returns a response on behalf of the user. The response accepts, rejects or redirects the request

VAD Voice activity detection

VIP CISCO: Versatile Interface Processor

VLSI very large scale integration

VoIP Voice over Internet protocol

VPIM Voice profile for Internet messaging

VQ vector quantization

VSELP vector sum excited linear prediction

WFQ Weighted Fair Queuing

wRED Weighted Random Early Detection

WSNR weighted SNR (signal to noise ratio)

XML Extended markup language

Zone A H.323 zone is the set of all H.323 endpoints, MC, MCUs and gateways managed by a single gatekeeper

Index